D1757393

DRILL HALL LIBRARY
MEDWAY

HUMAN RIGHTS AND THE PROTECTION OF PRIVACY IN TORT LAW

In its case law, the European Court of Human Rights has acknowledged that national courts are bound to give effect to Article 8 of the European Convention of Human Rights (ECHR), which sets out the right to private and family life, when they rule on controversies between private individuals. Article 8 of the ECHR has thus been accorded *mittelbare Drittwirkung* or indirect 'third-party' effect in private law relationships.

The German law of privacy, centring on the 'allgemeines Persönlichkeitsrecht', has quite a long history, and the influence of the European Court of Human Rights' interpretation of the ECHR has led to a strengthening of privacy protection in the German law. This book considers how English courts could possibly use and adapt structures adopted by the German legal order in response to rulings from the European Court of Human Rights to strengthen the protection of privacy in the private sphere.

Hans-Joachim Cremer is Professor of Public Law and Legal Philosophy at the University of Mannheim since 2000. He earned his doctorate at the University of Heidelberg. His dissertation on legal protection against expulsion and deportation won the University's Ruprecht Karls Award in 1995. In 1999 he completed his *Habilitation* at Heidelberg. His post-doctoral thesis investigates the methodology of constitutional interpretation.

The University of Texas at Austin Studies in Foreign and Transnational Law

General Editors: Sir Basil Markesinis and Dr Jörg Fedtke

The UT Studies in Foreign and Transnational Law series aims to publish books covering various aspects of foreign, private, criminal and public law, as well as transnational law. This broad ambition of the Series underlines the General Editors' belief that in a shrinking world there is a growing need to expand our knowledge of other legal orders – national or supranational – and to publish books discussing comparative methodology rather than mere descriptions of foreign systems.

Titles in the Series

The French Civil Code
J.-L. Halpérin, transl. T. Weir (2006)

Judicial Recourse to Foreign Law
B. Markesinis and J. Fedtke (2006)

International Negotiation in the Twenty-First Century
A. Plantey, transl. F. Meadows (2007)

Civil Disobedience and the German Courts
P. Quint (2007)

Human Rights in the Private Sphere
D. Oliver & J. Fedtke (2007)

Italian Private Law
G. Alpa & V. Zeno-Zencovich (2007)

Freedom of Expression
V. Zeno-Zencovich (2008)

Pure Economic Loss
V. Valentine Palmer (2008)

Introduction to Spanish Private Law
T. Rodríguez de las Heras Ballell (2009)

Printed in Great Britain
by Amazon

24218487R00249

3035973

HUMAN RIGHTS AND THE PROTECTION OF PRIVACY IN TORT LAW

A Comparison between English and German Law

Hans-Joachim Cremer

Routledge·Cavendish
Taylor & Francis Group
LONDON AND NEW YORK

First published 2011 by Routledge-Cavendish
2 Park Square, Milton Park, Abingdon, Oxon, OX14 4RN
Simultaneously published in the USA and Canada
by Routledge-Cavendish
270 Madison Avenue, New York, NY 10016

Routledge-Cavendish is an imprint of the Taylor & Francis Group,
an informa business

© 2011 Hans-Joachim Cremer

Typeset in Sabon by Swales & Willis Ltd, Exeter, Devon

Printed and bound in Great Britain by CPI Antony Rowe,
Chippenham, Wiltshire

All rights reserved. No part of this book may be reprinted or
reproduced or utilised in any form or by any electronic,
mechanical, or other means, now known or hereafter
invented, including photocopying and recording, or in any
information storage or retrieval system, without permission in
writing from the publishers.

British Library Cataloguing in Publication Data
A catalogue record for this book is available from the British Library

Library of Congress Cataloging in Publication Data
Cremer, Hans-Joachim.
Human rights and the protection of privacy in tort law: a comparison between English and
German law / Hans-Joachim Cremer.
p. cm.
1. Privacy, Right of—Germany. 2. Human rights—Germany. 3. Privacy,
Right of—England. 4. Human rights—England. 5. International and municipal
law—Germany. 6. International and municipal law—England. I. Title.
KJC1676.C74 2010
342.7308'58—dc22
2010009716

ISBN10: 0–415–47704–2 (hbk)
ISBN13: 978–0–415–47704–8 (hbk)

ISBN10: 0–203–84357–6 (ebk)
ISBN13: 978–0–203–84357–4 (ebk)

22 SEP 2011
DRILL HALL LIBRARY

Contents |

European Court of Human Rights

European Commission of Human Rights

European Court of Justice:

German Federal Constitutional Court (*Bundesverfassungsgericht*):

xxii | Table of cases

German Federal Court of Justice (*Bundesgerichtshof*):

European Law

Treaty on European Union (TEU)

European Convention on Human Rights (ECHR)

German Law

Grundgesetz (GG); Basic Law for the Federal Republic of Germany

Bürgerliches Gesetzbuch (BGB); German Civil Code

Foreword

Concerns about privacy are universal and have grown in intensity as modern technology has enhanced the ability of the state and individuals to collect, to collate, and to disseminate information about human beings and their activities. The amount of personal information that public authorities and private organisations thus accumulate across the globe is staggering and, potentially, harmful and even dangerous to those concerned. This development, though helpful in some respects, has also resulted in considerable tension between individual freedom and the public interest to be informed about events and the lives and activities of the members of society.

Far less universal, however, are the legal responses. Historical experience, diverging views of what the public may know and what should remain private, different conceptualisations of core human rights such as privacy, dignity, and freedom of expression, but also factual differences such as the ability of the press to influence the law, are some of the factors that can explain the variety of approaches found in Europe and elsewhere. But should this be so? The world is shrinking, and information – whether true or false – travels faster and further than ever before, and without much regard for jurisdictional boundaries; the incentives for using personal information are identical in most societies – as are the reasons that individuals may have for trying to keep things private; and common legal instruments, such as the European Convention on Human Rights, call for more harmonisation of national legal practice.

That is one side of the argument in favour of greater (but not necessarily complete) harmonisation; the other is learning from the experience of others. In England, for instance, there is a wide spread fear that a stronger recognition of privacy rights would flood the courts with vexatious litigation. Those who, as a matter principle, are scared of change or even adaptation in any form, voice another fear. Would a more rationalised protection of privacy stunt free speech? That is where observing carefully the experience of other countries can be helpful for it may confirm or help dispel (unfounded?) fears about what might happen if English law where to move closer to that found in most European systems.

A precondition for any harmonisation or, even, convergence, is dialogue and this, in turn, requires an open mind. As General Editors of this Series we cannot ensure the second but we can encourage the first by providing reliable information about the experiences of other major and socio-economically similar systems. Indeed, this series has already provided a number of valuable, we believe, contributions to this field of human endeavour. It is thus with great pleasure that we present this new volume by Professor Dr. Hans-Joachim Cremer of the University of Mannheim, which is devoted entirely to a comparative analysis of the complex legal problems surrounding the protection of privacy.

Professor Cremer is in a unique position to bridge the gap between the Common law and Continental Europe. Educated in Germany and the USA, he is an expert on German public law, but also deeply aware of the European influences on national jurisdictions. He has also spent much time and effort on the study of English common law perspectives on privacy. Thus, while a Visiting Professor at the Institute of Global Law at University College London, he delivered a brilliant series of lectures on this subject which were further enriched by his artistic ability to produce unique and humorous cartoons to illustrate his points. For various reasons we were unable to reproduce these illustrations in this book but his narrative provides a detailed and up-to-date account of the historical roots, development, and likely future direction of the rich case law surrounding the German *allgemeines Persönlichkeitsrecht*, the complex interaction between German courts and the European Court of Human Rights, as well as ideas and inspiration for lawyers and judges with a Common law background drawn from the German experience – and vice versa.

This book is thus warmly commended to lawyers, politicians and journalists from *both* sides of the Channel in the hope that even if it fails to make them any wiser it will certainly make them better informed.

Sir Basil Markesinis QC, FBA
Oxford

Professor Dr. Jörg Fedtke
Tulane Law School, New Orleans

Preface

How do human rights and tort law connect? A decade ago this might have seemed to be quite a puzzling question. But ever since the European Court of Human Rights (ECtHR) delivered its judgment in the case of *Von Hannover v. Germany*, it has been quite obvious that the States bound by the European Convention on Human Rights (ECHR) can be held responsible for a violation of the right to respect for private life if their tort law, as interpreted and applied by their domestic courts, does not sufficiently protect celebrities against press publications of photographs taken from their private life.

For the German constitutional lawyer, it is rather a commonplace that the fundamental rights guaranteed in the Basic Law, the German constitution, have a 'radiating effect' (*'Ausstrahlungswirkung'*) on private law, especially *Deliktsrecht*, tort law. What has become known as *'die mittelbare Drittwirkung der Grundrechte'* was acknowledged by the *Bundesverfassungsgericht*, the German Federal Constitutional Court, as early as 1958 in its famous judgment in the case of *Lüth*.

When Professor Sir Basil Markesinis, QC, DCL, FBA, then Professor of Common and Civil Law, University College London and holder of the Jamail Regents Chair at the University of Texas at Austin, invited me to co-teach part of his Comparative Tort Law course at University College London (UCL) in 2005, and again in 2007, he gave me the wonderful opportunity to explore this constitutional law aspect of German *Deliktsrecht* more deeply and to connect this immersion into the problems of *Drittwirkung* with my interest in the European Convention on Human Rights and Fundamental Freedoms. I owe Sir Basil great thanks for this kind invitation and his generous hospitality during my stays – and especially for his confidence and trust in me, whom at first he did not know personally. Ever since we first spoke on the telephone, I have been humbled by his kindness and his friendship. His confidence and trust seem to have radiated onto Professor Dr. Jörg Fedtke, A.N. Yiannopoulos Professor in Comparative and International Law at Tulane University Law School, whom I got to know as the then Director of the Institute of Global Law at UCL and who has also become a true friend. Both of them proposed that I take up the subject of 'Human Rights and the

Protection of Privacy in Tort Law' in the form of a book to be included in their series 'Studies in Foreign and Transnational Law'. For this I am grateful as well as for my two editors' patience and forbearance during the time it took me to write the manuscript.

Looking at the book as I hold it in my hands now, I can say that it contains the kind of research I most enjoy: reading, presenting and commenting on court decisions.

My hope is that it might give an English speaking audience insights into German constitutional law, which could be made to bear fruit for the interpretation and application of the European Convention on Human Rights, which in turn influences the case-law of domestic courts of other States Parties to the Convention such as the United Kingdom.

After retracing the *Von Hannover* case in detail and investigating how far human rights obligations under the Convention concern both the domestic law on relations of private parties *inter se* and judicial decisions in private law disputes, the book attempts to discover the argumentative 'structure' of *mittelbare Drittwirkung*, i.e., of how constitutional rights affect private law relations between private persons. This is done by what I call a reconstructive reading of the *Lüth* judgment, looking at this decision from the perspective of the present-day *Grundrechtsdogmatik* – the fundamental principles of reading and construing constitutionally guaranteed basic rights as basically accepted in theory and practice. This reconstructive reading shows *mittelbare Drittwirkung* to be the result of basic rights obligations binding the State when having to solve controversies between private parties in which one party encroaches upon the other: Basic rights generate both the duty to protect the 'victim's' basic rights and the duty to respect the 'encroacher's' basic rights, the limitation of which (to be undertaken for the sake of the 'victim's' protection) especially demands adherence to the principle of proportionality. The analysis of the triangle of legal relations between the State and the two parties reveals the 'structure' of *mittelbare Drittwirkung*. This structure, as I finally attempt to show, is not a specific trait of German constitutional law. Rather, it is the consequence of any system of fundamental rights binding States in which these rights are assigned to individuals and impose upon governmental powers, and especially the judiciary, not only duties to respect but also duties to protect rights and freedoms. While the ECtHR has interpreted the Convention to include both negative and positive obligations, the Court up to now has left undecided how negative and positive obligations under the ECHR relate in cases involving controversies between private parties. Using the insights into *mittelbare Drittwirkung* under German constitutional law allows us to clarify how the duty to respect and the duty to protect are both relevant for the analysis and decision of cases in which private parties, in making use of their respective freedoms run into conflict. This clarification can, and this would be my hope, make the application of ECHR guarantees to legal relations between private parties more rational and comprehensible and thus render the outcome of cases before national courts and the ECtHR more readily foreseeable.

If this attempt is successful, it will not only be Sir Basil Markesinis and Jörg Fedtke whom I owe thanks. My senior research assistant, Anne-Sophie Ritter, has accompanied this project from the start, helping to collect materials, drafting the addendum, co-ordinating the technical work on the manuscript and, especially, critically discussing my ideas as they evolved. Student researchers Natalie Ackermann, Julia Bechtel, Marius Fröschle, Stefan Jacob, Yasemin Keskintepe and Christian Werthmüller were involved in setting up the tables of abbreviations, cases and legislation. I am grateful to them all.

Hans-Joachim Cremer
Mannheim, 2010

Abbreviations |

Art.	Article/*Artikel*
BGB	Bürgerliches Gesetzbuch
BGHZ	Entscheidungen des Bundesgerichtshofs in Zivilsachen
BVerfGE	Entscheidungen des Bundesverfassungsgerichts (collection of the decisions edited by the Justices of the Court)
ebd.	ebenda
ECHR	European Convention on Human Rights *or* Reports of the European Court of Human Rights (present collection of decisions)
EComHR	European Commission of Human Rights
ECR	European Court Reports
ECtHR	European Court of Human Rights
et seq.	et sequens
EWCA	England and Wales Court of Appeal
f.	folgende
FamRZ	Familienrechts-Zeitschrift
GG	Grundgesetz
HGB	Handels-gesetzbuch
ibid.	*ibidem*
i.e.	for example
KUG	Kunsturhebergesetz
LG	*Landgericht* (Regional Court)
lit.	literature
MLR	The Modern Law Review
n.	note(s)
no.	number (in references to ECtHR judgments and decisions, and to EComHR decisions, this is the application number)
NZLR	New Zealand Law Reports
OLG	*Oberlandesgericht* (Court of Appeal)
Rep.	Reports of Judgments and Decisions (European Court of Human Rights until 1998)
sec.	section
StGB	Strafgesetzbuch
TEU	Treaty on European Union
UKHL	United Kingdom House of Lords
vgl.	verglichen

Chapter 1:
Aspects of comparison and the European Convention on Human Rights in the context of German law

1.1 Intrusions, disturbances, unwelcome publications

Privacy matters. The need for privacy protection is evident. This is so not only with a view to state authorities' activities – which can deeply invade the private sphere as two cases before the *Bundesverfassungsgericht*, the German Federal Constitutional Court, show. One of these concerns the powers of the *Verfassungsschutzbehörde*, the authority for protection of the constitution, of the German constituent state of North-Rhine Westfalia to collect data by secretly infiltrating computers ('online searches').[1] In the other case the *Bundesverfassungsgericht* declared certain new provisions of the Federal Telecommunications Act (*Telekommunikationsgesetz – TKG)* nul and void. These require suppliers of telecommunications services to store, for a period of six months, specific traffic and locations data. These data are created when mobile and landline telephones, email and internet are used so that they may be retrieved for the purposes of criminal prosecution, the warding off of substantial dangers to public security and the performance of intelligence tasks.[2]

The individual is also in need of protection when other individuals or private parties invade their private sphere. A surprising example comes from the book *Chronicles*, in which Bob Dylan writes about his experiences during the time when he lived in Woodstock with his family at the end of the 1960s. Their house apparently was under a constant siege not only by newspaper, television and radio reporters, but also by political enthusiasts and fans of his music, all of whom trespassed on his land.[3]

This episode alone might suffice to show the relevance of privacy protection for celebrities. Yet if we look at judgments by German courts, the cases brought by Princess Caroline of Monaco, now Princess Caroline von

---

[1] *Bundesverfassungsgericht*, judgment of 27 February 2008–1 BvR 370, 595/07–, BVerfGE 120, 274.
[2] *Bundesverfassungsgericht*, judgment of 2 March 2010–1 BvR 256/08, 263/08, 586/08.
[3] *Dylan* (2005), 116–118.

Hannover, against magazine publishers are the most prominent. The Princess in these cases sought to have the publication of pictures showing her and members of her family prohibited.[4] Another victim of paparazzi photographers has been Sabine Christiansen, a television news anchor woman and talk show host, who successfully filed suit against the republication of a photograph showing her going shopping in Puerto Andratx on the island of Mallorca.[5] Quite similarly, Heide Simonis, after losing her office as Prime Minister of the *Land* of Schleswig-Holstein, was pursued, observed and photographed by reporters and photographers of a prominent tabloid in situations, some of which the courts judged to have nothing to do with her official functions or her political career, but strictly to belong to the sphere of her private life.[6] Ms Christiansen also suffered intrusions of yet another quality when aerial photographs of the *finca* where she spends her holidays and which, due to its location in a nature reserve, is not easily accessible, were published in a television guide together with a description of the route leading to the estate. Although details of the normative legal background of such cases will be given later, the German courts have interestingly conceded that the publication of images showing the outer walls of private premises has the potential to violate the personality right. But in this specific case, in balancing the general personality right and the freedom of the press, they found Ms Christiansen only to have a right to demand the precise description of the route leading to the *finca* not to be published; the photographs as such were thus allowed to circulate.[7]

Privacy seems to be a scarce commodity. In the age of the Internet it is waning even more. Gossip sites are alarmingly fast in presenting the latest 'news' on the private life of celebrities. Internet culture itself seems to seduce even ordinary people to disclose personal information and images of themselves.[8] The media's money-driven appetite for private information on politicians, music or movie stars and other famous people appears insatiable and ever growing.[9] We need only to remember the case of the news reports on an alleged sex scandal

---

[4]See only *Bundesgerichtshof*, judgment of 19 December 1995 –VI ZR 15/95–, 1996 Neue Juristische Wochenschrift 1128 = BGHZ 131, 332; *Bundesverfassungsgericht*, judgment of 15 December 1999–1 BvR 653/96–, BVerfGE 101, 361 – *Caroline von Monaco II*. Also see European Court of Human Rights, *Von Hannover v. Germany*, no. 59320/00, judgment of 24 June 2004, ECHR 2004-VI.
[5]See *Bundesgerichtshof*, judgment of 1 July 2008 –VI ZR 243/06–, 2008 Neue Juristische Wochenschrift, 3138.
[6]See *Bundesgerichtshof*, judgment of 24 June 2008 –VI ZR 156/06–, 2008 Neue Juristische Wochenschrift 3134.
[7]*Bundesgerichtshof*, judgment of 9 December 2003 –VI ZR 373/02–, 2004 Neue Juristische Wochenschrift 762 (also quoting the *Kammergericht's* judgment).
[8]Cf. *Adorján* (2008), who gives the example that hardly more than an hour after Heath Ledger was found dead in his New York apartment on Tuesday, 22 January 2008, TMZ.com, a celebrity-gossip site, had the news.
[9]Cf. *Stadler* (2008).

of the former President of the Fédération Internationale de l'Automobile ('FIA'), Max Mosley, who successfully sued the News Group Newspapers Limited for damages for infringement of privacy before the High Court.[10]

But it is not only the media, envisaged as reporters and journalists, probing into the private sphere. Pressure to disclose facts of one's personal life may also come from other sources generating a public interest. This could, for example, be seen when a group of American physicians, in full-page newspaper advertisements, demanded that John McCain, who at the time was running for US President as the Republican candidate, make documents on his health condition and on the history of his illness available to the public.[11] On the other hand, politicians appear more and more tempted to exploit their own private lives in order to make use of the media for their political purposes, which has especially been discussed with a view to French President Nicolas Sarkozy.[12] There are worries that the loss of the private sphere, whether suffered or surrendered, is deeply changing society, especially by opening large spaces of the public sphere to 'waves of moralisation,' tabloid journalism and political populism. In ancient Athens, privacy was said to have been preserved and protected within the *oikos* while the public debates in the *agora*, admittedly in a somewhat idealised view, were conducted without looking into a speaker's private sphere seeing only the better argument prevail. Today, however, emotions count – whether we look at readers, viewers, Internet users, or voters. With persons becoming more important than substantive policies, political success is linked to personal reputation, and confidence in a person can be won or lost by disclosing how someone acts or behaves in private matters.[13] In this perspective privacy protection might be seen to gain not only societal, but political importance.[14] Perhaps privacy protection must even be accorded constitutional weight in the meaning of relevance for the functioning of democracy.

It is true that celebrities are those who seem to have the most substantial interest in privacy protection, if not for reasons of really wanting to preserve a personal sphere of liberty, then, as sometimes emphasised, but for reasons of selling glimpses of their private lives as dearly as possible. This is an attitude which privacy protection through tort law may well inspire and promote. However, as Bob Dylan rightly points out, 'privacy is something you can sell, but you can't buy it back.'[15]

---

[10][2008] EWHC 1777 (QB).
[11]*Gerste* (2008).
[12]See *Zitzmann* (2008a); *Zitzmann* (2008b).
[13]See the article by the professor of sociology and the science of the media, *Imhof* (2008). Cf. also *Barendt* (2005), 231–2.
[14]Cf. *Fenwick Phillipson* (2006), 809; *Habermas* (1994), 445–6, 449. An interesting aspect of unveiling the personal thoughts of individual kept private is highlighted by the publication of the diaries of Claretta Petacci, the lover of Benitto Mussolini, the comments on which however not always seem to have been written with seriousness. See *Woller* (2010).
[15]*Dylan* (2005), 118.

All of these considerations, however, should not let us forget the importance of privacy protection for ordinary people. With progressing knowledge and technology in the field of genetic analysis, privacy matters for the workers of car factories whose employer demands them to undergo a blood test before hiring them, and for customers seeking health or life insurance should the insurer demand their genes to be screened in order to assess the probability of having to make payments.

Let us turn to tort-law[16] protection of privacy, and especially consider the protection against the publication of images, upon which this book will very much concentrate not only because it is, in a twofold meaning of the word, illustrative, but also because it is of quite practical relevance. And this is so not only for the rich and the beautiful, as can be shown by cases decided by courts in Germany where privacy protection under the heading of *Schutz des allgemeinen Persönlichkeitsrechts* (protection of the general personality right) reaches back into the middle of the twentieth century.[17]

In some instances people who are close to celebrities can indirectly benefit from the famous person's right to demand a magazine not to publish pictures of him. For instance, when Oliver Kahn won his suit against the publisher of the magazine *Frau im Spiegel*, his new girlfriend was *de facto* also protected against the publication of the photograph which showed her with the soccer star during their holiday in St Tropez.[18]

Similarly, Princess Caroline's children share in the protection afforded to their mother by Article 2(1) in combination with Article 1(1) of the *Grundgesetz*[19]: The *Bundesverfassungsgericht* extends the protection of a parent's personality right, as guaranteed by constitutional law, to include parental care for children. The reason given for this is that Article 6(1) and (2) of the *Grundgesetz*, protecting the family and acknowledging the parents' 'natural right' to raise and educate their children, reinforces the parent's personality right. Article 6 of the *Grundgesetz* is read as obliging the state to secure those living conditions of a child which are essential for growing up healthy and to which parental care most prominently belongs.[20]

---

[16] Tort law with respect to German law is, for the purposes of this book, understood to comprise not only the Deliktsrecht of the Bürgerliches Gesetzbuch, the German Civil Code, but also especially other provisions of law regulating non-contractual relations of private persons and affording either claims for damages or rights to demand from another person to stop, and to refrain from, certain behaviour if it violates the other's rights.

[17] See only *Bundesgerichtshof*, judgment of 25 May 1954 – I ZR 211/53 (*Schacht*), 1954 Neue Juristische Wochenschrift 1404 = 1954 Juristenzeitung 698 = BGHZ 13, 334; judgment of 14 February 1958 – I ZR 151/56 (*Herrenreiter*), 1958 Neue Juristische Wochenschrift 827 = 1958 Juristenzeitung 571 = BGHZ 26, 349. See also Chapter 3.

[18] *Bundesgerichtshof*, judgment of 3 July 2007 – VI ZR 164/06–, 2008 Neue Juristische Wochenschrift 749.

[19] The *Grundgesetz für die Bundesrepublik Deutschland*, the Basic Law for the Federal Republic of Germany, is the German constitution.

[20] *Bundesverfassungsgericht*, (n. 4) – *Caroline von Monaco II*.

Metaphorically, Article 6 of the *Grundgesetz* thus solidifies and strengthens the constitutional law foundation on which a parent's personality right rests. In this specific case, a violation of Princess Caroline's right under Articles 2(1) and 1(1) of the *Grundgesetz* was established to have occurred by the civil courts' failure to enjoin the publisher of magazines, in which pictures showing the Princess together with her children had been printed, from republishing the images.[21]

Even though the press has a right to include in their coverage of a celebrity a person who steps into the limelight at the side of the prominent figure, this does not mean that the celebrity's companion will lose all protection against the publication of images which were illegally made in the past.[22] People close to stars may even have a right of their own to seek an injunction against the publication of pictures even if these show them in the company of the celebrity, as the case of the girlfriend of German singer *Herbert Grönemeyer* demonstrates.[23]

Being a public figure or having some connection with a celebrity, however, is in no way a necessary requirement for the protection of an individual's personality right under German law. As needs to be conceded, fame and publicity do play a role not only for the possibility of justifying a person's inclusion in a public debate, but also for both assessing the intensity of an infringement of the personality right and for considering the question of whether monetary compensation can be claimed.[24] Nevertheless even ordinary people enjoy protection. For example, a person whose picture the media accidentally, or without any justification, connect with news of public interest can have a right to compensation for damages. This can be demonstrated by a rather old case of a young man whose image in 1959 was shown out of context in connection with a weekly news reel (*Wochenschau*) report on spectacular murders and a public debate on the death penalty.[25]

More recently, German civil courts granted compensation for a violation of the personality right to the guardian of a mentally ill person after a newspaper, having mistaken the images of the guardian and the ward, had added the guardian's picture to a report titled, 'Lunatic Beats Up Senior Citizen'.[26]

---

[21]*Bundesverfassungsgericht* (n. 4), 395–396 – *Caroline von Monaco II.*
[22]*Bundesgerichtshof*, judgment of 19 October 2004 –VI ZR 292/03–, 2005 Neue Juristische Wochenschrift 594. The constitutional complaint against this judgment were not admitted for decision by the *Bundesverfassungsgericht*, see *Bundesverfassungsgericht, 1st chamber of the 1st Senate,* decision of 21 August 2006–1 BvR 2606/04, 1 BvR, 2845/04, 1 BvR 2846/04, 1 BvR 2847/04–, 2006 Neue Juristische Wochenschrift 3406 = 2006 Europäische Grundrechte-Zeitschrift 599.
[23]*Bundesgerichtshof*, judgment of 19 June 2007 –VI ZR 12/06– *(Grönemeyer)*, 2007 Neue Juristische Wochenschrift 3440.
[24]Cf. *Sprau* (2010), para. 124.
[25]*Bundesgerichtshof*, judgment of 5 January 1962 –VI ZR 72/61–, 1962 Neue Juristische Wochenschrift 1004.
[26]*Oberlandesgericht München*, judgment of 22 October 2003–21 U 2540/03–, 2004 Neue Juristische Wochenschrift 959.

Not dissimilar are two other cases. In one of these, a photograph showing a catholic priest during church services was printed as an illustration of a magazine report on cases of sexual abuse of children by priests. The caption to the pictures falsely indicated him, upon being reported to the police by a girl victim, to have admitted to six further offences. The civil courts granted the claim for compensation for damages against the publisher and one of the reporters.[27] In the other case, a monthly magazine published an article on the sexual abuse of a schoolgirl by a higher secondary school teacher in Cologne. The subtitle of the story gave the teacher's name without any indication that this was not the offender's real name, but a pseudonym invented by the editorial staff. A teacher at a higher secondary school in the region (in Siegburg), who had nothing to do with the case, but whose true name matched the pseudonym, successfully sued the editor for damages resulting form the violation of his personality right.[28]

To sum up: Privacy protection matters.

1.2 Outline of the book

The following study intends to look at a special constellation of privacy protection, in which two 'levels' need to be distinguished. At the *national level*, a State's tort law provides protection by granting compensation for all, or at least for certain, interferences with privacy, while at the *international level*, the European Convention on Human Rights (ECHR) has developed standards for privacy protection. For those States which are High Contracting Parties to, and therefore bound by, the Convention under public international law, this means that they must respect the Convention standards and that, more specifically, their national law of privacy protection must comply with the Convention requirements – at least as to the results brought about. Consequently, a comparison of the national rules of privacy protection and of the ECHR standards is called for. At the same time, different national 'schemes' of protecting privacy through tort law *quasi* become 'connected' as they are equally bound by human rights standards existing at the international, more specifically, at the European level. This book seeks to explore such 'connectedness' with a view to German *Deliktsrecht* and English tort law, thus choosing a civil law and a Common Law legal system for comparison.

It will especially concentrate on how human rights, whether guaranteed at the national or at the international level, influence private law; one intention being to show how an analysis of *mittelbare Drittwirkung* of basic rights under German constitutional law might allow a theoretical reconstruction of

---

[27]*Landgericht Trier*, judgment of 26 October 1995–6 O 57/95–, LEXIS NEXIS; *Oberlandesgericht Koblenz*, judgment of 20 December 1996 –10 U 1667/95–, 1997 Neue Juristische Wochenschrift 1375.

[28]*Landgericht Bonn*, judgment of 4 June 1992 –15 O 440/91–, LEXIS NEXIS. That the claimant also was a local politician was an aspect not specifically addressed in the merits of the judgment.

the European Court of Human Rights' (ECtHR's) handling of applications alleging the Convention to have been violated by civil court decisions in private-law cases. I hope to help clarify how individual rights guaranteed by the ECHR apply in cases before the ECtHR, which are rooted in private-law controversies. As both German *Deliktsrecht* and English tort law, as will be shown, must adapt to Convention requirements, understanding the mechanism through which human rights affect legal relations between private parties will be helpful for the English as well as the German courts. We will see that in both countries tort law provides privacy protection, as far as misuse of information or photographs is concerned. But we will have to keep in mind that English tort law, in contrast to German *Deliktsrecht*, knows no tort of breach of privacy similar to the interference with the *allgemeines Persönlichkeitsrecht* under German law. Having acknowledged a violation of this general right to one's personality as a *Delikt*, German law will be able to absorb the evolving European standards for the protection of the right to respect for one's private life under Article 8 ECHR. A similar adaptation might be more difficult for the English courts. English law may therefore have to be developed in order to avoid the danger of incompatibility with Convention.

1.3 Comparative aspects of the study

1.3.1 The comparative setting

This first sketch of the intention of the following study reveals a special comparative setting, which ought to be explored in more detail.

Someone embarking on the comparison of laws is not infrequently confronted with the question: Why compare laws? What is the justification for comparing the legal situation in different countries, especially considering the way the courts decide certain kinds of cases in one country, with the situation in another country? Isn't it *l'art pour l'art*? Some scholars think legal comparisons would be worthwhile even without an immediate practical utility as a science is not in need of a justification in such terms. Rather, they say, just as no one asks the astronomer for which practical purposes he is probing the sky with his telescope, comparative legal studies could be justified by pure curiosity, by the fact that one wants to learn about other legal orders and wants to know what is equal, similar and different. That theoretical insights to be gained by comparison – especially growing awareness of peculiarities of one's 'own' legal system, i.e. the one in which one lives – may prove to be of practical usefulness is something these scholars, of course, will not deny.[29]

---

[29]Cf. *Sacco* (2001), 13 et seq., paras. 1 et seq. See especially, ibid., 23, para. 18: '*Die Rechtsvergleichung ist reine Erkenntnis.*' On the practical usefulness of comparisons see: *Markesinis* (2003), 157–82; *Markesinis / Fedtke* (2009), 347–9.

1.3.2 The practical utility of legal comparisons

1.3.2.1 Comparisons required by law

In some cases, practical utility, in the sense of relevance for legal practice, will be obvious. This is especially true when legal provisions applicable to a case, i.e. 'positive law', require the judge to compare. Let us have a look at some examples.

One can be found in German family law. According to sec. 1357 of the *Bürgerliches Gesetzbuch* (BGB), the German Civil Code, each marital partner is entitled to enter into transactions for the adequate procurement of the necessities of life with (legal) effects for the other marital partner. Such transactions create rights and obligations for both marital partners unless the circumstances call for a deviation from this principle. This provision intends to enable the marital partners individually to engage in legal transactions with sufficient independence and autonomy for the purposes of the 'procurement of the necessities' of the couple's life; the one marital partner especially is not to depend on the other partner's consent for such transactions if they are to create rights and obligations for both of them. Thus, even where only one partner acts, the couple economically forms a single unit. The legal capacity to act with legal effect for both marital partners is especially important where one partner takes care of all matters of the household.[30] In cases in which the laws of a foreign state apply to the couple's matrimonial property,[31] Article 16(2) of the *Einführungsgesetz zum Bürgerlichen Gesetzbuche* (EGBGB), the Introductory Law to the German Civil Code, provides that to transactions within the country, i.e. *cum grano salis* within Germany, sec. 1357 BGB shall apply accordingly, however only insofar as sec. 1357 BGB is more favourable to third parties, acting in good faith, than the foreign law. Insofar as Article 16(2) EGBGB is concerned with persons who, within Germany, conclude contracts with one marital partner where foreign marital law applies to the couple, its intention is to protect these persons contracting with one of the spouses in their *bona fide* expectation that, as is the rule for couples married according to German law, both marital partners will be debtors of contractual obligations. But as sec. 1357 BGB will only apply if it is, in the specific case, *more favourable* than any corresponding rule in the matrimonial law of the foreign state.[32] Thus, if such a case were brought in the German civil courts, these would have to compare sec. 1357 BGB and the corresponding foreign provisions of law.

---

[30]See sec. 1356(1), second sentence, BGB. As to Sec. 1357 see *Brudermüller* (2010), § 1357 BGB.
[31]German law provides that the question the laws of which state apply to matrimonial property is to be answered in parallel to which laws are applicable to the marital relation and its effects as such. See Article 15(1) of the *Einführungsgesetz zum Bürgerlichen Gesetzbuche* (EGBGB).
[32]See *Heldrich* (2010), EG 16, para. 3.

Looking at a different field of German law, we encounter a rule saying that German criminal law shall apply to all offences committed against a German national if the act, at the place of its commission, is an offence punishable under criminal law (sec. 7(1) of the *Strafgesetzbuch*, StGB, the German Criminal Code).[33] The requirement that the act must be punishable at the place of its commission pertains to the specific circumstances of the case (including the absence of legal justification or grounds for excluding culpability).[34] Furthermore, the foreign criminal law need not qualify the offence identically, if only it is a criminal offence. Nevertheless, the necessity of a legal comparison of the German and the foreign criminal law is undeniable.

If we jump to the level of European Union law, Article 6(3) of the Treaty on European Union, as revised by the Treaty of Lisbon, provides that fundamental rights, as guaranteed by the European Convention for the Protection of Human Rights and Fundamental Freedoms and as they result from the constitutional traditions common to the Member States, shall constitute general principles of the Union's law. Insofar as it is necessary to establish which fundamental rights result from the Member States' constitutional traditions, a comparative study is unavoidable.[35]

---

[33]German criminal law will also apply according to sec. 7(1) StGB if the place of commission of the act against a German national is not subject to any criminal jurisdiction.

[34]See *Hans-Heinrich Jescheck* (1988), 156; *Eser* (1994), § 7, para. 8.

[35]As to the development of fundamental rights standards binding the European Communities before Art. 6 TEU and its predecessor norms entered into force, see European Court of Justice, judgment of 17 December 1970, case 11/70, *Internationale Handelsgesellschaft* (1970) ECR 1125, paras. 3–4: '3 Recourse to the legal rules or concepts of national law in order to judge the validity of measures adopted by the institutions of the Community would have an adverse effect on the uniformity and efficacy of Community law. The validity of such measures can only be judged in the light of Community law. In fact, the law stemming from the Treaty, an independent source of law, cannot because of its very nature be overridden by rules of national law, however framed, without being deprived of its character as Community law and without the legal basis of the Community itself being called in question. Therefore the validity of a Community measure or its effect within a Member State cannot be affected by allegations that it runs counter to either fundamental rights as formulated by the constitution of that state or the principles of a national constitutional structure. 4 However, an examination should be made as to whether or not any analogous guarantee inherent in Community law has been disregarded. In fact, respect for fundamental rights forms an integral part of the general principles of law protected by the Court of Justice. The protection of such rights, whilst inspired by the constitutional traditions common to the Member States, must be ensured within the framework of the structure and objectives of the Community. It must therefore be ascertained, in the light of the doubts expressed by the Verwaltungsgericht, whether the system of deposits has infringed rights of a fundamental nature, respect for which must be ensured in the Community legal system.' See also European Court of Justice, judgment of 13 December 1979, case 44/79, *Liselotte Hauer v. Land Rheinland-Pfalz*, (1979) ECR 3727, paras. 14–15: '14 As the Court declared in its judgment of 17 December 1970, *Internationale Handelsgesellschaft* (1970) ECR 1125, the question of a possible infringement of fundamental rights by a measure of the Community institutions can only be judged in the light of Community law itself. The introduction of special criteria for assessment stemming from the legislation or constitutional law of a particular Member State would, by

These three examples, almost randomly picked, demonstrate that a provision of the law can quite straightforwardly require a comparison with foreign law. What the examples have in common is that the comparison is called for by the very provision which determines that the result of the comparison is to be legally relevant. This is so in the case of sec. 16(2) EGBGB which demands sec. 1357 BGB be applied in favour of creditors of a foreign couple who in good faith believe German marital law applies to a contract with this couple, if sec. 1357 BGB is more favourable to the creditor than the foreign law – as well as in the case of sec. 7 StGB which requires an act to be criminally punishable in the place where this act was committed in order for German criminal law to apply. Similarly, Article 6(3) of the Treaty on European Union demands looking at the common constitutional traditions of the Member States in order to establish certain fundamental rights as general principles of the Union's law, which as part of the Union's primary law, rank equal to the law of the Treaty.

1.3.2.2 The need for legal comparisons in the context of the European Convention on Human Rights

1.3.2.2.1 COMPLIANCE WITH THE CONVENTION

The comparative situation we encounter in relation to the requirements of the European Convention on Human Rights as to the protection of privacy against interference by private persons are somewhat different. This is clearly so from the Convention's point of view. Here, as we shall see, the Convention, as interpreted by the ECtHR, demands the States Parties to afford one private party protection against another private party's intrusion on privacy. This is an obligation at the level of public international law, contained in a human rights treaty. By ratifying the Convention the High Contracting Parties have committed themselves to respecting the Convention

---

damaging the substantive unity and efficacy of Community law, lead inevitably to the destruction of the unity of the Common Market and the jeopardizing of the cohesion of the Community. 15 The Court also emphasised in the judgment cited, and later in the judgment of 14 May 1974, *Nold* (1974) ECR 491, that fundamental rights form an integral part of the general principles of the law, the observance of which it ensures, that in safeguarding those rights, the Court is bound to draw inspiration from constitutional traditions common to the Member States, so that measures which are incompatible with the fundamental rights recognised by the constitutions of those states are unacceptable in the Community, and that, similarly, international treaties for the protection of human rights on which the Member States have collaborated or of which they are signatories, can supply guidelines which should be followed within the framework of Community law. That conception was later recognised by the joint declaration of the European Parliament, the Council and the Commission of 5 April 1977, which, after recalling the case-law of the Court, refers on the one hand to the rights guaranteed by the constitutions of the Member States and on the other hand to the European Convention for the Protection of Human Rights and Fundamental Freedoms of 4 November 1950 (Official Journal C 103, 1977, p. 1).'

guarantees. Article 1 ECHR says: 'The High Contracting Parties shall secure to everyone within their jurisdiction the rights and freedoms defined in Section I of this Convention.'

Whether or not they comply with this obligation, is a question we would hardly address as one of comparative law. It is a matter of compliance. From the perspective of public international law, the 'behaviour' of a State and its institutions compose the 'facts' to which the norms of public international law are applied. This also holds true in the special circumstances in which the ECtHR exercises its jurisdiction to decide on inter-state cases according to Article 33 ECHR or on individual applications according to Article 34 ECHR. A Contracting State can especially, though not exclusively, in inter-state cases, be found to have violated the Convention or one of the protocols thereto because it has enacted a certain statute or other *abstract* provision of law – with the norm as such constituting the State's behaviour infringing a Convention guarantee. More frequently, however, and typically in individual applications, it is the *interpretation and application* of provisions of national law which are alleged to have violated an individual right under the ECHR. If the ECtHR finds that there has actually been such a violation, the judgment has a binding effect on the State Party against which the application is directed.[36] Article 46 ECHR makes this clear by providing: 'The High Contracting Parties undertake to abide by the final judgment of the Court in any case to which they are parties.'

Even if it is an individual judgment by a national court, or an individual act or decision by an administrative authority, which has violated an applicant's right under the Convention, there are good reasons to assume that the State which the ECtHR has found to be responsible for this violation is under an obligation to investigate whether the individual violation was strictly *predetermined* by an abstract rule of law and, if so, to change its law in order to avoid a repetition of the violation of the same individual, as established by the ECtHR judgment, or foreseeable *equal* violations in *parallel* cases. Even where a case decided by the ECtHR in favour of a specific applicant concerned *discretionary* acts of national courts or authorities (the violations thus not having been strictly programmed), or where other cases are only similar without being connected through the same applicable provision of law, it is quite plausible to consider the State which the ECtHR has found to be in violation of the ECHR to be bound to avoid similar infringements in parallel cases.[37] The best legal explanation for this obligation, however, is not the

---

[36] This is, of course, not to say that there is no binding effect of a judgment finding no violation to have occurred. In such a case, however, the respondent State is not burdened by the judgment. Rather it is the applicant who must be content with the outcome of the case and cannot, through a second, identical application, bring the identical case before the ECtHR a second time.

[37] Cf. sec. 10(2) of the Human Rights Act 1998, which gives a Minister or Her Majesty in Council power to take remedial action if it appears to a Minister of the Crown or Her Majesty in Council that, having regard to a finding of the European Court of Human Rights made after the coming

binding effect of the ECtHR judgment in the sense of *res judicata*, but rather the *normative* binding force of the Convention provision concerned.

In order to adapt its law to the requirements of the Convention for these cases, which are merely parallel as they are normatively not pre-determined by law at the national level, the State Party might be said to be in need of legal 'comparisons' because cases have to be tested whether they are truly in parallel to the case decided by the ECtHR or whether they can for some reason be distinguished. Common Law lawyers will, however, probably shake their heads at such an understanding of legal comparison, and quite rightly so, as here, too, compliance with the Convention is concerned. There will be special force to this objection against qualifying such operations for the sake of compliance as 'comparative' with a view to the United Kingdom. For there, the Human Rights Act 1998 in its sec. 3(1) requires, quite abstractly, primary legislation and subordinate legislation, so far as it is possible, to be read and given effect in a way which is compatible with the Convention rights. It is quite evident that in so far the Human Rights Act 1998 is opening the gate for the *normative* effects of the ECHR to flow in.

1.3.2.2.2 THE RELEVANCE OF ECTHR JUDGMENTS AND THE NEED TO COMPARE

The Human Rights Act 1998 also deals with the relevance of the ECtHR's pronouncements for judicial authorities in the United Kingdom. Sec. 2(1), lit. (a), of the Human Rights Act 1998 places a court or tribunal determining a question which has arisen in connection with a Convention under the obligation to take into account *any judgment, decision, declaration or advisory opinion* of the European Court of Human Rights, *whenever made or given*, so far as, in the opinion of the court or tribunal, it is relevant to the proceedings in which that question has arisen. As broadly as the ECtHR's pronouncements are declared relevant here, this provision clearly goes beyond merely activating the *res judicata* rule for ECtHR decisions and judgments within the domestic legal sphere. Rather, it determines that the British courts sieve through the ECtHR case-law (as well as its declarations and advisory opinions) in order to find out *what the ECHR law is*. If we are correct in understanding this to mean that the British courts, where they have to decide a case in which Convention rights are concerned, need to take into account judgments and decisions by the ECtHR in cases in which the United Kingdom was *not* the respondent State, then we are closer to saying that a *comparative* investigation is required.

---

into force of this section of the Human Rights Act 1998 in proceedings against the United Kingdom, a provision of legislation is incompatible with an obligation of the United Kingdom arising from the Convention. Thus the Human Rights Act 1998 seems to be able to deal with all of the situations described.

It is true that it is only the law of the Convention in the abstract which (as far as the Human Rights Act 1998 implements it in the United Kingdom's domestic legal order) is relevant for the British courts (there being, *ratione personae*, no binding effect resulting from *res judicata*). But when the ECtHR decides on an application brought against *another State*,[38] the rights guaranteed by the Convention are necessarily interpreted and applied, albeit with a view to the specific circumstances of the case. The Court itself does not tire of emphasising its 'case-by-case' approach to explicating and applying the Convention. The relevant circumstances of a case, however, are both factual and normative, the normative character of the case being determined by the law binding the respondent State, which regularly is its national law. When the Human Rights Act 1998 requires British courts to take into account the ECtHR's case-law, this will not only involve 'pealing' away the ECtHR's strictly case-specific findings in order to disclose the normative heart of the decision or judgment. The British courts will also have to look at restatements of Convention law, which the ECtHR has made in tailoring the normative obligations under the ECHR to the details of the factual and (national) normative setting of the case, and to examine whether these specific restatements will 'attach' themselves to similar settings under United Kingdom law.

Let us have a look at two examples.

1.3.2.2.2.1 First example: The accessione invertita *under Italian law and the functioning of British rules on the limitation of land recovery actions* The first one might appear to be 'far away' from the law of the United Kingdom, but can, exactly for this reason, help us to understand what is meant here. In Italy, judge-made law, and subsequently statutory law, have acknowledged the so-called *accessione invertita* or *occupazione acquisitiva*, an indirect form of expropriation: Where an administrative authority has illegally occupied a piece of land, the public power *ab initio* becomes the owner of this land without any formal act of expropriation as soon as facilities of public interest have been installed there; the transfer of the property coming about at the very moment the public facility is completed. If the occupation of the land was initially authorised for a certain period of time, the transfer of property is, as of law, effected as soon as the time period has expired.[39]

---

[38]The ECtHR can only decide cases brought against States Parties, not against individuals or other non-governmental actors. This can be seen by looking at Section II of the ECHR, which deals with the European Court of Human Rights: According to Article 34, first sentence, ECHR, individual applications can be made by 'any person, non-governmental organisation or group of individuals claiming to be the victim of a violation by one of the High Contracting Parties of the rights set forth in the Convention or the protocols thereto.' For inter-state cases Article 33 ECHR provides: 'Any High Contracting Party may refer to the Court any alleged breach of the provisions of the Convention and the protocols thereto by another High Contracting Party.'

[39]ECtHR, *Sciarrotta et al. v. Italy*, no. 14793/02, judgment of 12 January 2006, paras. 21–49.

It is hardly conceivable that there is any similar provision or rule in the law of the United Kingdom to which the ECtHR's evaluation of the indirect expropriation according to Italian law might be applied in parallel. Apparently of consequently little interest is the ECtHR's finding in cases of the application of the *accessione invertita* – for instance, in its judgment on *Sciarrotta et al. v. Italy* – that there was an interference in the applicant's rights under Article 1 of the (first) Protocol to the ECHR, which amounted to a violation of the said article as the legal foundation of this interference, though not missing altogether, did not comply with the requirements of the rule of law (*la prééminence du droit*).[40] But if we reconsider the last two sentences just written, the necessity of a comparative approach stands out clearly: In order to find out whether a 'similar' provision or rule exists in British law, we must make a legal comparison, first determining the purpose and effects as well as the underlying scheme of the *accessione invertita*, then scanning British law for a provision with resemblance.

If we are not all too strict in excluding comparability, we might – I ask the reader forgiveness for my speculations – conceive of a situation in which the British courts might well spend some thought on whether the ECtHR judgment might be relevant, and thereby 'take' it 'into account' within the meaning of sec. 2(1), lit. (a), of the Human Rights Act 1998. It is not too difficult to imagine English courts to be confronted with a case in which a public facility was set up on a piece of private land in England, without any legal basis or justification for such use of the land, and the owner now demands the facility to be broken down and the land to be returned, however only after the time limit[41] for bringing action for the recovery of the land has expired.

In such a case it might well be relevant to learn that the ECtHR regarded the *accessione invertita* as a *de facto* expropriation falling within the scope of Article 1(1), second sentence, of the (first) Protocol to the ECHR and that the requirement that deprivations of possessions need to be 'provided for law' is influenced by the general principle of the rule of law to the effect that domestic legal norms need to be sufficiently accessible, precise and foreseeable. In comparing the cases the English judges will immediately see that in their case the former owner did lose title to the land upon the expiry of the limitation period – whether based on sec. 17 of the Limitation Act 1980[42] (in case the

---

[40]ECtHR, *Sciarrotta* (n. 39), paras 70–74. Also see: ECtHR, *Genovese et al. v. Italy*, no. 9119/03, paras 63–77; *Prenna et al. v. Italy*, no. 69907/01, judgment of 9 February 2006, paras 60–70; *Immobiliare Cerro s.a.s. v. Italy*, no. 35638/03, judgment of 23 February 2006, paras. 74–89; see also ECtHR, *Belvedere Alberghiera S.r.l v. Italy*, no. 31524/96, judgment of 30 May 2000, paras. 20–36, 51–63.

[41]See sec. 15 (in combination with Schedule 2) of the Limitation Act 1980.

[42]According to its sec. 37(1), the Limitation Act 1980, subject to express exceptions in the Act or in other enactments, provided in this Act, shall apply to proceedings by or against the Crown in like manner as it applies to proceedings between subjects. Sec. 37(3) of the Limitation Act 1980 provides that, for the purposes of sec. 37, proceedings by or against the Crown include:

land was not registered) or on sec. 75(1) of the Land Registration Act 1925 (in case of registered land). But they will be able to refer to the ECtHR's judgment in the case of *J.A. Pye (Oxford) Ltd and J.A. Pye (Oxford) Land Ltd v. the United Kingdom*[43] and to point out the *decisive difference* of their case and that of *Sciarrotta et al. v. Italy*: In their case, the loss of land is brought about *neither* by a legislative provision which permitted the State to transfer, or which *ipso iure*, automatically transferred, ownership to the State in the particular circumstances of the instalment of public facilities, *nor* by a social policy of transfer of ownership to the State.

The legislative intention of the British rules on limitation of action for recovery of land is not to deprive owners of their ownership, but rather to regulate questions of title in a system in which, historically, 12 years' adverse possession has been sufficient to extinguish the former owner's right to re-enter or to recover possession, the new title depending on the principle that unchallenged lengthy possession gave a title. The English courts will therefore regard the (former) owner to be affected, not by a 'deprivation of possessions' within the meaning of the second sentence of the first paragraph of Article 1 of the (first) Protocol to the Convention, but rather by a 'control of use' of land within the meaning of the second paragraph of the provision. The statutory provisions which resulted in the applicant companies' loss of beneficial ownership were thus not intended to deprive paper owners of their ownership, but rather to regulate questions of title in a system in which, historically, 12 years' adverse possession was sufficient to extinguish the former owner's right to re-enter or to recover possession, and the new title depended on the principle that unchallenged lengthy possession gave a title. The provisions of the 1925 and 1980 Acts, which were applied to the applicant companies, are part of the general land law, and are designed to regulate, among other things, limitation periods in the context of the use and ownership of land as between individuals. The applicant companies were therefore affected, not by a 'deprivation of possessions' within the meaning of the second sentence of the first paragraph of Article 1 ECHR, but rather by a 'control of use' of land within the meaning of the second paragraph of the provision.[44]

(a) proceedings by or against Her Majesty in right of the Duchy of Lancaster; (b) proceedings by or against any Government department or any officer of the Crown as such or any person acting on behalf of the Crown; and (c) proceedings by or against the Duke of Cornwall. As to actions for the recovery of land see also sec. 37(4) of the Act.

[43] ECtHR (GC), *J.A. Pye (Oxford) Ltd and J.A. Pye (Oxford) Land Ltd v. the United Kingdom*, no. 44302/02, judgment of 27 August 2007, paras. 64–66 (concerning sec. 15, and para. 1 of Schedule 1, of the Limitation Act 1980). The judgment found sec. 17 of the Limitation Act 1980 and sec. 75(1) of the Land Registration Act 1925 merely to be provisions for the control of the use of property which were compatible with Article 1 of the (first) Protocol to the ECHR.

[44] ECtHR (GC), *J.A. Pye (Oxford) Ltd and J.A. Pye (Oxford) Land Ltd* (n. 43), paras. 65–66. The facts of the *Pye* judgment can be distinguished from the fictitious case discussed as it concerned a controversy between private parties, whereas in the fictitious case the rules on limitation operate to the benefit of the State.

1.3.2.2.2.2 Second example: Deprivation of liberty and medication in a private psychiatric clinic without consent Let us take a look at a second example. It is taken from the ECtHR's case *Storck v. Germany*.[45] Of this complex case,[46] to which we will come back later, it is but a small segment. The case concerned judgments by the German courts in the case of a woman claiming to have been deprived of her liberty, *inter alia*, by being placed in a locked ward (*geschlossene Station*) at a private psychiatric institution in Bremen. The applicant had lodged an action for damages against the clinic, claiming that her detention had been illegal under German law and that the medical treatment she received had been contraindicated; her forcible detention and the medical treatment had ruined both her physical and mental health.

While the Bremen Regional Court (*Landgericht Bremen*) allowed the action, the Bremen Court of Appeal (*Oberlandesgericht Bremen*), reversed this judgment. The Court of Appeal left open the question whether the applicant had a compensation claim in tort (*Schadensersatzanspruch aus unerlaubter Handlung*) on account of her unlawful deprivation of liberty or on account of the damage caused to her body by her medical treatment: In any event, such a claim would be time-barred under sec. 852(1) of the Civil Code, which provided for a three-year time-limit.[47]

In its judgment on the *Storck* case, the ECtHR found there to have been an interference imputable to the respondent State with the applicant's right to liberty as guaranteed by Article 5(1) of the Convention as the Bremen Court of Appeal 'failed to interpret the provisions of civil law' relating to the applicant's claims of compensation for deprivation of her liberty 'in contract and tort in the spirit of Article 5'.[48]

The ECtHR judged the applicant to have been deprived of her liberty within the meaning of Article 5(1) ECHR.[49] However, the facts were not fully clear. There was no doubt that her placement in a locked ward under the continuous supervision and control of the clinic personnel amounted to a deprivation of liberty objectively.[50] But in the Court's eyes, a person can only be considered to have been deprived of his liberty 'if, as an additional subjective element, he has not *validly consented* to the confinement in question.'[51] Whether the applicant had done so, was doubtful. What was clear, however, was that having just reached the age of majority and not having been placed under guardianship, she was considered to have the (legal) capacity to

---

[45]ECtHR, *Storck v. Germany*, no. 61603/00, judgment of 16 June 2005, ECHR 2005-V.
[46]For reasons of complexity the case cannot be discussed here in every detail. For a thorough analysis, see *Cremer* (2008).
[47]ECtHR, *Storck* (no. 45), para. 36.
[48]ECtHR, *Storck* (no. 45), para. 99.
[49]ECtHR, *Storck* (no. 45), para. 77.
[50]ECtHR, *Storck* (no. 45), para. 73.
[51]ECtHR, *Storck* (no. 45), para. 74 (emphasis added by the author).

consent or object to her admission and treatment in hospital. Although, undisputedly, she did not sign the clinic's admission form prepared on the day of her arrival, she did come to the clinic herself, accompanied by her father.[52] Nevertheless, the applicant maintained to have been detained *against* her will.[53]

The ECtHR, in effect, leaves the question of whether the applicant had initially validly given her consent *undecided*, emphasising that 'the right to liberty is too important in a democratic society for a person to lose the benefit of the Convention protection for the single reason that he may have given himself up to be taken into detention'.[54] With this, the Court turns away from the question of *initial* consent and addresses problems of 'the *continuation* of the applicant's stay in the clinic',[55] considering 'the key factor in the present case to be that – as is uncontested – the applicant tried on several occasions to escape'; she had to be shackled in order to prevent her from absconding and brought back to the clinic by the police when she managed to escape on one occasion.[56]

The judgment then distinguishes two alternative constellations: Presuming that she had the capacity to consent, the Court under these circumstances is unable to discern any factual basis for the assumption that the applicant agreed to her *continued* stay in the clinic. The court writes: 'In the alternative, assuming that the applicant was no longer capable of consenting following her treatment with strong medication, she cannot in any event be considered to have validly agreed.'[57] In other words, whether a person detained validly revokes his or her initial consent or after being detained loses his or her initially existing capacity to consent, there is an interference with the right under Article 5(1) ECHR, which is in need of justification.

In the *Storck* case, the applicant's (continued) confinement in the clinic against her will is regarded as 'a breach of her right to liberty as guaranteed by Article 5 § 1 of the Convention'[58] as it was not in compliance with the relevant German laws. Before this background, the Bremen Court of Appeal's judgment, although it concerned no more than the damages claims against the clinic, is found to violate the Convention's guarantee of the right to liberty. As far as the damages claims were based on *Deliktsrecht*, German tort law,[59] the

---

[52]ECtHR, *Storck* (no. 45), para. 75.

[53]ECtHR, *Storck* (no. 45), para. 69.

[54]ECtHR, *Storck* (no. 45), para. 75 with reference to ECtHR, *De Wilde, Ooms and Versyp v. Belgium*, no. 2832/66, 2835/66, 2899/66, judgment of 18 June 1971, Series A no. 12, p. 36, para. 65; *H.L. v. the United Kingdom*, no. 45508/99, ECHR 2004-IX, para. 90.

[55]ECtHR, *Storck* (no. 45), para. 76 (emphasis added by the author).

[56]ECtHR, *Storck* (no. 45), para. 76.

[57]ECtHR, *Storck* (no. 45), para. 76.

[58]ECtHR, *Storck* (no. 45), para. 113, see also paras. 109–110.

[59]Questions of contract law are omitted here. As to these see ECtHR, *Storck* (no. 45), paras. 96–98 (concerning deprivation of liberty), paras. 146–147 (concerning medication against the applicant's will).

ECtHR judged the Bremen Court of Appeal to have construed sec. 852 BGB too narrowly. According to this provision of the German Civil Code, in the version in force at the relevant time, compensation claims in tort are time-barred three years after the date on which the victim learned of the damage and of the person liable to compensate him.[60] In the ECtHR's eyes, the Bremen Court of Appeal's view regarding the moment at which time started to run was too restrictive because it found that 'the applicant, being conscious that she had allegedly been deprived of her liberty against her will, had had sufficient knowledge to bring a compensation claim while she was still being detained in the clinic.'[61] The ECtHR reached the conclusion that the Bremen Court of Appeal's interpretation of sec. 852 BGB did not comply with the spirit of Article 5(1) ECHR. The ECtHR did so by comparing the national courts' approach with the principles which it has developed under the Convention with respect to the calculation of the six-month time-limit laid down in Article 35(1) of the Convention for the initiation of proceedings before the Court. It reiterated the consistence of the Convention institutions, holding that this rule has to be applied without excessive formalism, having regard to the particular circumstances of the case, and that there may be, in particular, special circumstances – for example, where the applicant's mental state rendered him incapable of lodging a complaint within the prescribed period – that can interrupt or suspend the running of time for the purposes of limitation.[62] The ECtHR continued verbatim:

---

[60]ECtHR, *Storck* (no. 45), para. 63.

[61]This evaluation of the judgment by the Bremen Court of Appeal is rather doubtful. The *Oberlandesgericht Bremen*, judgment of 22 December 2000–3 U 99/98–, JURIS, para. 29, had found that the plaintiff (the applicant before the ECtHR) had had knowledge of allegedly having been placed and held there against her will *ever since* her stay in the defendant's clinic (*'seit dem Klinikaufenthalt bei der Beklagten'*). As the first headnote – although, admittedly, not an official part of the judgment – says, in a case in which the deprivation of liberty and the physical harm is alleged to be the result of hospitalisation and medication without consent the time begins to run at the end of the stay in the clinic at the latest (*'Die Verjährungsfrist beginnt spätestens mit der Beendigung des stationären Klinikaufenthalts, wenn der Freiheitsentzug und die Körperverletzung durch angeblich ohne Einwilligung erfolgte Klinikunterbringung und medikamentöse Behandlung eingetreten sein sollen.'*). The Bremen Court of Appeal left it at that, at least with regard to the alleged deprivation of liberty, and did not pronounce on when exactly the three years' time began to run. However, it must be conceded that the Court did expressly find the plaintiff to have known from the start that she was being medicated allegedly against her will. Nevertheless, it ought to be observed that it was sufficient for the Court to demonstrate that the plaintiffs action, brought in 1997, was clearly time-barred, since she had been released from the clinic in 1980.

[62]ECtHR, *Storck* (no. 45), para. 95 with reference to ECtHR, *Toth v. Austria*, no. 11894/85. judgment of 12 December 1991, Series A no. 224, pp. 22–23, para. 82; and EComHR, *K. v. Ireland*, no. 10416/83, decision of 17 May 1984, Decisions and Reports (DR) 38, p. 160, *H. v. the United Kingdom and Ireland*, no. 9833/82, Commission decision of 7 March 1985, DR 42, 57.

Having regard to this, the Court considers that the Court of Appeal, in its interpretation of the provisions on the limitation period, did not have sufficient regard to the right to liberty laid down in Article 5 § 1 of the Convention. In particular, that court did not consider the applicant's situation while being detained, in that she had in reality been incapable of bringing an action in court. Contrary to the Regional Court, it also took no account of the difficulties she had encountered after her release from the clinic. The applicant had been treated with strong medication at the time of her release and long afterwards. It is undisputed that, at that time, she was suffering from serious physical disorders and, in particular, lost the ability to speak for more than eleven years (from 1980 to 1991/92). She was also deemed to be mentally ill until she finally obtained two expert reports to the contrary in 1994 and 1999. Furthermore, it has to be noted that the applicant was refused access to the medical file concerning her treatment at the clinic before she brought her action in the Bremen Regional Court. In this connection, the Court also takes into consideration the fact that, as a result of a decision of the Marburg Regional Court produced by the applicant, time did not start running for the purposes of limitation under Article 852 of the Civil Code before the person concerned had access to his medical file.[63]

In parallel to this finding of a violation of Article 5(1) ECHR, the ECtHR held that the Bremen Court of Appeal's judgment had also violated Article 8 ECHR. The applicant's medical treatment against her will was regarded as an interference with her right to respect for private life.[64] This interference was imputable to the State, *inter alia*, on account of the courts' failure to interpret the national law in the spirit of Article 8[65] and was not justified under Article 8(2) ECHR.[66] Referring to its findings regarding Article 5(1)[67] the ECtHR in particular held that 'the Court of Appeal, in its interpretation of the provisions governing the time-limit for bringing the compensation claim – including the possibility of interrupting or suspending the running of time for the purposes of limitation – did not have sufficient regard to the applicant's poor state of health during and following her treatment at the clinic.'[68] Thus, the Court of Appeal failed to interpret the provisions of German civil law relating to the applicant's compensation claim arising from her medical treatment 'in the spirit of her right to respect for her private life under.'

A case similar to that of Ms *Storck* can well be imagined in the United Kingdom, especially as populations all over Europe are over-aging and there

---

[63]ECtHR, *Storck* (no. 45), para. 96.
[64]ECtHR, *Storck* (no. 45), paras. 142–143.
[65]ECtHR, *Storck* (no. 45), paras. 145, 147–148.
[66]ECtHR, *Storck* (no. 45), paras. 152–153.
[67]ECtHR, *Storck* (no. 45), paras. 92–99.
[68]ECtHR, *Storck* (no. 45), para. 147.

are more and more people who, in consequence of age-related dementia or for other reasons, lack the capacity to consent when they are placed in a medical or psychiatric hospital or a nursing home, or lose this capacity afterwards.[69] With regard to the condition that valid consent will exclude the subjective component of a deprivation of liberty within the scope of Article 5(1) ECHR, or of a violation of the right to private life under Article 8 ECHR, the ECtHR's abstract explanations can be of some relevance for British courts when they judge cases of medical treatment, especially medication, and deprivation of liberty allegedly without the consent of the person concerned. They are *normative* specifications of the Convention's guarantees which, as far as possible, need to be complied with[70] when interpreting and applying British statutory law according to sec. 3(1) of the Human Rights Act 1998, and which are also to be taken into account by British courts as the content of an ECtHR decision, as provided by sec. 2(1), lit. (a), of the Human Rights Act 1998. Legal comparison of cases under British law and the *Storck* case will insofar not appear as very urgent or relevant.

But what if a case parallel to that of Ms *Storck* were brought in an English court? Imagine a plaintiff claiming damages for torts of trespass to the person, more specifically battery for medical treatment without the patient's consent,[71] and false imprisonment[72] in a private clinic. However, the plaintiff files his suit against the medical personnel more than ten years after having been released from the clinic. In such a case the British court,[73] in order to fully comprehend the meaning of the ECtHR's judgment for the operation of limitation periods for damages claims, will need to look at sec. 852 BGB, in its version applicable to the *Storck* case. The judge will see that according to sec. 852 BGB (in the version at the time of application) compensation claims in tort are time-barred three years after the date on which the victim learned of the damage and of the person liable to compensate him and that a violation

---

[69]Cf. the Mental Capacity Act 2005.

[70]In this respect it is often pointed out that the judgments of the ECtHR, while not being binding authoritative interpretations, do have persuasive authority. See *Grabenwarter* (2009), § 16, para. 9; *Ress* (1996), 350.

[71]Cf. Murphy (2007), 238, 298, who, at 234, gives as a working definition: 'Battery is any act of the defendant that directly and intentionally or negligently causes some physical contact with the person of the claimant without the claimant's consent.' As to the possibility of an injection against the claimant's will constituting the tort of battery, see *Freeman v. Home Office* (No. 2) [1984] 1 All ER 1036, CA; affirmed [1984] QB 524. Making a patient swallow medicine against his or her will will also involve an unpermitted, direct contact since it is irrelevant whether there is any physical harm (see *Murphy*, ibid., 239).

[72]*Murphy* (n. 71), 246, defines: 'An act of the defendant which directly and intentionally (or possibly negligently) causes the confinement of the claimant within an area delimited by the defendant.' He doubts however whether the courts would allow a claim based on negligent false imprisonment, ibid., 247.

[73]Their willingness to test how far the conditions of a particular tort match the relevant provisions of the ECHR under the Human Rights Act 1980, is underlined by *Murphy* (n. 71), 233 (cf. also ibid., 6–7, 249).

of ECHR guarantees was seen in its restrictive interpretation and handling by the German civil courts.

At the same time, the judge will be aware that, both as to the medication of a patient against his or her will and to detention without consent, the action brought in the British court concerns personal injuries within the meaning of sec. 11 of the Limitation Act 1980.[74] This provision of British law stands in the context of tort law[75] and serves similar purposes as sec. 852 BGB does in the context of German *Deliktsrecht*. The parallels being obvious, sec. 2(1), lit. (a), of the Human Rights Act 1998 will consequently clearly require taking the ECtHR's judgment in the *Storck* case into account, as far as it concerns sec. 852 BGB - eventually in order to obey sec. 3(1) of the Human Rights Act 1998 and read, and give effect to, sec. 11 (and sec. 33) of the Limitation Act 1980 in a way which is compatible with the Convention rights.

That torts are committed intentionally does not exclude them from falling within the scope of this section as can be concluded from the House of Lords decision in *A v. Hoare, C v. Middlesbrough Council, X and another v. London Borough of Wandsworth, H v. Suffolk County Council, Young v. Catholic Care (Diocese of Leeds) and others*.[76] If so,[77] according to this provision, an action shall not be brought after the expiration of a period of three years beginning either from the date on which the cause of action occurred, or from the date of knowledge[78] (if later) of the person injured.[79] In such a case,

---

[74]Which, according to its first paragraph, applies to any action for damages for negligence, nuisance or breach of duty (whether the duty exists by virtue of a contract or of provision made by or under a statute or independently of any contract or any such provision) where the damages claimed by the plaintiff for the negligence, nuisance or breach of duty consist of or include damages in respect of personal injuries to the plaintiff or any other person.

[75]Cf. *Murphy* (n. 71), 3–4 as to the definition and functions of tort law.

[76][2008] UKHL 6, overruling *Stubbings v. Webb*, [1993] 1 All ER 322.

[77]The person injured must, however, not die during the limitation period, see sec. 11(5) of the Limitation Act 1980.

[78]Sec. 14 of the Limitation Act 1980 defines the date of a person's knowledge for purposes of secs. 11 and 12 as the date on which he first had knowledge of the following facts (a) that the injury in question was significant; and (b) that the injury was attributable in whole or in part to the act or omission which is alleged to constitute negligence, nuisance or breach of duty; and (c) the identity of the defendant; and (d) if it is alleged that the act or omission was that of a person other than the defendant, the identity of that person and the additional facts supporting the bringing of an action against the defendant; and knowledge that any acts or omissions did or did not, as a matter of law, involve negligence, nuisance or breach of duty is irrelevant. For the purposes of sec. 14 an injury is significant if the person whose date of knowledge is in question would reasonably have considered it sufficiently serious to justify his instituting proceedings for damages against a defendant who did not dispute liability and was able to satisfy a judgment (sec. 14(2)). For the purposes of this section a person's knowledge includes knowledge which he might reasonably have been expected to acquire (a) from facts observable or ascertainable by him; or (b) from facts ascertainable by him with the help of medical or other appropriate expert advice which it is reasonable for him to seek; but a person shall not be fixed under this subsection with knowledge of a fact ascertainable only with the help of expert advice so long as he has taken all reasonable steps to obtain (and, where appropriate, to act on) that advice (sec. 14(3)).

[79]Sec. 11(3) and (4) of the Limitation Act 1980.

however, sec. 33 of the Limitation Act 1980 enables the court, in which the action has been brought,[80] to direct that sec. 11 of the Act shall not apply to the action, or shall not apply to any specified cause of action to which the action relates, if it appears to the court that it *would be equitable* to allow an action to proceed having regard to the degree to which the provisions of section 11 or 11A or 12 of the Act prejudice the plaintiff or any person whom he represents, and to any decision of the court under sec. 33(1) of the Act would prejudice the defendant or any person whom he represents. This power to exclude the time limit for actions in respect of personal injuries by discretion seems to give it considerable flexibility[81] allowing for an adaptation to the requirements of the Convention as spelled out in the *Storck* judgment. There appears to be considerable leeway as the court shall have regard 'to all the circumstances of the case'.[82] The discretion expressly afforded by sec. 33 of the 1980 Act can be *contrasted* with sec. 852 BGB's wording not mentioning judicial discretion and with its restrictive application by the German courts. Through this contrast, the *Storck* judgment may cause the British court, insofar as it regards the case brought before it to be sufficiently similar, to change the way it uses its discretion under sec. 33 of the Limitation Act 1980. The British judge will probably, through the ECtHR's *Storck* judgment especially, be dissuaded from applying sec. 33 restrictively.

The need for comparison thus comes about through sec. 2(1), lit. (a), of the Human Rights Act 1998 insofar as it requires the judiciary to take into account decisions and judgments by the ECtHR in cases of applications against third States. Unlike Article 16(2) EGBGB, sec. 7(1) StGB, or Article 6(3) of the Treaty on European Union, sec. 2(1), lit. (a), of the Human Rights Act 1998 does not direct the courts immediately to compare normative standards. Rather it, *inter alia*, declares the ECtHR's decisions and judgments to be relevant. But such relevance needs to be proven and requires that the 'case' decided by the ECtHR is comparable. As the 'case', as we have seen, is

---

[80]See sec. 33(7) of the Limitation Act 1980.

[81]Cf. *Murphy* (n. 71), 654–655.

[82]Sec. 33(3) of the Limitation Act 1980. Only 'in particular', and thus not exclusively, is the court, according to sec. 33(3), to have regard to (a) the length of, and the reasons for, the delay on the part of the plaintiff; (b) the extent to which, having regard to the delay, the evidence adduced or likely to be adduced by the plaintiff or the defendant is or is likely to be less cogent than if the action had been brought within the time allowed by section 11 [by section 11A] or (as the case may be) by section 12; (c) the conduct of the defendant after the cause of action arose, including the extent (if any) to which he responded to requests reasonably made by the plaintiff for information or inspection for the purpose of ascertaining facts which were or might be relevant to the plaintiff's cause of action against the defendant; (d) the duration of any disability of the plaintiff arising after the date of the accrual of the cause of action; (e) the extent to which the plaintiff acted promptly and reasonably once he knew whether or not the act or omission of the defendant, to which the injury was attributable, might be capable at that time of giving rise to an action for damages; (f) the steps, if any, taken by the plaintiff to obtain medical, legal or other expert advice and the nature of any such advice he may have received.

influenced by fact and law, especially the law governing the respondent third State's conduct, comparability will depend on the degree of similarity or difference between this State's law and the law which the British courts are bound to apply.

1.4 The German courts and the ECHR

1.4.1 The implementation of the ECHR and its status and rank in German law

The examples we have just looked at mirror the situation of British courts in the context of the Human Rights Act 1998. When we turn to the effects of the European Convention on Human Rights and of the decisions and judgments of the ECtHR on German courts – which, despite a differently structured domestic legal context, show some similarities – we can see that difficulties arise from the way the ECHR, as a public international law treaty, is implemented in German law. Unfortunately, these difficulties require an analysis, which only in the end will show its relevance for German *Deliktsrecht*. But only if we understand the status and the effects of the Convention within the German legal order (and also the effects of single ECtHR judgments) as interpreted by the *Bundesverfassungsgericht* can we hope to comprehend the Convention's influence on the tort-law-based protection of privacy in controversies between private parties. This influence of the Convention is of a normative nature. As our look at the Human Rights Act 1998 has shown, it is different from the *res judicata* effects of single judgments against the state. In order to understand the normative meaning of Convention provisions, the national courts will need to take the ECtHR's case-law into consideration. And this will require them to take a comparative look at judgments against third states in situations similar to the constellations of the cases before them. In this respect the situations in the United Kingdom and Germany do not differ. But let us now look at the implementation of the ECHR in German law.

In order to be ratified, the Convention as a treaty 'relating to subjects of federal legislation' required the consent or participation, in the form of a federal law, of the bodies responsible in such a case for the enactment of federal law according to Article 59(2) of the *Grundgesetz* (*Grundgesetz*).[83] This means that a Federal statute consenting to the Convention, enacted by the *Bundestag*, the Federal Parliament, and the *Bundesrat*, the Federal Council,[84] was required by constitutional law before the Convention could be ratified. This

---

[83] The same holds true for each protocol to the Convention ratified by Germany.

[84] Through which, according to Article 50 of the *Grundgesetz*, the Länder, the constituent states of the Federal Republic of Germany, participate in the Federation's legislation and administration and in matters of the European Union.

Federal statute of consent makes the ECHR applicable within the Federal Republic of Germany's legal order, by way of a *Rechtsanwendungsbefehl*[85] ordering it to be effective and to be applied by the domestic courts and authorities. Simultaneously, it defines the Convention's rank within the hierarchy of norms. Despite some constitutional lawyers' arguments to the contrary, the provisions of the Convention are, within the German legal order, regarded as superior neither to Federal statutes nor to the *Grundgesetz*[86] as the constitution.[87] This causes problems in the case of substantive incompatibility since a derogation of Convention norms within the German legal order brought about by domestic rules of collision, such as supremacy of constitutional law[88] or, for conflicting norms of equal rank, *lex posterior derogat legi priori*, will necessarily lead to a breach of the Convention in the sphere of public international law by making national law prevail. That the Convention, as a treaty concluded by the Federation nevertheless is to be accorded equal rank with Federal statutes,[89] has been pointed out by the *Bundesverfassungsgericht*,[90] especially in a rather problematic decision of 2004.[91]

---

[85]As to the *Rechtsanwendungsbefehl* contained in the statute consenting to a Treaty (including the EC Treaty) and its effect see: *Bundesverfassungsgericht*, decision of 25 July 1979–2BvL 6/77–, BVerfGE 52, 187 (199) – '*Vielleicht*' decision; decision of 10 November 1981–2 BvR 1058/79–, BVerfGE 59, 63 (90) – *Eurocontrol II*; 22 October 1986–2 BvR 197/83–, BVerfGE 73, 339 (375) – *Solange II*; decision of 8 April 1987–2 BvR 687/85–, BVerfGE 75, 223 (244) – *Kloppenburg*; decision of 29 October 1987–2 BvR 624, 1080, 2029/83–, BVerfGE 77, 170 (209–210) – *chemical weapons depots*; judgment of 28 January 1992–1 BvR 1025/82, 1 BvL 16/83 and 10/91–, BVerfGE 85, 191 (204) – *prohibition of night work*; judgment of 12 October 1993–2 BvR 2134, 2159/92–, BVerfGE 89, 155 (190) – *Maastricht*; Judgment of 12 July 1994–2 BvE 3/92, 5/93, 7/93, 8/93–, BVerfGE 90, 286 (364) – *Out-of-area missions*. See also the Görgülü decision, infra, n. 91. Cf. *Bundesverfassungsgericht*, decision of 21 December 1997–2 BvL 6/95–, BVerfGE 97, 117 (124) – *continued validity of GDR criminal law*.

[86]Note that in consequence of its ranking equally with Federal statutes, the Convention has supremacy over the law of the *Länder*, the constituent states of the Federation.

[87]See *Bleckmann* (1994), 152 et seq.; *Frowein* (1987), 1770; *Ress* (1996), 353; *Ress* (1987), 1790 et seq.; *Walter* (1999), 961 et seq. For an overview see: *Hoffmeister* (2001), 365 et seq.; *Sommermann* (1989), 391 et seq.

[88]But see *Steinberger* (1992), pp. 525 et seq., para. 61, according to whom general rules of public international law rank equal with the constitution (but see *infra*, n. 91; see also *Steinberger*, *op. cit.*, paras. 58 et seq. as to theories assigning general rules of public international law supremacy over the *Grundgesetz*).

[89]This is different from the general rules of international law, which, according to Article 25, first sentence, of the *Grundgesetz*, take precedence even over Federal laws (but not over the constitution).

[90]*Bundesverfassungsgericht*, decision of 26 March 1987–2 BvR 589/79, 740/81 und 284/85–, BVerfGE 74, 358 (370) – *presumption of innocence*.

[91]*Bundesverfassungsgericht*, decision of 14 October 2004–2 BvR 1481/04–, BVerfGE 111, 307 (315–316, 316–317) – *Görgülü* (ibid., 318, *obiter* denying general rules of public international law equal rank with the constitution).

1.4.2 The Görgülü *decision of the* Bundesverfassungsgericht

1.4.2.1 *The facts of the case as decided by the ECtHR*

This decision in the *Görgülü* case, which has been heavily criticised,[92] highlighted problems resulting from the Convention's ranking equally with Federal statutes and below the constitution. The case concerned a controversy over the parental custody of, and the right of access to, a child, Christofer. Only after the biological father and the mother had separated and contact between the two had broken off, did Christofer's father learn of his son's birth. However, the mother had released the child for adoption immediately after his birth. Upon this, the child was given to foster parents. The *Wittenberg* Local Court (*Amtsgericht Wittenberg*) transferred the sole parental custody of Christofer to his father. The *Naumburg* Higher Regional Court (*Oberlandesgericht Naumburg*) reversed this decision and suspended the father's right of access to his son. Because the father's constitutional complaint was not accepted for decision by the *Bundesverfassungsgericht*,[93] he filed an application with the ECtHR under Article 34 ECHR.

1.4.2.2 *Effects of an ECtHR judgment according to the Convention as exemplified by the ECtHR's* Görgülü *judgment*

The ECtHR in its judgment of 26 February 2004 found the Naumburg Higher Regional Court to have violated the applicant's right to respect for family life under Article 8 ECHR by refusing the applicant custody of his child and by suspending the applicant's access to his child for one year without sufficient justification.[94] With a view to the High Contracting Parties obligation under Article 46 ECHR 'to abide by the final judgment of the Court in any case to which they are parties', execution being supervised by the Committee of Ministers, the Court pointed out that it follows, *inter alia*, that a judgment in which the Court finds a breach imposes on the respondent State a legal obligation not just to pay those concerned the sums awarded by way of just satisfaction, but also to choose, subject to supervision by the Committee of Ministers, the general and/or, if appropriate, individual measures to be adopted in their domestic legal order to put an end to the violation found by the Court and to redress so far as possible the effects. Furthermore, subject to monitoring by the Committee of Ministers, the respondent State

---

[92]As to the discussion sparked off by the *Bundesverfassungsgericht*'s *Görgülü* decision, see: *Breuer* (2005), 412; *Buschle* (2005), 293 et seq.; *Cremer* (2004), 683 et seq.; *Esser* (2005), 348 et seq.; *Frowein (2005)*, 279 et seq.; *Gruppl Stelkens* (2005), 133 et seq.; *Klein* (2004), 1176 et seq.; *Kadelbach* (2005), 480 et seq.; *Meyer-LadewiglPetzold* (2005), 15 et seq.; *Rohleder* (2009), 196 et seq., 343; *Weber* (2006), 911.

[93]*Bundesverfassungsgericht*, 3rd Chamber of the First Senate, decision of 31 July 2001–1 BvR 1174/01.

[94]ECtHR, *Görgülü v. Germany*, no. 74969/01, judgment of 26 February 2004, paras. 41–51.

remains free to choose the means by which it will discharge its legal obligation under Article 46 of the Convention, provided that such means are compatible with the conclusions set out in the Court's judgment.[95] The court
expressly specified the meaning of Article 46 ECHR in the Görgülü case saying: 'In the case at hand this means making it possible for the applicant to at
least have access to his child.'

This explication by the ECtHR of the effects of its very decision in the
Görgülü case omitted any indication that Article 46 ECHR could only require
the Federal Republic of Germany to enable the applicant access to his son *as
long as* the factual situation had not changed. This is quite essential. One need
only imagine – and let me stress that the following is strictly hypothetical –
that, in the *Görgülü* case, the father might at a time after the delivery of the
ECtHR judgment have attempted to contact his child using force, and in this
context might have seriously disturbed or even disrupted an as yet tender
emotional and social bond with the child. Such a development would undeniably give the German courts leeway to decide differently from what the
ECtHR spelled out in its *Görgülü* judgment. As the binding effects of *res judicata* are limited *ratione personae, ratione materiae* and *ratione temporis*,[96]
such a change of circumstances would take the case outside the bounds of the
ECtHR judgment's *case-specific* binding effects[97] (however leaving all applicable *normative* requirements of the Convention guarantees themselves
untouched).

1.4.2.3 The development in the Görgülü case after the ECtHR judgment

It might well be that the ECtHR's 'over-assertiveness' in defining the *Görgülü*
judgment's *res judicata* effects induced the *Bundesverfassungsgericht* –
notwithstanding some Convention-friendly inputs – to give a rather sceptical
assessment of the binding effects of Strasburg judgments against Germany
within the domestic legal order.[98] It had opportunity to do so after the
Naumburg Higher Regional Court reversed a further decision of the
Wittenberg Local Court, which had transferred parental custody to

[95]ECtHR (n. 94), para. 64 referring to ECtHR (GC), *Scozzari and Giunta v. Italy*, nos. 39221/98
and 41963/98, ECHR 2000-VIII, para. 249.
[96]For details see: *Cremer* (2010), paras. 56–58 (as to the *extent* of obligations resulting from the
ECtHR's finding a violation in a specific case against a State Party, see ibid., paras. 59–69 [as to
the consequences in Germany's domestic legal order, paras. 70–89]; as to effects of ECtHR judgments for *parallel* cases, see ibid., paras. 90–110 [as to the consequences in Germany's domestic
legal order, paras. 111–113]).
[97]*Frowein* (2007), 261 (263–264).
[98]The *Bundesverfassungsgericht*'s oscillation between 'friendliness' towards public international
law and especially ECHR law, on the one hand, and fending off impacts of ECtHR judgments
amounts to the *Görgülü* decision spelling out the *Karlsruhe uncertainty principle* (for a detailed
discussion, see *Cremer* [n. 92], 693–698).

Christofer's father and, as a measure of interim judicial relief, had allowed him access to his son. The *Naumburg* judges had expressly stated their opinion that the ECtHR's judgment was only binding on the Federal Republic of Germany as a subject of public international law, but not on its organs or administrative agencies, and especially not on its courts as these were independent bodies of the judiciary according to Article 97(1) of the *Grundgesetz*; the judgment's effects, subject to a change of domestic law, *de jure* and *de facto* went no further than establishing and declaratorily sanctioning what the ECtHR deemed to be a violation of law having occurred in the past.[99] Against the Higher Regional Court's decision the father lodged a constitutional complaint.

1.4.2.4 Extension of the range of constitutional complaints in cases of non-compliance with an ECtHR judgment by German courts

The *Bundesverfassungsgericht* – and this is one of the undeniably positive parts of its decision – found the *Naumburg* Higher Regional Court to have infringed the father's constitutional right under Article 6 of the *Grundgesetz* in combination with the *Rechtsstaatsprinzip* for not sufficiently having taken into account the ECtHR's judgment of 26 February 2004.[100] In doing so, the *Bundesverfassungsgericht* – a second pro-Convention aspect of its decision – makes a remarkably progressive innovation by pronouncing that it must at least be possible to complain in the course of proceedings before the *Bundesverfassungsgericht* that organs of the state have disregarded, or have failed to take into account, a decision of the ECtHR.[101] This can only mean that in such a case a constitutional complaint can be lodged based upon the allegation that, for instance, a decision of a German court has, by disregarding an ECtHR judgment, violated a basic right guaranteed by the *Grundgesetz* in combination with the *Rechtsstaatsprinzip* (rule of law).[102]

It needs to be underlined that the Court does not deviate from its consistent ruling[103] that a constitutional complaint cannot be founded directly on the allegation of a breach of an ECHR guarantee.[104] Rather, it opens a side-track: The *Bundesverfassungsgericht* extends the priority of statutory law, being based in Article 20(3) of the *Grundgesetz* as one component of the *Rechtsstaatsprinzip*,[105] to include the Convention, because it has the rank and status of a Federal statute. From this, the Constitutional Justices conclusively

---

[99] *Oberlandesgericht Naumburg*, – 14. ZS –3-. FamS–, decision of 30 June 2004–14 WF 64/04–, 2004 Familienrechts-Zeitschrift (FamRZ), 1510 (1511).
[100] *Bundesverfassungsgericht* (n. 91), 330 – *Görgülü*.
[101] *Bundesverfassungsgericht* (n. 91), 329–330 – *Görgülü*.
[102] See *Bundesverfassungsgericht* (n. 91), 317 – *Görgülü*.
[103] See BVerfGE 10, 271 [274]; 34, 384 [395]; 41, 126 [149]; 64, 135 [157]); 74, 102 (128).
[104] *Bundesverfassungsgericht* (n. 91), 315 – *Görgülü* expressly excludes the possibility of lodging a contitutional complaint on the basis of an alleged violation of a Convention right.
[105] But see also Article 28(1), first sentence, of the *Grundgesetz*.

argue that the Convention 'must be respected by the judiciary ('*muss ... beachtet werden*')[106] – but in no way different from a Federal statute. The effects of a judgment of the ECtHR at the international level are defined in the Convention.[107] The *Rechtsanwendungsbefehl*[108] i.e. the order to apply the treaty given by the German Federal statute consenting to the Convention – transposes the rules on the effects of ECtHR judgments into the national legal order,[109] albeit subject to compatibility with higher ranking or otherwise derogating domestic law (on which the *Görgülü* decision expounds[110]). Consequently, a violation of obligations to comply with an ECtHR judgment is quite consistently regarded as a breach of the judiciary's duty to respect and to obey the law according to the *Rechtsstaatsprinzip's* rule of the priority of statutory law. Insofar as such a breach of an objective principle of constitutional law affects the protective sphere of a constitutionally guaranteed basic right, this basic right, as such, is violated and a constitutional complaint, if otherwise[111] raised admissibly, is well-founded.

Meanwhile, the *Bundesverfassungsgericht* has acknowledged the possibility of a constitutional complaint relying on a breach of the Convention in combination with the *Rechtsstaatsprinzip* not only where the *res judicata* effects of an ECtHR judgment are concerned,[112] but also where a regular court in reaching its decision has disregarded, or failed sufficiently to take into account, '*die Rechtsprechung des Europäischen Gerichtshofs für Menschenrechte*', i.e. the European Court of Human Rights' case-law as such.[113]

I.4.2.5 The Bundesverfassungsgericht's *reservations against the binding effects of ECtHR judgments within the German domestic legal order:* Berücksichtigen *instead of* beachten

The *Bundesverfassungsgericht*'s scepticism, however, shows that it not only again and again points to the undeniable possibility of ECHR norms running

---

[106]*Bundesverfassungsgericht* (n. 91), 326– *Görgülü*.
[107]See Articles 41, 44 and 46 ECHR.
[108]See *supra*, at and in n. 85.
[109]Cf. *Frowein* (1986), 845 (850).
[110]Cf. *supra*, at n. 85 et seq. See also *infra*, at n. 117 et seq.
[111]'Otherwise' here meaning apart from the requirement of a substantial, and not *a limine* rejectable, allegation by the complainant of a violation of his or her basic rights (see sec. 90(1) of the *Gesetz über das Bundesverfassungsgericht (Bundesverfassungsgerichtsgesetz–BVerfGG)* and Article 93(1) no. 4a of the *Grundgesetz*).
[112]As in the *Görgülü* case.
[113]*Bundesverfassungsgericht*, decision of 26 February 2008–1 BvR 1602, 1606, 1626/07–, BVerfGE 120, 180 (218, 209–210) – *Caroline von Monaco III*: '*Verfehlt ist die Rüge der Beschwerdeführerin zu 3), der Bundesgerichtshof habe mit dem von ihm gefundenen Entscheidungsergebnis die Rechtsprechung des Europäischen Gerichtshofs für Menschenrechte missachtet oder nicht hinreichend berücksichtigt. Eine solche Rüge kann – gestützt auf das einschlägige deutsche Grundrecht – im verfassungsgerichtlichen Verfahren erhoben werden* (vgl. BVerfGE 111, 307 [323 ff., 329 f.]). *Sie ist vorliegend aber nicht begründet.*'

into conflict with domestic law, but shows a general tendency to interpret German law as calling for the national norm to prevail. With a view to the domestic situation, it consistently avoids clearly and unreservedly speaking of a duty to respect (*beachten*) and to comply with an ECtHR judgment. Instead it prefers saying that the German authorities, especially the courts, must no more than take into account, *berücksichtigen*, judgments of the Strasbourg Court:

> If the [European] Court [of Human Rights] has established a violation of the Convention in a specific application procedure involving the Federal Republic of Germany [as respondent] and if this violation continues, the decision of the [European] Court [of Human Rights] must be taken into account, which means that the competent authorities or courts must be clearly seen to take the judgment into consideration and, as the case may be, *to give comprehensible reasons why they nevertheless will not adopt the legal opinion expressed at the level of public international law.*[114]

While avoiding the demand of strict compliance is understandable with a view to the difficulty of solving conflicts between the Convention and German constitutional and Federal law, the emphasis is obviously on *non*-compliance. The *Bundesverfassungsgericht* stresses that the binding effect of the ECtHR judgments does not allow German administrative authorities or courts to deviate from the order of competencies or from their obedience to law and justice under Article 20(3) of the *Grundgesetz*.[115] When they are required to take the Convention and the judgments of the ECtHR into account, this means that they must neither fail to take an ECtHR judgment into consideration; nor must they simply 'enforce' it schematically.[116]

Symptomatic is the definition the Court gives for '*berücksichtigen*': The provisions of the Convention as interpreted by the ECtHR need to be taken notice of and applied to the case 'insofar as the application does not violate higher ranking law, especially constitutional law'.[117] The reservation is undeniably necessary. However, the Court then seems to back off from this quite

---

[114]*Bundesverfassungsgericht* (n. 91), 324 – *Görgülü*: '*Hat der Gerichtshof in einem konkreten Beschwerdeverfahren unter Beteiligung der Bundesrepublik Deutschland einen Konventionsverstoß festgestellt und dauert dieser Verstoß an, so ist die Entscheidung des Gerichtshofs im innerstaatlichen Bereich zu berücksichtigen, das heißt die zuständigen Behörden oder Gerichte müssen sich mit der Entscheidung erkennbar auseinander setzen und gegebenenfalls nachvollziehbar begründen, warum sie den völkerrechtlichen Rechtsauffassung gleichwohl nicht folgen.*' – The *Görgülü* decision (see (n. 91), 324–328) shows the *Bundesverfassungsgericht* to recognise special problems in multi-polar basic rights conflicts. As to this argument see *infra*, at n. 138 et seq., and also *Cremer* (n. 92), 697 (see also 695–698); idem (n. 96), paras. 85–87; *Grupp/Stelkens*, (n. 92), 141; *Meyer-Ladewig/Petzold* (n. 92), 17.
[115]*Bundesverfassungsgericht* (n. 91), 323 – *Görgülü*.
[116]*Bundesverfassungsgericht* (n. 91), 323–324 – *Görgülü*.
[117]*Bundesverfassungsgericht* (n. 91), 329 (see also 325–328) – *Görgülü*.

clear statement step by step when it continues: 'The Convention norm as interpreted by the [European] Court [of Human Rights] must *at least be included* in the finding of the decision, the [national] Court being under the duty *at least duly to consider* it. In a factual situation which has changed in the meantime, or in a different factual setting, the courts will have to examine what constituted the specific violation of the Convention and *why the change of the factual basis does not allow the application to the case.* In this context it will always be of relevance what taking the judgment into account means in the system of the respective field of law. Even at the level of Federal law *the Convention*[118] *does not automatically enjoy supremacy over other Federal law*, especially when it has not yet been the object of the judgment of the [European] Court [of Human Rights] in this context.'[119]

It is true that the *Bundesverfassungsgericht*'s evaluation of the effects of Convention norms within the German domestic legal sphere – and the Court's tendency to explicate and expound on cases justifying not complying with an ECtHR judgment (obviously including the case of a judgment binding Germany[120]) – might well be considered not unlike what the United Kingdom has laid down in the Human Rights Act 1998. We have seen that sec. 2(1), lit. (a) of the 1998 Act places a court or tribunal determining a question which has arisen in connection with a Convention right under the obligation *to take into account* any judgment, decision, declaration or advisory opinion of the European Court of Human Rights, whenever made or given, so far as, in the opinion of the court or tribunal, it is relevant to the proceedings in which that question has arisen. Sec. 3(1) of the Human Rights Act 1998 requires primary legislation and subordinate legislation to be read and

---

[118]The *Bundesverfassungsgericht* here is pointing to conflicts between the Convention and equally ranking German law. Before, it dealt with conflicts between the Convention (ranking equal to Federal statutes) and higher ranking law, especially the *Grundgesetz* as the constitution and supreme law of the land.

[119]*Bundesverfassungsgericht* (n. 91), 329 – *Görgülü* (emphasis added by the author). The complete passage reads: '"*Berücksichtigen" bedeutet, die Konventionsbestimmung in der Auslegung des Gerichtshofs zur Kenntnis zu nehmen und auf den Fall anzuwenden, soweit die Anwendung nicht gegen höherrangiges Recht, insbesondere gegen Verfassungsrecht verstößt. Die Konventionsbestimmung muss in der Auslegung des Gerichtshofs jedenfalls in die Entscheidungsfindung einbezogen werden, das Gericht muss sich zumindest gebührend mit ihr auseinander setzen. Bei einem zwischenzeitlich veränderten oder bei einem anderen Sachverhalt werden die Gerichte ermitteln müssen, worin der spezifische Konventionsverstoß nach Auffassung des Gerichtshofs gelegen hat und warum eine geänderte Tatsachenbasis eine Anwendung auf den Fall nicht erlaubt. Dabei wird es immer auch von Bedeutung sein, wie sich die Berücksichtigung der Entscheidung im System des jeweiligen Rechtsgebietes darstellt. Auch auf der Ebene des Bundesrechts genießt die Konvention nicht automatisch Vorrang vor anderem Bundesrecht, zumal wenn es in diesem Zusammenhang nicht bereits Gegenstand der Entscheidung des Gerichtshofs war.*'

[120]This is so because the *Bundesverfassungsgericht* addresses the case that 'a factual situation' has changed 'in the meantime' and distinguishes it from the case of 'a different factual setting' (see the quotation *supra*, at n. 119).

given effect in a way which is compatible with the Convention rights so far as it is possible to do so. This rule, however, does not apply to primary legislation and subordinate legislation whenever enacted; it does not affect the validity, continuing operation or enforcement of any incompatible primary legislation; and it does not affect the validity, continuing operation or enforcement of any incompatible subordinate legislation if (disregarding any possibility of revocation) primary legislation prevents removal of the incompatibility. Sec. 6(1) declares it unlawful for a public authority (which term includes British courts and tribunals[121]) to act in a way that is incompatible with a Convention right. But again, this provision does not apply if (a) as the result of one or more provisions of primary legislation, the authority could not have acted differently; or (b) in the case of one or more provisions of, or made under, primary legislation which cannot be read or given effect in a way which is compatible with the Convention rights, the authority was acting so as to give effect to or enforce those provisions.

1.4.2.6 The Bundesverfassungsgericht's emphasis on the German legal order's Völkerrechtsfreundlichkeit and simultaneous failure to consistently construe this principle

1.4.2.6.1 THE GERMAN LEGAL ORDER'S SENSITIVITY TO OBLIGATIONS UNDER PUBLIC INTERNATIONAL LAW

What the German *Bundesverfassungsgericht* ought to have emphasised in the *Görgülü* judgment is that the Federal Republic of Germany cannot simply shrug off obligations under public international law by refusing to accord norms of the Convention or judgments by the ECtHR effect within the domestic legal sphere. Where there is an irreconcilable collision between Convention law and domestic law, German courts, by obeying German law and disregarding ECHR obligations, would make the Federal Republic of Germany breach treaty obligations – if only 'on the outside', i.e. in its relations with the other High Contracting Parties to the Convention. If the *Grundgesetz* actually is 'friendly' towards public international law – as the *Bundesverfassungsgericht* even in the *Görgülü* decision emphasises expressly and with considerable energy and conviction[122] – then the starting point for

---

[121]Sec. 6(3) of the Human Rights Act 1998.
[122]*Bundesverfassungsgericht* (n. 91), 317–318 – *Görgülü*. The Court points to various Articles of the *Grundgesetz*: Article 24 enabling international co-operation (through the transfer of sovereign powers to international organisations); Article 23 (allowing participation in the European Union; Article 25, second sentence, giving priority to the general rules of public international law even over Federal statutes within the domestic legal order); Article 24(2) (enabling accession to a system of mutual collective security); Article 24(3) (requiring the Federation to accede to agreements providing for general, comprehensive, and compulsory international arbitration); Article 26 (declaring acts tending to and undertaken with intent to disturb the peaceful relations

an evaluation of the *res judicata* effects of an ECtHR judgment ought to be that the German courts are basically obliged to *respect and comply with* the ECtHR judgment, and that the case that domestic law cannot be understood to allow such respect and compliance ought to be the *extreme and rare exception*. These would have been the adequate consequences to be drawn from the '*Völkerrechtsfreundlichkeit des Grundgesetzes*', the friendliness and openness of the *Grundgesetz* towards public international law.[123]

1.4.2.6.2 *VÖLKERRECHTSFREUNDLICHKEIT* AND ITS CONSEQUENCES FOR THE INTERPRETATION OF GERMAN LAW

While the *Bundesverfassungsgericht*'s *Görgülü* decision thus shows some ambiguities in defining the relation of German law and ECHR law, the decision does restate two principles of the German legal order's *Völkerrechtsfreundlichkeit*, whose importance can hardly be underestimated.

The first of these principles is that, 'independent of the time of its entering into force, national law is to be interpreted in harmony with public international law as far as possible (...).'[124] In this context the Court refers to a decision of 26 March 1987,[125] which gives an explanation for the 'radiating effect' of the Convention on the interpretation of German law: '(...) [I]t must not be assumed that the legislature, as far as it has not clearly so indicated, intends to deviate from public international law obligations of the Federal Republic of Germany or to allow the violation of such obligations.'[126] This can be seen as part of a larger picture: If the German legal order's 'friendliness' towards public international law is constitutionally required, *Völkerrechtsfreundlichkeit* thus being a principle of the *Grundgesetz*, and if, according to Article 20(3) of the *Grundgesetz*, the legislature must respect the constitutional order, then there seems to be a general constitutional obligation not to enact laws breaking, or permitting the breach of, public international law – notwithstanding the possibility that there might be cases in which national law might have the power at least internally to deviate from public international law, especially as within German domestic law, the constitution ranks highest.

From a principled normative point of view, however, it would be highly problematic, without proof or certainty, to suppose that the *Bundestag* and the *Bundesrat* had the will to act contrary to the *Grundgesetz*, and thus also

---

between nations, especially to prepare for a war of aggression, to be unconstitutional); and finally the Preamble (declaring the commitment of the German people, as an equal member of a united Europe, to peace in the world).

[123] As to this see: BVerfGE 6, 309 (362 f.); 18, 112 (117 f., 120 f.); 31, 58 (75 f.); 58, 1 (41); 63, 343 (379 f.); 75, 1 (17). See also *Fiedler* (2000), 11 et seq.

[124] *Bundesverfassungsgericht* (n. 91), 324 (see also 317, 329, 330) – *Görgülü*.

[125] *Bundesverfassungsgericht*, decision of 26 March 1987–2 BvR 589/79, 740/81 und 284/85–, BVerfGE 74, 258 – *presumption of innocence*.

[126] *Bundesverfassungsgericht* (n. 125), 370 – *presumption of innocence*.

contrary to the principle of *Völkerrechtsfreundlichkeit*. Consequently there can be no presumption of the legislature's intention to violate public international law obligations binding Germany. Where a law is enacted with the will to resist, or even to breach, public international law – for instance, in the context of participating in establishing a new rule of customary law[127] – the legislature must make a clear indication; the clearest way being an express statement.

The duty to interpret German law in concord with public international law generally rules out the application of the principle *lex posterior derogat legi priori* in cases in which a Federal law has been made at a date following the date of enacting a Federal statute consenting to a treaty according to Article 59 of the *Grundgesetz*. It also basically excludes assigning a rule of Federal law, for reasons of its being *lex specialis*, priority over a provision of incorporated treaty law. Rather the Convention, as such a treaty, despite its ranking below the constitution, is part of the normative context into which the provisions of the Federal statute must be fitted through interpretation. This also holds true for German private law, including tort law, on which we will concentrate below.

I.4.2.6.3 *VÖLKERRECHTSFREUNDLICHKEIT* AND THE INTERPRETATION OF CONSTITUTIONAL LAW

The *Bundesverfassungsgericht*'s decision of 26 March 1987 pronounced a second principle linked to the first, but more dramatic. This principle specifically concerns the ECHR. The Court pointed out a 'legal effect, which the Convention's entry into force has for the relation between the basic rights of the *Grundgesetz* and related human rights of the Convention':

> For the interpretation of the *Grundgesetz* both the content and the state of development of the European Convention on Human Rights need to be taken into consideration as far as this does not lead to a limitation or abridgment of the basic rights protection under the *Grundgesetz*, an effect, which the Convention itself however wills and intends to be excluded (Article 60 ECHR[128]). Insofar, the case-law and practice [*die Rechtsprechung*] of the European Court of Human Rights serve as an interpretative tool [*Auslegungshilfe*[129]] for the determination of the

---

[127]The constitutional limits for which of course must be respected; cf. as to the principle of *Völkerrechtsfreundlichkeit*, *supra*, n. 122 and n. 123.

[128]Now Article 53 ECHR: 'Nothing in this Convention shall be construed as limiting or derogating from any of the human rights and fundamental freedoms which may be ensured under the laws of any High Contracting Party or under any other agreement to which it is a Party.'

[129]The word *Auslegungshilfe* is given a strong meaning by translating it with 'interpretative tool'. I understand this strong meaning to accord with the *Bundesverfassungsgericht*'s intention in the decision of 26 March 1987 (*Bundesverfassungsgericht* (n. 125), 370 – *presumption of innocence*). However, it is also open to a weaker meaning amounting to 'something helpful in interpreting the constitution'.

contents and scope of *Grundgesetz*'s basic rights and rule-of-law principles [*rechtsstaatliche Grundsätze*].[130]

The *Görgülü* decision endorses this expressly.[131]
The consequence is that within the German legal order the Convention
exerts a radiating effect not only on statutes and sub-statutory norms, but
also influences constitutional law by helping to determine the contents of
basic rights and constitutional principles.

1.4.2.6.4 CONSEQUENCES OF THE GERMAN CONSTITUTION'S RECEPTIVITY FOR PUBLIC INTERNATIONAL LAW AND A MOVE AWAY FROM THE *GÖRGÜLÜ* DECISION'S SCEPTICISM BY THE *BUNDESVERFASSUNGSGERICHT*'S FIRST SENATE

Above we saw that the *Bundesverfassungsgericht* opened the possibility of
indirectly basing a constitutional complaint on the allegation of a violation of
a Convention guarantee.[132] While the Second Senate's *Görgülü* decision[133]

---

[130]*Bundesverfassungsgericht* (n. 125), 370 – *presumption of innocence*: 'Wenn das
Bundesverfassungsgericht sich zur Definition der Unschuldsvermutung auf den Wortlaut des Art.
6 Abs. 2 EMRK bezogen hat (BVerfGE 35, 311 [320]), der in der Bundesrepublik den Rang von
Verfassungsrecht nicht genießt, so beruht dies auf der rechtlichen Wirkung, die das Inkrafttreten
der Konvention auf das Verhältnis zwischen den Grundrechten des Grundgesetzes und ihnen ver-
wandten Menschenrechten der Konvention hat. Bei der Auslegung des Grundgesetzes sind auch
Inhalt und Entwicklungsstand der Europäischen Menschenrechtskonvention in Betracht zu
ziehen, sofern dies nicht zu einer Einschränkung oder Minderung des Grundrechtsschutzes nach
dem Grundgesetz führt, eine Wirkung, die die Konvention indes selbst ausgeschlossen wissen will
(Art. 60 EMRK). Deshalb dient insoweit auch die Rechtsprechung des Europäischen Gerichtshofs
für Menschenrechte als Auslegungshilfe für die Bestimmung von Inhalt und Reichweite von
Grundrechten und rechtsstaatlichen Grundsätzen des Grundgesetzes.'
[131]*Bundesverfassungsgericht* (n. 91), 317, 329 – *Görgülü*. Yet again, the Court blurs the meaning
of the principle set up in *Bundesverfassungsgericht* (n. 125), 370 when, *ibid.*, 329, it mingles the
duty to interpret *constitutional law* in concord with the Convention as explicated by the ECtHR,
and the duty to comply with the *res judicata* effects of an ECtHR judgment (limited *ratione materiae, personae et temporis*), saying: 'The *Grundgesetz*, through Article 1(2) of the *Grundgesetz*,
accords special protection to the core substance of international human rights. This [sc.- protec-
tion] in combination with Article 59(2) of the *Grundgesetz* is the foundation of the constitutional
duty to employ the European Convention on Human Rights, in its specific development, as an
interpretative tool [*Auslegungshilfe*] when applying German basic rights (cf. BVerfGE 74, 358
[370]). As long as leeway for interpretation and balancing is open within the bounds of methodo-
logical standards, German courts are under the duty to give priority to an interpretation conforming with the Convention. This only does not apply if respecting the judgment of the [European]
Court [of Human Rights], for instance because the factual basis has changed, clearly violates conflicting statutory law or provisions of the German constitution, especially also the basic rights of
third parties.' – As to the endorsement of the rule set out in *Bundesverfassungsgericht* (n. 125), 370
– *presumption of innocence*, see also *Bundesverfassungsgericht*, decision of 29 May 1990–2 BvR
254, 1343/88–, BVerfGE 82, 106 (120); decision of 14 November 1990–2 BvR 1462/87–,
BVerfGE 83, 119 (128).
[132]See *supra*, after n. 100.
[133]*Bundesverfassungsgericht* (n. 91), 329–330 – *Görgülü*. See *supra*, at n. 101.

concentrated on the situation that *a decision* of the ECtHR has not been duly considered, the First Senate in the *Caroline von Monaco III* case[134] pronounced that it is possible to complain in the course of proceedings before the *Bundesverfassungsgericht* that organs of the state have disregarded, or have failed to take into account, *the European Court of Human Rights' case-law as such*. In doing so it pointed out that the complaint of non-compliance with the ECtHR's case-law will need to rely on the German basic right specifically applicable.[135]

In the context of the *Caroline von Monaco III* decision, this part connects with a passage that deals with the limited standard of constitutional review applied by the *Bundesverfassungsgericht* to decisions of regular courts. According to its consistent holding, the Court will restrict its examination to whether the regular courts, in interpreting and applying the provisions of sub-constitutional law and especially in balancing conflicting legal values, have sufficiently respected the influence of constitutionally guaranteed basic rights.[136] This restrictive standard is what, according to the *Caroline von Monaco III* decision, also applies when the question arises whether the regular courts have fulfilled their task of fitting the judgments of the ECtHR into the specifically regulated parts of the German legal order ('*Teilrechtsordnungen der deutschen Rechtsordnung*').[137]

This last statement is clearly made with reference to the *Görgülü* decision. There, one of the main reasons for the *Bundesverfassungsgericht*'s First Senate to be sceptical about a strong influence of ECtHR judgments on subsequent German court decisions were the difficulties it foresaw arising in multi-polar basic rights conflicts.[138] The arguments show the Court to be especially reluctant to make ECtHR judgments influential when the German courts are concerned with the same case; but they go beyond this constellation. For the solution of multi-polar basic rights conflicts the German courts have, as the Court emphasises, through their case-law already created '*nationale Teilrechtssysteme*', i.e. 'sub-systems' of the domestic legal order, in which they have brought conflicting basic rights into a balance by spelling out differentiating rules for specific groups of cases.[139] In the Second Senate's opinion, the 'sub-systems' therefore do not allow ECtHR judgments to be inserted into these case-law-made specific sets of rules in a schematic way.

---

[134]*Bundesverfassungsgericht* (n. 113), 218, 209–210 – *Caroline von Monaco III*. See *supra*, at n. 113.

[135]*Bundesverfassungsgericht* (n. 113), 218 – *Caroline von Monaco III*.

[136]*Bundesverfassungsgericht* (n. 113), 209–210 – *Caroline von Monaco III*.

[137]*Bundesverfassungsgericht* (n. 113), 210 – *Caroline von Monaco III*.

[138]*Bundesverfassungsgericht* (n. 91), 324–328 – *Görgülü*. See *supra*, n. 114 with further references.

[139]*Bundesverfassungsgericht* (n. 91), 327 – *Görgülü*. The Court is not very specific about what these sub-systems are; apart from the sphere of the protection of the personality right, it merely points to the fields of family and immigration law.

Rather the rules need to be adapted carefully. Especially as to the effects of an ECtHR judgment in the same case, the *Görgülü* decision[140] sees the German courts in need of taking into account that, at the European level, in cases of individual applications (Article 34 ECHR), only one of the parties of a private-law controversy also has the status of a party before the ECtHR, there being no guarantee that the other party will even be heard in Strasbourg.[141]

While it is doubtful whether the 'sub-systems' cannot, contrary to what the Second Senate's *Görgülü* decision implies, quite easily adapt to what ECtHR holds, be it for a specific case or in general,[142] the First Senate's attitude seems more relaxed. In its eyes, there is no sufficient justification for the *Bundesverfassungsgericht* to correct a regular court's decision when the balancing of legal positions in complex, especially multi-polar, conflicts might have a different outcome when reviewed.[143] It continues:

> However, a violation of the constitution leading to reprehension of the decision complained of exists where the protective sphere [*Schutzbereich*] of a basic right, which needs to be respected, has been determined wrongly or incompletely or its weight has been judged incorrectly thereby having been incorrectly included in the balancing or where the balancing is incompatible with other standards [*Vorgaben*] of constitutional law, especially for failing to have sufficiently taken into account such requirements [*Maßgaben*] of the European Convention on Human Rights as constitutional law demands to be respected.[144]

The Court's specification that constitutional law also encompasses the courts' duty to take sufficiently into account such requirements of the ECHR as constitutional law demands to be respected, may have a tautological touch. But it easily connects not only with the rule, as highlighted by the *Görgülü* decision, that obedience to law and justice, as required of the courts under Article 20(3) of the *Grundgesetz*, demands respect for the Convention[145] and

---

[140]*Bundesverfassungsgericht* (n. 91), 328 – *Görgülü*.

[141]This is due to the general procedural situation of individual complaints against civil court decisions before the ECtHR: The application is made by one of the parties against the State Party. The other party to the underlying private-law controversy only may be heard (see Article 36(2) ECHR).

[142]See *Grupp/Stelkens*, (n. 92), 140 et seq.

[143]*Bundesverfassungsgericht* (n. 113), 210 – *Caroline von Monaco III*.

[144]*Bundesverfassungsgericht* (n. 113), 210 – *Caroline von Monaco III*: 'Ein Verfassungsverstoß, der zur Beanstandung der angegriffenen Entscheidung führt, liegt aber vor, wenn der Schutzbereich eines hierbei zu beachtenden Grundrechts unrichtig oder unvollkommen bestimmt worden ist oder sein Gewicht unrichtig bemessen und auf diese Weise fehlerhaft in die Abwägung einbezogen worden ist oder wenn die Abwägung sonstigen Vorgaben des Verfassungsrechts widerspricht, insbesondere auch verfassungsrechtlich zu beachtende Maßgaben der Europäischen Menschenrechtskonvention nicht hinreichend berücksichtigt worden sind.'

[145]*Bundesverfassungsgericht* (n. 91), 325–326 – *Görgülü*.

creates a duty to take ECtHR judgments into account.[146] It must also be read in the context of the (constitutional) requirement to interpret the basic rights guaranteed by the German *Grundgesetz* with reference to the ECHR, using the Convention guarantees as *Auslegungshilfe*, as interpretative tools[147] – which in the light of the *Völkerrechtsfreundlichkeit* of the *Grundgesetz* can only mean that the German basic rights are to be read as conforming with Convention law as far as possible.

I.4.2.6.5 THE CONVENTION'S INFLUENCE ON THE INTERPRETATION OF GERMAN CONSTITU-TIONAL LAW IN THE CONTEXT OF *MITTELBARE DRITTWIRKUNG* AS EXEMPLIFIED BY THE *CAROLINE VON MONACO III* CASE

Admittedly, the *Caroline von Monaco III* decision does not elaborate on the interpretation of basic rights in conformity with the ECHR. But a closer look at the case reveals where and how along the lines of this decision the Convention can influence the answer to the question whether basic rights under the German *Grundgesetz* have been infringed.

The case concerned photographs of Princess Caroline von Hannover (formerly of Monaco) in different volumes of two German magazines, the republication of which she had sought to be prohibited by the German courts.[148] All of the pictures were used as illustrations for text articles. The first magazine had printed three pictures, which, so the Princess alleged, violated her privacy: One photograph, showing the Princess together with her husband, Prince Ernst August von Hannover, on a street in St Moritz, was added to an article covering the severe illness of her father, Prince Rainier of Monaco. A similar photograph was attached to a story on the couple's stay in this Swiss winter sports resort. A third picture illustrating an article on the Princess's expected return to Monaco showed the couple using a chairlift during a skiing tour. The photograph in the second magazine, the printing of which the Princess claimed to be a violation of her personality rights, accompanied an article reporting on celebrities who were said to be letting their mansions and castles to private tenants. The Princess filed suits against the magazine publishers in the German civil courts, seeking injunctions prohibiting the pictures to be republished.

The outcome of these proceedings, as pronounced in judgments by the *Bundesgerichtshof*, Federal Court of Justice, as the final court of appeal, was that the Princess's suits were successful in all but one case. Only in the first case against the first magazine publisher was the publication of the picture added to the report on Prince Rainier's illness judged to be justified. In all the other cases the publishers were enjoined from republishing the photographs,

---

[146]*Bundesverfassungsgericht* (n. 91), 316, 323–328 – *Görgülü*.
[147]See *supra*, at n. 130.
[148]The following paragraph is a condensed summary of *Bundesverfassungsgericht* (n. 113), 182–195 – *Caroline von Monaco III*.

which led the magazine publishers, who alleged that their rights under Article 5(1), second sentence, of the *Grundgesetz* had been violated by the injunctions, to lodge constitutional complaints against the civil court decisions with the *Bundesverfassungsgericht*. Princess Caroline directed a constitutional complaint of her own, based on the allegation of a violation of her rights under Articles 2(1) and 1(1) of the *Grundgesetz*, against the civil courts' refusal to grant her protection against the publication of the first picture.

The *Bundesverfassungsgericht* found only the second publisher's complaint to be well-founded. The questions of German constitutional law, which these cases concern, are rooted in the so-called *mittelbare Drittwirkung* of basic rights, which will be discussed in detail in Chapter 4. Suffice it to say here that the fundamental legal phenomenon of *mittelbare Drittwirkung* is that constitutionally guaranteed basic rights, although according to Article 1(3) of the *Grundgesetz* considered to create immediate obligations only for the powers of the state, do influence legal relations between private parties and thus the decisions of civil courts in controversies concerning such private-law relations. Chapter 4 will attempt to analyse the structures of *mittelbare Drittwirkung* in the hope of not only making this difficult inter-relatedness of German constitutional law and German private law more comprehensible, but also of convincing the reader that these structures might plausibly be detected at the level of the European Convention on Human Rights to affect private-law relations and could well be put to work by the European Court of Human Rights in cases in which it reviews court decisions on private-law controversies. This is a further comparative aspect of this book.

But let us turn back to the *Caroline von Monaco III* decision. What Chapter 4 will try to explicate in detail, is indicated when the *Bundesverfassungsgericht* defines its starting point for the evaluation of the cases as to whether the civil court judgments have violated constitutional rights of the three different complainants:

With regard to the magazine publishers, who had been forbidden to republish certain pictures, the Court says that the civil court injunctions against them 'interfered with the protective sphere (*Schutzbereich*) of the basic right of freedom of the press under Article 5(1), second sentence, of the *Grundgesetz* by prohibiting the publication of the photographs'.[149]

As to the rejection of Princess Caroline's application for an injunction against the republication of the photograph used in the context of the article on her father's illness, the Court sees the Princess's 'basic right to protection of the personality' ('*Grundrecht ... auf Schutz der Persönlichkeit*') under Article 2(1) in combination with Article 1(1) of the *Grundgesetz* negatively affected, the German word being '*beeinträchtigt*';[150] '*beeinträchtigt*' is a term

---

[149]*Bundesverfassungsgericht* (n. 113), 196 – *Caroline von Monaco III*.
[150]*Bundesverfassungsgericht* (n. 113), 197 – *Caroline von Monaco III*.

difficult to grasp dogmatically, but quite obviously the word is used with the intention of avoiding the term '*eingreifen*' (to interfere with). '*Eingreifen*' is shunned because the *Bundesverfassungsgericht* here is examining whether the courts have violated Articles 2(1) and 1(1) of the *Grundgesetz* by failing to protect the Princess's personality sufficiently.

In terms of constitutional law, the question the civil courts had to decide in the case of each of the pictures was whether they were under a duty to *protect* the Princess's basic right under Article 2(1) in combination with Article 1(1)[151] by enjoining the magazine publishers from any further publication, i.e. by *restricting* the freedom of the press. Chapter 4 will try to show that this is precisely the structure of *mittelbare Drittwirkung*: In a conflict between private parties the basic right of one of the parties suffers an intrusion resulting from the other party's exercise of their basic right; and it is a matter for authorities of the state, especially the courts, to decide whose constitutionally guaranteed right is to suffer a set-back: Must the first party tolerate the encroachment by the second party? Or can it demand to be protected by the states, or, in other words, can it demand the state to limit the second party in exercising their right? What is essential for the *Caroline von Monaco III* case is that the *Bundesverfassungsgericht* regards the constitution in such cases to require a balancing of the conflicting basic rights – i.e. in the case of the Princess of Monaco, a balancing of the right to protection of one's personality, on the one hand, and the freedom of the press, on the other hand, when the civil courts decide in these cases.[152] And here is where the ECHR comes in: If one starts out looking at a case from the press's point of view, the question is whether Article 5(1), second sentence, of the *Grundgesetz* can be restricted by the civil courts for the purpose of protecting the personality and privacy of a private individual. One then finds that according to Article 5(2) of the *Grundgesetz* the freedom of the press finds its limits in the provisions of *allgemeine Gesetze*, i.e. of the laws of general application.[153] The *Bundesverfassungsgericht* regards the ECHR, and more specifically Article 8(1) ECHR guaranteeing the right to respect for one's private life, as belonging among these laws of general application.[154] But what is more, the *Caroline von Monaco III* decision regards the protection required by Article 8(1) ECHR to correspond with the personality protection under German constitutional law, the parallel including the necessity of balancing privacy protection with the freedom of expression.[155]

Such a balancing likewise proves necessary if an evaluation of the case chooses the personality right or right to privacy as the starting point. The

---

[151]Nowhere, however, does *Bundesverfassungsgericht* (n. 113) – *Caroline von Monaco III*, use the German technical term '*Schutzpflicht*'.

[152]See especially *Bundesverfassungsgericht* (n. 113), 199–203 – *Caroline von Monaco III*.

[153]For details see *infra*, Chapter 4.

[154]*Bundesverfassungsgericht* (n. 113), 200 – *Caroline von Monaco III*.

[155]*Bundesverfassungsgericht* (n. 113), 200–201 – *Caroline von Monaco III*.

Bundesverfassungsgericht in this perspective points out that the limitations laid down in Article 2(1) of the *Grundgesetz* apply to the right to protection of the personality under Article 2(1) in combination with Article 1(1) of the *Grundgesetz*.[156] As an element of the constitutional order limiting the rights under Article 2(1), the Court – in parallel to what it says to Article 5(2) – again addresses the Convention: Article 10 ECHR (after its incorporation into domestic law) restricts the constitutionally protected personality right. Just as the freedom of expression under Article 10 ECHR needs to be fine-tuned with the right to respect for another's private life under Article 8(1) ECHR, the right guaranteed by Article 2(1) in combination with Article 1(1) of the *Grundgesetz* needs to be balanced against the freedom of the press under Article 5(1) of the *Grundgesetz*.[157]

As to the latter balancing of constitutional rights, i.e. basic rights guaranteed by the German *Grundgesetz*, the *Bundesverfassungsgericht* demands special weight to be given to the freedom of expression as guaranteed under Article 10(1) ECHR.[158] Later on, the Court seems to blend the standards altogether, when it says:

> It is in principle in harmony with the protection guaranteed to the press under Article 5(1) of the *Grundgesetz* that the European Court of Human Rights considers it as necessary to judge whether it is admissible to publish images of persons for the purpose of reporting by the press by way of balancing the interests of the protection of the private sphere and the freedom of expression.[159]

---

[156] *Bundesverfassungsgericht* (n. 113), 201 – *Caroline von Monaco III*. In terms of *Dogmatik*, it is quite surprising to see the Court address limitation clauses of basic rights in the context of what essentially is a discussion of *Schutzpflichten*, duties to protect basic rights (especially against intrusion by other private parties). However, as Chapter 4 will show, the *Bundesverfassungsgericht* has not yet clearly acknowledged *mittelbare Drittwirkung* to be inextricably connected to *Schutzpflichten*. Rather Chapter 4 will offer a reconstructive reading of the *Lüth* judgment in the context of the Court's case-law, which will try to make plausible that *mittelbare Drittwirkung* is the resultant of the joint 'operation' of protective duties for the basic right of one party in a private-law controversy (requesting protection against another party's intrusion into the protective sphere of this very right) and the duty to respect the basic rights which the other party uses thereby intruding into the first party's sphere.

[157] *Bundesverfassungsgericht* (n. 113), 202–203 – *Caroline von Monaco III*.

[158] *Bundesverfassungsgericht* (n. 113), 203 – *Caroline von Monaco III*.

[159] *Bundesverfassungsgericht* (n. 113), 218 – *Caroline von Monaco III*: 'In grundsätzlichem Einklang mit dem von Art. 5 Abs. 1 GG der Presse verbürgten Schutz sieht es auch der Europäische Gerichtshof für Menschenrechte als erforderlich an, über die Zulässigkeit der Veröffentlichung von Personenbildnissen aus Anlass einer Presseberichterstattung im Wege einer Abwägung der Belange des Schutzes der Privatsphäre und der Äußerungsfreiheit zu entscheiden.'

1.5 Looking ahead

This blending of *Grundgesetz* and ECHR requirements, in my opinion, points to the influence the Convention guarantees have on the interpretation and operation of basic rights guaranteed under German constitutional law – especially in cases of controversies between private parties. If ECHR rights thus, albeit only as interpretative tools (*Auslegungshilfe*), influence German basic rights, then the problems resulting from the formal status of the Convention as ranking equivalent to a Federal statute within the German domestic legal order seem to dissolve – something which interestingly can only be assessed through a comparison of the situation under the *Grundgesetz* taken alone (i.e. hypothesising the ECHR's influence to be absent) and the situation under the Convention. The Convention appears all the more influential in Germany – especially in cases of privacy protection through tort law as the *Caroline von Monaco III* case shows. But this case is little more than an echo of its immediate predecessor, a case, which after its decision by the *Bundesverfassungsgericht* was taken to Strasbourg, where the ECtHR set a milestone in its judgment of 2004 in the case of *Hannover v. Germany*.[160] This case and the reverberations caused by the ECtHR judgment will be explored in the next chapter.

---

[160] ECtHR, *Hannover* (no. 4).

Chapter 2:
The European Court of Human Rights' *Caroline von Hannover* judgment and its reverberations

2.1 The Case of *Caroline von Hannover*

The case of *Caroline von Hannover* decided by the ECtHR[1] is well-known among lawyers. It has influenced not only the jurisprudence of German courts, but, through its interpretation of Article 8 ECHR and its acknowledgement of the effects of Convention guarantees in controversies between private parties, radiates into the High Contracting Parties' legal orders – at least by force of the persuasive authority of the Court's jurisprudence – thus affecting decisions by domestic courts. The House of Lords has been most attentive to the Strasbourg judicature.

2.1.1 A sketch of the facts

For a long time, Princess Caroline of Hannover has attracted the attention of the media. As the eldest daughter of the late Prince Rainier III of Monaco, she is the president of certain humanitarian or cultural foundations and also represents the ruling family at events such as the Red Cross Ball and the opening of the International Circus Festival. She does not, however, perform any function within or on behalf of the State of Monaco or one of its institutions.[2] Since the early 1990s the Princess had been trying in a number of European countries to prevent the publication of photos about her private life in the tabloid press.[3]

The case decided by the ECtHR evolved before the German courts.[4] It might best be told as the story of the press seeing its publishable photo files on

---

[1] ECtHR, *Von Hannover v. Germany*, no. 59320/00, judgment of 24 June 2004, ECHR 2004–VI.

[2] ECtHR, *Von Hannover* (n. 1), § 8.

[3] ECtHR, *Von Hannover* (n. 1), § 9.

[4] As to the facts see *Bundesgerichtshof*, judgment of 19 December 1995 –VI ZR 15/95–, 1996 Neue Juristische Wochenschrift 1128 = BGHZ 131, 332; *Bundesverfassungsgericht*, judgment of 15 December 1999 –1 BvR 653/96–, BVerfGE 101, 361 (362–371) – *Caroline von Monaco II*; ECtHR, *Von Hannover* (n. 1), §§ 18–38.

the Princess shrinking gradually, instance by instance. The case concerned images published by the publishing company, Burda, in the German magazines, *Bunte* and *Freizeit Revue*, and by the publishing company, Heinrich Bauer, in the German magazine, *Neue Post*. The photos illustrate articles on aspects of Princess Caroline's life, very often speculating on love affairs or her family situation, which have no apparent, direct connection with any of her official functions. They show scenes such as the Princess horse-back riding, shopping with a bag slung over her shoulder, skiing on a holiday in Zürs/Arlberg, leaving her house in Paris, and, tripping over an obstacle and falling down while dressed in a swimsuit and wrapped up in a bathing towel. There are also pictures of the Princess and Prince Ernst August von Hannover, visiting a horse show in Saint-Rémy-de-Provence, playing tennis and both putting their bicycles down.[5] All of these situations, as people in the street would be sure to say, belong to the Princess's 'private life'.

In the course of the court proceedings, one picture and a group of other photographs gained special importance. The one picture showed the Princess sitting with the actor Vincent Lindon at the far end of a restaurant courtyard in Saint-Rémy-de-Provence.[6] The other photographs formed a group insofar as they depicted Caroline together with her children.[7]

2.1.2 Proceedings before the German civil courts

There were three sets of proceedings before the German courts.[8] It will suffice to retrace the first set as it shows all the relevant legal aspects of publishing celebrity photographs in the media. At the same time, it is not necessary to comment on the German court decisions insofar as the Princess's claims for protection against the publication of the contested images in magazines in France were rejected.[9]

With a view to any further publication of a number of the photographs described above in Germany, Princess Caroline sought an injunction against the Burda publishing company relying on her rights under the *Kunsturhebergesetz* (KUG), the German Copyright (Acts Domain) Act.[10] Section 22(1) KUG provides that images can only be disseminated or shown in public with the express approval of the person concerned. However, this is

---

[5]ECtHR, *Von Hannover* (n. 1), §§ 11–17.

[6]ECtHR, *Von Hannover* (n. 1), § 11.

[7]ECtHR, *Von Hannover* (n. 1), §§ 12, 13.

[8]See ECtHR, *Von Hannover* (n. 1), §§ 18–26, §§ 27–32, §§ 33–38 (third set).

[9]As to sec. 38 of the *Einführungsgesetz in das bürgerliche Gesetzbuch* (Introductory Act to the Civil Code) read as barring the application of Article 9 of the French Civil Code, see *Bundesgerichtshof* (n. 4), 1128, 1131; see also *Oberlandesgericht Hamburg*, judgment of 8 December 1994 –3 U 64/94 –, 1995 Neue Juristische Wochenschrift – Rechtsprechungsreport 790–793. Cf. ECtHR, *Von Hannover* (n. 1), §§ 19, 21. See also *Michael* (2007), 360–1.

[10]As to the roots of this statute, see *Markesinis/Unberath* (2002), 78; *Michael* (2007), 361–70.

only a general rule. It suffers certain exceptions under sec. 23(1) KUG, the first of which is that images portraying an aspect of contemporary society (*Bildnisse aus dem Bereich der Zeitgeschichte*) can be disseminated or shown in public. However, this right of dissemination or public display does not comprise a publication interfering with a legitimate interest either of the person concerned or, if the person has died, of his relatives (sec. 23(2) KUG). As far as publication is barred by sec. 22(1) KUG, it is generally accepted that the person whose image is concerned has a right to forbearance if there is imminent danger of dissemination or public display by another person.[11]

Under sec. 23(1) KUG, the courts had, in a long line of decisions, developed a rather rigid differentiation using the concept of '*Person der Zeitgeschichte*', a figure of contemporary society. A '*relative*' figure of contemporary society is a person who has attracted interest by being involved in an event of contemporary society with the consequence of the publication of this person's image being allowed within the context of this event. In contrast, an '*absolute*' figure of contemporary society, i.e. a person who for reasons of status and importance receives public attention, is himself or herself an object of contemporary society.[12] In the case of Princess Caroline, the civil courts of the first and second instances made use of this distinction.

The Hamburg Regional Court (*Landgericht*) and Appellate Court (*Oberlandesgericht*) rejected the claim on the grounds of the Princess's being a figure of contemporary society *par excellence*, '*eine absolute Person der Zeitgeschichte*'.[13] It denied her protection, arguing that the right to protection of people's private life stopped at their front door. Even if the barrier between the public interest in reporting and privacy were drawn at the garden fence or the wall around the park, all the photos of the applicant had been taken exclusively in public places. She therefore had to tolerate publication without her consent. The Hamburg Court of Appeal confirmed the Regional Court's judgment. Though the constant hounding by photographers may have made her daily life difficult, it arose from a legitimate desire to inform the general public.[14]

---

[11]*Sprau* (2010), Einf v § 823, § 18 (for details see *ibid.*, §§ 19–27). The right to forbearance is construed analogous to sec. 1004 BGB. This provision grants the owner of property, whether movables or immovables, a right to removal and prevention of infringement: If, absent an obligation to tolerate, property rights are infringed upon other than by dispossession or ouster, the owner can demand of the infringer to remove the infringement. If further infringements are imminent, the owner can petition for a preventive injunction.

[12]For a summary see *Bundesgerichtshof*, judgment of 6 March 2007 –VI ZR 51/06, 2007 Neue Juristische Wochenschrift 1977 (1978) (= 2007 Europäische Grundrechtezeitschirft 499; the following quotations, see ns. 186 et seq., refer to the publication in Neue Juristische Wochenschrift).

[13]*Oberlandesgericht Hamburg* (n. 9), 791–792. See also *Bundesgerichtshof* (n. 4), 1128; *Bundesverfassungsgericht* (n. 4), 365–366 – *Caroline von Monaco II*; ECtHR, *Von Hannover* (n. 1), §§ 19, 21.

[14]*Oberlandesgericht Hamburg* (n. 9), 792. See also *Bundesgerichtshof* (n. 4), 1128;

The *Bundesgerichtshof* (the German Federal Court of Justice) confirmed that the Princess was an 'absolute' figure of contemporary society. For such a conclusion, the Court said (somewhat tautologically, one might find), it was decisive that public opinion considered images of such persons as important and worthy of being taken note of for the sole reason of these persons being who they are ('*daß die öffentliche Meinung Bildwerke über sie als bedeutsam und um der dargestellten Person willen der Beachtung wert findet*'). In this case the public had a real informational interest, which needed to be acknowledged. This rule applied to monarchs, heads of state or prominent politicians, and was, therefore, equally valid in the case of the Princess, who was the eldest daughter of the then ruling Prince of Monaco.[15]

However, the *Bundesgerichtshof* pointed out that there were limits to the publishing of images of figures of contemporary history. According to sec. 23(2) KUG, a legitimate interest of the person concerned could stand against publication. This had to be assessed by balancing the public's interest in being informed (Article 5 of the *Grundgesetz*) against the personality right of the depicted person (Article 2 of the *Grundgesetz*).[16]

Even a figure of contemporary society enjoyed the right to respect for one's private sphere, thus not having to suffer photographs taken of themselves within the core sphere of their privacy; for instance, within their home.[17] Only in exceptional conditions, when dominant public interests justified such an interference, could the publication of images from this sphere be admissible.[18] Consequently, the *Bundesgerichtshof* disagreed with the lower courts insofar as they had restricted the private sphere to spaces secluded from the public within a person's own home. Even figures of contemporary society *par excellence* were entitled to respect for their private life. Pointing to the historic roots of the Copy Right (Arts Domain) Act, the Court found this respect not to be limited to the home.[19]

Bundesverfassungsgericht (n. 4), 365–366) – *Caroline von Monaco II*; ECtHR, *Von Hannover* (n. 1), §§ 19, 21.

[15] *Bundesgerichtshof* (n. 4), 1129 with reference to *Kammergericht Berlin*, , judgment of 12 October 1927 – 10 U 11325/27 – 1928 Juristische Wochenschrift 363 – *Kaiser Wilhelm II*; *Amtsgericht Ahrensböck*, judgment of 9 March 1920, 1920 Deutsche Juristenzeitung 596 – *Reichspräsident Ebert and Reichswehrminister Noske*; Bundesgerichtshof, judgment of 14 November 1995 – VI ZR 410/94 – 1996 Neue Juristische Wochenschrift, 593 – *Bundeskanzler*; Oberlandesgericht München, judgment of 6 December 1962 – 6 U 2160/61 – 1964 Archiv für Urheber- und Medienrecht 322 – *Kanzlerkandidat*.

[16] *Bundesgerichtshof* (n. 4), 1129.

[17] *Bundesgerichtshof* (n. 4), 1129 referring to *Bundesgerichtshof*, judgment of 10 May 1957 –I ZR 234/55–,1957 Neue Juristische Wochenschrift 1315 = BGHZ 24, 200 (208); judgment of 10 November 1961 –I ZR 78/60–, GRUR 1962, 211 (212) – *Hochzeitsbild*; judgment of 9 June 1965 –I b ZR 126/63–,1965 Neue Juristische Wochenschrift 2148 – *Spielgefährtin*.

[18] *Bundesgerichtshof* (n. 4), 1129 referring, inter alia, to *Bundesgerichtshof*, 26.01.1965 –VI ZR 204/63–, 1965 Juristenzeitung 411 (413) – *Gretna Gree*.

[19] *Bundesgerichtshof* (n. 4), 1129 quoting *Stenographischer Bericht über die Verhandlungen des Reichstages* 1905/1906, Annex. vol. II, 1526, 1541.

Outside their home, however, they could not rely on the protection of their privacy unless they had retired to a secluded place – away from the public eye (*in eine örtliche Abgeschiedenheit*) – where it was objectively clear to everyone that they wanted to be alone and where, confident of being away from prying eyes, they behaved in a given situation in a manner in which they would not behave in a public place. Unlawful interference with the protection of that privacy could therefore be made out if photos were published that had been taken secretly or by catching unawares a person who had retired to such a place.[20] This was the case where someone was watching the person concerned *quasi* through a keyhole, clandestinely taking pictures, or where someone took him or her by surprise, thus preventing the victim from reacting in time and getting prepared to be photographed. While taking pictures inside the home strictly requires consent (even in the case of a figure of contemporary society *par excellence*), a person might *quasi* take the sphere of privacy outside the house and then need to have a right to the same protection.[21]

Retreating to a secluded place, unaware of being photographed, was exactly the situation in which the picture of the Princess, sitting with the actor Vincent Lindon at the far end of a restaurant courtyard in Saint-Rémy-de-Provence, was taken. The applicant and her boyfriend had withdrawn to the far end of a restaurant courtyard with the clear aim of being out of the public eye. Therefore, the *Bundesgerichtshof* found a legitimate interest to stand against the publication of this photograph without the Princess's consent. The exception of sec. 23(1) KUG thus did not apply, and the Princess enjoyed protection under sec. 22 KUG against the publication.[22]

However, the Federal Court dismissed the remainder of her appeal. Sec. 23 KUG did not allow the same degree of protection as might Article 9 of the Code Civil in France.[23] Rather, the public had a legitimate interest in being shown a figure of contemporary society *par excellence*, in learning how this person, as an individual, moves and behaves in public, even outside his or her public functions. The public's informational interest could only be overridden by a legitimate interest of the person concerned within the meaning of sec. 23(2) KUG. Such an interest of the Princess's was, the Court found, absent with regard to the images of her in public, whether riding, canoeing, cycling, shopping or being in the street.[24] The applicant had to tolerate the publication of photographs in which she appeared in a public place even if they were

---

[20]*Bundesgerichtshof* (n. 4), 1129–1130 as summarised by ECtHR, *Von Hannover* (n. 1), § 23.

[21]*Bundesgerichtshof* (n. 4), 1130.

[22]*Bundesgerichtshof* (n. 4), 1130; the summary by ECtHR, *Von Hannover* (n. 1), § 23 has been used here too.

[23]The *Bundesgerichtshof*, *inter alia*, refers to *Cour de Cassation*, Bulletin des arrets, Chambres civiles, avril 1988, 1. Ch. civ. Nr. 98, p. 67 – *Farah Diba*; *Tribunal de grande instance de Paris*, Recueil Dalloz Sirey 1977, Jurisprudence pp. 364 et seq. – *Caroline von Monaco*.

[24]*Bundesgerichtshof* (n. 4), 1130–1131.

photos of scenes from her daily life and not photos showing her exercising her official functions.

2.2 Excursus *on the general personality right*

Before we look into the judgments of the *Bundesverfassungsgericht* and the European Court of Justice in this case, it seems advisable at least briefly to look at the *Bundesgerichtshof*'s case-law concerning the general personality right, *das allgemeine Persönlichkeitsrecht*. This right is a pivotal point in the Court's *Caroline II* judgment, just presented as the Court construes the meaning of sec. 23(2) KUG on the foundation of the personality right: In balancing the respective legal positions in the conflict between the protection of the *absolute Person der Zeitgeschichte* against the publication of an image and the public's right to see, and learn about, this figure of contemporary society par excellence, the *Bundesgerichtshof* attributes special importance to the protection of the private sphere. The right to respect for the private sphere, the Court explains, emanates from the general personality right, which assigns to every individual a protected sphere for conducting his life autonomously. This right includes the right to be let alone, 'to belong to oneself' *(sich selbst gehören).*[25] Consequently, the courts have, after the Second World War,[26] attached special importance, both in public and in private law, to the right to respect the private sphere as a constitutionally guaranteed basic right, which encompasses the right to one's own image.[27]

In German private law there is no general provision of a tort of unlawful interferences with another person's personality.[28] Rather, the courts in general rely on sec. 823(1) of the German Civil Code *(Bürgerliches Gesetzbuch – BGB)*, according to which someone who, willingly or through negligence, unlawfully infringes life, body, health, freedom, property or another right of another person owes this person compensation for redress of damages. As in the special case of sec. 22(1) KUG, the person who has suffered such an unlawful infringement has a right both to demand the infringer to stop the interference and, if there is imminent danger, to refrain from repeating it.[29]

---

[25]*Bundesgerichtshof* (n. 4), 1129. The *Bundesgerichtshof* refers to BVerfGE 34, 238 (245ff.); BVerfGE 35, 202 (220); it also points to the situation under the law of the USA referring to *Katz v. United States*, 389 Supreme Court (1967), 347, 350–351.; *Warren/Brandeis* (1890), 193 et seq.; *Götting* (1995), pp. 168 et seq., 174.

[26]For a concise overview of the development leading to the acknowledgement of the general right to one's personality, see *Markesinis/ Unberath* (n. 10), German Tort Law, 74–79.

[27]*Bundesgerichtshof* (n. 4), 1129, with further references.

[28]There are, however, specific provisions such as secs. 22 and 23 KUG, see *supra*, at n. 10.

[29]See *supra*, n. 11.

2.2.1 The development of the general personality right by the civil courts

2.2.1.1 The changing constitutional background of the Bürgerliches Gesetzbuch

Privacy and the wider concept of the personal autonomy are – especially in the light of the history of the BGB[30] – not contained in sec. 823(1) BGB's list of specific interests, the infringement of which leads to a right to compensation against the infringer. Consequently, the initial core question of privacy protection is whether these interests might be included in 'another right' within the meaning of the provision – which would require the existence of a right with an absolute power of exclusion (*absolutes Recht*). It is this which the German civil courts acknowledged after the Second World War. They could do so as the *Bürgerliches Gesetzbuch* of 18 August 1896,[31] in force since 1 January 1900, needed to be read and construed before a new constitutional background. The supreme law of the land was no longer the Constitution of the German Empire of 1871, nor the Weimar Constitution of 1919, but the *Grundgesetz*, which most prominently placed the protection of basic rights, and most prominent respect for and protection of human dignity, in its very first section.

Almost exactly five years after the *Grundgesetz* entered into force for the western part of Germany, the *Bundesgerichtshof* drew the conclusion from the basic rights and accepted the general personality right as a right protected under sec. 823(1) BGB when it decided the *Schacht* case.[32] The attorney of Dr Schacht, acting on his client's instructions, wrote a letter to a company which in one of its weekly journals had criticised Dr Schacht's political activity during the national-socialist regime and the years after the war. Instead of answering, the company published the attorney's letter, with omissions of certain material from the Nuremberg judgment concerning Dr Schacht, as one of several 'Letters from Readers'. The attorney sued the company, demanding it to recall its statement that he had sent a reader's letter to the company. The *Bundesgerichtshof* found the Court of Appeal wrongly not to have examined whether the claim was justified on grounds of an infringement of the plaintiff's personality rights. In the light of the guarantee of human dignity in Article 1 of the *Grundgesetz* and the right to free development of one's personality under Article 2(1) of the *Grundgesetz*, it qualified the general personality right as a *constitutionally guaranteed fundamental right*:

---

[30]See *Markesinis/Unberath* (n. 10), 74. See also *Bundesverfassungsgericht*, decision of 14 February 1973 –1 BvR 112/65–, BVerfGE 34, 269 (270–271) – *Soraya*.
[31]Reichsgesetzblatt 1896, 195.
[32]*Bundesgerichtshof*, judgment of 25 May 1954 –I ZR 211/53– (*Schacht*), 1954 Neue Juristische Wochenschrift 1404 = BGHZ 13, 334.

After the *Grundgesetz* now recognises the right of the human being to respect for his dignity (Article 1 of the *Grundgesetz*) and the right to free development of his personality even as a private right, to be respected by everyone as far as this right does not violate the rights of others or contravene the constitutional order or good morals (Article 2 of the *Grundgesetz*), the general personality right must be regarded as a constitutionally guaranteed basic right (…).[33]

Only briefly did the Court point to limitations of this right and the need to bring it into a balance with other justified private or public needs.[34] Then it went on to acknowledge verbal expressions of a definite thought as an emanation of the author's personality right. Independent of copyright law, this right protected both against an unauthorised publication of private notes and against reproduction with unauthorised alterations, as they posed the danger of spreading a false picture of the author's personality.

At this point it is worth mentioning that it is established case-law that sec. 823(1) BGB operates differently in cases of an interference with the general personality right than in cases of infringements of life, body, health, freedom or property. While these infringements, if established, create a presumption of unlawfulness, rebuttable only by proving a ground for justification, interference with the personality right only amounts to a tort under sec. 823(1) BGB if a balancing of the interests involved positively shows the personality right to prevail.[35] This balancing can be quite complex, as it needs to include aspects of the severity and of the nature of the intrusion, on the one hand, but also counter-positions, on the other, such as a legitimate public interest, or the interferences resulting from the exercise especially of the freedom of expression, the freedom of the press, or the freedom of art; the structures of the balancing operation, having been developed case by case, are not always obvious.[36] We will see that the balancing is the decisive turning point in the *Caroline von Hannover* case.

---

[33]*Bundesgerichtshof* (n. 32), 1405: 'Nachdem nunmehr das Grundgesetz das Recht des Menschen auf Achtung seiner Würde (Art. 1 GG) und das Recht auf freie Entfaltung seiner Persönlichkeit auch als privates, von jedermann zu achtendes Recht anerkennt, soweit dieses Recht nicht die Rechte anderer verletzt oder gegen die verfassungsmäßige Ordnung oder das Sittengesetz verstößt (Art 2 GrundG), muß das allgemeine Persönlichkeitsrecht als ein verfassungsmäßig gewährleistetes Grundrecht angesehen werden (vgl Enneccerus/Nipperdey (1952) , § 78 I 2; Enneccerus/Lehmann (1954), §§ 233 2c; Coing (1947), 642).'

[34]As to this see the discussions of the judgment by *Coing* (1954); *Gamm* (1955) 1827. See also *Bundesgerichtshof*, judgment of 2 April 1957 –VI ZR 9/56–, 1957 Neue Juristische Wochenschrift 1146 = BGHZ 24, 72.

[35]*Sprau* (n. 11), § 823, para. 95. See especially *Bundesgerichtshof* (n. 34); judgment of 24 October 1961 –VI ZR 204/60–, 1962 Neue Juristische Wochenschrift 32 = BGHZ 36, 77.

[36]See *Sprau* (n. 11), § 823, paras. 96–109, who lists the relevant case-law.

2.2.1.2 The initial interpretation of constitutionally guaranteed basic rights as law immediately binding private parties – unmittelbare Drittwirkung

The *Schacht* judgment gives the impression that the personality right is a constitutional right, a position which seems very heavily to have been influenced by the theories of *Hans Carl Nipperdey* and actually was very clearly adopted by the *Bundesgerichtshof* in its judgment on the *Krankenpapiere* case concerning the allegedly unlawful disclosure of health documents:[37]

> It [sc. the court of appeal] is rightly assumed that the provisions in Articles 1 and 2 of the *Grundgesetz*, in which the inviolability of human dignity is expressed and everyone's right to free development of his personality is acknowledged as far as he does not violate the rights of others and does not offend the constitutional order or good morals, guarantee a basic right which is not only directed against the state and its organs but is also valid in private-law relations vis-à-vis anyone (…). For no differently can it be understood that in Article 1(1), second sentence, it is declared to be the duty of all state powers to respect and to protect human dignity, and that Article 1(3) has transformed the basic rights laid down in the following provisions, among these the right freely to develop one's personality, into immediately applicable law binding the legislature, the executive and the judiciary. Accordingly the conclusion becomes inevitable that the general personality right is to be regarded as 'another right' within the meaning of sec. 823(1) BGB (…).

What is put down here echoes in the *Bundesgerichtshof*'s *Herrenreiter* judgment. It concerned the co-owner of a brewery, who was active as a gentleman show-jumper (*Herrenreiter*). A manufacturer of pharmaceuticals advertised a drug widely believed to increase sexual potency using posters of a show-jumper. The posters were based on an original photograph showing the businessman. The courts found him to be recognisable despite the pictures having been retouched before being used for the poster. The businessman sued the manufacturer for damages. The *Bundesgerichtshof* affirmed the grant of the claim by the lower courts' judgments, finding that the dissemination of the poster without the plaintiff's permission injured his personality rights, as specifically protected under the KUG.[38] The claim for damages principally

---

[37]*Bundesgerichtshof* (n. 34), 1146. The Court refers, *inter alia*, to *Nipperdey* (1954), 1–50 (18, 37); Enneccerus,/Nipperdey (1952), § 78 I 2; *Hubmann (1953)*, pp 104, 106 et seq., 127 et seq., 139. The *Bundesgerichtshof* thus acknowledged the immediate third-party effect of basic rights, *die mittelbare Drittwirkung der Grundrechte*. At the time it was able to refer to a similar interpretation of constitutional law being endorsed, *inter alia*, by *Wernicke (1950)*, Article 1 comment II 1c; *Hamann* (1956), Art 1 Bem B; Denecke (1956), Vorbem II vor § 1; *Heimerich* (1956), 249 (251); *contra*: *von Mangoldt/ Klein* (1957), 65–66, 147.

[38]*Bundesgerichtshof*, judgment of 14 February 1958 –I ZR 151/56– (*Herrenreiter*), 1958 Neue Juristische Wochenschrift 827 = BGHZ 26, 349.

had a legal basis in sec. 823(2) BGB in combination with sec. 22 KUG. It was, however, doubtful whether immaterial damages could be claimed. Sec. 253 BGB, in the version applicable at the time, excluded compensation for immaterial damages when this was not expressly foreseen by the law. The *Bundesgerichtshof* nevertheless applied sec. 847 BGB, which in cases of physical injury or deprivation of liberty granted a right to compensation for immaterial damages. The Court based this analogy on the effects of the changed constitutional background of private law. The original intent of the BGB that there could be no private-law protection of a general personality right was overruled by the guarantee of human dignity (Article 1(1) of the *Grundgesetz*) and the right to free development of the personality (Article 2(1) of the *Grundgesetz*).

With a view to the connection between constitutional and private law, the following excerpt from the *Herrenreiter* judgment seems of special importance, although, upon closer examination, it leaves the qualification of the personality right in limbo:

> Already in the judgment BGHZ 13, 334, 338, the Senate stated that the inviolability of human dignity and the right to free development of the personality protected under Articles 1, 2 of the *Grundgesetz* are also to be recognised as a private-law right which is to be respected by everyone in private legal relations insofar as this right does not violate the rights of others or contravenes the constitutional order or good morals. This so-called general personality right [*allgemeines Persönlichkeitsrecht*] thus is also accorded legal validity within the private system of private law and, as 'another right' it enjoys legal protection under sec. 823(1) BGB (...).
>
> Articles 1 and 2 of the *Grundgesetz* protect, and this has binding effect also for the judiciary, what has been called *die menschliche Personhaftigkeit* [the quality of a human being as a person]; thereby they even acknowledge one of the supra-legal basic values of the legal order [*einen der übergesetzlichen Grundwerte der Rechtsordnung*]. Thus they directly protect the internal sphere of the personality which basically is subject only to self-determination, exercised in freedom and self-responsibility, and the violation of which is characterised by primarily causing so-called immaterial damages, damages resulting in a diminution of the personality. To respect this sphere and not to invade it unauthorised is a legal requirement [*Gebot*] flowing from the *Grundgesetz* itself. Equally a consequence of the *Grundgesetz* is the necessity in case of a violation of this sphere to grant protection against the damages typical of the violation.[39]

---

[39] *Bundesgerichtshof* (n. 38), 829: '*Bereits in der Entscheidung BGHZ 13, 334, 338 hat der Senat ausgesprochen, daß die durch das Grundgesetz Art 1, 2 geschützte Unantastbarkeit der Menschenwürde und das Recht auf freie Entfaltung der Persönlichkeit auch als bürgerlichrechtliches, von jedem im Privatrechtsverkehr zu achtendes Recht anzuerkennen ist, soweit dieses*

As the *Schacht* judgment (BGHZ 13, 334) here is read as recognising the rights under Articles 1(1) and 2(1) of the *Grundgesetz* 'as a private-law right', this could mean no more than that equivalent protection is acknowledged to exist in private law. But then Articles 1 and 2 of the *Grundgesetz* are understood 'directly' to 'protect' the internal sphere of the personality right. Moreover, from the perspective taken by the *Herrenreiter* judgment, respect of, and non-interference with, the personality sphere are required by a norm 'flowing from the *Grundgesetz* itself' (*'das sich aus dem Grundgesetz selbst ergibt'*) – which, as it might seem, binds not only the state but also private parties.

2.2.1.3 The Bundesgerichtshof's move away from unmittelbare Drittwirkung

In 1961 the *Bundesgerichtshof* made a new approach to the problem of compensation for immaterial damages in cases of personality right infringements, detaching the solution from sec. 847 BGB (which it had before[40] applied by way of an analogy). The judgment's new solution is best understood as, for reasons of constitutional law, restricting sec. 253 BGB in its scope so as no longer to exclude compensation for immaterial damages, and more specifically, compensation aimed at granting satisfaction, in cases of infringements of the personality right.[41] In the *Ginsengwurzel* case a professor of international and ecclesiastical law who, having mistakenly been called one of the most renowned experts in the field of ginseng root research in a journal, had to discover that the producer of a tonic containing ginseng was referring to an alleged scientific opinion of his as to the potency of ginseng, including its quality as an aphrodisiac, in a brochure advertising the tonic. A comparable reference was furthermore used by the ginseng producer in an editorial note printed together with an advertisement for his tonic in the February 1958

Recht nicht die Rechte anderer verletzt oder gegen die verfassungsmäßige Ordnung oder das Sittengesetz verstößt. Diesem sog allgemeinen Persönlichkeitsrecht kommt mithin auch innerhalb der Zivilrechtsordnung Rechtsgeltung zu und es genießt als 'sonstiges Recht' den Schutz des § 823 Abs 1 BGB (vgl auch BGHZ 24, 12ff).
  'Die Art 1 und 2 des Grundgesetzes schützen, und zwar mit bindender Wirkung auch für die Rechtsprechung, das, was man die menschliche Personhaftigkeit nennt; ja sie erkennen in ihr einen der übergesetzlichen Grundwerte der Rechtsordnung an. Sie schützen damit unmittelbar jenen inneren Persönlichkeitsbereich, der grundsätzlich nur der freien und eigenverantwortlichen Selbstbestimmung des Einzelnen untersteht und dessen Verletzung rechtlich dadurch gekennzeichnet ist, daß sie in erster Linie sogenannte immaterielle Schäden, Schäden, die sich in einer Persönlichkeitsminderung ausdrücken, erzeugt. Diesen Bereich zu achten und nicht unbefugt in ihn einzudringen, ist ein rechtliches Gebot, das sich aus dem Grundgesetz selbst ergibt. Ebenso folgt aus dem Grundgesetz die Notwendigkeit, bei Verletzung dieses Bereiches Schutz gegen die der Verletzung wesenseigentümlichen Schäden zu gewähren.'
[40] *Bundesgerichtshof* (n. 38).
[41] *Bundesgerichtshof*, judgment of 19 September 1961 –VI ZR 259/60– (*Ginsengwurzel*), 1961 Neue Juristische Wochenschrift 2059 = BGHZ 35, 363.

edition of a magazine. With a view to the qualification of the personality right protected under sec. 823(1) BGB, the *Bundesgerichtshof* said:

> By acknowledging a general personality right of the human individual and granting it the protection of sec. 823(1) BGB, the judiciary has for the purposes of private law drawn conclusions following from the rank which the *Grundgesetz* assigns the dignity of the human personality and the protection of its free development. The construction of the private-law protection of the personality, having progressed under the influence of the value decisions of the *Grundgesetz*, would, however, be incomplete and insufficient if an infringement of the personality right would not trigger any sanction adequate to the immaterial interference.[42]

It is recommendable to leave aside the details of the problem of compensation at this point and to concentrate only on the relation of private and constitutional law presented here. The *Ginsengwurzel* judgment quite evidently does not speak of constitutionally guaranteed basic rights being applicable, as such, in the relations of private parties *inter se*. Rather, it understands the courts to have 'drawn conclusions' from constitutional law 'for the purposes of private law'.

2.2.2 The *Bundesverfassungsgericht*'s re-interpretation of the *Bundesgerichtshof*'s case-law: The *allgemeines Persönlichkeitsrecht* as a right existing under private law

In its decision of 14 February 1973 the *Bundesverfassungsgericht* had to decide upon the constitutionality of the civil court's extension of compensation to covering immaterial damages caused by serious violations of the personality right.[43] The *Soraya* case concerned a fictitious interview with Princess Soraya Esfandiary-Bakhtiary, the ex-wife of the Shah of Iran, published by a weekly magazine. The civil courts had granted the Princess monetary compensation for this grave interference with her personality right.[44] In the summary it gives of the development of the civil court's case-law,

---

[42]*Bundesgerichtshof* (n. 41), 2060: '*Indem die Rechtsprechung ein allgemeines Persönlichkeitsrecht des Menschen anerkannte und ihm den Schutz des § 823 Abs 1 BGB zubilligte, zog sie für das Zivilrecht die Folgerungen, die sich aus dem Rang ergeben, den das Grundgesetz der Würde der menschlichen Persönlichkeit und dem Schutz ihrer freien Entfaltung beimißt. Die unter dem Einfluß der Wertentscheidung des Grundgesetzes erfolgte Ausbildung des zivilrechtlichen Persönlichkeitsschutzes wäre aber lückenhaft und unzureichend, wenn eine Verletzung des Persönlichkeitsrechts keine der ideellen Beeinträchtigung adäquate Sanktion auslösen würde.*'
[43]*Bundesverfassungsgericht* (n. 30) – *Soraya*.
[44]*Bundesverfassungsgericht* (n. 30), 276–278 – *Soraya*.

the *Bundesverfassungsgericht* presents an interesting restatement of the *Bundesgerichtshof*'s *Schacht* judgment:

It [sc. the *Bundesgerichtshof*] pronounced that the right to respect for dignity and free development of the personality, protected by Articles 1 and 2 of the *Grundgesetz*, was also a private-law right, to be respected by everyone. It enjoyed the protection of sec. 823(1) BGB; the decision whether this right had been infringed, however, required a careful and detailed balancing of values and interests.[45]

This rephrasing indicates that the *Bundesverfassungsgericht* distances itself from the idea that the general personality right must be regarded as a constitutionally guaranteed basic right ('*als ein verfassungsmäßig gewährleistetes Grundrecht angesehen werden [muß]*'), as the *Schacht* judgment had put it.[46] It can rather be understood to regard the general personality right to be of a private-law nature, more specifically, a private right which the civil courts have acknowledged to exist under the constitution's '*Ausstrahlungswirkung*' on private law, its radiating effect. When the *Bundesverfassungsgericht*, for the sake of delimiting its own scope of constitutional review, describes the situation in which the civil courts had had to decide the *Soraya* case, this becomes quite clear:

The court procedure in which the contested judgments were rendered was a private-law controversy [*bürgerliche Rechtsstreitigkeit*] which was to be decided according to the rules of private law [*Privatrechtsordnung*]. The *Bundesverfassungsgericht*'s task is not to interpret and apply private law as such. However, the objective order of values [*objektive Wertordnung*] contained in the basic rights provisions of the constitution also affects private law; it is valid as a fundamental constitutional determinant [*verfassungsrechtliche Grundentscheidung*] for all fields of law. It is for the *Bundesverfassungsgericht* to secure respect for this 'radiating effect' ['*Ausstrahlungswirkung*'] of the constitution. Therefore it will examine whether the decisions of the civil courts are based on a fundamentally wrong conception of the scope and effective force of a basic right or whether the outcome of the decision itself violates basic rights of one of the parties (…).[47]

---

[45] *Bundesverfassungsgericht* (n. 30), 271–272 – *Soraya*: '*Er sprach aus, das durch die Art. 1 und 2 GG geschützte Recht auf Achtung der Würde und der freien Entfaltung der Persönlichkeit sei auch ein bürgerlich-rechtliches, von jedermann im Privatrechtsverkehr zu achtendes Recht. Das allgemeine Persönlichkeitsrecht genieße den Schutz des § 823 Abs. 1 BGB; die Entscheidung, ob dieses Recht verletzt sei, bedürfe jedoch einer sorgsamen und ins einzelne gehenden Güter- und Interessenabwägung.*'

[46] See *supra*, n. 33.

[47] *Bundesverfassungsgericht* (n. 30), 279–280 – *Soraya*: '*Das gerichtliche Verfahren, in dem die*

The *Bundesverfassungsgericht* goes on to specify that in the *Soraya* case the civil courts had applied sec. 823(1) BGB to an infringement of the *'allgemeines Persönlichkeitsrecht'*, which the *Bundesgerichtshof* counted among the rights to which the tort law provision extends. It implicitly qualifies this consistent holding as a development *'im Bereich der zivilrechtlichen Dogmatik'*,[48] which over the years had led to the general personality right being recognised as a consolidated component of the private-law order (*'nunmehr zum festen Bestandteil unserer Privatrechtsordnung geworden ist'*).[49] A distinction between the effects of basic rights, directly guaranteed by the constitution, and the general personality right becomes apparent in the subsequent paragraph:

> The *Bundesverfassungsgericht* has no cause to oppose this established case law of the *Bundesgerichtshof*'s for reasons of constitutional law. The value system of the basic rights centres on the human personality freely developing within the social community, and its dignity (...). Respect and protection are owed to it by all state powers (Article 1 and Article 2(1) of the *Grundgesetz*). Such protection can rightly especially be demanded for the human being's private sphere, the realm in which he wishes to be let alone, to make his decisions in self-responsibility and not to suffer interference of any kind (...). It is this protective purpose which in the field of private law is served by the legal construction of the general personality right; it fills lacunae in the protection of the personality, which had remained despite the acknowledgement of single specific personality rights and for various reasons had been felt more and more intensely over time. The *Bundesverfassungsgericht* has therefore never reprimanded the acknowledgement of the general personality right in the established case-law of the civil courts.[50]

---

angegriffenen Entscheidungen ergangen sind, war eine bürgerliche Rechtsstreitigkeit, die nach der Privatrechtsordnung zu entscheiden war. Das Bundesverfassungsgericht hat die Auslegung und Anwendung des bürgerlichen Rechts als solche nicht nachzuprüfen. Die in den Grundrechtsnormen der Verfassung enthaltene objektive Wertordnung wirkt jedoch auch auf das Privatrecht ein; sie gilt als verfassungsrechtliche Grundentscheidung für alle Bereiche des Rechts. Die Beachtung dieser "Ausstrahlungswirkung" der Verfassung sicherzustellen, obliegt dem Bundesverfassungsgericht. Es prüft deshalb, ob die Entscheidungen der Zivilgerichte auf einer grundsätzlich unrichtigen Auffassung von der Reichweite und Wirkkraft eines Grundrechts beruhen oder ob das Entscheidungsergebnis selbst Grundrechte eines Beteiligten verletzt (s. dazu allgemein BVerfGE 7, 198 [205 ff.]; 18, 85 [92 f.]; 30, 173 [187f., 196 f.]; 32, 311 [316]).'
[48]Which is almost impossible to translate into English, *Dogmatik quasi* being the theoretical reconstructive systematisation of the law, with *zivilrechtliche Dogmatik* specifically concerning private law.
[49]*Bundesverfassungsgericht* (n. 30), 280–281 – *Soraya*.
[50]*Bundesverfassungsgericht* (n. 30), 281–282 – *Soraya*: *'Das Bundesverfassungsgericht hat keinen Anlaß, dieser Rechtsprechung des Bundesgerichtshofs von Verfassungs wegen*

Here it becomes obvious that the *Bundesverfassungsgericht* places the legal construction of the general personality right in the context of private law. It is to private-law relations that the *allgemeines Persönlichkeitsrecht* applies as a private right.[51] Only this position is compatible with the *Bundesverfassungsgericht*'s consistent interpretation of basic rights as not immediately binding private parties, which takes its first roots in the *Lüth* judgment of 1958,[52] which will be discussed *in extenso* below in Chapter 4. It is noteworthy that the Court follows *Günter Dürig's* conception of *mittelbare Drittwirkung*,[53] although it also refers to *Nipperdey*,[54] who favoured the direct application of basic rights in private-law relations.[55]

2.2.3 The terminological confusion caused by the *Bundesverfassungsgericht* in its *Eppler* judgment of 1980

The consistency of the *Bundesverfassungsgericht*'s position can also be retraced throughout its judgments and decisions up until 1980. Except for an *obiter dictum* five months after the *Bundesgerichtshof* had delivered its *Schacht* judgment,[56] the *Bundesverfassungsgericht* never used the term

---

entgegenzutreten. Das Wertsystem der Grundrechte findet seinen Mittelpunkt in der innerhalb der sozialen Gemeinschaft sich frei entfaltenden menschlichen Persönlichkeit und ihrer Würde (BVerfGE 6, 32 [41]; 7, 198 [205]). Ihr gebührt Achtung und Schutz von seiten aller staatlichen Gewalt (Art. 1 und 2 Abs. 1 GG). Solchen Schutz darf vor allem die private Sphäre des Menschen beanspruchen, der Bereich, in dem er allein zu bleiben, seine Entscheidungen in eigener Verantwortung zu treffen und von Eingriffen jeder Art nicht behelligt zu werden wünscht (BVerfGE 27, 1 [6]). Diesem Schutzzweck dient im Bereich des Privatrechts auch die Rechtsfigur des allgemeinen Persönlichkeitsrechts; sie füllt Lücken im Persönlichkeitsschutz aus, die hier trotz Anerkennung einzelner Persönlichkeitsrechte verblieben und im Laufe der Zeit aus verschiedenen Gründen immer fühlbarer geworden waren. Das Bundesverfassungsgericht hat deshalb die Anerkennung eines allgemeinen Persönlichkeitsrechts in der Rechtsprechung der Zivilgerichte nie beanstandet (s. besonders BVerfGE 30, 173 [194 ff.]; 34, 118 [135 f.] sowie Beschluß vom 31. Januar 1973 – 2 BvR 454/71 – Abschn. B II 2 [= BVerfGE 34, 238 (246 et seq.)]).'

[51]See *Bundesverfassungsgericht*, decision of 25 July 1979–2 BvR 878/74–, BVerfGE 52, 131 (169), where attempts to alter criminal law provisions by making unauthorised medical treatment a new offence are commented saying that the protective purpose pursued in the context of criminal law reform was, in the context of private law, served by the legal construction of the general personality right. Interestingly, *Bundesverfassungsgericht* (n. 30), 281 – *Soraya* is quoted: '*Dem hier angesprochenen Schutzzweck dient im Bereich des Zivilrechts bereits die Rechtsfigur des allgemeinen Persönlichkeitsrechts* (vgl. BVerfGE 34, 269 [281]; ...).'

[52]*Bundesverfassungsgericht*, judgment of 15 January 1958–1 BvR 400/51–, BVerfGE 7, 198 – *Lüth*.

[53]See *Günter Dürig (1958)*, Art. 1 Abs. III, § 127; Art. 2 Abs. I, §§ 56–58; *idem* Dürig (1956), 157–190.

[54]*Bundesverfassungsgericht* (n. 30), 275, 281, 290 – *Soraya*.

[55]See *supra*, n. 37.

[56]*Bundesverfassungsgericht*, judgment of 20 October 1954–1 BvR 527/52–, BVerfGE 4, 52 (57): '*Denn auch wenn man Art. 6 Abs. 2 GG als eine Konkretisierung des in Art. 2 Abs. 1 GG*

'*allgemeines Persönlichkeitsrecht*' to describe even a partial content of the basic right guaranteed under Article 2(1) of the *Grundgesetz*. This cannot be seen as something unintentional since constitutional complainants as well as other applicants before the Court again and again expressly resorted to the '*allgemeines Persönlichkeitsrecht*' argument in their applications.[57] Not until its decision of 3 June 1980[58] did the *Bundesverfassungsgericht* speak of 'the general personality right guaranteed by Article 2(1) in combination with Article 1(1)' ['*das durch Art. 2 Abs. 1 i.V.m. Art. 1 Abs. 1 GG verfassungsrechtlich gewährleistete allgemeine Persönlichkeitsrecht*']. Then obviously forgetful of the careful distinctions made earlier,[59] it did this saying that there was an interference with the general personality right where utterances were put in someone's mouth which this person had not done and which infringed the social assertive claim defined by this person.[60]

2.2.4 The strict distinction between the 'zivilrechtliches allgemeines Persönlichkeitsrecht' and the 'verfassungsrechtliches Persönlichkeitsrecht'

The unfortunate terminological confusion, caused by importing the phrase '*allgemeines Persönlichkeitsrecht*' into constitutional law and theory, has lasted up until today. However, in 1998 the *Bundesverfassungsgericht* had to decide on constitutional complaints raised by a publishing company against civil court judgments ordering it to print counter-statements and a rectification in two of its magazines because of the title pages and cover stories of two

---

begründeten allgemeinen Persönlichkeitsrechts betrachtet, ist neben der Sonderbestimmung des Art. 6 Abs. 2 GG im elterlichen Erziehungsrecht für eine Anwendung des Art. 2 Abs. 1 GG kein Raum.' (For even if one regards Article 6(2) of the *Grundgesetz* as a specification of the general personality right based in Article 2(1) of the *Grundgesetz*, there is no room for applying Article 2(1) of the *Grundgesetz* beside the special provision of Article 6(2) of the *Grundgesetz* in the context of the parental right to educate [their children].).

[57] For a prominent example see *Bundesverfassungsgericht* (n. 52), 232–232 – *Lüth*.

[58] *Bundesverfassungsgericht*, decision of 3 June 1980 –1 BvR 185/77–, BVerfGE 54, 148 (153) – *Eppler*.

[59] See *supra*, n. 50. See also *Bundesverfassungsgericht*, 5 June 1973–1 BvR 536/72–, BVerfGE 35, 202 (224) – *Lebach*: '*Das Gesamtverständnis der Vorschriften [sc. §§ 22, 23 KUG] hat sich seit Inkrafttreten des Grundgesetzes dahin gewandelt, daß das Recht am eigenen Bild als ein Ausschnitt, eine besondere Ausprägung des allgemeinen Persönlichkeitsrechts angesehen wird, das aus Art. 1 und 2 GG entwickelt worden ist (...).*' ('Since the *Grundgesetz* entered into force, the overall interpretation of the provisions [sc. secs. 22, 23 KUG] has changed in the direction that the right to one's own picture is considered as a segment, a specification of the general personality right, which has been developed out of Articles 1 and 2 of the *Grundgesetz* (...).').

[60] *Bundesverfassungsgericht* (n. 58), 155 – *Eppler* ('... *bedeutet es gleichfalls einen Eingriff in das allgemeine Persönlichkeitsrecht, wenn jemandem Äußerungen in den Mund gelegt werden, die er nicht getan hat und die seinen von ihm selbst definierten sozialen Geltungsanspruch beeinträchtigen*').

of their editions.[61] One of the magazines had reported that Princess Caroline of Monaco was planning to wed again; the other had announced the famous German swimmer Franziska van Almsick intending to marry. The civil courts had – in procedures of interim judicial relief – applied sec. 11 of the Hamburg Press Act obliging the publisher and the editor of a periodical to print a counter-statement by the person concerned in reaction to a statement of fact having been printed in the periodical, and had ordered a counter-statement of Princess Caroline in the first case, and of Ms van Almsick in the second case, to be placed on the front page of the respective magazines. Ms van Almsick, and the man said to be her boyfriend and the wedding candidate, had additionally been successful with their claims and the publishing company had to print a rectification saying that the two had no intention to marry.[62] These claims were based on secs. 823 and 1004 BGB and the allegation that the personality rights of the two plaintiffs had been infringed. The details of the *Bundesverfassungsgericht*'s judgment need not be given here. It is more important, rather, to note that with regard to secs. 823 and 1004 BGB the Court speaks of '*das (zivilrechtliche) allgemeine Persönlichkeitsrecht*',[63] 'the general personality right (of private-law)', and clearly distinguishes it from '*das verfassungsrechtliche Persönlichkeitsrecht*', the constitutionally guaranteed personality right'.[64]

Even more outspoken is a decision by the First Chamber of the First Senate of the *Bundesverfassungsgericht* of 22 August 2006.[65] It refused to entertain the constitutional complaint raised by a manufacturer who had used a picture of the then already deceased Marlene Dietrich for the advertisement of the photo-copying machines it sells. The German civil courts had ordered the manufacturer to supply information and subsequently also to pay a licence fee to the only child and sole heir of Ms Dietrich. In denying that the civil courts had overstepped the limits of *zivilrechtliche Rechtsfortbildung*, the progressive development of private law by the judges, the panel consisting of three Constitutional Justices, stated:

The constitutional, and the private-law, personality rights are not identical. Consequently, the *Bundesverfassungsgericht* will not examine civil court decisions as to whether they have correctly applied the private-law provisions serving the protection of the personality right. Constitutional review [*(d)ie verfassungsgerichtliche Kontrolle*] is restricted to [sc. the

[61]*Bundesverfassungsgericht*, decision of 14 January 1998–1 BvR 1861/93, 1864/96, 2073/97–, BVerfGE 97, 125 – *Caroline von Monaco I*.
[62]*Bundesverfassungsgericht* (n. 61), 126–130, 130–133, 133–137.
[63]*Bundesverfassungsgericht* (n. 61), 148.
[64]*Bundesverfassungsgericht* (n. 61), 149.
[65]*Bundesverfassungsgericht, Erste Kammer des Ersten Senats*, decision of 22 August 2006–1 BvR 1168/04–, JURIS = 2006 Neue Juristische Wochenschrift 3409.

civil courts'] taking into account standards of constitutional law for the interpretation of sub-constitutional law (...).[66]

The restriction of the standard of review to norms of the constitution (which we will encounter again and again) is in line with what the First Senate, sitting as a full court, had already said in the *Soraya* judgment.[67] This restriction is founded on the distinction which needs to be made between the general personality right as '*ein anderes Recht*' within the meaning of sec. 823 BGB, i.e. within the realm of private law, and the protection of the personality right under Article 2(1) of the *Grundgesetz* in combination with Article 1(1) of the *Grundgesetz*.[68] This is completely consistent with the prevailing theory of German constitutional law. For it is generally not accepted that basic rights – with some certain exceptions such as Article 9(3) of the *Grundgesetz*[69] – exert immediate effects in relations exclusively involving private parties: According to Article 1(3) of the *Grundgesetz* the basic rights bind the legislative, executive and judicial powers as directly applicable law. In contrast, a private party cannot violate another private party's basic rights as such. The obligations created by basic rights burden those who possess public, or if one applies a broad understanding, governmental, powers. Consequently, basic rights have no *unmittelbare Drittwirkung*, no immediate third-party effects. If this is accepted, the general personality right as 'another right' within the meaning of sec. 823(1) BGB, which can be infringed by another private party, must be of a different quality: It must be a private right. And it must not be confused with the *constitutionally guaranteed* general personality right emanating from Articles 2(1) and 1(1) of the *Grundgesetz* – for which highly unfortunately today the legal term *allgemeines Persönlichkeitsrecht* is also used.[70]

---

[66]*Bundesverfassungsgericht* (n. 65), § 30: '*Verfassungsrechtliches und zivilrechtliches Persönlichkeitsrecht sind nicht identisch. Dementsprechend überprüft das Bundesverfassungsgericht zivilgerichtliche Entscheidungen nicht darauf, ob sie die dem Persönlichkeitsschutz dienenden zivilrechtlichen Normen richtig angewandt haben. Die verfassungsgerichtliche Kontrolle beschränkt sich auf die Berücksichtigung verfassungsrechtlicher Maßgaben für die Interpretation des einfachen Rechts (...).*' See also *Bundesverfassungsgericht*, decision of 26 February 2008–1 BvR 1602, 1606, 1626/07–, BVerfGE 120, 180 (214–215), where the *Bundesverfassungsgericht* (First Senate) distinguishes the '*Kernbereich der Privatsphäre*' ('core sphere of privacy') from the '*grundrechtlich gewährleisteter Kernbereich*' (the 'core sphere guaranteed by basic rights').

[67]See *supra*, n. 47.

[68]See especially, *Hoffmann-Riem* (2009), 22–23.

[69]Which not only guarantees the right to form associations (in the sense both of trade unions and employers' associations) for the purposes of preserving and developing working and economic conditions, but also expressly declares any agreement intending to restrict or hinder the exercise of such right to be invalid.

[70]*Sprau* (n. 11), § 823, § 84; *Bundesverfassungsgericht*, 2009 Neue Juristische Wochenschrift 3409; *Hoffmann-Riem* (n. 58), 23.

2.3 The Case of *Caroline von Hannover* – continued

The *excursus* on the development of the *allgemeines Persönlichkeitsrecht* hopefully helps to understand what the *Bundesverfassungsgericht* says at the beginning of its judgment on the merits of the constitutional complaint raised by Princess Caroline of Monaco against the *Bundesgerichtshof*'s judgment. If we indeed tell the story of the case as that of the press's shrinking photo file on the Princess, the *Bundesgerichtshof* had quasi struck out the one picture showing the Princess and actor Vincent Lindon sitting at the far end of a restaurant courtyard in Saint-Rémy-de-Provence. Before the *Bundesverfassungsgericht*, the Princess was seeking more protection against the publication of images of her, alleging violations of Articles 2(1) and 1(1) of the *Grundgesetz*.[71] She was successful as far as the photographs depicted her together with her children.

2.3.1 The constitutional law situation in the abstract

The *Bundesverfassungsgericht* opens its elaboration on the abstract questions of constitutional law, which clearly pave the way for the merely partial success of the Princess's constitutional complaint, with the following words:

> I. The contested judgments affect the complainant's general personality right under Article 2(1) in combination with Article 1(1) of the *Grundgesetz*.
> 1. The protection of the general personality right also pertains to images of a person made by a third person.
> a) It is the function of this basic right to secure elements of the personality which are not the object of the *Grundgesetz*'s special guarantees of liberty, but are of no less constituent relevance for the personality (...). The necessity of such a gap-filling guarantee exists especially with a view to new dangers to the development of the personality mostly arising in the context of scientific-technological progress (...). A specific claim for legal protection must therefore be classified as one of the various aspects of the personality right mainly according to the danger for the personality which can be discerned in the specific circumstances of the case at hand.[72]

After what was said above, it is clear that the *Bundesverfassungsgericht* is only addressing the general personality right as a *constitutionally* guaranteed right, but not as a private right within the scope of sec. 823(1) BGB. With a view to the specific case, the Court – after saying that no one has a general and

---

[71] *Bundesverfassungsgericht* (n. 4), 371–376 – *Caroline von Monaco II*.
[72] *Bundesverfassungsgericht* (n. 4), 379–380 – *Caroline von Monaco II*.

extensive, exclusive right to determine how (and especially by which image) to present him- or herself, or to be presented, to others[73] – distinguishes two aspects of the personality right: autonomy as to one's image and the protection of a private sphere.

2.3.1.1 Autonomy as to one's image as an aspect of the personality right

The first of these is '*das Recht am eigenen Bild*', autonomy as to one's image, which guarantees the individual the possibility to influence and to decide whether and how far others may take one's photograph or make other kinds of recordings.[74] The Court sees dangers to the personality right, and the corresponding need for protection, primarily arising from the growing potential of reproducing images, spreading them around and putting them into new settings and contexts.[75] The Princess's case, however, did not concern questions of manipulating or distorting images, but only touched the aspect of distributing images to a larger public audience.

2.3.1.2 Protection of the private sphere as a further aspect of the personality right

The *Bundesverfassungsgericht* contrasts self-determination with a view to one's image with the '*Schutz der Privatsphäre*', the protection of the private sphere, which according to the Court is determined thematically and spatially:

2.3.1.2.1 PRIVATE MATTERS

On the one hand, it [sc. the protection of the private sphere] covers affairs which are typically classified as 'private' because of their informational content since a public discussion or presentation of these is considered as improper, making them known is felt to be embarrassing or can cause disadvantageous reactions, as is the case with looking into oneself in writing a diary (BVerfGE 80, 367), with confidential communication among spouses (BVerfGE 27, 344), in the sphere of sexuality (BVerfGE), with socially divergent behaviour (BVerfGE 44, 353) or with illnesses (BVerfGE 32, 373). If there were no protection against others collecting information here, looking into oneself, uninhibited communication among people close to one another, sexual development or seeking

---

[73]*Bundesverfassungsgericht* (n. 4), 380–381 – *Caroline von Monaco II.*

[74]*Bundesverfassungsgericht* (n. 4), 381 – *Caroline von Monaco II*, pointing to the close relation with the '*Recht am eigenen Wort*', autonomy as to one's (spoken) word (with reference to *Bundesverfassungsgericht*, decision of 31 January 1973–2 BvR 454/71–, BVerfGE 34, 238 [246] – *tape-recording*).

[75]*Bundesverfassungsgericht* (n. 4), 381–382 – *Caroline von Monaco II.*

medical treatment would be impaired or impossible although these are forms of behaviour protected by basic rights.[76]

2.3.1.2.2 SPACES OF PRIVACY

On the other hand, the protection pertains to a spatial sphere, in which the individual can find himself again, can relax or let himself go (cf. BVerfGE 27, 1 [6]). This sphere also offers the opportunity to behave in a way which is not for the public to perceive and the observation or presentation of which by outsiders would be embarrassing or disadvantageous to the person concerned. But essentially it is a sphere in which he has the possibility to be free from public observation and thus from self-control thereby [sc. by public observation] forced upon him. If such spaces of retreat no longer existed, the individual could be psychically overburdened as he would incessantly have to be cautious of his impression on others and of whether he is behaving correctly. He would lack those phases of time which are necessary for the development of the personality and without which it [sc. the personality] would be lastingly impaired.[77]

2.3.1.2.3 CELEBRITIES AND POLITICIANS NOT EXCLUDED FROM PRIVACY PROTECTION

The *Bundesverfassungsgericht* then concedes that a private sphere is not only reserved to 'ordinary people':

Such a need for protection also exists for persons who because of their rank or reputation, their office or influence, their abilities or deeds find public attention. Who, whether willingly or unwillingly, has become a person of public life, does not thereby lose his right to a private sphere, out of reach of the public's eyes. This also holds true for democratically elected office holders, who do have to answer for the fulfilment of their official functions [*ihre Amtsführung*] in public, and to this degree must tolerate public attention, but not for their private life as far as this does not affect the exercise of their official functions.[78]

2.3.1.2.4 PRIVATE SPHERES OUTSIDE THE HOME

The *Bundesverfassungsgericht* then, for the purposes of constitutional law, quite obviously retraces what the *Bundesgerichtshof* had said elaborating on the private-law protection of privacy: It would be insufficient if the private

---

[76]*Bundesverfassungsgericht* (n. 4), 382 – *Caroline von Monaco II.*

[77]*Bundesverfassungsgericht* (n. 4), 382–383 – *Caroline von Monaco II.*

[78]*Bundesverfassungsgericht* (n. 4), 383 – *Caroline von Monaco II.*

sphere were restricted to the walls of the home or the boundaries of one's plot of land.[79] Especially with a view to secret photography or (image) recording, the *Bundesverfassungsgericht* concludes that 'the individual must principally have the possibility to move about free from public observation in open, but nevertheless secluded spaces of nature or in places which are clearly separated from the general public'.[80] Unsurprisingly, the Court feels unable to determine the boundaries of the private sphere outside the home in the abstract. It rather leaves this sphere to be specifically delimited on a case-by-case basis: 'As the question is whether the individual has a justified expectation of not being watched or rather has gone into places where he is moving under the eyes of the public, the secludedness which is the prerequisite for the protection of the private sphere outside one's own home can even be missing in enclosed spaces.'[81] Places where the individual is among an indefinite number of people, is one of a crowd, lie outside the sphere of the privacy protection guaranteed by Article 2(1) in combination with Article 1(1) of the *Grundgesetz*. Such places cannot simply be redefined by the individual. They cannot be turned into part of his private sphere by his showing a behaviour which typically is not displayed in public: 'It is not his behaviour, whether alone or with others, which constitutes the private sphere, it is the objective setting of the place at the time in question. Therefore, if he behaves in places not showing the characteristics of secludedness as if he were not being watched, he himself eliminates the need for protection with a view to behaviour which as such is not intended for the public.'[82]

2.3.1.2.5 PRIVACY AND COMMERCIALISATION

These thoughts lead to an important aspect of privacy protection, that of commercialisation, as to which the *Bundesverfassungsgericht* is quite reserved:

> Protection of the private sphere against being observed by the public [*vor öffentlicher Kenntnisnahme*] is furthermore lost if someone himself agrees to certain affairs being made public, which are normally considered to be private, for instance by concluding exclusive contracts allowing matters of his private sphere to be reported on. The constitutional law protection of the private sphere under Article 2(1) in combination with Article 1(1) of the *Grundgesetz* is not provided for the sake of the commercialisation of one's own person. Admittedly, no one is prevented from opening private spheres in such a way. But then he cannot invoke

---

[79]*Bundesverfassungsgericht* (n. 4), 383 – *Caroline von Monaco II*.
[80]*Bundesverfassungsgericht* (n. 4), 384 – *Caroline von Monaco II*.
[81]*Bundesverfassungsgericht* (n. 4), 384 – *Caroline von Monaco II*.
[82]*Bundesverfassungsgericht* (n. 4), 384–385 – *Caroline von Monaco II*.

the protection of the private sphere as a shield against the public [*den öffentlichkeitsabgewandten Persönlichkeitsschutz*] at the same time. The expectation that the environment will take only limited or no notice of the affairs or manners of behaviour in a sphere functioning as a refuge must therefore be expressed both in more than an incidental way and consistently. This also holds true for the case that the decision to allow, or to tolerate, certain events in one's private sphere to be reported on is revoked.[83]

2.3.1.2.6 REINFORCEMENT OF PRIVACY PROTECTION FOR PARENTS

Up to this point this abstract description of the constitutional foundation of privacy protection seems to cause no conflict with the protection which the *Bundesgerichtshof* accorded the personality right in private law. At the same time the *Bundesverfassungsgericht* then underlines the special need for protecting children in their undisturbed development and their sensitivity to disturbances while growing up:[84]

It is foremost the parents who are responsible for the development of the personality of a child. As far as education depends on undisturbed relations with the children, the special basic rights protection of children does not only exert a reflexive effect beneficial to the father or the mother (cf. also BVerfGE 76, 1 [44 et seq.]; 80, 81 [91–92]). Rather the specific care and attention for the children also falls within the protective sphere of Article 2(1) in combination with Article 1(1) of the *Grundgesetz*. The protective power of the general personality right then is reinforced through Article 6(1) and (2) of the *Grundgesetz*, which places the state under the duty to secure the living conditions of the child which are necessary for its growing up healthy and among which parental care is especially to be counted (cf. BVerfGE 56, 363 [384]; 57, 361 [382–383]; 80, 81 [90 et seq.]).[85]

While the Court again points to the necessity of a case-by-case specification of what this reinforcement of personality protection means, it singles out one important consequence, i.e. that 'the protection of the general personality right can principally apply in favour of the specific parent-child relationship even where the conditions of spatial seclusion have not been met.'[86]

---

[83]*Bundesverfassungsgericht* (n. 4), 385 – *Caroline von Monaco II*.
[84]*Bundesverfassungsgericht* (n. 4), 385 – *Caroline von Monaco II*.
[85]*Bundesverfassungsgericht* (n. 4), 385–386 – *Caroline von Monaco II*.
[86]*Bundesverfassungsgericht* (n. 4), 386 – *Caroline von Monaco II*.

2.3.2 Preparing the special ground for assessing the civil court judgments

2.3.2.1 The Constitutionality of secs. 22, 23 KUG

After this abstract elaboration on special aspects of the constitutional protection of the personality right, the *Bundesverfassungsgericht* first explains that secs. 22 and 23 KUG are constitutional. It emphasises the '*abgestuftes Schutzkonzept*' they contain. This scheme of variable protection takes into account not only the individual's wish to be protected against his image being used, but also the interests of the public and the media.[87]

2.3.2.2 The scope of constitutional review: No predetermination of civil court decisions by constitutional law

Then the Court turns to what is again and again reiterated in decisions on constitutional complaints against civil court judgments or decisions: the scope and intensity of constitutional review. We have encountered the 'formula' twice.[88] Yet the rephrasing done by the *Bundesverfassungsgericht* in its *Caroline von Monaco II* judgment makes it especially clear that constitutional law strictly predetermines neither how the civil courts are to interpret the provisions of private law nor how they are to decide specific cases:

> The interpretation and application of provisions of private law, which are in conformity with the constitution, is the task of the civil courts. In fulfilling this task [*dabei*], however, they must respect the meaning and scope of the basic rights affected by their decisions in order for their [sc. the basic rights'] value-defining meaning also to be preserved at the level of applying the law (cf. BVerfGE 7, 198 [205 et seq.]). This requires a balancing of the conflicting protective values of the basic rights [involved], which is to be performed within the framework of the conditions [*Tatbestandsmerkmale*] of the private-law provisions as far as they leave room for interpretation, and which must take into account the special circumstances of the case (cf. BVerfGE 99, 185 [196]; constant holding of the Court). As the legal controversy, irrespective of the basic rights influence, retains its private-law nature and must be solved by the private law, as interpreted under the guidance of the basic rights, the *Bundesverfassungsgericht* is limited to examining whether the civil courts have paid sufficient respect to the influence of the basic rights (cf. BVerfGE 18, 85 [92–93]). In contrast, it is not its task to prescribe how

---

[87]*Bundesverfassungsgericht* (n. 4), 386–388 – *Caroline von Monaco II*.
[88]See *supra* at n. 45 and n. 67.

the civil courts ought to decide the controversy as to its outcome (cf. BVerfGE 94, 1 [9–10]). Only then is there a violation of basic rights leading to reproof of a contested decision if it has been neglected that in interpreting and applying provisions of private law, compatible with the constitution, basic rights needed to be respected; if the scope of protection of the rights to be respected has been wrongly or imperfectly defined or their weight has been misjudged so that the balancing of the legal positions on both sides within the framework of the private-law provision suffers (cf. BVerfGE 95, 28 [37]; 97, 391 [401]), and the decision is founded on this failure.[89]

2.3.2.3 Balancing the personality right and freedom of the press

In the case of the photo publication of Princess Caroline the constitutional '*allgemeines Persönlichkeitsrecht*' needed to be brought into a balance with the competing basic right protecting the publisher of the magazines: freedom of the press as guaranteed by Article 5(1), second sentence, of the *Grundgesetz*. The *Bundesverfassungsgericht* understands this liberty to give the press autonomy to decide what is printed, what is not, and how the selected contents are presented. It discerns the press as an essential ingredient for the functioning of democracy, but denies that its contribution to the forming of individual and public opinions is restricted to the political sphere.[90] Expressly, the Court includes entertainment in the constitution's functional guarantee of the freedom of the press.[91] The forming of opinions which the freedom of the press serves can, in the Court's eyes, sometimes more lastingly be effected by combining, mixing or even fusing, information and entertainment ('infotainment').[92] Furthermore the *Bundesverfassungsgericht* even goes one step further: In the Court's eyes, even mere entertainment cannot *ab initio* be denied relevance to the formation of opinions. Entertainment falling within the scope of Article 5(1), second sentence, of the *Grundgesetz* also includes reporting on persons, especially celebrities, who can stand for certain values or attitudes, serve as role models or contrasting negative examples. This is the reason for the public's interest in such people and the various dimensions of their lives:[93]

> With regard to persons involved in political life such an interest of the public audience has always been acknowledged as legitimate from the perspective of democratic transparency. But even for other persons of

---

[89]*Bundesverfassungsgericht* (n. 4), 388 – *Caroline von Monaco II.*
[90]*Bundesverfassungsgericht* (n. 4), 389 – *Caroline von Monaco II.*
[91]*Bundesverfassungsgericht* (n. 4), 389 – *Caroline von Monaco II.*
[92]*Bundesverfassungsgericht* (n. 4), 389–390 – *Caroline von Monaco II.* Cf. as to the danger of depoliticising public communication *Habermas* (1994), 455–6.
[93]*Bundesverfassungsgericht* (n. 4), 390 – *Caroline von Monaco II.*

public life it cannot be principally denied. Insofar it is one of the functions of the press to present people irrespective of certain functions or events, this presentation therefore also falling within the protective sphere of the right to freedom of the press. No earlier than in the balancing with conflicting personality rights can it be of relevance whether questions essentially concerning the public are discussed seriously and matter-of-factly, or matters of a merely private nature, only satisfying curiosity, are exposed (cf. BVerfGE 34, 269 [283]).[94]

2.3.3 Rejecting the constitutional complaint as unfounded in all but one point

All these considerations prepare the scene for the *Bundesverfassungsgericht*'s evaluation of the civil court judgments which Princess Caroline alleged to have infringed her rights under Articles 2(1) and 1(1) of the *Grundgesetz*. It is hardly surprising to see the Court accept the judgment by the *Bundesgerichtshof*, which had corrected the lower courts' opinion according to which the protection of the private sphere was restricted to the home,[95] largely as complying with the requirements of constitutional law.

The abstract discussion of the constitutional-law setting paves the way for the Court to regard the *Bundesgerichtshof*'s handling of secs. 22, 23 KUG as constitutional. Defining the meaning of 'images portraying an aspect of contemporary society' according to the informational interest of the public opens sec. 23(1) no. 1 KUG wide enough to include the full breadth of the liberty guaranteed by Article 5(1), second sentence, of the *Grundgesetz*, with the freedom of the press, as shown above, covering not only political or historical information but also merely entertaining 'news'.[96] The *Bundesverfassungsgericht* furthermore regards the distinction between 'absolute' and 'relative' persons of contemporary society under secs. 22, 23 KUG as compatible with constitutional requirements. The permission to publish images of absolute persons of contemporary society, even insofar as these show them in other contexts than fulfilling official functions, is expressly endorsed with a view to preserving the press's constitutionally guaranteed field of activity.[97] In the Court's eyes, the countervailing general personality right is sufficiently protected as sec. 23(2) KUG prohibits publication in case of an interference with the 'legitimate interests' of the person concerned. Such 'legitimate interests' may well stand against the publication of the image not

---

[94] *Bundesverfassungsgericht* (n. 4), 391 – *Caroline von Monaco II*.
[95] *Bundesverfassungsgericht* (n. 4), 396 – *Caroline von Monaco II* therefore judges the lower courts' judgments to have violated Article 2(1) in combination with Article 1(1) of the *Grundgesetz*.
[96] *Bundesverfassungsgericht* (n. 4), 391–392 – *Caroline von Monaco II*.
[97] *Bundesverfassungsgericht* (n. 4), 392–393 – *Caroline von Monaco II*.

only of a 'relative', but even of an 'absolute', person of contemporary society. Sec. 23(2) thus gives room for granting sufficient protection of the personality right.[98] The *Bundesverfassungsgericht* especially supports the *Bundesgerichtshof*'s extension of privacy protection to places of seclusion outside the home.[99] It acknowledges the relevance of the methods of photography or (image) recording, especially of the person being caught unawares, but takes this one decisive step further by pointing out that photography or filming as such can violate the private sphere outside the home, even if it is not established that the images were made secretly or by taking the 'victim' by surprise.[100] Thus, according to the *Bundesverfassungsgericht*'s evaluation, sec. 23(2) KUG, as interpreted by the *Bundesgerichtshof*, allows sufficient protection of the personality right, while, at the same time, it does not strictly forbid publishing pictures from the everyday life of an 'absolute' person of contemporary society.

All in all, secs. 22, 23 KUG allow for a balancing of the general personality right on the one hand, and freedom of the press on the other, which is in agreement with what Articles 2(1) and 1(1) as well as Article 5(1), second sentence, of the *Grundgesetz* require.[101] These specific provisions of private law lend themselves to an interpretation and application which pays due respect to all the conflicting basic rights involved. They are thus open for the influence of constitutionally guaranteed basic rights, for their 'radiating effect' ('*Ausstrahlungswirkung*').[102]

The *Bundesgerichtshof*'s ruling was quite in harmony with the constitutional requirements as spelled out in the *Bundesverfassungsgericht*'s judgment. Therefore, the photographs from Princess Caroline's everyday life were rightly judged to be publishable.[103] However, as already mentioned, the *Bundesverfassungsgericht* found fault in the final civil judgment insofar as it had also considered the publisher to be allowed to print the images showing Princess Caroline with her children. Here the *Bundesgerichtshof* had failed to take the reinforcing effect of Article 6 of the *Grundgesetz* into account when interpreting secs. 22, 23 KUG in the light of Articles 2(1) and 1(1) of the *Grundgesetz* and the constitutional standards of the personality-right protection. As it could not be excluded that the *Bundesgerichtshof* would have reached a different result if it had assessed the basic rights situation correctly, the *Bundesverfassungsgericht* insofar quashed its decision and remitted the case to the *Bundesgerichtshof*.[104]

---

[98]*Bundesverfassungsgericht* (n. 4), 393 – *Caroline von Monaco II*.

[99]*Bundesverfassungsgericht* (n. 4), 393–394 – *Caroline von Monaco II*.

[100]*Bundesverfassungsgericht* (n. 4), 393–394 – *Caroline von Monaco II*.

[101]*Bundesverfassungsgericht* (n. 4), 391–392 – *Caroline von Monaco II*.

[102]See *supra*, at n. 47.

[103]*Bundesverfassungsgericht* (n. 4), 395–396 – *Caroline von Monaco II*.

[104]*Bundesverfassungsgericht* (n. 4), 396 – *Caroline von Monaco II*.

The number of printable photographs in the magazines' files was thus further diminished.

2.4 The ECtHR's judgment in the *Caroline von Hannover* case

Princess Caroline took her case to Strasbourg. Submitting her application under Article 34 ECHR, Caroline claimed that the German court decisions, as they stood after the *Bundesverfassungsgericht*'s judgment of 15 December 1999 had largely upheld the *Bundesgerichtshof*'s final judgment, infringed her right to respect for her private and family life as guaranteed by Article 8 ECHR.

It is well-known that the ECtHR agreed with the Princess. Neither the press' right to freedom of expression, nor the public's interest in knowing about her outweighed the protection of her private life in the case. Even if a public interest were assumed to exist and a commercial interest of the magazines in publishing the photographs was conceded, those interests, in the Court's view, needed to yield to the applicant's right to the effective protection of her private life.[105] The German courts were found not to have struck a fair balance between each of the competing interests and thus to have violated Article 8 ECHR.[106]

In effect, the ECtHR says that none of the pictures in the magazines' files ought to have been permitted to be published. This result by itself contrasts with the evaluation of the legal situation by the German courts. Furthermore, the approach is of a different colour.

2.4.1 The ECtHR's approach to the case

2.4.1.1 The broad understanding of 'private life'

The Court has 'no doubt that the publication by various German magazines of photos of the applicant in her daily life either on her own or with other people falls within the scope of her private life'.[107] The *Bundesverfassungsgericht* would quite probably agree that the autonomy as to one's image (*das Recht am eigenen Bild*)[108] is affected as far as sec. 23(1) KUG allows the dissemination and public display of a person's image.[109] Nevertheless, the Karlsruhe

---

[105]ECtHR, *Von Hannover* (n. 1), §§ 76–77.
[106]ECtHR, *Von Hannover* (n. 1), §§ 79–80.
[107]ECtHR, *Von Hannover* (n. 1), § 53.
[108]See *supra*, at n. 74.
[109]*Bundesverfassungsgericht* (n. 4), 381–382, 387 – *Caroline von Monaco II* (the *Bundesverfassungsgericht*, ibid., 387, qualifies secs. 22, 23 KUG as part of the constitutional order, which, according to Article 2(1) of the *Grundgesetz*, must be respected in the free development of the personality right; these provisions thus are specifications of the limitation of the liberty guaranteed by Article 2(1).

Court seems quite hesitant to extend the private sphere protected under Article 2(1) of the *Grundgesetz* to places outside the home; it does so only with regard to 'objectively' secluded spaces.[110] Merely for the sake of indirectly protecting children does the *Bundesverfassungsgericht* take up a more courageous stance in the name of a parent's privacy protection.[111] In contrast, the ECtHR shows a more protective attitude from the start, as it reiterates that the concept of private life extends to aspects relating to personal identity, such as a person's name,[112] or a person's picture.[113] It continues by pointing out that private life includes a person's physical and psychological integrity, and that the guarantee afforded by Article 8 ECHR is primarily intended to ensure the development, without outside interference, of the personality of each individual in his or her relations with other human beings.[114] In the ECtHR's eyes, there is therefore a zone of interaction of a person with others, *even in a public context*, which may fall within the scope of 'private life'.[115] This concept of private life is quite broad, especially in that it also extends into the sphere of *public social interaction*.[116] This stands quite in contrast to the *Bundesverfassungsgericht*'s understanding of the private sphere as protected under Articles 2(1), 1(1) of the *Grundgesetz*. Not only is the *spatial* dimension of the private sphere, as understood by the

---

[110]See *supra*, at ns. 79–82.

[111]See *supra*, at ns. 83–86.

[112]With reference to ECtHR, *Burghartz v. Switzerland*, no. 16213/90, judgment of 22 February 1994, § 24, Series A no. 280–B, p. 28.

[113]ECtHR, *Von Hannover* (n. 1), § 50 with reference to ECtHR, *Schüssel v. Austria*, no. 42409/98, decision of 21 February 2002.

[114]ECtHR, *Von Hannover* (n. 1), § 50, referring, *mutatis mutandis*, to ECtHR, *Niemietz v. Germany*, no. 13710/88, judgment of 16 December 1992, § 29, Series A no. 251–B, p. 33; *Botta v. Italy*, no. 21439/93, judgment of 24 February 1998, *Reports of Judgments and Decisions* 1998–I, p. 422, § 32.

[115]ECtHR, *Von Hannover* (n. 1), § 50, referring, *mutatis mutandis*, to ECtHR, *P.G. and J.H. v. the United Kingdom*, no. 44787/98, § 56, ECHR 2001–IX, and *Peck v. the United Kingdom*, no. 44647/98, judgment of 28 January 2003, § 57, ECHR 2003–I. A different position is taken by Judge *Zupančič* in his concurring opinion: 'Privacy … is the right to be left alone. One has the right to be left alone precisely to the degree to which one's private life does not intersect with other people's private lives.' Similar is the tone of Judge *Cabral Barreto*'s concurring opinion: 'I agree with the majority that the private life of a public figure does not stop at their front door. However, it has to be acknowledged that, in view of their fame, a public figure's life outside their home, and particularly in public places, is inevitably subject to certain constraints.'

[116]There are, however, limits as can be seen by ECtHR, *Botta v. Italy*, no. 21439/93, judgment of 24 February 1998, *Reports of Judgments and Decisions* 1998–I, § 35: In this case, the Court found that the right asserted by the applicant, namely the right to gain access to the beach and the sea at a place distant from his normal place of residence during his holidays, concerned interpersonal relations of such broad and indeterminate scope that there can be no conceivable direct link between the measures the State was urged to take in order to make good the omissions of the private bathing establishments and the applicant's private life. Consequently, Article 8 was deemed not to be applicable.

Bundesverfassungsgericht, rather limited,[117] but its '*thematical*' expansion also seems to go no further than situations of solitary self-reflection or of close confidentiality as in relations between spouses, sexual partners, or between a patient and his physician.[118]

2.4.1.2 A closer look at the case-law referred to by the Court

2.4.1.2.1 THE CASE OF HALFORD V. THE UNITED KINGDOM

It might seem as though, in a second move, the ECtHR considerably restricted the scope of respect for private life, when it mentions that in its judgment in the *Halford v. the United Kingdom* case,[119] concerning the interception of telephone calls, it held that the applicant 'would have had a reasonable expectation of privacy for such calls'.[120] Reasonableness of expectation might be understood as a condition for privacy not easily fulfilled and thus as a restrictive element. Actually, however, Ms Halford at the relevant time was a high-ranking police officer and was using the internal telecommunications system operated at the Merseyside police headquarters. Thus, an interference with (and even a violation of) Article 8 ECHR was acknowledged in the *Halford* case *although* the telephone calls were not made from a privately owned home phone. Consequently, there was quite an extensive reading of Article 8.

2.4.1.2.2 OTHER CASES OF INTERFERENCES WITH 'PRIVATE LIFE' IN PUBLIC CONTEXTS

Not dissimilarly, it is no more than a tentative restriction of the protective scope of Article 8 which the ECtHR points to when it refers to (and apparently endorses) the Commission's consistent holding with respect to photographs taken by the police: The Court recalls that in judging whether photographs fell within the scope of the protection afforded by Article 8 against arbitrary interference by public authorities, 'the Commission had regard to whether the photographs related to private or public matters and whether the material thus obtained was envisaged for a limited use or was likely to be made available to the general public.'[121] Interestingly, in the *Friedl* case, referred to by the Court,[122] the Commission had attached 'weight to the assurances given by the respondent Government according to which the individual persons on the photographs taken remained anonymous in that no

---

[117]See *supra*, at ns. 110 and 111.
[118]See *supra*, at n. 76.
[119]ECtHR, *Halford v. the United Kingdom*, no. 20605/92, judgment of 25 June 1997, ECHR 1997–III, p.1016, § 45.
[120]ECtHR, *Von Hannover* (n. 1), § 51.
[121]ECtHR, *Von Hannover* (n. 1), § 52.
[122]Quoting ECtHR, *Friedl v. Austria*, no. 15225/89, judgment of 31 January 1995, Series A no. 305–B, Friendly Settlement.

names were noted down, the personal data recorded and photographs taken were not entered into a data processing system, and *no action was taken to identify the persons photographed* on that occasion by means of data processing.'[123] On these grounds, the Commission did not regard the police, by taking photographs of the applicant and retaining them, to have interfered with his right to respect for his private life.[124] Nevertheless, it did recognise an interference with the right guaranteed by Article 8(1) ECHR insofar as the police had questioned the applicant in order to establish his identity, and had recorded his personal data[125] In a consistent ruling, the Court found that the applicants in the case of *P.G. and J.H. v. the United Kingdom* had been deprived of their right to respect for private life as their voices had been secretly recorded while they were being charged at the police station and while staying in their police cell.[126]

It must be conceded that there are 'thematical' limits to the right to respect for private life under the Convention. The *Lupker* case,[127] not mentioned by the ECtHR, gives one example: The police had, for the purpose of a judicial investigation, used photographs which, having been either provided voluntarily in connection with applications for a passport or a driving licence or taken by the police in connection with a previous arrest, were kept in police or other official archives. In its decision in the *Lupker* case, the Commission denied there to be an interference with the right to private life: The photographs had not been taken in a way which constituted an intrusion upon the applicants' privacy; they were used solely for the purpose of the identification of the offenders in the criminal proceedings against the applicants; and there was no suggestion that they had been made available to the general public or used for any other purpose. Therefore, rights under Article 8 ECHR were not found to have been interfered with. The *Lupker* case was a point of reference in the Court's *Peck* judgment.[128] In the *Peck* case, the Brentwood Borough Council had recorded footage of the immediate aftermath of the applicant's suicide attempt, which had been recorded by a surveillance camera on a traffic island in the street, and had disclosed this material directly to the public in its *CCTV News* publication. In addition, the footage was passed on to the media for further broadcasting and publication purposes.[129] The ECtHR considered the Council by disclosing the relevant footage to have seriously interfered with the applicant's right to respect for his private life.[130]

---

[123]EComHR, *Friedl v. Austria*, no. 15225/89, decision of 19 May 1994, § 49 (emphasis added).
[124]EComHR, *Friedl* (n. 123), § 51.
[125]EComHR, *Friedl* (n. 123), § 52.
[126]ECtHR, *P.G. and J.H.* (n. 115), § 56.
[127]EComHR, *Lupker and Others v. the Netherlands*, no. 18395/91, decision of 7 December 1992.
[128]ECtHR, *Peck* (n. 115), § 61.
[129]ECtHR, *Peck* (n. 115), § 62 (see also §§ 9–23).
[130]ECtHR, *Peck* (n. 1), § 63. For a thorough discussion of the scope of private life 'after Hannover' see *Fenwick/Phillipson* (2006), 677–83.

Thus, as far as the taking, use, storage and disclosure of images by public authorities is concerned, the case-law of the Convention institutions presents a multi-faceted, differentiated picture, with some, but not all, public contexts falling outside the scope of Article 8 ECHR. Nevertheless, in comparison with the German understanding of the constitutionally protected *Privatsphäre* (sphere of privacy), the concept of 'private life' under the Convention is more inclusive from the start.

2.4.1.3 Interferences with privacy by private entities under the law of the Convention

2.4.1.3.1 POSITIVE OBLIGATIONS

The ECtHR makes it very clear that the *Von Hannover* case is not dealing with an interference in the right to respect for private life by a public authority or institution: 'In the present case the applicant did not complain of an action by the State, but rather of the lack of adequate State protection of her private life and her image.'[131] Furthermore, the ECtHR expressly addresses the aspect of *positive obligations* which the Convention places on the High Contracting Parties:

> The Court reiterates that although the object of Article 8 is essentially that of protecting the individual against arbitrary interference by the public authorities, it does not merely compel the State to abstain from such interference: in addition to this primarily negative undertaking, there may be positive obligations inherent in an effective respect for private or family life. These obligations may involve the adoption of measures designed to secure respect for private life even in the sphere of the relations of individuals between themselves (...). That also applies to the protection of a person's picture against abuse by others (...).[132]

Here we can detect a certain contrast to the *Bundesverfassungsgericht*. In its judgment in the same case, the Karlsruhe Justices had ventilated aspects of 'protecting' autonomy as to one's image and the private sphere. But not once did they even mention the word '*Schutzpflicht*', the constitutional duty to protect basic rights.[133] The ECtHR, however, neither elaborates on the nature of positive obligations. It is even reluctant to distinguish the boundary between the State's positive and negative obligations under Article 8 ECHR, as this boundary 'does not lend itself to precise definition'.[134] Rather, it contents itself with describing the applicable principles as 'similar': 'In both

---

[131]ECtHR, *Von Hannover* (n. 1), § 56.
[132]ECtHR, *Von Hannover* (n. 1), § 57.
[133]See especially *Bundesverfassungsgericht* (n. 4), 379–386 – *Caroline von Monaco II*.
[134]ECtHR, *Von Hannover* (n. 1), § 57.

contexts regard must be had to the fair balance that has to be struck between the competing interests of the individual and of the community as a whole; and in both contexts the State enjoys a certain margin of appreciation (...).'[135]

2.4.1.3.2 BALANCING THE CONFLICTING RIGHTS AND INTERESTS

Quite similar to the way the *Bundesverfassungsgericht* construes basic rights under German constitutional law, the ECtHR sees that the protection of private life needs to be balanced against the right to freedom of expression, as guaranteed by Article 10 of the Convention. Freedom of expression is said to constitute one of the essential foundations of a democratic society. The Court underlines the strength of the guarantee under Article 10 by reiterating that, subject to Article 10(2), 'it is applicable not only to 'information' or 'ideas' that are favourably received or regarded as inoffensive or as a matter of indifference, but also to those that offend, shock or disturb. Such are the demands of that pluralism, tolerance and broadmindedness without which there is no 'democratic society' (...).'[136] This perspective is, with a view to the German constitution, principally shared by the *Bundesverfassungsgericht*.[137] In the eyes of the ECtHR, the press plays an essential role in a democratic society: 'Although it must not overstep certain bounds, in particular in respect of the reputation and rights of others, its duty is nevertheless to impart – in a manner consistent with its obligations and responsibilities – information and ideas on all matters of public interest (...).'[138] The Court understands journalistic freedom also to cover possible recourse to a degree of exaggeration, or even provocation.[139] Furthermore it includes the publication of photographs among the protected activities.[140]

However, the photo publication is regarded as a somewhat delicate matter, with the protection of the rights and reputation of others taking on particular importance. The *Von Hannover* case, the Court says, concerns the dissemination not of 'ideas', 'but of images containing very personal or even intimate 'information' about an individual.'[141] Already, here, it points to the sometimes aggressive methods of collecting images: 'Furthermore, photos

[135]ECtHR, *Von Hannover* (n. 1), § 57. As to horizontal effects of Article 8 ECHR see *Fenwick/Phillipson* (2006), 666–77.
[136]ECtHR, *Von Hannover* (n. 1), § 58, referring to ECtHR, *Handyside v. the United Kingdom*, no. 5493/72, judgment of 7 December 1976, Series A no. 24, p. 23, § 49.
[137]See *supra*, at n. 90 et seq.
[138]ECtHR, *Von Hannover* (n. 1), § 58, referring to ECtHR, *Observer and Guardian v. the United Kingdom*, no. 13585/88, judgment of 26 November 1991, Series A no. 216, p. 29–30, § 59; and *Bladet Tromsø and Stensaas v. Norway* [GC], no. 21980/93, § 59, ECHR 1999–III.
[139]ECtHR, *Von Hannover* (n. 1), § 58, referring to ECtHR, *Prager and Oberschlick v. Austria*, no. 15974/90, judgment of 26 April 1995, Series A no. 313, p. 19, § 38; *Tammer v. Estonia*, no. 41205/98, § 59–63, ECHR 2001–I; and *Prisma Press v. France* (dec.), nos. 66910/01 and 71612/01, 1 July 2003.
[140]ECtHR, *Von Hannover* (n. 1), § 59.
[141]ECtHR, *Von Hannover* (n. 1), § 59.

appearing in the tabloid press are often taken in a climate of continual harassment which induces in the person concerned a very strong sense of intrusion into their private life or even of persecution.'[142]

Finally, the judgment highlights a component of the evaluation necessary to balance the protection of private life against the freedom of expression: the relevance of the contribution made by the photos or articles compared to the debate of general interest.[143]

2.4.2 Application of the ECHR standards to the case

In the ECtHR's opinion, all of the photographs in the magazines' files ought to have been deleted – more exactly, considered unpublishable. In applying the standards derived from Articles 8 and 10 ECHR, the Court ventilates all of the essential arguments brought forth by the parties and the German judges up to then. Yet it weighs them differently.

2.4.2.1 The different weighing of the competing positions by the ECtHR

2.4.2.1.1 LESS (OR EVEN NO?) WEIGHT OF FREEDOM OF EXPRESSION OUTSIDE A DEBATE OF GENERAL INTEREST

From the start, the Court makes it clear that its evaluation centres on 'a fundamental distinction' to be made 'between reporting facts – even controversial ones – capable of contributing to a debate in a democratic society relating to politicians in the exercise of their functions, for example, and reporting details of the private life of an individual who, moreover, as in this case, does not exercise official functions.'[144] This distinction is vital to balancing the different interests, especially as it very much determines the weight accorded to

---

[142]ECtHR, *Von Hannover* (n. 1), § 59.

[143]ECtHR, *Von Hannover* (n. 1), § 60, with recourse to ECtHR, *News Verlags GmbH & CoKG v. Austria*, no. 31457/96, § 52 et seq., ECHR 2000–I, and *Krone Verlag GmbH & Co. KG v. Austria*, no. 34315/96, § 33 et seq., 26 February 2002 (the subject in question was considered as a news item of 'major public concern'; and the published photographs 'did not disclose any details of [the] private life' of the person in question, see ibid., § 37). As an example of a case where the use of certain terms in relation to an individual's private life was not 'justified by considerations of public concern' and those terms did not '[bear] on a matter of general importance' the ECtHR quotes its *Tammer* judgment (*supra*, n. 139). Finally, the Court draws on its judgment *Èditions Plon v. France*, no. 58148/00, 18 May 2004, ECHR 2004–IV, to show that – as to the publication by President Mitterand's former private doctor of a book containing revelations about the President's state of health – protection under Article 8 ECHR could fade: The Court held that 'the more time that elapsed, the more the public interest in discussion of the history of President Mitterrand's two terms of office prevailed over the requirements of protecting the President's rights with regard to medical confidentiality' (*ibid.*, § 53) and held that there had been a breach of Article 10 (*ibid.*, § 55). See also *Barendt* (2005), 243–5.

[144]ECtHR, *Von Hannover* (n. 1), § 63.

the press's freedom of expression. Towards the end of the judgment, the Court clearly states that 'the decisive factor in balancing the protection of private life against freedom of expression should lie in the contribution that the published photos and articles make to a debate of general interest.'[145] Only by making such a contribution does 'the press exercise[s] its vital role of 'watchdog' in a democracy by contributing to 'impart[ing] information and ideas on matters of public interest' (…).'[146]

In the *Von Hannover* case, the ECtHR can discern 'no such contribution since the applicant exercises no official function and the photos and articles related exclusively to details of her private life.'[147] The photos of Princess Caroline in various German magazines showed her in scenes from her daily life, thus engaged in activities of a purely private nature.[148] She did not exercise any function within or on behalf of the State of Monaco or one of its institutions.[149]

Freedom of expression and the public's interest to be informed are not assigned much weight in the specific case: While the Court concedes that the public, in general, has a right to be informed, and that this is an essential right in a democratic society, it is very cautious when it says 'that, in certain special circumstances, can even extend to aspects of the private life of public figures, particularly where politicians are concerned.'[150] In the absence of any such connection to political or public debate and thus, any contribution to a debate of general interest, the Court perceives the sole purpose for publishing the photos and articles in question to be, 'the curiosity of a particular readership regarding the details of the applicant's private life.'[151] It concludes, under these circumstances, that 'freedom of expression calls for a narrower interpretation.'[152] Justification for this restrictive attitude towards the freedom of expression is derived from Resolution 1165 (1998) of the Parliamentary Assembly of the Council of Europe on the right to privacy,[153] whose eighth paragraph reads: 'It is often in the name of a one-sided interpretation of the right to freedom of expression, which is guaranteed in Article 10 of the European Convention on Human Rights, that the media invade people's privacy, claiming that their readers are entitled to know everything about public figures.' The Court is very much tempted to deny any public interest in the

---

[145]ECtHR, *Von Hannover* (n. 1), § 76.
[146]ECtHR, *Von Hannover* (n. 1), § 63, here quotes ECtHR, *Observer and Guardian* (n. 138).
[147]ECtHR, *Von Hannover* (n. 1), § 76 (see also § 65).
[148]ECtHR, *Von Hannover* (n. 1), § 61.
[149]ECtHR, *Von Hannover* (n. 1), § 62 (see also § 64: 'The situation here does not come within the sphere of any political or public debate because the published photos and accompanying commentaries relate exclusively to details of the applicant's private life.').
[150]ECtHR, *Von Hannover* (n. 1), § 64 with reference to ECtHR, *Èditions Plon* (n. 143).
[151]ECtHR, *Von Hannover* (n. 1), § 65.
[152]ECtHR, *Von Hannover* (n. 1), § 66.
[153]ECtHR, *Von Hannover* (n. 1), § 67.

photographs of the Princess concerned. It is steadfastly convinced that the public has no 'legitimate'(!)[154] interest 'in knowing where the applicant is and how she behaves generally in her private life even if she appears in places that cannot always be described as secluded and despite the fact that she is well known to the public.'[155] Only hypothetically does it concede that, absent any contribution to a general debate, there might possibly be a public interest. With all arguments reinforcing the press's position for the sake of an open society's democratic discourse having become threadbare, the manifest economic interests of the magazines in publishing the pictures come shining through.[156] This deconstruction of the publisher's argumentation, however, does not make the Court completely deny Article 10 ECHR to be applicable. But, while it might even be hinting to some scepticism insofar, it does strip the freedom of expression of its weight in being balanced against the right to respect for private life.

2.4.2.1.2 IS STRASBOURG'S APPROACH TO FREEDOM OF THE PRESS PRINCIPALLY DIFFERENT FROM KARLSRUHE'S?

It is worth having a closer look at the difference between the ECtHR's approach and the *Bundesverfassungsgericht*'s approach.

The German Constitutional Justices accept that freedom of the press extends to reporting on celebrities for the sole sake of their being 'points of crystallisation for approval or disapproval' and fulfilling 'functions of role-models or contrasting figures.'[157] Expressly, it is acknowledged as one of the functions of the press protected under Article 5(1), second sentence, of the *Grundgesetz* to present people irrespective of certain functions or events.[158] The fact that it might merely be curiosity, or as one might want to phrase this

---

[154] The word 'legitimate' is used quite often throughout the judgment (see ECtHR, *Von Hannover* [n. 1], §§ 51, 69, 77, 78). In a way it encapsulates the result of the balancing operation necessary. Cf. the concurring opinion of Judge *Cabral Barreto*. Judge *Zupančič* in his concurring opinion favours a test as to whether there was a 'reasonable expectation of privacy', construed along the lines of ECtHR, *Halford* (n. 119), and permitting a 'nuanced approach to every new case'. He is careful to warn of the danger of a circuitous reasoning, and considers both reducing the 'reasonableness' of the expectation of privacy to the balancing test, and understanding reasonableness as, 'an allusion to informed common sense, which tells us that he who lives in a glass house may not have the right to throw stones.'

[155] ECtHR, *Von Hannover* (n. 1), § 77.

[156] ECtHR, *Von Hannover* (n. 1), § 77: 'Even if such a public interest exists, as does a commercial interest of the magazines in publishing these photos and these articles, in the instant case those interests must, in the Court's view, yield to the applicant's right to the effective protection of her private life.'

[157] *Bundesverfassungsgericht* (n. 4), 390 – *Caroline von Monaco II*: 'Sie werden zu Kristallisationspunkten für Zustimmung oder Ablehnung und erfüllen Leitbild – oder Kontrastfunktionen.'

[158] *Bundesverfassungsgericht* (n. 4), 391 – *Caroline von Monaco II*.

more pejoratively – voyeurism – is accorded relevance only in the balancing of interests required to solve the conflict between the freedom of expression and the need for protecting the personality right.[159]

In both the *Bundesverfassungsgericht*'s and the ECtHR's argumentation the decisive context is that of striking the balance. At the level of German constitutional law, however, freedom of the press, where it cannot draw on its functions within a democratic society, stands on the chessboard as a queen, at the Convention's level, only as a pawn. Not inconceivably, the *Bundesverfassungsgericht* might appear to be more inclined to regard the guarantee of freedom of the press as, at least *prima facie*, content-neutral, thus leaving it to the press to decide what is worth reporting on. The Karlsruhe Court might thus be attaching more weight to this liberty.[160] However, such a perception does not pay due respect to the ECtHR's protectiveness of Article 10 ECHR, which is clearly demonstrated in its case-law.[161] The Court has, for instance, albeit with regard to the press's 'vital role of "public watchdog"' emphasised the importance of news reporting based on interviews, holding that 'it is not for the Court, any more than it is for the national courts, to substitute its own views for those of the press as to what techniques of reporting should be adopted by journalists.'[162] Punishment for assisting in the dissemination of statements made by another person in an interview would, the Court has said, seriously hamper the contribution of the press to the discussion of matters of public interest and should not be envisaged unless there are particularly strong reasons for doing so.[163]

The decisive contrast between the ECtHR and the German *Bundesverfassungsgericht* is that the Strasbourg Court estimates the need for protecting private life higher than the Karlsruhe Justices. While there is common ground insofar as – in the ECtHR's words – 'the fundamental importance of protecting private life from the point of view of the development of every human being's personality,' under the Convention, that protection, as already mentioned, in principle 'extends beyond the private family circle and

---

[159]*Bundesverfassungsgericht* (n. 4), 391 – *Caroline von Monaco II*.

[160]See *supra*, at ns. 90 et seq. See, as a contrast, Judge *Zupančič* in his concurring opinion in the *Von Hannover* case: '... I believe that the courts have to some extent and under American influence made a fetish of the freedom of the press.'

[161]See only as to restrictions on the freedom of the press based on 'protection of the reputation of others': ECtHR, *Krone Verlag GmbH & Co. KG* (n. 143), and *Krone Verlag GmbH & Co. KG (No. 2)*, no. 40284/98, judgment of 6 November 2003; as well as especially ECtHR, *Özgür Gündem ./. Türkei*, no. 23144/93, judgment of 16 March 2000, ECHR 2000–III.

[162]ECtHR, *Bergens Tidende and Others v. Norway*, no. 26132/95, judgment of 2 May 2000, § 57, ECHR 2000–IV.

[163]ECtHR, *Thoma v. Luxembourg*, no. 38432/97, judgment of 29 March 2001, § 62, ECHR 2001–III; *Jersild v. Denmark*, no. 15890/89, judgment of 23 September 1994, Series A no. 298, pp. 25–26, § 35. See also ECtHR, *Krone Verlag GmbH & Co. KG (No. 4)*, no. 72331/01, judgment of 9 November 2006, § 34.

also includes a social dimension.'[164] '[A]nyone, even if they are known to the general public, must be able to enjoy a "legitimate expectation" of protection of and respect for their private life.'[165] Although these aspects are also discussed by the *Bundesverfassungsgericht*, the ECtHR puts more emphasis on 'the context in which these photos were taken – without the applicant's knowledge or consent – and the harassment endured by many public figures in their daily lives'[166] and on 'new communication technologies which make it possible to store and reproduce personal data' as well as on 'to the systematic taking of specific photos and their dissemination to a broad section of the public.'[167] All of this increases the necessity of 'vigilance in protecting private life.'[168]

2.4.2.2 Evaluation of the German courts' application of secs. 22, 23 KUG

In the ECtHR's eyes, the German courts have failed 'to ensure the effective protection of the applicant's private life'.[169] The Court has never tired of emphasising 'that the Convention is intended to guarantee not rights that are theoretical or illusory but rights that are practical and effective'.[170] The protection afforded to an 'absolute' figure of contemporary society by the German courts under sec. 23 KUG is regarded as insufficient. As it conveys very limited protection for their private life or the right to control the use of their image, the ECtHR only considers it – conceivably – appropriate for politicians exercising official functions. 'However, it cannot be justified for a "private" individual, such as the applicant, in whom the interest of the general public and the press is based solely on her membership of a reigning family whereas she herself does not exercise any official functions.'[171]

---

[164]ECtHR, *Von Hannover* (n. 1), § 69. But see *supra*, n. 115.
[165]ECtHR, *Von Hannover* (n. 1), § 69.
[166]ECtHR, *Von Hannover* (n. 1), § 68. The Court regards this point to be illustrated in particularly striking fashion by the photos taken of Princess Caroline at the Monte Carlo Beach Club tripping over an obstacle and falling down, as these photos had apparently been taken secretly at a distance of several hundred metres, probably from a neighbouring house, whereas journalists and photographers' access to the club was strictly regulated.
[167]ECtHR, *Von Hannover* (n. 1), § 70.
[168]ECtHR, *Von Hannover* (n. 1), § 70.
[169]ECtHR, *Von Hannover* (n. 1), § 78.
[170]ECtHR, *Von Hannover* (n. 1), § 71, referring to ECtHR, *Artico v. Italy*, no. 6694/74, judgment of 13 May 1980, Series A no. 37, p. 15–16, § 33.
[171]ECtHR, *Von Hannover* (n. 1), § 72. Cf. the position of Judge *Cabral Barreto* in his concurring opinion: 'The applicant is, in my view, a public figure and information about her life contributes to a debate of general interest. The general interest does not have to be limited to political debate. As pointed out by the Parliamentary Assembly certain facts relating to the private lives of public figures, particularly politicians, may indeed be of interest to citizens. If that is true of politicians it is also true for all other public figures in whom the public takes an interest.'

The Court furthermore is doubtful of the legal certainty of the distinction drawn between figures of contemporary society '*par excellence*' and 'relatively' public figures and the consequences respectively attached. While individuals need to know exactly when and where they are in a protected sphere or, on the contrary, in a sphere in which they must expect interference from others, especially the tabloid press, the Princess, as a figure of contemporary society '*par excellence*', 'cannot – in the name of freedom of the press and the public interest – rely on protection of her private life unless she is in a secluded place out of the public eye and, moreover, succeeds in proving it (which can be difficult). Where that is not the case, she has to accept that she might be photographed at almost any time, systematically, and that the photos are then very widely disseminated even if, as was the case here, the photos and accompanying articles relate exclusively to details of her private life.'[172] These considerations lead the Court to the conclusion that 'the criterion of spatial isolation, although apposite in theory, is in reality too vague and difficult for the person concerned to determine in advance. In the present case merely classifying the applicant as a figure of contemporary society "*par excellence*" does not suffice to justify such an intrusion into her private life.'[173] Regardless of the State's having a 'margin of appreciation', the Court therefore found there to have been a breach of Article 8 ECHR.[174]

2.4.3 Does the ECtHR overstep the limits of its competence in demanding national courts to interpret domestic law in conformity with the Convention?

In this context one aspect deserves to be highlighted: When discussing the protective scheme developed by the German courts under secs. 22, 23 KUG, the ECtHR finds that the KUG 'has to be interpreted narrowly to ensure that the State complies with its positive obligation under the Convention to protect private life and the right to control the use of one's image'.[175] The national lawyer might be quite disturbed to see an international court of law making prescriptions on how to interpret provisions of a domestic statute. However,

---

[172]ECtHR, *Von Hannover* (n. 1), § 73–74.

[173]ECtHR, *Von Hannover* (n. 1), § 75.

[174]A stronger differentiation is advocated by Judge *Cabral Barreto* in his concurring opinion on the following grounds: 'Admittedly, determining the limit of a public figure's private life is no easy task. Furthermore, a strict criterion might lead to solutions that do not correspond to the "nature of things". It is clear that if the person is in an isolated spot everything that happens there must be covered by the protection of private life. It appears to me, however, that the criterion of spatial isolation used by the German courts is very restrictive. In my view, whenever a public figure has a "legitimate expectation" of being safe from the media his or her right to private life prevails over the right to freedom of expression or the right to be informed. It will never be easy to define in concrete terms the situations that correspond to this "legitimate expectation" and a case-by-case approach is therefore justified.'

[175]ECtHR, *Von Hannover* (n. 1), § 72.

keep in mind that the Court had to deal with the question of whether Germany had fulfilled its positive obligations under Article 8 ECHR, in other words, whether it had sufficiently and effectively protected Princess Caroline against intrusions into her private life by the press. In order to perform such a task, Germany as a state must rely on its institutions, more specifically on its laws and their interpretation and application by the German courts of justice. Compliance with the normative standards of the Convention as an international human rights treaty concerns the whole of the State Party, as the behaviour of each of its institutions, in principle, forms part of the behaviour of the High Contracting Party as such. Furthermore, cases can only be brought in the ECtHR 'after all domestic remedies have been exhausted' (Article 35(1) ECHR). As States Parties are under an obligation to provide 'an effective remedy before a national authority' (Article 13 ECHR), cases will necessarily, or at least regularly, have been dealt with by such a national authority, most regularly by the national courts. Especially in a case in which the respondent state is alleged to have violated positive obligations under the Convention, it is quite logical that the courts will have dealt with the question of their fulfilment – though perhaps only applying domestic law and thus only answering the question whether such obligations exist according to national norms. Therefore it is quite 'natural' for the ECtHR to examine an application under Article 34 (or Article 33) ECHR by looking at the decisions of the national courts.

Moreover, the Court itself has indicated that it does not understand itself to be some kind of ultimate court of appeal or review. In no way is it a simple extension of the domestic judicial systems. Rather, its function is to decide on applications against States Parties alleging there to have been a violation of the rights guaranteed by the Convention. With hindsight, the Court has commented on its *Von Hannover* judgment. In the *Storck* case[176] the Court reiterated 'that it is not its function to deal with errors of fact or law allegedly committed by the national courts and that it is in the first place for the national authorities, notably the courts, to interpret national law.'[177] At the same time, however, it reasserted its power 'to examine whether the effects of such an interpretation are compatible with the Convention.'[178] It continued:

> In securing the rights protected by the Convention, the Contracting States, notably their courts, are obliged to apply the provisions of national law in the spirit of those rights. Failure to do so can amount to a violation imputable to the State of the Convention Article in question. In this connection, the Court reiterates that the Convention is intended to

---

[176]ECtHR, *Storck v. Germany*, no. 61603/00, judgment of 16 June 2005, 2005-V.
[177]ECtHR, *Storck* (n. 176), § 93.
[178]ECtHR, *Storck* (n. 176), § 93, with reference to ECtHR, *Platakou v. Greece*, no. 38460/97, judgment of 11 January 2001, § 37, ECHR 2001-I.

guarantee not rights that are theoretical or illusory but rights that are practical and effective (...).[179]

The obligation to apply domestic law in conformity with the Convention does not presuppose the 'immediate' applicability of the Convention guarantees, although the Convention has now become an integral part of the domestic legal order of all States Parties.[180] Instead this obligation is no more than an emanation of the treaty's binding force. When a High Contracting Party's authorities, especially its courts, tune provisions of domestic law to the requirements of the ECHR rights and freedoms, they merely participate in a way of ensuring the State's compliance with the Convention.

2.5 Reactions of the German *Bundesgerichtshof*

The ECtHR's judgment reserved the question of whether Princess Caroline was to be awarded just satisfaction in application of Article 41 ECHR.[181] In the end, a friendly settlement was reached, according to which the Federal Republic of Germany agreed to pay the applicant a global sum of EUR 115,000, this sum comprising EUR 10,000 in compensation for non-pecuniary damage and EUR 105,000 for costs and expenses, including tax.[182]

The German courts were barred from dealing with the case again. Only with the 2. *Justizmodernisierungsgesetz* (2nd Act on the Modernisation of the Judiciary), which entered into force on 31 December 2006, was sec. 580 of the German Code on Civil Procedure (Zivilprozessordnung – ZPO) changed[183] to allow a reopening of proceedings when the ECtHR has found Germany to have violated the Convention or one of its Protocols, and the respective judgment is based on this violation.[184]

---

[179]ECtHR, *Storck* (n. 176), § 93, with reference to ECtHR, *Artico* (n. 170), § 33, and *Von Hannover* (n. 1), § 71. For a critical discussion of horizontal effects of ECHR rights see *Kay* (2005).

[180]Resolution Res(2004)3 of the Committee of Ministers of the Council of Europe on judgments revealing an underlying systemic problem (adopted by the Committee of Ministers on 12 May 2004, at its 114th Session).

[181]ECtHR, *Von Hannover* (n. 1), § 85.

[182]ECtHR, no. 59320/00, judgment of 28 July 2005 (just satisfaction and friendly settlement).

[183]The Federal Government, which drafted the bill, intended to approximate the situation of civil proceedings to that of criminal proceedings under sec. 359 no. 6 of the Code of Criminal Procedure (Strafprozessordnung – StPO); see *Entwurf der Bundesregierung*, Bundestagsdrucksache [BT-Drs.] 16/3038 of 19 October 2006, p. 25 and pp. 38 et seq. As sec. 580 of the Code of Civil Procedure is also applicable to proceedings before the labour courts, the administrative courts, the social courts and the tax courts, it has caused a far-reaching change of the relevance of ECtHR judgments; this had been intended by the Federal Government (*Entwurf der Bundesregierung, ibid.*, p. 39).

[184]Cf. the Recommendation of the Committee of Ministers of the European Council of 19 January 2000 (694th session) Nr. R (2000) 2, HRLJ 2000, 272 et seq., point II ('Encourages the Contracting Parties, in particular, to examine their national legal systems with a view to ensuring that there exist adequate possibilities of re-examination of the case, including reopening

Nevertheless, the German courts reacted to the ECtHR's *Von Hannover* judgment. It has been mentioned that the *Bundesverfassungsgericht*'s *Görgülü* decision, delivered four months after the ECtHR's *Von Hannover* judgment, was understood as a move to fight back the influence of the Convention and the jurisprudence of the ECtHR on German law. However, the *Bundesgerichtshof* clearly showed deference to the Strasbourg Court and adapted its interpretation of secs. 22, 23 KUG to the standards developed in the ECtHR's *Von Hannover* judgment. This adaptation was endorsed by the *Bundesverfassungsgericht* as compatible with the basic rights of the constitution.[185]

2.5.1 The Bundesgerichtshof's judgment of 6 March 2007 in yet another Princess Caroline case

A leading case in this respect again concerned Princess Caroline.[186] Again, she sought protection against the publisher of a magazine in which pictures of her and her husband were printed. Before the German courts, her motion for judgment was aimed at enjoining the publisher from the republication of photographs. All of the pictures were used as illustrations for text articles. One photograph, showing the Princess together with her husband, Prince Ernst August von Hannover, on a street in St Moritz, was added to an article covering the severe illness of her father, Prince Rainier of Monaco. A similar photograph was attached to a story on the couple's stay in this Swiss winter sports resort. A third picture, showing the couple using a chairlift during a skiing tour, illustrated an article on the Princess's expected return to Monaco in order to attend the 'Rose Ball'.[187]

2.5.1.1 The new scheme of variable protection ('abgestuftes Schutzkonzept') under secs. 22, 23 KUG

In its judgment on appeal from the Hamburg Higher Regional Court (*Oberlandesgericht Hamburg*), the *Bundesgerichtshof* recalled the distinction between 'relative' and 'absolute' figures of contemporary society

---

of proceedings, in instances where the Court has found a violation of the Convention, especially where: (i) the injured party continues to suffer very serious negative consequences because of the outcome of the domestic decision at issue, which are not adequately remedied by the just satisfaction and cannot be rectified except by re-examination or reopening, and (ii) the judgment of the Court leads to the conclusion that (a) the impugned domestic decision is on the merits contrary to the Convention, or (b) the violation found is based on procedural errors or shortcomings of such gravity that a serious doubt is cast on the outcome of the domestic proceedings complained of.').

[185]*Bundesverfassungsgericht*, decision of 26 February 2008–1 BvR 1602, 1606, 1626/07–, BVerfGE 120, 180 – *Caroline von Monaco III*.
[186]*Bundesgerichtshof* (n. 12), 1977.
[187]*Bundesgerichtshof* (n. 12), 1977. See also *Bundesverfassungsgericht* (n. 185), 182–195 – *Caroline von Monaco III*.

as it had evolved under secs. 22, 23 KUG.[188] It also comprehensively restated the new '*agestuftes Schutzkonzept*', the new scheme of variable protection, which the courts had developed, starting with its own judgment of 19 December 1995[189] and the *Bundesverfassungsgericht*'s judgment in the *Caroline von Monaco II* case;[190] meanwhile the principles of the ECtHR's judgments in the cases of *Von Hannover v. Germany* and *Karhuvaara und Iltalehti v. Finland*,[191] had also been taken into account.[192]

The new scheme of variable protection moves away from the rigidity of the distinction between 'absolute' and 'relative' figures of contemporary society by readjusting the test applied in assessing whether an image can be disseminated or shown in public because it portrays 'an aspect of contemporary society' ('*Bildnisse aus dem Bereich der Zeitgeschichte*'). The interpretation of this condition takes the interests of the public into consideration. Consequently, the balancing of the conflicting rights and basic rights of the depicted person on the one hand,[193] and the press on the other,[194] is already required at this stage. A normative standard needs to be applied, which must pay due respect both to freedom of the press and to the protection of the personality and its sphere of privacy. In this respect, the public's interest in being fully informed of contemporary society (*das Zeitgeschehen*) is essential. With a view to freedom of the press the scope of *Zeitgeschehen* is to be understood broadly. But limits are set to the interest in being informed. The intrusion into the personal sphere of the person whose image is used is restricted by the principle of proportionality, which will not always allow disclosure and publication. The *Bundesgerichtshof* considers it impossible to draw a clear line where the informational interest of the public ends. Rather this needs to be decided on a case-by-case basis, taking into account the details of the specific circumstances.[195]

The Court understands the ECtHR's criticism of the concept of 'absolute' figures of contemporary society to centre around the question of when such a

---

[188]*Bundesgerichtshof* (n. 12), 1978. See *supra*, at ns. 12 et seq.

[189]*Bundesgerichtshof* (n. 4). See *supra*, at ns. 15 et seq.

[190]*Bundesverfassungsgericht* (n. 4) – *Caroline von Monaco II*. See *supra*, at ns. 71 et seq.

[191]ECtHR, *Karhuvaara und Iltalehti v. Finland*, no. 53678/00, judgment of 16 November 2004, ECHR 2004–X.

[192]*Bundesgerichtshof* (n. 12), 1978, additionally points to the following decisions by the *Bundesverfassungsgericht*: *Bundesverfassungsgericht, 1st Chamber of the First Senate*, decision of 26 April 2001–1 BvR 758/97–, 2001 Neue Juristische Wochenschrift 1921 (1924 et seq.); decision of 13 June 2006–1 BvR 565/06–, 2006 Neue Juristische Wochenschrift 2835; decision of 2 Mai 2006–1 BvR 507/01–, 2006 Neue Juristische Wochenschrift 2836; and to judgments of its own: *Bundesgerichtshof*, judgment of 9 October 2004 –VI ZR 292/03–, 2005 Neue Juristische Wochenschrift 594; judgment of 15. November 2005 –VI ZR 286/04–, 2006 Neue Juristische Wochenschrift 599.

[193]Article 8 ECHR; Articles 2(1) and 1(1) of the *Grundgesetz*.

[194]Article 10 ECHR; Article 5(1), second sentence, of the *Grundgesetz*.

[195]*Bundesgerichtshof* (n. 12), 1978.

public figure may be the object of reporting by the media.[196] Its reaction is to point out that the civil courts must not deny protection of the private sphere for the sole reason that a public figure's picture has not been taken secretly in a situation in which he or she had retreated to a secluded place. Rightly perceived, this not only followed from the ECtHR's opinion of what the Convention demanded, but even before had already been a necessary consequence of the (new) scheme of variable protection.[197] Accordingly, even when a person's image can, in principle, be disseminated without the person's consent with a view to events of contemporary society within the meaning of sec. 23(1) no. 1 KUG, such a dissemination may be prohibited if this interferes with a legitimate interest of the person.[198]

It follows, the *Bundesgerichtshof* says, that there is room for an exception from the requirement of the person's consent only if reporting pertains to an event of contemporary history, the concept of which must not, however, be construed too narrowly. Pointing to the framers' intent, and also to the public's need for information on contemporary history (*Zeitgeschichte*), the Court says that contemporary history comprises not only affairs and events of historical or political importance, but the contemporary society ('*das Zeitgeschehen*') in general, and thus all questions of general relevance to society. Thus it is determined by the public interest ('*Interesse der Öffentlichkeit*'). Despite the ECtHR's more constrained conception of what contributes to a debate of general interest,[199] the *Bundesgerichtshof* remains convinced that articles (or broadcasts) aimed at entertainment can very well affect the formation of opinions, sometimes exerting more influence than matter-of-fact information.[200]

The Court regards itself in harmony with the ECtHR in its belief that freedom of the press in its core guarantees the press to have sufficient leeway to decide according to editorial criteria what the public is interested in, albeit within the limits of the law – the process of the forming of opinions lastly determining what actually is in the public interest. It is, the Court believes, up to the press to take the editorial decision as to what it will present to the public as worthy of its attention. This is seen in connection with the prohibition of censorship under the German constitution (Article 5(1), third sentence, of

---

[196]*Bundesgerichtshof* (n. 12), 1978.
[197]*Bundesgerichtshof* (n. 12), 1978–1979.
[198]*Bundesgerichtshof* (n. 12), 1979.
[199]See *supra*, at ns. 144 et seq.
[200]*Bundesgerichtshof* (n. 12), 1979, as reference for the original intent pointing to *Ebermayer*, in: *Stengleins*, Kommentar zu den Strafrechtlichen Nebengesetzen des Deutschen Reiches, 5th ed., vol. I, § 23 KUG annotation 1; *Stenographische Berichte über die Verhandlungen des Reichstags* (Stenographic reports of the debates of the Parliament of the German Empire), XI. *Legislaturperiode* (10th Legislative Period), I. *Session* 1905/1906, *erster Sessionsabschnitt* (first chapter of sessions), *Aktenstück* (file) no. 30, p. 1540–1541 and I. *Lesung* (first reading) 25 January 1906, vol. 214, p. 819.

the *Grundgesetz*). That the ECtHR pointed to certain bounds which must not be overstepped by the press is understood to pertain to the balancing of freedom of the press and the public's interest in being informed on the one hand, and the protection of the private sphere on the other hand.[201]

Balancing is also called for under sec. 23(2) KUG, with the informational value of an object of reporting being of special relevance. The greater the importance of a piece of information to the public, the more easily the public's interest can overcome the interest of the person concerned not to disclose this information. In the alternative, the protection of the personality of the person concerned has (relatively) more weight when the informational value is low. The readers' interest merely to be entertained – the Court says quite in line with the ECtHR[202] – normally weighs less and is not worthy of protection. The *Bundesgerichtshof* holds these considerations to be valid even in cases of people who have reached a high degree of publicity. Therefore, even with a view to a figure of contemporary society it is not irrelevant whether media coverage can contribute to a substantive debate and thus goes beyond mere satisfying curiosity. This does not, in the eyes of the Court, exclude the possibility that a person's fame can influence the value of a piece of information. In any case, whether assessing the informational value or answering the question whether an event belongs to contemporary history, one must apply a broad understanding of the concept of *Zeitgeschichte*.[203]

The Court also pointed out that, if an image is connected with a text article, this has to be taken into account when the courts assess its informational value.[204]

2.5.1.2 Applying the new scheme

In this specific case, the Court concluded that the picture showing the Princess and her husband during their holiday in St Moritz belonged to the core of their sphere of privacy and had no connection to contemporary history. Its publication without consent was thus prohibited. The same conclusion was reached with respect to the photograph showing the Princess in a skiing lift. The Court conceded that the article on the 'Rose Ball' in Monaco might be regarded as reporting on an event of contemporary society arousing public

---

[201]*Bundesgerichtshof* (n. 12), 1979.

[202]See *supra*, at n. 151.

[203]*Bundesgerichtshof* (n. 12), 1979. The *Bundesgerichtshof* sees this way of reconciling the protection of privacy and the freedom of the press as consistent with the ECtHR, *Von Hannover* (n. 1), § 76; furthermore it denies any conflict with the binding effect of *Bundesverfassungsgericht* (n. 4) – *Caroline von Monaco II* under sec. 31 of the *Gesetz über das Bundesverfassungsgericht* (*Bundesverfassungsgerichtsgesetz – BVerfGG*) (as to this see also *Hoffmann-Riem* [n. 58], 21–22).

[204]*Bundesgerichtshof* (n. 12), 1980.

interest. But the photograph, taken by intrusion into the private sphere of a skiing holiday, had nothing to do with the article.[205]

The *Bundesgerichtshof* reached a different conclusion with a view to the photo attached to the report on Prince Rainier's illness. Although it also showed the Princess and her husband during their vacation and thus in a private situation, its connection with the article created a context with an affair of contemporary society. Freedom of the press disallowed making its protection dependent on the quality of a press product or its contents. As an illustration of how the Prince's family members were behaving while he lay ill, the publication of the photograph in connection with the article interfered with no legitimate interest of Princess Caroline's and was allowed.[206]

2.5.1.3 Confirmation in two parallel cases

In two decisions on the same day, in proceedings brought by Princess Caroline, the *Bundesgerichtshof*, relying on the same standards, found the republication of images of the Princess and her husband to be prohibited by sec. 22 KUG, the exception of sec. 23(1) no. 1 KUG not applying. One case was essentially parallel to the case involving the use of a holiday photograph scene used for the illustration of an article on Prince Rainier's illness, but concerned a different magazine.[207] In the other case, the picture accompanied an article reporting on celebrities who were said to be letting their mansions and castles to private tenants.[208] It hardly occurred by chance that the *Bundesgerichtshof* delivered the judgments simultaneously. Obviously, the Court meant to emphasise the new *abgestuftes Schutzkonzept*, the new scheme of variable protection, and to send a signal to Strasbourg that it had definitely adjusted its interpretation of sec. 23(1) KUG to the Convention requirements.

2.5.2 The Bundesverfassungsgericht's decision in the Caroline von Monaco III case

Against the first judgment,[209] discussed in detail above,[210] and the judgments of the lower courts in the same case, constitutional complaints were raised by

---

[205]*Bundesgerichtshof* (n. 12), 1980.

[206]*Bundesgerichtshof* (n. 12), 1980–1981, the *Bundesgerichtshof* pointing out that the image as such did not by itself effect a violation of its own, there being no indication of the photographs having been taken secretly or by using (special) technical means.

[207]*Bundesgerichtshof*, judgment of 6 March 2007 –VI ZR 14/06–, 2007 Europäische Grundrechtezeitschrift 504.

[208]*Bundesgerichtshof*, judgment of 6 March 2007 –VI ZR 52/06–, 2007 Europäische Grundrechtezeitschrift 503. See also the judgment in the proceedings brought by Princess Caroline's husband, Ernst August von Hannover, concerning the same picture: *Bundesgerichtshof*, judgment of 6 March 2007 –VI ZR 13/06–, 2007 Neue Juristische Wochenschrift 1981.

[209]*Bundesgerichtshof* (n. 12).

[210]*Supra*, at ns. 186 et seq.

Princess Caroline and the publisher concerned. The other publisher concerned also took the judgments in the case last mentioned, concerning the article on celebrities' estates,[211] to Karlsruhe. The *Bundesverfassungsgericht*'s decision on these complaints[212] has been referred to above[213] as well as in the Chapter 1. There it was pointed out that the *Bundesverfassungsgericht* regards the judgments, insofar as they forbid the republication of certain images, to interfere with the right to freedom of the press under Article 5(1), second sentence, of the *Grundgesetz*.[214] Conversely, the rejection of the Princess's application for an injunction against the republication of the photograph used in the context of the article on her father's illness, was seen negatively to affect ('*beeinträchtigen*') the Princess's 'basic right to protection of the personality' ('*Grundrecht ... auf Schutz der Persönlichkeit*') under Article 2(1) in combination with Article 1(1) of the *Grundgesetz*. However, the Court omitted using the German technical term '*Schutzpflicht*', although a violation of such a duty to protect is quite obviously what it meant.[215] The cases, whether viewed from the perspective of the press or from the perspective of the person whose image is concerned, always require the civil courts to balance conflicting basic rights.[216]

2.5.2.1 The inter-relatedness of German constitutional law and the ECHR

At the end of Chapter 1, we already saw the intertwining of German constitutional law and ECHR guarantees. Not only does Article 8 ECHR, as an *allgemeines Gesetz* within the meaning of Article 5(2) of the *Grundgesetz*, define limits to freedom of the press (Article 5(1), second sentence, of the *Grundgesetz*).[217] Article 10 ECHR, itself guaranteeing freedom of expression, forms part of the constitutional order within the meaning of Article 2(1) of the *Grundgesetz* and thus limits the scope of constitutional protection for the personality right.[218] Moreover, the Court reiterates that the interpretation of German constitutional law needs to respond to the Convention, whose guarantees principally serve as interpretative tools ('*Auslegungshilfen*') for determining the contents and scope of basic rights.[219]

---

[211]*Bundesgerichtshof*, judgment of 6 March 2007 –VI ZR 52/06–, 2007 Europäische Grundrechtezeitschrift 503.
[212]*Bundesverfassungsgericht* (n. 185) – *Caroline von Monaco III*.
[213]*Supra* at n. 185.
[214]*Bundesverfassungsgericht* (n. 185), 196 – *Caroline von Monaco III*.
[215]*Bundesverfassungsgericht* (n. 185), 197 – *Caroline von Monaco III*.
[216]See especially *Bundesverfassungsgericht* (n. 185), 199–203 – *Caroline von Monaco III*.
[217]*Bundesverfassungsgericht* (n. 185), 200 – *Caroline von Monaco III*.
[218]*Bundesverfassungsgericht* (n. 185), 202–203 – *Caroline von Monaco III*.
[219]This is expressly stated, see *Bundesverfassungsgericht* (n. 185), 200–201 – *Caroline von Monaco III* (see also *ibid.*, 208 ['*die bei der Auslegung der deutschen Grundrechte bedeutsamen Vorgaben der Europäischen Menschenrechtskonvention*'], 218).

2.5.2.2 *The Constitutionality of the new scheme of variable protection under secs. 22, 23 KUG*

The *Bundesverfassungsgericht*, in principle, regards the variable scheme of protection developed under secs. 22, 23 KUG to be compatible with the constitution.[220] It emphasises the relevance of whether an image contains information relevant to the public, but – in line with its *Caroline von Monaco II* judgment[221] – sees such relevance to exist even insofar as celebrities serve as role models or contrasting figures.[222] Furthermore, the Court is not willing to exclude entertainment from the scope of public interest and thus from the scope of freedom of the press as guaranteed under Article 5(1) of the *Grundgesetz*.[223] The Court warns, however, that recognising reporting by the press to be important for the public's and the individuals' formation of opinions does not automatically mean that the protection of a person's image, founded on the personality right, must always yield.[224] On the one hand, the balancing required must respect the autonomy of the press to decide what it considers fit to print, the weight of the informational interest (notwithstanding that it is not for the courts to qualify contents as valuable or invaluable), and an image's connection with the text of an article.[225] On the other hand, account must be taken of the methods of taking pictures, the intensity of an infringement of the personality right connected with an image as such, and legitimate expectations of privacy, whether – and this especially appears to modify the standards developed in the *Caroline von Monaco II* judgment – inside or outside places of seclusion.[226] Relevance in this context is furthermore assigned to the onus of presentation and burden of proof in civil procedure.[227] Freedom of the press must be seen in its function to contribute to the forming of opinions in a democratic society. There is a presumption that whatever the press decides to print makes such a contribution. But the fact that it is a public figure from whose private or everyday life an image is taken does not in itself justify assuming that the protection of this person's personality right must yield to the press' interest in public disclosure.[228]

---

[220] See especially *Bundesverfassungsgericht* (n. 185), 211–215 – *Caroline von Monaco III*. There, at 211, the *Bundesverfassungsgericht* acknowledges the *Bundesgerichtshof* to have leeway to modify the '*Schutzkonzept*', the scheme of protection, under secs. 22, 23 KUG; especially giving up the concept of 'figures of contemporary society' was anything but unconstitutional. The *Bundesverfassungsgericht* understands its own *Caroline von Monaco II* judgment (*Bundesverfassungsgericht* [n. 4]) not to bar such modification and specification under sec. 31 BVerfGG (cf. also n. 203), but merely to have pronounced on the constitutionality of the scheme as developed at that time.

[221] *Bundesverfassungsgericht* (n. 4), 390 – *Caroline von Monaco II*.

[222] *Bundesverfassungsgericht* (n. 185), 203–204 – *Caroline von Monaco III*.

[223] *Bundesverfassungsgericht* (n. 185), 204–205 – *Caroline von Monaco III*.

[224] *Bundesverfassungsgericht* (n. 185), 205 – *Caroline von Monaco III*.

[225] *Bundesverfassungsgericht* (n. 185), 205–207 – *Caroline von Monaco III*.

[226] *Bundesverfassungsgericht* (n. 185), 207 – *Caroline von Monaco III*.

[227] *Bundesverfassungsgericht* (n. 185), 207–208 – *Caroline von Monaco III*.

[228] *Bundesverfassungsgericht* (n. 185), 208–209 – *Caroline von Monaco III*.

2.5.2.3 The Bundesverfassungsgericht's evaluation of the application of the scheme by the civil courts

The *Bundesverfassungsgericht* regards the civil courts' judgment for the most part to be compatible with the constitution. The constitutional complaints were thus rejected as unfounded.[229] There was a different outcome only for the constitutional complaint of the publisher of the magazine containing the article reporting on celebrities who were said to be letting their mansions and castles to private tenants. The Court found that the civil courts failed to examine the informational content of the article. When Hollywood stars and members of the aristocracy rented their estates to private tenants, this might very well induce readers to social criticism, which could very well initiate a debate of general interest to the public. Using a small photograph showing the Princess and her husband together with other people as an illustration was no more than a minor intrusion into the private sphere. The civil courts' balancing thus had not paid due respect to the requirements of freedom of the press under Article 5(1), second sentence, of the *Grundgesetz*.[230]

2.5.2.4 The Bundesverfassungsgericht's careful attention to the Convention guarantees as construed by the ECtHR

The way in which the *Bundesverfassungsgericht* refers to the ECtHR's case-law in the *Caroline von Monaco III* decision must not be overlooked. It shows respect for the ECtHR's *Von Hannover* judgment. In the context of Article 5(2) of the *Grundgesetz* the *Bundesverfassungsgericht* states that Article 8(1) ECHR, in certain cases, guarantees an individual the right to be protected by the state's courts against the publication of images taken from this individual's everyday life.[231] Thus, when the *Von Hannover* judgment is quoted here, it not only explicates a limitation of the freedom of the press guaranteed under Article 5(1), second sentence, of the *Grundgesetz*, with Article 8 ECHR being addressed as a provision of an act of general legislation ('*allgemeines Gesetz*') within the meaning of Article 5(2) of the *Grundgesetz*. The *Bundesverfassungsgericht* also expressly points to the constitutional guarantee of the personality right and the protection of private life afforded by Article 8(1) ECHR being in harmony insofar as the latter refers to the 'sum of the personal, social and economic relations which are constitutive of the private life of every human being'.[232] This may well be understood as bringing constitutional and Convention requirements in line, especially as only in the previous paragraph of the *Caroline von Monaco III* decision the *Bundesverfassungsgericht* mentions the role of the Convention and the

---

[229] *Bundesverfassungsgericht* (n. 185), 215–220 – *Caroline von Monaco III*.
[230] *Bundesverfassungsgericht* (n. 185), 220–223 – *Caroline von Monaco III*.
[231] *Bundesverfassungsgericht* (n. 185), 201 – *Caroline von Monaco III*.
[232] *Bundesverfassungsgericht* (n. 185), 201 – *Caroline von Monaco III*.

ECtHR's jurisprudence as interpretative tools to be applied when construing the meaning and scope of basic rights guaranteed under the *Grundgesetz*.[233] A contribution of harmonising the norms of the *Grundgesetz* and the ECHR can also be seen in the reference to the ECtHR's judgments in the cases of *Minelli v. Switzerland*[234] and *Gurgenidze v. Georgia* with a view to the need for balancing the rights under Article 8 and Article 10 ECHR.[235]

When the *Bundesverfassungsgericht* discusses Article 10 ECHR as a provision of law belonging to the constitutional order limiting personality protection under Articles 2(1) and 1(1) of the *Grundgesetz*, it again refers to ECtHR judgments to show that the Convention protection includes the press's right to publish photographs,[236] its restriction again requiring a balancing.[237] Pointing to ECtHR judgments, it goes on to say that '[i]n balancing the conflicting legal values, taking into account the presumption, emanating from Article 5(1) of the *Grundgesetz* (…), that reporting by the press aiming at a contribution to the formation of a public opinion is allowed, the freedom of expression guaranteed by Article 10(1) ECHR is to be accorded special weight where reporting by the press contributes to matters of general interest (…).'[238] The *Gurgenidze* judgment serves as a point of reference for the *Bundesverfassungsgericht* when it points out that the scope of the protection afforded by secs. 22 et seq. KUG, reinforced by Article 2(1) in combination with Article 1(1) of the *Grundgesetz*, is influenced by whether a piece of information is given general publicity through the mass media, thus no longer being known only to a limited group of persons.[239] One can even detect an attempt by the Constitutional Justices to reconcile their inclusion of entertainment in the scope of freedom of the press under Article 5(1), second sentence, of the *Grundgesetz* with the ECtHR's case-law, when they argue that, if an article (or broadcast) were denied relevance for the formation of opinions for the sole reason that it was presented in an entertaining way, not only the basic right under the German constitution, but also the substance of Article 10 ECHR could be violated.[240]

---

[233]*Bundesverfassungsgericht* (n. 185), 200 – *Caroline von Monaco III*.

[234]ECtHR, *Minelli v. Switzerland*, no. 14991/02, decision of 14 June 2005; *Gurgenidze v. Georgia*, no. 71678/01, judgment of 17 October 2006, §§ 38 et seq.

[235]*Bundesverfassungsgericht* (n. 185), 200 – *Caroline von Monaco III*.

[236]*Bundesverfassungsgericht* (n. 185), 202 – *Caroline von Monaco III* quotes ECtHR, *Verlagsgruppe News GmbH (No. 2)*, no. 10520/02, judgment of 14. December 2006, § 29; *Von Hannover* (n. 1), § 59; *Gurgenidze* (n. 234), § 55.

[237]*Bundesverfassungsgericht* (n. 185), 202 – *Caroline von Monaco III* quotes ECtHR, *Gurgenidze* (n. 234), § 37.

[238]*Bundesverfassungsgericht* (n. 185), 203 – *Caroline von Monaco III* quoting ECtHR, *Karhuvaara und Iltalehti* (n. 191), § 40; *Tønsbergs Blad and Others v. Norway*, no. 510/04, judgment of 1 March 2007, § 82.

[239]*Bundesverfassungsgericht* (n. 185), 203 – *Caroline von Monaco III* referring to ECtHR, *Gurgenidze* (n. 234), § 55. The *Bundesverfassungsgericht* later (*ibid.*, 218) also refers to § 59 of the *Gurgenidze* judgment.

[240]*Bundesverfassungsgericht* (n. 185), 204 – *Caroline von Monaco III* points to ECtHR,

The *Bundesverfassungsgericht* stresses that under both constitutional law and the Convention, the national courts enjoy a margin of appreciation in assessing the informational value of media reports and their illustrations.[241] It is furthermore aware of the ECtHR's inclination to let the guarantee under Article 10 ECHR prevail if media publications show a connection to a substantive debate of general interest.[242] It also fine-tunes its own evaluation to the ECtHR's classification of Princess Caroline as not being a politician, but nevertheless a public figure.[243] It points out that the ECtHR has acknowledged that Article 10 ECHR protects a contribution to a general debate especially when it enables public control of the private behaviour of influential people engaged in economic, cultural or media activities,[244] and that the ECtHR has criticised national courts for applying too restrictive a standard in assessing whether there is a public interest when the media report on aspects of the private life of a person outside the official or political sphere.[245] According to the ECtHR's case-law it suffices if the media, at least to a certain extent, covers questions of political or other relevance.[246] The *Bundesverfassungsgericht* also emphasises that in the *Von Hannover* case the ECtHR did not principally exclude the possibility of an article or broadcast on matters of general concern illustrated with images showing a public figure's everyday life; it only denied there to be a sufficient informational value in Princess Caroline's case.[247]

All of this proves the *Bundesverfassungsgericht*'s efforts to harmonise the standards of the constitution and the Convention. The *Bundesverfassungsgericht* is taking the ECHR's and the ECtHR's influence on German constitutional law seriously and trying to reconcile its case-law with that of the Strasbourg Court. The *Grundgesetz* is flexible enough to allow such an adaptation.

Wirtschafts-Trend-Zeitschriften-Verlagsgesellschaft mbH v. Austria, no. 66298/01 et al., judgment of 13 December 2005, §§ 49–50.

[241] *Bundesverfassungsgericht* (n. 185), 208 – *Caroline von Monaco III* with reference to ECtHR (GC), *Dickson v. The United Kingdom*, no. 44362/04, judgment of 4 December 2007, §§ 77 et seq.

[242] *Bundesverfassungsgericht* (n. 185), 208 – *Caroline von Monaco III* refers to ECtHR (GC), *Lindon and Others v. France*, no. 21279/02, judgment of 22 October 2007, § 45; (GC) *Pedersen and Baadsgaard v. Denmark*, no. 49017/99, judgment of 17 December 2004, §§ 68–69.

[243] *Bundesverfassungsgericht* (n. 185), 219 – *Caroline von Monaco III* points to ECtHR, *Gurgenidze* (n. 234), § 57; *Sciacca v. Italy*, no. 50774/99, judgment of 11 January 2005, §§ 27 et seq.

[244] *Bundesverfassungsgericht* (n. 185), 219 – *Caroline von Monaco III* relying on *Tønsbergs Blad and Others* (n. 238), §§ 87–88; *Verlagsgruppe News GmbH (No. 2)* (n. 236), §§ 35 et seq.; *Minelli* (n. 234).

[245] *Bundesverfassungsgericht* (n. 185), 219–220 – *Caroline von Monaco III* with reference to ECtHR, *Tønsbergs Blad and Others* (n. 238), § 87.

[246] *Bundesverfassungsgericht* (n. 185), 220 – *Caroline von Monaco III* with reference to ECtHR, *Karhuvaara und Iltalehti v. Finland* (n. 191), § 45.

[247] *Bundesverfassungsgericht* (n. 185), 220 – *Caroline von Monaco III* with reference to ECtHR, *Von Hannover* (n. 1), § 64.

2.5.3 The Bundesgerichtshof's *adherence to the new scheme of variable protection*

The *Bundesgerichtshof* has upheld the balancing test required under secs. 22, 23 KUG,[248] especially because the new variable scheme of protection under secs. 22, 23 KUG was, as has just been shown, considered constitutional by the *Bundesverfassungsgericht*. Recently the *Bundesgerichtshof* applied this scheme to photographs and film clips shown in a television broadcast reporting on one of the grandchildren of the late Prince Rainier of Monaco.[249] Interestingly, the Court left undecided whether the same test would have to be applied to the assessment of whether the broadcasting of a (spoken) text report could be prohibited in application of secs. 1004(1), 823(1) BGB in combination with Articles 2(1) and 1(1) of the *Grundgesetz*. The Court rather contented itself with finding that the report (of which, as it was held, single parts could not be assessed separately, but which had to be considered as a whole) was covered by the freedom of broadcasting under Article 5 of the *Grundgesetz*. It concerned the plaintiff's behaviour in the social, if not even in the public, sphere, and was furthermore quite favourable to him. Therefore, the plaintiff's personality right was affected only slightly. Consequently, the television report was allowed to be rebroadcast.[250]

2.6 The impact of the ECtHR's expansive reading of 'private life' (Article 8 ECHR) on the British courts: *The Campbell v. MGN Ltd* case

On 6 May 2004, less than two months before the ECtHR decided the *Von Hannover* case, the House of Lords delivered their judgment in *Campbell v. MGN Ltd*.[251] This is said to be the most frequently cited judgment in the field of the protection of privacy in tort law.[252] It has been followed as a precedent:[253]

---

[248]See, for instance, Bundesgerichtshof, judgment of 3 July 2007 –VI ZR 164/06–, 2008 Neue Juristische Wochenschrift 749.
[249]*Bundesgerichtshof*, judgment of 10 March 2009 –VI ZR 261/07–, 2009 Neue Juristische Wochenschrift 1499 (1500–1501).
[250]*Bundesgerichtshof* (n. 249), 1501–1502.
[251][2004] UKHL 22.
[252]*Harpwood* (2009), 407.
[253]The following judgments expressly refer to the House of Lords' *Campbell* judgment: *CC v. AB*, [2006] EWHC 3083 (QB), 2006 WL 3485386; *Associated Newspapers Limited v. His Royal Highness the Prince of Wales*, [2006] EWCA Civ 1776; *McKennitt v. Ash*, [2005] EWHC 3003 (QB). Other judgments apply the same test: *Bluck v. The Information Commissioner*, –2007– WL 4266111; *Kay and Others and Another (FC) v. London Borough of Lambeth and Others*, [2006] UKHL 10; *Long Beach Limited and Denis Christel Sassou Nguesso v. Global Witness Limited*, [2007] EWHC 1980 (QB); *David Murray v. Express Newspapers plc, Big Pictures (UK) Limited*, [2007] EWHC 1908 (Ch). Some judgments predate the House of Lords' judgment, but nevertheless follow a similar line of argument: *A v. B & C*, [2002] EWCA Civ 337; *Attorney General v. Guardian Newspapers No 2*, [1990] 1 A.C. 109; *Jean F Jones v. University*

Although in English law certain aspects of privacy are protected in the context of different torts, such as private nuisance, trespass to land, libel, defamation, or malicious falsehood,[254] there is no generalised tort of infringement of privacy.[255] The House of Lords refused to acknowledge its existence not only in *Wainwright v. Home Office*, but also in *Campbell v. MGN Ltd.*[256] Nevertheless, the *Campbell* judgment shows that considerable protection against the misuse of information, including the unjustified publication of images, is provided by the law of 'breach of confidence'.

2.6.1 The facts of the case

The main facts of the case, as concisely summarised by Baroness Hale of Richmond, are the following: The *Daily Mirror* (the *Mirror*) published a front page article titled: 'Naomi: I am a drug addict', which was not based on any public confession she had made. Having discovered that she was attending meetings of Narcotics Anonymous (NA) and knowing enough about those meetings, the newspaper constructed an article based on what they thought was going on. The front page article had a small picture of Ms Campbell emerging from the first meeting. The fuller article, spread across two pages, showed a larger picture of her and others outside a building with a prominent cafe signboard in the foreground. The others' faces were pixillated. The article gave a full account of her history of difficult behaviour but was sympathetic to the seriousness of her attempts to undergo therapy and overcome her addiction. Ever since the hearing before the trial judge, the parties had accepted[257] that the *Mirror* was entitled to publish the fact that Ms Campbell was a drug addict and was having therapy since she had publicly denied any involvement with illegal drugs. Claiming that the paper, in contrast, was entitled neither to disclose the fact and details of her attending

---

of *Warwick*, [2003] EWCA Civ 151; *In re S (FC) (a child)*, [2004] UKHL 47; *Wainwright v. Home Office*, [2003] UKHL 53.

[254]*Lord Hoffmann*'s speech in Wainwright v. Home Office, [2003] UKHL 53, § 18. See also: *Murphy* (2007), 385; *Harpwood* (n. 252), 407; and especially, *Neil*, (1999). See also *Gordon Kaye (by Peter Froggatt his next friend) v. Andrew Robertson and Sport Newspapers Ltd*, Court of Appeal, 23 February 1990, [1991] FSR 62 (also reproduced in *Markesinis/ Unberath* [n. 10], 493–499). This case is said to have had a decisive impact on the drafting of the Calcutt Report of 1990 ('Report of the Committee on Privacy and Related Matters', Cm. 1102), see: *Markesinis/ Unberath* (n. 10), 500 (reproducing the Report's Summary of Recommendations, ibid., 500–502); see also *Wright* (2001), 163–4.

[255]*Lord Hoffmann* in Wainwright v. Home Office, [2003] UKHL 53, § 18. See also: *Harpwood* (n. 252), 407; *Murphy* (n. 254), 385.

[256][2004] UKHL 22 (see not only the speeches of the dissenters Lord Nicholls of Birkenhead, § 11, and Lord Hoffmann, § 43; but also the speech of Baroness Hale of Richmond, § 133: 'But the courts will not invent a new cause of action to cover types of activity which were not previously covered: ...').

[257]See Lord Nicholls, [2004] UKHL 22, § 24.

meetings of NA nor to illustrate the story with covert photography of her in the company of other participants in the meeting, Ms Campbell brought proceedings for damages for breach of confidence and infringement of privacy. At trial only the former was pursued (along with a claim under the Data Protection Act 1998 which, it was agreed, added nothing to the claim for breach of confidence). While the trial judge granted the claim, the Court of Appeal reversed its decision.[258]

2.6.2 Breach of confidence as a tort

By a 3:2 majority, the House of Lords allowed Ms Campbell's appeal and restored the trial judge's order.

The House of Lords' decision is attributed special importance because it acknowledges breach of confidence as a tort under common law.[259] Although not all of the members of the House address this problem, the two dissenters do, of whom Lord Hoffmann points out that the difference of opinion within the House 'relates to a very narrow point which arises on the unusual facts of this case.'[260] Lord Nicholls refers to the history of breach of confidence as a cause of action, which was granted by courts of equity in order to afford protection to the wrongful use of private information. Originally the cause of action was based on improper use of information disclosed by one person to another in confidence, the information having to be of a confidential nature. But the gist of the cause of action, Lord Nicholls demonstrates, 'was that information of this character had been disclosed by one person to another in circumstances "importing an obligation of confidence" even though no contract of non-disclosure existed'.[261]

While the confidence referred to in the phrase 'breach of confidence' originally was the confidence arising out of a confidential relationship, his Lordship describes this cause of action now to have 'firmly shaken off the limiting constraint of the need for an initial confidential relationship' and to have 'changed its nature'.[262] In apparent congruence with the House, he points to the recognition of this development by the judgment of Lord Goff of Chieveley in *Attorney General v Guardian Newspapers Ltd (No 2)*[263] and regards '[t]he essence of the tort' better to be 'encapsulated now as misuse of private information'.[264] Thus Lord Nicholls expressly speaks of a 'tort', and

---

[258][2004] UKHL 22, §§ 127–131. A more detailed statement of the facts is given by Lord Nicholls, ibid., §§ 2–10.
[259]Cf. *Murphy* (n. 254), 385–386.
[260][2004] UKHL 22, § 36.
[261][2004] UKHL 22, § 13, quoting Megarry J in *Coco v AN Clark (Engineers) Ltd* [1969] RPC 41 at 47–48.
[262][2004] UKHL 22, § 14.
[263][1988] 3 All ER 545 at 658–659, [1990] 1 AC 109 at 281.
[264][2004] UKHL 22, § 14.

no longer of a cause of action under equity. 'This tort affords respect for one aspect of an individual's privacy.'[265] Presumably in the same vein, Lord Hoffmann says breach of confidence 'was' an equitable remedy,[266] underlines 'the capacity of the common law to adapt itself to the needs of contemporary life',[267] and considers the relationship between the freedom of the press and 'the common law right of the individual to protect personal information.'[268]

Lord Hope of Craighead also refers to Lord Goff, who had set out 'three limiting principles to the broad general principle that a duty of confidence arises when confidential information comes to the knowledge of a person where he has notice that the information is confidential.'[269] These limiting principles are the following:[270] (1) '[T]he principle of confidentiality only applies to information to the extent that it is confidential. In particular, once it has entered what is usually called the public domain (…) then, as a general rule, the principle of confidentiality can have no application to it.' (2) '[T]he duty of confidence applies neither to useless information, nor to trivia.' (3) '[A]lthough the basis of the law's protection of confidence is that there is a public interest that confidences should be preserved and protected by the law, nevertheless that public interest may be outweighed by some other countervailing public interest which favours disclosure. This limitation may apply, as the learned judge pointed out, to all types of confidential information. It is this limiting principle which may require a court to carry out a balancing operation, weighing the public interest in maintaining confidence against a countervailing public interest favouring disclosure.'[271]

2.6.3 The turning point of the case

This test was applied by the House to the *Campbell* case, being divided – as it is said[272] – only on the application of the third principle.

Counsel for Ms Campbell had, as Lord Nicholls points out, 'placed the information published by the newspaper into five categories: (1) the fact of Miss Campbell's drug addiction; (2) the fact that she was receiving treatment; (3) the fact that she was receiving treatment at NA; (4) the details of the treatment – how long she had been attending meetings, how often she went, how

---

[265][2004] UKHL 22, § 15. As to the development of the remedy see *Fenwick/Phillipson* (2006), 721–70 (see also 771–809).

[266][2004] UKHL 22, § 44.

[267][2004] UKHL 22, § 46.

[268][2004] UKHL 22, § 55.

[269][2004] UKHL 22, § 85. See also Lord Hoffmann, § 47.

[270]See Lord Walker of Gestingthorpe, *OBG Limited and others (Appellants) v. Allan and others (Respondents), Douglas and another and others (Appellants) v. Hello! Limited and others (Respondents), Mainstream Properties Limited (Appellants) v. Young and others and another (Respondents)*, [2007] UKHL 21, § 272.

[271][1988] 3 All ER 545 at 658–659, [1990] 1 AC 109 at 281.

[272]Lord Walker of Gestingthorpe (n. 270), [2007] UKHL 21, § 272.

she was treated within the sessions themselves, the extent of her commitment, and the nature of her entrance on the specific occasion; and (5) the visual portrayal of her leaving a specific meeting with other addicts.'[273]

2.6.4 The dissenters' position

Information within the first two categories was unanimously considered publishable. As to the third through fifth categories, Lord Nicholls was sceptical of whether the information deserved protection under breach of confidence.[274] Yet, he essentially solves 'the tension between privacy and freedom of expression' in the case in favour of the press.[275] In his opinion, the claim failed even with regard to the images. The photographs, the taking of which Ms Campbell had not complained, conveyed no private information beyond that discussed in the article; there was nothing undignified or distraught about her appearance.[276]

Lord Hoffmann sees freedom of the press in conflict with the common law right of the individual to protect personal information and raises the question of 'the extent to which it is necessary to qualify the one right in order to protect the underlying value which is protected by the other.'[277] Applying a test of proportionality, he also concludes that the appeal ought to be dismissed. In his words the issue at the heart of the case is:

> Where the main substance of the story is conceded to have been justified, should the newspaper be held liable whenever the judge considers that it was not necessary to have published some of the personal information? Or should the newspaper be allowed some margin of choice in the way it chooses to present the story?[278]

In Lord Hoffmann's eyes, the press ought to be allowed a substantial degree of latitude,[279] for which it was relevant that for many years Ms Campbell and the media had 'both fed upon each other'.[280] He is careful to point out that '[t]his does not deprive Ms Campbell of the right to privacy in respect of areas of her life which she has not chosen to make public.' In essence, his Lordship sees the information contained in categories (3) and (4) to make no substantial addition to the bare revelation that she was a drug addict seeking therapy.

---

[273][2004] UKHL 22, § 23.
[274][2004] UKHL 22, §§ 25–27.
[275][2004] UKHL 22, §§ 28.
[276][2004] UKHL 22, §§ 29–32.
[277][2004] UKHL 22, § 55.
[278][2004] UKHL 22, § 61.
[279][2004] UKHL 22, §§ 62–70.
[280][2004] UKHL 22, § 66.

In the light of the *Von Hannover* case, Lord Hoffmann's opinion of the photographs is noteworthy. Not only is a photograph to him 'in principle information no different from any other information' with the consequence that the same principles apply.[281] His phrasing of an unjustified invasion of the privacy of personal information takes into account both the possibility of privacy in public places and the method of photography:

> In my opinion, therefore, the widespread publication of a photograph of someone which reveals him to be in a situation of humiliation or severe embarrassment, even if taken in a public place, may be an infringement of the privacy of his personal information. Likewise, the publication of a photograph taken by intrusion into a private place (for example, by a long distance lens) may in itself be such an infringement, even if there is nothing embarrassing about the picture itself.[282]

His evaluation of the case led him to deny there to be any unjustified invasion of privacy.

2.6.5 The majority's point(s) of view

Lord Hope of Craighead classified the information about Ms Campbell's receiving therapy as private and, in contrast to the Court of Appeal, found the trial judge's analogy with information about details of a medical condition or its treatment convincing.[283] In his eyes,[284] it normally would not be necessary to go on and ask whether it would be highly offensive for it to be published.[285] Notwithstanding, his Lordship did elaborate on his position that insofar the decisive question was 'what a reasonable person of ordinary sensibilities would feel if she was placed in the same position as the claimant and faced with the same publicity.'[286] He found that the Court of Appeal had failed to carry out the required balancing exercise.[287] The outcome of this balancing –

---

[281] [2004] UKHL 22, § 72.

[282] [2004] UKHL 22, § 75, with reference to *Hellewell v Chief Constable of Derbyshire*, [1995] 4 All ER 473 at 476, [1995] 1 WLR 804 at 807; and Lord Mustill in *R v Broadcasting Standards Commission, ex p BBC*, [2000] 3 All ER 989 at 1002, [2001] QB 885 at 900 (para 48): 'An infringement of privacy is an affront to the personality, which is damaged both by the violation and by the demonstration that the personal space is not inviolate.'

[283] [2004] UKHL 22, §§ 91–95.

[284] [2004] UKHL 22, § 96.

[285] A test the trial judge used following Gleeson CJ in *Australian Broadcasting Corp v Lenah Game Meats Pty Ltd* (2001) 185 ALR 1, and which Lord Hope identified as taken from the law of the USA (Restatement of the Law of Torts (Second) (1977) p 383, art 652D), with Gleeson CJ quoting *William L Prosser*, Privacy (1960) 48 Calif LR 383 (396–397).

[286] [2004] UKHL 22, § 99; see §§ 96–101, with reference to Nicholson J in *P v D*, [2000] 2 NZLR 591 (601, § 39) and Restatement of the Law of Torts (Second) (n. 285), p 387, comment c1 (a) of art 652D.

[287] [2004] UKHL 22, § 104.

as he saw it – was that there was an unjustifiable infringement of Ms Campbell's right to privacy.[288] Decisions about the publication of material that is private to the individual, Lord Hope says, raises issues that are not simply about presentation and editing:

> Any interference with the public interest in disclosure has to be balanced against the interference with the right of the individual to respect for their private life. The decisions that are then taken are open to review by the court. The tests which the court must apply are the familiar ones. They are whether publication of the material pursues a legitimate aim and whether the benefits that will be achieved by its publication are proportionate to the harm that may be done by the interference with the right to privacy.[289]

Although Lord Hope, too, points to the importance of journalistic freedom and accords the respondent publisher 'a reasonable margin of appreciation in taking decisions as to what details needed to be included in the article to give it credibility,'[290] he found Ms Campbell's right to respect for her private life to prevail.[291] Interestingly, this conclusion rests essentially on the publication of the photographs, without which he would have been inclined to regard the balance between the competing rights to have been 'about even.'[292] Again, in light of the *Von Hannover* case, it is remarkable that Lord Hope acknowledges that the right to respect for private life can be infringed upon by publishing pictures taken in a public street. When he states that a 'person who just happens to be in the street when the photograph was taken and appears in it only incidentally cannot as a general rule object to the publication of the photograph,' this even reminds us of the '*relative Person der Zeitgeschichte*' under sec. 23 KUG.[293] The situation, however, is judged to be different 'if the public nature of the place where a photograph is taken was simply used as background for one or more persons who constitute the true subject of the photograph.'[294] Attaching some weight to the fact that Ms Campbell had been photographed surreptitiously and that the photograph was not self-explanatory, Lord Hope concludes that any person in Ms Campbell's position would have seen the publication of the images in conjunction with the article as a gross interference with her right to respect for her private life. This, according to Lord Hope, outweighed the defendants' right to freedom of expression.[295]

---

[288][2004] UKHL 22, § 125.
[289][2004] UKHL 22, § 113.
[290][2004] UKHL 22, § 112, see also § 120.
[291][2004] UKHL 22, § 124.
[292][2004] UKHL 22, § 121.
[293]See *supra*, at n. 12.
[294][2004] UKHL 22, § 122.
[295][2004] UKHL 22, § 123–124.

Starting from the position that 'the "reasonable expectation of privacy" is a threshold test which brings the balancing exercise into play,'[296] Baroness Hale concentrates on weighing freedom of expression against the right to respect for one's private life. In Lord Hoffmann's speech we find the sentence: 'We value the freedom of the press but the press is a commercial enterprise and can flourish only by selling newspapers.'[297] What might appear to be in a dialectic struggle is taken to the higher plane of synthesis by Baroness Hale when she connects the press's economic interest with freedom of the press:

> One reason why press freedom is so important is that we need newspapers to sell in order to ensure that we still have newspapers at all. It may be said that newspapers should be allowed considerable latitude in their intrusions into private grief so that they can maintain circulation and the rest of us can then continue to enjoy the variety of newspapers and other mass media which are available in this country. It may also be said that newspaper editors often have to make their decisions at great speed and in difficult circumstances, so that to expect too minute an analysis of the position is in itself a restriction on their freedom of expression.[298]

But her Ladyship sees a strong counter-interest in respect for private life, emphasising that '[i]t has always been accepted that information about a person's health and treatment for ill-health is both private and confidential.'[299] Thus 'all of the information about Miss Campbell's addiction and attendance at NA which was revealed in the Mirror article was both private and confidential, because it related to an important aspect of Miss Campbell's physical and mental health and the treatment she was receiving for it.'[300] The article contained information, the value of which Baroness Hale quite obviously does not see as equal to that of political, intellectual, or artistic speech and expression. In her eyes, any educational value is diminished by the lack of consent and thus of co-operation of the person concerned.[301] It is the risk of harm done by the disclosure of the information, especially by the destruction of the NA as a safe haven to a drug addict at the 'fragile' stage of doing therapy, which led Baroness Hale to conclude that there was no justification for disclosing the fact that Ms Campbell was attending NA meetings, the fact

---

[296][2004] UKHL 22, § 137. Baroness Hale, *ibid.*, reveals that Gleeson CJ in *Australian Broadcasting Corp v Lenah Game Meats Pty Ltd (*2001) 185 ALR 1 at 13 (§ 42) had not intended to provide an exclusive test by stating that 'disclosure or observation of information or conduct would be highly offensive to a reasonable person of ordinary sensibilities.'

[297][2004] UKHL 22, § 77 (see also § 66).

[298][2004] UKHL 22, § 143.

[299][2004] UKHL 22, § 145, pointing to ECtHR, *Z. v. Finland*, no. 22009/93, judgment of 25 January 1996, ECHR 1997-I, § 95.

[300][2004] UKHL 22, § 147.

[301][2004] UKHL 22, §§ 148–150.

that she had been doing so for some time, and with some regularity, and the photographs of her either arriving at or leaving the premises where meetings took place.[302] Baroness Hale's position as to the images, however, is in contrast with the ECtHR's *Von Hannover* judgment, which acknowledged private life to extend beyond the home into a social sphere where photographing someone without consent interfered with this person's right under Article 8 ECHR. Baroness Hale considers the photographs portraying Ms Campbell's leaving a specific meeting *by themselves* not to be objectionable:

> We have not so far held that the mere fact of covert photography is sufficient to make the information contained in the photograph confidential. The activity photographed must be private. If this had been, and had been presented as, a picture of Naomi Campbell going about her business in a public street, there could have been no complaint. She makes a substantial part of her living out of being photographed looking stunning in designer clothing. Readers will obviously be interested to see how she looks if and when she pops out to the shops for a bottle of milk. There is nothing essentially private about that information nor can it be expected to damage her private life. It may not be a high order of freedom of speech but there is nothing to justify interfering with it.[303]

2.6.6 The core problem of balancing privacy and freedom of the press

While Lord Carswell agrees with Lord Hope and Baroness Hale as to the outcome of the case, he is quite close to the dissenters when he underlines 'the importance of allowing a proper degree of journalistic margin to the press to deal with a legitimate story in its own way, without imposing unnecessary shackles on its freedom to publish detail and photographs which add colour and conviction.'[304] His speech makes it very clear that the conclusion to be reached by balancing 'is by no means self-evident.'[305] Rather, it 'depends on the weight which one attributes to several factors.' 'Weighing and balancing these factors is a process which may well lead different people to different conclusions.'[306]

That there is a subjective element to the weighing and balancing can be seen in all of the speeches. But what again is common to them is that all of their Lordships were clearly inspired and influenced by the ECHR and the

---

[302][2004] UKHL 22, §§ 151–159 (especially §§ 153, 157).
[303][2004] UKHL 22, § 154, referring to Randerson J in *Hosking v Runting* [2003] 3 NZLR 385 and an unreported decision of the [New Zealand] Court of Appeal of 25 March 2004.
[304][2004] UKHL 22, § 169.
[305][2004] UKHL 22, § 169.
[306][2004] UKHL 22, § 168.

jurisprudence of the ECtHR. This especially shows in the House's apparent unanimity in the following points: (1) In the balancing exercise required under the tort of breach of confidence, Articles 8 and 10 ECHR must be taken into account. Yet, as neither the right to respect for private life nor freedom of expression is accorded prevalence over the other *a priori*,[307] their respective weight in the specific case must be assessed in order to decide whether the interests of privacy or of publication will dominate the outcome.[308] (2) The need for privacy protection can arise even when an individual is in a public place.[309] (3) Article 10 ECHR requires the press to have considerable journalistic and editorial freedom, especially when it fulfills its function as a 'public watchdog' within a democratic society.[310] A similar attentiveness towards the Strasbourg jurisprudence might well have enabled the German *Bundesverfassungsgericht* to prevent its *Caroline von Monaco II* judgment of 1999 from being successfully challenged before the ECtHR.

2.6.7 How do the Convention rights affect the balancing under the law of breach of confidence?

Lord Nicholls points out that the influence of the ECHR and the ECtHR's jurisprudence in the area of the common law had been significant for some years. The provisions of Articles 8 and 10 ECHR, and the interaction of these two articles, had 'prompted the courts of this country to identify more clearly the different factors involved in cases where one or other of these two interests is present.'[311]

The Human Rights Act 1998 has changed the legal situation in England. However, if we look at the way the speeches deal with the 1998 Act, it is hard to detect a common understanding.

---

[307]See [2004] UKHL 22, §§ 55 (Lord Hoffmann); § 111 (Lord Hope); § 138 (Baroness Hale).

[308]See especially [2004] UKHL 22, §§ 18–20, 29 (Lord Nicholls); §§ 49–55, 59 (Lord Hoffmann); §§ 86, 103–111, 113, 117 (Lord Hope relying on ECtHR, *Dudgeon v. the United Kingdom (No. 2)*, no. 7525/76, judgment of 22 October 1981, § 52, Series A no. 45; *Tammer v. Estonia* (n. 139), § 59; *Goodwin v. the United Kingdom*, no. 17488/90, judgment of 27 March 1996, § 40, ECHR 1996–II); §§ 133–132, 137–141 (Baroness Hale); §§ 167–170 (Lord Carswell).

[309]See especially [2004] UKHL 22, §§ 18–20, 29 (Lord Nicholls); §§ 49–55, 59 (Lord Hoffmann); §§ 86, 103–111, 113, 117 (Lord Hope relying on ECtHR, *Dudgeon v. the United Kingdom (No. 2)*, no. 7525/76, judgment of 22 October 1981, § 52, Series A no. 45; *Tammer v. Estonia* (n. 139), § 59; *Goodwin v. the United Kingdom*, no. 17488/90, judgment of 27 March 1996, § 40, ECHR 1996–II); §§ 133–132, 137–141 (Baroness Hale); §§ 167–170 (Lord Carswell).

[310]*Id v. Denmark* (n. 163); *Observer and Guardian* (n. 138), § 59; *Fressoz and Roire*, loc. cit., §§ 54, 65; *Bladet Tromsø and Stensaas* [GC] [n. 138]) ; § 169 (Lord Carswell).

[311][2004] UKHL 22, § 16. Cf. *Wright* (2001), 24–7, 33; *Markesinis/Fedtke* (2009), 266–72.

Lord Nicholls leaves it undecided 'whether the duty imposed on courts by s[ec.] 6 of the 1998 Act extends to questions of substantive law as distinct from questions of practice and procedure.'[312]

Lord Hoffmann points out the following:

> Until the 1998 Act came into force, there was no equivalent in English domestic law of Article 8 of the convention or the equivalent articles in other international human rights instruments which guarantee rights of privacy. So the courts of the United Kingdom did not have to decide what such guarantees meant. Even now that the equivalent of Article 8 has been enacted as part of English law, it is not directly concerned with the protection of privacy against private persons or corporations. It is, by virtue of sec. 6 of the 1998 Act, a guarantee of privacy only against public authorities. Although the convention, as an international instrument, may impose upon the United Kingdom an obligation to take some steps (whether by statute or otherwise) to protect rights of privacy against invasion by private individuals, it does not follow that such an obligation would have any counterpart in domestic law.[313]

Presumably, Lord Hoffmann interprets sec. 6 of the 1998 Act, though applicable to courts and tribunals, not to place them under the duty of making new law – for instance by acknowledging a new tort of invasion into privacy. He does, however, seem to accept that the Convention influences the jurisprudence of the English courts, unfortunately without clarifying whether this is legally effected by sec. 6, when he says: 'What human rights law has done is to identify private information as something worth protecting as an aspect of human autonomy and dignity.'[314]

He discerns 'a shift in the centre of gravity of the action for breach of confidence when it is used as a remedy for the unjustified publication of personal information,' tracing 'the incremental changes' back to the new approach's focusing 'upon the protection of human autonomy and dignity – the right to control the dissemination of information about one's private life and the right to the esteem and respect of other people.'[315] The German constitutional lawyer might detect in these words a description of a *radiating effect* of the Convention on English law – parallel to the '*Ausstrahlungswirkung*' the *Bundesverfassungsgericht* assigns to basic rights in relation to private law – as his Lordship continues:

---

[312][2004] UKHL 22, § 18.
[313][2004] UKHL 22, § 49.
[314][2004] UKHL 22, § 50.
[315][2004] UKHL 22, § 51.

These changes have implications for the future development of the law. They *must* influence the approach of the courts to the kind of information which is regarded as entitled to protection, the extent and form of publication which attracts a remedy and the circumstances in which publication can be justified.[316]

The duty to acknowledge this radiating effect can easily be understood to have been created by sec. 6 of the Human Rights Act 1998.

Lord Hope draws attention to the fact that '[t]he language has changed following the coming into operation of the 1998 Act and the incorporation into domestic law of arts 8 and 10 of the convention:'[317]

> We now talk about the right to respect for private life and the countervailing right to freedom of expression. The jurisprudence of the European Court of Human Rights offers important guidance as to how these competing rights ought to be approached and analysed.

Lord Hope, however, doubts whether the result of the 1998 Act is that the centre of gravity, as Lord Hoffmann said, has shifted. Instead, it seems to him that the balancing exercise to which the ECtHR's guidance is directed is essentially the same exercise as before, 'although it is plainly now more carefully focused and more penetrating.'[318] He quotes Lord Woolf CJ as saying[319] that new breadth and strength is given to the action for breach of confidence by these articles.[320]

Lord Hope's position seems clear in that the Human Rights Act 1998 makes it 'the court's duty as a public authority' under sec. 6(1), which sec. 12(4) reinforces, 'not to act in a way which is incompatible with' Article 10 ECHR.[321] Thus, he considers the House bound by the Convention through the 1998 Act when it decides on a case of alleged breach of confidence, but also respects the special mention of the freedom of expression required by sec. 12(4) of the Act. Lord Hope, however, expressly also looks at the case from Ms Campbell's point of view applying Article 8 ECHR.[322]

Baroness Hale's speech starts out by summarising 'some big questions' the Campbell case raises and which directly concern the influence of the ECHR on English law – among others:

---

[316][2004] UKHL 22, § 52 (emphasis added).
[317][2004] UKHL 22, § 86.
[318][2004] UKHL 22, § 86. See also ibid., § 106, where Lord Hope points out that the balancing exercise was already part of English law.
[319]*A v B* [2002] 2 All ER 545 at [4].
[320][2004] UKHL 22, § 86.
[321][2004] UKHL 22, § 114.
[322][2004] UKHL 22, §§ 119–124.

How is the balance to be struck between everyone's right to respect for their private and family life under art 8 of the European Convention for the Protection of Human Rights and Fundamental Freedoms 1950 (as set out in Schedule 1 to the Human Rights Act 1998) and everyone's right to freedom of expression, including the freedom to receive and impart information and ideas under art 10? How do those rights come into play in a dispute between two private persons?[323]

Her basic answer points to 'the basic principles which have emerged from the Court of Appeal in the wake of the 1998 Act':

The 1998 Act does not create any new cause of action between private persons. But if there is a relevant cause of action applicable, the court as a public authority must act compatibly with both parties' convention rights.[324]

With a view to the action for breach of confidence she quotes Lord Woolf CJ in *A v B* (a company) as saying:[325]

[Articles 8 and 10] have provided new parameters within which the court will decide, in an action for breach of confidence, whether a person is entitled to have his privacy protected by the court or whether the restriction of freedom of expression which such protection involves cannot be justified. The court's approach to the issues which the applications raise has been modified because under sec. 6 of the 1998 Act, the court, as a public authority, is required not to act 'in a way which is incompatible with a Convention right'. The court is able to achieve this by absorbing the rights which Articles 8 and 10 protect into the long-established action for breach of confidence. This involves giving a new strength and breadth to the action so that it accommodates the requirements of those articles.

Thus Baroness Hale obviously endorses Lord Woolf's position that it is sec. 6 of the Human Rights Act 1998 which places the courts, as public authorities within the scope of that provision, under the duty to apply English law in conformity with the Convention rights.

So far, the situation appears quite similar to that of German law. We have seen that the Convention ranks equal to a Federal statute within the German legal order, but that, nevertheless, German sub-constitutional law, whether Federal or *Land* law and even if enacted at a later date, must be interpreted in conformity with the Convention. What is more, the principles of the

[323][2004] UKHL 22, § 126.
[324][2004] UKHL 22, § 132.
[325][2002] EWCA Civ 337 at [4], [2002] 2 All ER 545 at [4], [2003] QB 195.

constitution and the basic rights as set out in the *Grundgesetz* need to be interpreted in harmony with the Convention.[326] Quite apparently, the British courts have taken great care to 'absorb' what the ECHR guarantees require – even before the 1998 Act.

2.6.8 The structure of the Convention's impact on English law

The task of conforming to the requirements of the Convention, however, is not an easy one since the ECtHR, as has been shown, takes a dynamic approach to the interpretation and application of its guarantees. As the *Von Hannover* judgment, which is a milestone in the ECtHR's jurisprudence with a view to the effects of Convention rights on decisions in controversies between private parties, was delivered at a later date, it is unfortunate, but only natural, that the *Campbell v. MGN Ltd* judgment does not take it into account. Even taken one by one, however, the speeches of the House of Lords do not convey a clear picture of how exactly the Convention rights influence the tort of breach of confidence.

Lord Nicholls regards it as 'sufficient to recognise that the values underlying Articles 8 and 10 are not confined to disputes between individuals and public authorities,' this approach having been adopted by the courts in several recent decisions where individuals have complained of press intrusion.[327] Thus, he does not think of his evaluation of the case as an operation including the *application* of Articles 8 and 10 ECHR as such; it is only the underlying values which are relevant. When both Articles are engaged he sees 'a difficult question of proportionality arise,'[328] on the exact answer to which his speech does not expound as its argument is essentially based on denying Ms Campbell's privacy interests to have any serious weight.[329]

In Lord Hoffmann's eyes, when human rights law has brought to the surface that human autonomy and dignity identify private information as something worth protecting,[330] this 'has raised inescapably the question of why it should be worth protecting against the state but not against a private person.'[331] This might sound very much like his acceptance of *unmittelbare Drittwirkung* of Convention rights, of their being directly applicable in relations between private parties. Lord Hoffmann is aware of the resulting difficulties:

> There may of course be justifications for the publication of private information by private persons which would not be available to the state – I

---

[326]See Chapter 1, at ns. 124 et seq., see also at ns. 90 et seq.
[327][2004] UKHL 22, § 18.
[328][2004] UKHL 22, § 20.
[329][2004] UKHL 22, §§ 28–35.
[330]*Supra*, at n. 314.
[331][2004] UKHL 22, § 50.

have particularly in mind the position of the media, … – but I can see no logical ground for saying that a person should have less protection against a private individual than he would have against the state for the publication of personal information for which there is no justification. Nor, it appears, have any of the other judges who have considered the matter.[332]

With a view especially to the relationship between the right to freedom of the press and the common law right of the individual to protect personal information, Lord Hoffmann starts out by stating that both reflect important civilised values. However, as neither can be given effect in full measure without restricting the other, he raises the question of how they ought to be reconciled in a particular case.[333] His solution is a test of necessity and proportionality:

> There is in my view no question of automatic priority. Nor is there a presumption in favour of one rather than the other. The question is rather the extent to which it is necessary to qualify the one right in order to protect the underlying value which is protected by the other. And the extent of the qualification must be proportionate to the need.[334]

The test apparently needs to be applied from the perspective of each of the parties involved. Lord Hoffmann's speech can be understood as examining the intrusiveness of the *Mirror*'s article and photographs on Ms Campbell's privacy, on the one hand, and the intensity of a setback to be suffered by the press if the personal information were protected against publication, on the other.[335]

In Lord Hope's speech one finds[336] that he is willing to follow Sedley LJ in *Douglas v Hello! Ltd in* that Article 10 and Article 8 ECHR deserve equal respect[337] and that considerations of proportionality principally determine the outcome of a case involving the alleged unjustified publication of private information.[338] The proportionality test, then, is given more contour. After the press's editorial freedom has been touched upon,[339] Lord Hope makes it clear that 'decisions about the publication of material that is private to the individual raise issues that are not simply about presentation and editing':[340]

---

[332][2004] UKHL 22, § 50. Cf. as to the merely indirect horizontal effects of the ECHR in relations between private parties *Wright* (2001), 27–33.

[333][2004] UKHL 22, § 55.

[334][2004] UKHL 22, § 55, referring to see Sedley LJ in *Douglas v. Hello* [2001] 2 All ER 289 at 324, [2001] QB 967 at 1005 (§ 137).

[335]Cf. [2004] UKHL 22, §§ 56–77.

[336][2004] UKHL 22, § 111.

[337][2001] 2 All ER 289 at 322, [2001] QB 967 at 1003 (§ 133).

[338][2001] 2 All ER 289 at 324, [2001] QB 967 at 1005 (§ 137).

[339][2004] UKHL 22, § 112.

[340][2004] UKHL 22, § 113.

> Any interference with the public interest in disclosure has to be balanced against the interference with the right of the individual to respect for their private life. The decisions that are then taken are open to review by the court. The tests which the court must apply are the familiar ones. They are whether publication of the material pursues a legitimate aim and whether the benefits that will be achieved by its publication are proportionate to the harm that may be done by the interference with the right to privacy. The jurisprudence of the European Court of Human Rights explains how these principles are to be understood and applied in the context of the facts of each case. Any restriction of the right to freedom of expression must be subjected to very close scrutiny. But so too must any restriction of the right to respect for private life. [341]

This seems to point to a necessity of evaluating a specific case first from the perspective of the one Convention right concerned, then from the perspective of the other, competing, right, quite similar to that of Lord Hoffmann's. Yet when Lord Hope puts this test to work, something interesting shows: In deference to sec. 12(4) of the Human Rights Act 1998,[342] he starts out asking whether the objective of the restriction on the Article 10 right is sufficiently important to justify limiting the fundamental right to freedom of expression which the press assert on behalf of the public. Then he goes on to examine whether the means chosen to limit the art 10 right are rational, fair and not arbitrary and impair the right as minimally as is reasonably possible.[343] While this may look like a classical approach in the light of the ECHR, it is interesting to see that Lord Hope discerns as the objective of the restriction on freedom of expression 'the protection of Miss Campbell's right under art 8 to respect for her private life'. Again, the German constitutional lawyer would think that this objective is an emanation of *Schutzpflichten*, positive obligations, under Article 8 ECHR, but Lord Hope does not elaborate on any such duty to protect. Even when he changes his perspective to that of Ms Campbell, he discusses her protection (of which he never loses sight) in terms of *interference* with her private life by the press:

> As for the other side of the balance, a person's right to privacy may be *limited* by the public's interest in knowing about certain traits of her personality and certain aspects of her private life, as L'Heureux-Dubi and Bastarache JJ in the Supreme Court of Canada recognised in *Aubry v Editions Vice-Versa Inc* [1998] 1 SCR 591 at 616 (paras 57–58). But it is not enough to *deprive* Miss Campbell of her right to privacy that she is a celebrity and that her private life is newsworthy. A margin of

---

341 [2004] UKHL 22, § 113.
342 [2004] UKHL 22, § 114.
343 [2004] UKHL 22, § 115.

appreciation must, of course, be given to the journalist. Weight must be given to this. But to treat these details merely as background was to undervalue the importance that was to be attached to the need, if Miss Campbell *was to be protected*, to keep these details private. And it is hard to see that there was any *compelling need for the public to know* the name of the organisation that she was attending for the therapy, or for the other details of it to be set out. [344]

Baroness Hale's approach is quite similar to Lord Hope's. Her speech reflects on the difficulties which arise when there is a conflict between two Convention rights:

> The application of the proportionality test is more straightforward when only one convention right is in play: the question then is whether the private right claimed offers sufficient justification for the degree of interference with the fundamental right. It is much less straightforward when two convention rights are in play, and the proportionality of interfering with one has to be balanced against the proportionality of restricting the other. As each is a fundamental right, there is evidently a 'pressing social need' to protect it.[345]

Baroness Hale thus addresses the essential structural problems involved when state courts must with binding force decide a controversy between private parties. She seems to point to the necessity of interfering or restricting each of the two rights in conflict, which sounds close to Lord Hoffmann's analysis. On the other hand she speaks of the need to protect every fundamental right. At the time of the judgment, she saw the Convention jurisprudence offering little help with this problem of applying ECHR rights to private controversies, the ECtHR having been concerned with whether *the state's* interference with privacy[346] or a restriction on freedom of expression[347] could be justified in the particular case. In the national court, the problem of balancing two rights of equal importance arises most acutely in the context of disputes between private persons. Looking back, one can only gain the impression that the subjectivity of the balancing Lord Carswell emphasised not only affects the weight attached to the legal interests involved, but also the underlying scheme of how Convention rights influence the balancing as such. Is the House truly agreed on the basic principles of law, as Lord Hoffmann implies?[348]

---

[344][2004] UKHL 22, § 120 (emphasis added).
[345][2004] UKHL 22, § 140.
[346]Reference is made to ECtHR, *Z v Finland* (n. 299).
[347]Reference is made to ECtHR, *Jersild* (n. 163); Fressoz and Roire (n. 310); *Tammer* (n. 139).
[348]*Supra*, at n. 260.

When it was said above that the *Campbell* judgment had de facto not been able to 'absorb' the Convention law as it was, afterwards, developed by the ECtHR in its *Von Hannover* judgment, this was not intended to imply that the Strasbourg court itself gave guidelines of any more clarity than the very learned and thoughtful speeches of the members of the House of Lords. In discussing the ECtHR's judgment we found that the Court not only reiterated that Article 8, though essentially protecting against arbitrary interference by the public authorities, 'does not merely compel the State to abstain from such interference: in addition to this primarily negative undertaking, there may be positive obligations inherent in an effective respect for private or family life' and that '[t]hese obligations may involve the adoption of measures designed to secure respect for private life even in the sphere of the relations of individuals between themselves.'[349] The Court furthermore stated:

> The boundary between the State's positive and negative obligations under this provision does not lend itself to precise definition. The applicable principles are, nonetheless, similar. In both contexts regard must be had to the fair balance that has to be struck between the competing interests of the individual and of the community as a whole; and in both contexts the State enjoys a certain margin of appreciation (...).[350]

How this balancing is to be understood was not explicated. Decisive questions remain unanswered: Where do the positive and/or negative obligations come into play? Even more basic, is the Court at all right in applying the Convention guarantees in cases concerning 'the relations of individuals between themselves', especially their private-law relations? Could a deeper look into the Court's jurisprudence help gain a better understanding of the paths along which Convention law enters the legal sphere in which private individuals encounter one another? Might the structures of the ECHR rights' legal effects on private parties' *inter se* relations, and, more principally, the reason for the Convention's relevance in such contexts then stand out more clearly? This is what the following chapter intends to explore.

---

[349] ECtHR, *Von Hannover* (n. 1), § 57.
[350] ECtHR, *Von Hannover* (n. 1), § 57.

Chapter 3:
Drittwirkung under the ECHR: Human rights obligation of state authorities and their influence on judicial decisions in private law disputes

Do the rights guaranteed by the European Convention on Human Rights bear on legal relationships between private individuals? And, if so, how can the Convention's human rights and fundamental freedoms be understood to affect private individuals *inter se*? Both of these questions are inter-connected. The first seems to have been answered in the affirmative by the ECtHR in its *Von Hannover* judgment. This clear and definite statement of legal principle might, from a theoretical point of view, appear doubtful, and thus weak, upon closer examination. Exploring the validity of the principle by probing into the Court's case-law, however, is not only worthwhile for the observers in the ivory tower, but it can simultaneously help gain a better understanding of how the Convention law can, or must, be construed in order for international human rights guarantees to affect private-law relations. This again will affect the legal systems of the States Parties to the Convention, albeit through different channels, as exemplified in the preceding chapter by sec. 6 of the Human Rights Act 1998, on the one hand, and Article 59 of the Basic Law and the Federal statutes of consent to the Convention and its Protocols, on the other.

3.1 State responsibility for acts of private persons

At first glance, the Convention in its very first Article[1] gives the impression that it is only the States Parties that shall be bound by the Convention rights. This notion easily allows for and, as the ECtHR's case-law shows, actually includes, the possibility that acts of a private person are attributed to a State Party in such a way as to establish the State's responsibility under the Convention. In the case of *Costello-Roberts v. the United Kingdom*, which may well be seen as the leading case in this respect, the Court held that the act of a headmaster of an independent school may engage the responsibility of

---

[1]Article 1 reads: 'The High Contracting Parties shall secure to everyone within their jurisdiction the rights and freedoms defined in Section I of the Convention.'

the United Kingdom under the Convention if it proves to be incompatible with Article 3 or Article 8 or both.[2] In exploring whether there has been a violation of rights guaranteed under the ECHR, the judgment treats the corporal punishment of the applicant, although it is the behaviour of the organ of a private institution, in exactly the same way as it would review an act of a State authority.[3] Apart from pointing to the State's obligation under Article 2 of Protocol No. 1 to secure to children their right to education (in the context of which a school's disciplinary system is seen to fall),[4] the judgment relies on two arguments: First, in the United Kingdom, independent schools co-exist with a system of public education. Second and more importantly, the State cannot absolve itself from responsibility by delegating its obligations to private bodies or individuals.[5]

It is this second argument upon which the ECtHR relies in two quite recent cases, which may serve to underline the principle that the Convention binds 'the State', i.e. public authorities in a broad sense, and does not as such, or 'immediately', apply to relations between private legal subjects.[6] Both cases show that it is – both in terms of substantive and procedural ECHR law – essential for the Court to establish the responsibility of the State.[7]

In the case of *Wos v. Poland* the applicant had applied to the Polish-German Reconciliation Foundation (*Fundacja Polsko-Niemieckie Pojednanie* – 'the Foundation') for compensation on account of having been subjected to forced labour during the German occupation of Poland in the course of the Second World War. His application was turned down. The Polish Government had set up the Foundation under an Agreement of 16 October 1991 concluded with the Federal Republic of Germany for the purposes of providing financial assistance to victims of Nazi persecution. The Foundation, however, was not a governmental agency.[8] This provided a basis

---

[2]ECtHR, *Costello-Roberts v. the United Kingdom*, no. 13134/87, judgment of 25 March 1993, § 28.

[3]See ECtHR, *Costello-Roberts* (n. 2), §§ 29–32 (as to Article 3 ECHR) and §§ 33–36 (as to Article (ECHR). However, ECtHR, *Storck v. Germany*, no. 61603/00, judgment of 16 June 2005, §§ 100–107, places the Costello-Roberts judgment (§§ 26–28) in the context of questions of 'compliance with the State's positive obligations'.

[4]ECtHR, *Costello-Roberts* (n. 2), § 27, drawing a parallel to Article 28 of the United Nations Convention on the Rights of the Child of 20 November 1989.

[5]ECtHR, *Costello-Roberts* (n. 2), § 27, referring, mutatis mutandis, to the Van der Mussele v. Belgium, no. 8919/80, judgment of 23 November 1983, Series A 70, pp. 14–15, paras. 28–30.

[6]*Frowein* (2009), Article 1, para. 16.

[7]There are two legal dimensions of this responsibility of the State: The restriction of the binding effect of the ECHR guarantees to the States parties is an aspect of the *substantive* law of the Convention, which corresponds with the *procedural* setting that an application by a 'person, non-governmental organisation or group of individuals' can only be brought against 'one of the High Contracting Parties' (Art. 34, first sentence, ECHR; see: *Frowein*, in: Frowein/ Peukert (2009), Article 1, para. 17).

[8]ECtHR, *Wos v. Poland*, no. 22860/02, dec. of 1 March 2005, ECHR 2005-IV, §§ 8, 20 et seq.

upon which the Polish Government argued that, as the Foundation was a fully independent entity operating under private law, the State could not be held responsible for its actions or decisions concerning individual applications for financial assistance.[9] The ECtHR did not agree, although it did concede that the Polish State did not exercise a pervasive influence in the daily operations of the Polish-German Reconciliation Foundation: The State did not have direct influence over the decisions taken by the Foundation in respect of individual claimants. Nevertheless, the State's role was crucial in establishing the overall framework within which the Foundation operated.[10] Substantial means of, at least indirectly, influencing the Foundation's operation were at the Government's disposal. The Court referred to three important aspects: (1) the manner in which the Foundation's governing bodies were created; (2) the wide scope of regulatory powers exercised by those governing bodies in respect of the benefits paid under the first compensation scheme; and (3) those governing bodies' powers regarding the appointment and dismissal of the Foundation's adjudicating bodies. The Court also pointed to the supervisory powers which were exercised in respect of the Foundation by the competent minister.[11] Thus, the fact that the task of compensating Nazi victims had been delegated to the Foundation did not relieve the State of its responsibility under the Convention.[12] The Court says:

> [T]he exercise of State powers which affects Convention rights and freedoms raises an issue of State responsibility regardless of the form in which these powers happen to be exercised, be it for instance by a body whose activities are regulated by private law.[13]

The *Wos* decision[14] shows that a State cannot shed its responsibility simply by installing a private-law entity which it vests with 'independent' regulatory powers. The basic rule on which the decision rests is that private-law subjects neither are bound by the substantive law of the Convention nor can in terms of the Convention's procedural law be respondents to an application under

---

[9]ECtHR, *Wos* (n. 8), § 54.
[10]ECtHR, *Wos* (n. 8), § 71 (in combination with §§ 61–67).
[11]ECtHR, *Wos* (n. 8), §§ 61–67, see the summary in the final judgment of 8 June 2006, ECHR, 2006–VII, § 51.
[12]ECtHR, *Wos* (n. 8), § 74, pointing to, *mutatis mutandis*, its Van der Mussele (n. 5) Costello-Roberts (n. 2; p. 58, § 27) judgments. The Court does not regard it to be decisive for the question of State responsibility *ratione personae* that a State chooses a form of delegation in which some of its powers are exercised by another body; such a transfer of competences under an international agreement to a body operating under private law is not excluded by the Convention provided that Convention rights continue to be secured (ECtHR, *Wos* [n. 8], § 73, quoting as reference, *mutatis mutandis*, ECtHR [GC], *Matthews v. the United Kingdom*, no. 24833/94, judgment of 28 February 1999, § 32, ECHR 1999–I).
[13]ECtHR, *Wos* (n. 8), § 72.
[14]Which was confirmed by the final judgment (n. 11), §§ 51–54.

Article 34 ECHR. Where an individual is affected by acts of private-law entities or agents, the Court will look behind the legal construction in order to see whether it is not, in 'reality', the State that is at work.

This is confirmed by a brief look at the case of *Sychev v. Ukraine*.[15] The applicant had tried to enforce a judgment against the State-owned Lenina coal mine ('LCM') awarding him payment of arrears in industrial disablement benefits. After the LCM had been declared bankrupt, the writ of enforcement was transferred to the competent liquidation commission, established in the insolvency procedure, which then, however, remained inactive. Not until 2004, more than three years after the writ of enforcement had been re-transferred to the Bailiffs' Office in 2001, was the enforcement completed.[16] The ECtHR held the State responsible for the inactivity of the liquidation commission, even though the Ukrainian government argued that it was a private-law body.[17] It refused to embark on a discussion of whether the liquidation commission was or was not in itself a State authority. Rather, it found it sufficient to note that the body in question exercised certain State powers at least as regards the execution of court judgments. Expressly referring to the case of *Wos v. Poland*, the Court points out that the fact that a State chooses a form of delegation in which some of its powers are exercised by another body cannot be decisive for the question of State responsibility ratione personae: The exercise of State powers which affects Convention rights and freedoms raises an issue of State responsibility regardless of the form in which these powers happen to be exercised, be it for instance by a body whose activities are regulated by private law.[18]

As indicated above,[19] the responsibility of the State is relevant both for the substantive binding effects of the Convention and as a procedural requirement for the admissibility of an application under Article 34(1) ECHR. Lack of responsibility *ratione personae* makes an application inadmissible as it then is 'incompatible with the provisions of the Convention or the protocols thereto' within the meaning of Article 35 § 3 ECHR.[20] The point of reference for a State's responsibility both as an admissibility requirement and as the basis of the binding effects of the Convention's substantive law is Article 1 ECHR.[21]

---

[15]ECtHR, *Sychev v. Ukraine*, no. 4773/02, judgment of 11 October 2005, § 53.
[16]ECtHR, *Sychev* (n. 15), §§ 5–17, 19.
[17]ECtHR, *Sychev* (n. 15), § 52.
[18]ECtHR, *Sychev* (n. 15), § 54.
[19]*Supra*, n. 7, and in the main text at n. 7 and n. 14.
[20]*Grabenwarter* (2009), § 13, para. 40 (see also paras. 13–17); *Peukert* (2009), Article 35, para. 59 (see also Article 34, paras. 49–58).
[21]Cf. ECtHR, *Wos* (n. 8), § 60: 'The Court has consistently held that the responsibility of a State is engaged if a violation of one of the rights and freedoms defined in the Convention is the result of non-observance by that State of its obligation under Article 1 to secure those rights and freedoms in its domestic law to everyone within its jurisdiction (see, *mutatis mutandis*, *Young, James and Webster v. the United Kingdom*, nos. 7601/76 and 7806/77, judgment of 13 August

3.2 A closer look at Article 1 ECHR and obvious categories of the Convention's substantive requirements

Therefore, it seems advisable to explore the relevance of this provision, according to which the High Contracting Parties shall secure to everyone within their jurisdiction 'the rights and freedoms defined in Section I of the Convention'. This Section contains a list of quite 'classical' individual rights and freedoms, whose protective force we are quite used to seeing operate in legal relationships between a private individual and the State: The right to life (Article 2), the prohibition of torture (Article 3), the prohibition of slavery and forced labour (Article 4), the right to liberty and security (Article 5), the right to a fair trial (Article 6), the guarantee of no punishment without law (Article 7), the right to respect for private and family life (Article 8), freedom of thought, conscience and religion (Article 9), freedom of expression (Article 10), freedom of assembly and association (Article 11), the right to marry (Article 12), the right to an effective remedy (Article 13), and the prohibition of discrimination (Article 14). The Protocols add other important guarantees. These, however, need not be considered in detail in this context as the guarantees immediately contained in the Convention itself, when looked upon more closely, already show the relevant categories of State obligations which can be discerned.

3.2.1 The duty not to interfere

The States Parties commit themselves – albeit in most cases[22] not without limits – to refrain from interfering with 'spheres' of freedom reserved for private individuals, non-governmental organisations or groups of individuals:[23] It is 'the State' (including institutions and agents acting for the State[24]) which shall not subject anyone to torture or to inhuman or degrading treatment (Article 3). Without a justification meeting the Convention requirements, they shall

---

1981, § 49, Series A no. 44, p. 20). Article 1 makes no distinction as to the type of rule or measure concerned and does not exclude any part of the member State's "jurisdiction" from scrutiny under the Convention (see *United Communist Party of Turkey and Others v. Turkey*, no. 19392/92, judgment of 30 January 1998, § 29, Reports of Judgments and Decisions 1998–I, pp. 17–18). Furthermore, the State cannot absolve itself from responsibility *ratione personae* by delegating its obligations to private bodies or individuals (see, *mutatis mutandis*, *Costello-Roberts* (n. 2), § 27, Series A no. 247–C, p. 58). The undertakings given by a Contracting State under Article 1 of the Convention include, in addition to the duty to refrain from interfering with the enjoyment of the rights and freedoms guaranteed, positive obligations to take appropriate steps to ensure respect for those rights and freedoms within its territory (see, among other authorities, *Z and Others v. the United Kingdom* [GC], no. 29392/95, judgment of 10 May 2001, § 73, ECHR 2001–V).' See also ECtHR, *Sychev* (n. 15), §§ 53–54.
[22]But see Article 3 ECHR. Cf. also Article 15(2) ECHR forbidding derogation from Article 2, except in respect of deaths resulting from lawful acts of war, or from Articles 3, 4(1) and 7.
[23]Arg. ex Article 34, first sentence, ECHR.
[24]Attribution being a difficult problem, however, not to be discussed here.

not deprive any one of his life (Article 2), of his liberty (Article 5), they shall let private individuals be when they conduct their private and family lives, live in their homes and correspond with one another (Article 8), when they express their opinions, ideas, gather or distribute information (Article 10), peacefully assemble or associate with others (Article 11); and the States Parties shall respect their freedom of thought, conscience and religion (Article 9).

3.2.2 The duty of States to adjust their legal rules so that the treatment of private persons and entities meets certain standards

By merely abstaining from interference in these 'spheres', the States have not fulfilled all of their obligations under the Convention.[25] Rather, some of the provisions clearly require them to see to it that what might be called their 'legal infrastructure' meets certain standards. Let us look at some examples: If their existing rules do not already suffice, the States need to design the procedure of their courts of justice according to the requirements of Article 6, especially making sure that '[i]n the determination of his civil rights and obligations or of any criminal charge against him, everyone is entitled to a fair and public hearing within a reasonable time by an independent and impartial tribunal established by law' (Article 6(1), first sentence). Where they allow someone to be deprived of his liberty, they have to install the *habeas corpus* safeguards listed in Article 5. Furthermore, they have to ensure that '[e]veryone whose rights and freedoms as set forth in this Convention are violated shall have an effective remedy before a national authority notwithstanding that the violation has been committed by persons acting in an official capacity' (Article 13). These Convention requirements concern the activity of state institutions dealing with private persons, especially private individuals.

3.2.3 Duties to enact 'enabling' legislation

The Convention contains obligations of still another kind when, for instance, Article 12 says: 'Men and women of marriageable age have the right to marry and to found a family, according to the national laws governing the exercise of this right.' This provision implies that in a Contracting State there are laws allowing men and women to marry and to found a family: laws allowing the establishment of marital and familial relationships acknowledged by the State's legal order.[26] Such laws have an 'enabling' character as they make it

---

[25] *Harris/O'Boyle/Warbrick* (2009), 18–19, rightly point out that the ECtHR distinguishes between negative and positive obligations while human rights terminology has advanced to a 'tripartite typology': duties to respect, protect and fulfil human rights.

[26] Cf. ECtHR, *I. v. United Kingdom*, no. 25680/94, judgment of 11. July 2002 (GC), §§ 77 et seq.; *Christine Goodwin v. the United Kingdom*, no. 28957/95, judgment of 11 July 2002 (GC), §§ 97 et seq, RJD 2002 2002-VI. *Grabenwarter* (2008), § 22, paras. 59, 66.

legally possible for private individuals to enter into legal relationships with other private individuals. Similarly, insofar as Article 11 guarantees the freedom of association, and especially the right to form and to join trade unions, a State Party would completely fulfil its obligations only if it, in addition to refraining from interference with private individuals' activities to associate with others and actually organise themselves in groups, provided legal forms for such associations or corporations.[27]

3.2.4 Duties to regulate the behaviour of private individuals inter se

Reading the text of the Convention carefully, one finally discovers yet another category of duties: According to Article 2(1) '[e]veryone's right to life shall be protected by law.'[28] It is hardly surprising that, in the eyes of the ECtHR, 'the first sentence of Article 2 § 1 enjoins the State not only to refrain from the intentional and unlawful taking of life, but also to take appropriate steps to safeguard the lives of those within its jurisdiction.'[29] In the case of *Osman v. the United Kingdom*, in which the applicants complained of the authorities' failure to appreciate and to act on what they claimed was a series of clear warning signs that a specific person represented a serious threat to their, and their family's, physical safety,[30] the Court points out that '[i]t is common ground that the State's obligation in this respect extends beyond its primary duty to secure the right to life by putting in place effective criminal-law provisions to deter the commission of offences against the person backed up by law-enforcement machinery for the prevention, suppression and sanctioning of breaches of such provisions.'[31] The Grand Chamber found that 'those appearing before the Court' in the *Osman*[32] proceedings 'accepted [...]

---

[27]EComHR, *Lavisse v. France*, no. 14223/88, decision of 5 June 1991, DR 70, 218 (226); *Frowein/Peukert (2009)*, Art. 11, Para. 6; *Grabenwarter*, (2008), § 23, para. 88.; *Marauhn* (2005), § 4, para. 72; *Tomuschat*, (1993), p. 506.
[28]See also the French wording: 'Le droit de toute personne à la vie est protégé par la loi.'
[29]ECtHR, *Osman v. United Kingdom*, no. 23452/94, judgment of 28 October 1998, § 115; *Keenan v. United Kingdom*, no. 27229/95, judgment of 3 April 2001, § 89, both judgments referring to ECtHR, *L.C.B. v. the United Kingdom*, no. 23413/94, judgment of 9 June 1998, § 36, RJD 1998–III, 1403; *Calvelli and Ciglio v. Italy*, no. 32967/96, judgment of 17 January 2002, § 48, RJD 2002–I. Before the European Commission of Human Rights had in a series of cases acknowledged the existence of positive obligations under Article 2, see EcomHR, *Tugar v. Italy*, no. 22869/93, decision of. 18 October 1995, DR 83-A, 26; *X v. Ireland*, no. 6040/73, decision of 20 July 1973, YB 16 (1973), 388 (392); *Mrs. W. v. the United Kingdom*, no. 9348/81, judgment of 28 February 1983, DR 32, 190 (200); *Mrs. W. v. Ireland*, no. 9360/81, decision of 28 February 1983, DR 32, 211 (216); *K v. the United Kingdom and Ireland*, no. 9839/82, decision of 7 March 1985; *G v. the United Kingdom and Ireland*, no. 9837/82, decision of 4 March 1985, DR 47, 27.
[30]See ECtHR, *Osman* (n. 29), § 10 (for details see §§ 10–71).
[31]ECtHR, *Osman* (n. 29), § 115. Recently affirmed in ECtHR (GC), *Öneryıldız v. Turkey*, no. 48939/99, judgment of 30 November 2004, § 89; *Budayeva and Others v. Russia*, nos. 15339/02, 21166/02, 20058/02, 11673/02 and 15343/02, judgment of 20 March 2008, § 128.
[32]i.e. the applicants and their counsel and advisers; a delegate for the European Commission of Human Rights; finally, an agent, counsel and advisers of the British Government.

that Article 2 of the Convention may also imply in certain well-defined circumstances a positive obligation on the authorities to take preventive *operational* measures to protect an individual whose life is at risk from the criminal acts of another individual.'[33] In later judgments the ECtHR expressly endorsed this position as a position of its own.[34] Thus, under certain circumstances, Article 2 obliges the States Parties to stop one individual from attacking another individual's life.

Similarly, when Article 4 says, 'No one shall be held in slavery or servitude,' and, 'No one shall be required to perform forced or compulsory labour,' these provisions quite obviously demand not only that States improve 'their' behaviour[35] but that they also abolish 'slavery', 'servitude', and 'forced or compulsory labour', insofar as such situations exist among private persons.[36] In the ECtHR's opinion, limiting compliance with Article 4 only to direct action by the State authorities would amount to rendering it ineffective.[37] Thus, States Parties are not only forbidden to uphold, and, *a fortiori*, are precluded from newly introducing, a state-run system of 'slavery', 'servitude' or 'forced or compulsory labour'. As can be seen from the ECtHR's judgment in the *Siliadin* case,[38] States are also obliged to take measures securing that there is *among private individuals* neither 'forced labour' in the sense of 'work "exacted … under the menace of any penalty" and also performed against the will of the person concerned, that is work for which he "has not offered himself voluntarily"';[39] nor 'slavery', i.e. 'the status or condition of a person over

---

[33]ECtHR, *Osman* (n. 29), § 115.
[34]See, for example, ECtHR, *Keenan* (n. 29), § 89 (speaking not of 'well-defined' but of 'appropriate' circumstances); *Calvelli and Ciglio* (n. 29), § 51; *Kılıç v. Turkey*, no. 22492/93, decision of 20 March 2000, § 62, ECHR 2000–III, and *Mahmut Kaya v. Turkey*, no. 22535/93, decision of 28 March 2000, § 85, ECHR 2000–III. *Paul and Audrey Edwards*, cited above, § 54; *İlhan v. Turkey*, no. 22277/93, decision of 27 June 2000, [GC], § 91, ECHR 2000–VII.
[35]The exceptions listed in Article 4(3) ECHR do show the provisions of Article 4(1) and (2) to be addressed to the States Parties but, at the same time, do not prove oppression by private persons to be outside of the scope of the protection intended.
[36]See *Frowein* (2009), Article 1, para. 16.
[37]ECtHR, *Siliadin v. France*, no. 73316/01, judgment of 26 July 2005, § 89 (furthermore, this 'would be inconsistent with the international instruments specifically concerned with this issue', i.e. slavery, servitude and forced labour).
[38]ECtHR, *Siliadin* (n. 37), §§ 111 et seq.
[39]ECtHR, *Siliadin* (n. 37), § 117, gives the definition of 'forced or compulsory labour', quoting *Van der Mussele* (n. 5), § 34, Series A no. 70, p. 17. In the *Siliadin* case, the Court came to the conclusion that the applicant was, at the least, subjected to forced labour within the meaning of Article 4 of the Convention at a time when she was a minor (ibid., § 120), a point the Court emphasised. This was based on the following facts (ibid., §§ 109–110, 118–119): The applicant arrived in France from Togo at the age of 15 years and 7 months with a person who had agreed with her father that she would work until her air ticket had been reimbursed, that her immigration status would be regularised and that she would be sent to school. In reality, the applicant worked for this person for a few months before being 'lent' to Mr and Mrs B. working in their house without respite for approximately fifteen hours per day, with no day off, for several years, without ever receiving wages or

whom any or all of the powers attaching to the right of ownership are exercised';[40] nor servitude meaning, within the context of the Convention, 'an obligation to provide one's services that is imposed by the use of coercion'.[41] Under Article 4 of the Convention, the member States have positive obligations requiring the penalisation and effective prosecution of any act aimed at maintaining a person in such a situation.[42]

3.3 Expanding the category of duties to regulate the behaviour of private individuals *inter se* beyond what is obvious from the Convention's wording

However, when the ECtHR in its *Siliadin* judgment finds 'that the criminal-law legislation in force at the material time did not afford the applicant, a minor, practical and effective protection against the actions of which she was a victim,'[43] actions of private individuals amounting to forced labour and servitude within the meaning of Article 4 of the Convention,[44] this conclusion does not rest solely on the wording of that provision. Rather, it must be read in the context of a long line of cases falling *outside* the scope of provisions, which, like Articles 2 and 4, quite obviously require the State to regulate the conduct of private individuals *inter se*.[45] Nevertheless, the Court has in these

---

being sent to school, without identity papers and without her immigration status being regularised. She was accommodated in their home and slept in the children's bedroom. Although the applicant was not threatened by a 'penalty', she was in an equivalent situation in terms of the perceived seriousness of the threat. She was an adolescent girl in a foreign land, unlawfully present on French territory and in fear of arrest by the police. The Court denied that the applicant had performed the work of her own free will; it was evident that she had not been given any choice.

[40]ECtHR, *Siliadin* (n. 37), § 122, referring to the 1927 Slavery Convention (Article 1(1)).

[41]ECtHR, *Siliadin* (n. 37), § 124, the Court adding that 'servitude' 'is to be linked with the concept of "slavery" described above [sc. § 122]' (ibid., referring to ECHR, *Seguin v. France*, no. 42400/98, decision. of 7 March 2000). The Court found that the applicant, a minor at the relevant time, was by a couple Mr and Mr B, held in servitude within the meaning of Article 4 of the Convention (ibid., §§ 126–129). In addition to the fact that she was required to perform forced labour, this labour, as the Court notes, lasted almost fifteen hours a day, seven days per week. She had been brought to France by a relative of her father's, and had not chosen to work for Mr and Mrs B. As a minor, the applicant had no resources and was vulnerable and isolated, and had no means of living elsewhere than in the home of Mr and Mrs B., where she shared the children's bedroom as no other accommodation had been offered. She was entirely at Mr and Mrs B.'s mercy, since her papers had been confiscated and she had been promised that her immigration status would be regularised, which had never occurred. She was afraid of being arrested by the police, was not in any event permitted to leave the house, except to take the children to their classes and various activities, and, thus, had no freedom of movement and no free time. As she had not been sent to school, despite the promises made to her father, the applicant could not hope that her situation would improve and was completely dependent on Mr and Mrs B.

[42]ECtHR, *Siliadin* (n. 37), § 112.

[43]ECtHR, *Siliadin* (n. 37), § 148.

[44]See above, n. 39 and n. 41.

[45]For a comprehensive analysis of positive obligations under the ECHR see: *Krieger* (2006), paras. 23–117.

cases acknowledged that from the rights and freedoms which the Convention guarantees there flow positive obligations. It is to landmark decisions of this kind to which the *Siliadin* judgment expressly points when it recalls previously having stated 'that children and other vulnerable individuals, in particular, are entitled to State protection, in the form of effective deterrence, against such serious breaches of personal integrity' as the applicant had suffered.[46]

The Court's finding in the *Siladin* case, which held that the respondent State's *criminal-law legislation* did not meet the protective standards required by the Convention, appears to be quite in line with the leading case of *X and Y v. the Netherlands*. There the civil-law remedies which were available to the applicant, Ms X, who had been the victim of a rape,[47] were considered to be insufficient: As fundamental values and essential aspects of private life were at stake, effective deterrence was not only 'indispensable', but could 'be achieved only by criminal-law provisions.'[48] However, it should not be overlooked that the Court did take the civil-law remedies into account when it assessed the standard of protection in the respondent State's law.[49] Similarly, in the case of *Stubbings and others v. the United Kingdom*, the Court, after underlining that sexual abuse is unquestionably an abhorrent type of wrongdoing, with debilitating effects on its victims, found that '[c]hildren and other vulnerable individuals are entitled to State protection, in the form of effective deterrence, from such grave types of interference with essential aspects of their private lives.'[50] It then considered such protection to have been afforded in the instant case, relying on an evaluation of English criminal law,[51] but – and again this should not be neglected – immediately adding that '[i]n principle, civil remedies are also available provided they are sought within the

---

[46]ECtHR, *Siliadin* (n. 37), § 143. Besides the cases *X and Y v. the Netherlands* (see below, at n. 47 et seq.), *Stubbings* (see below, at n. 50 et seq.), and *A. v. the United Kingdom* (see below, n. 53), the Court referred to no. 25599/94, judgment of 23 September 1998, § 22, *Reports* 1998–VI, p. 2699, and the United Nations Convention on the Rights of the Child, Articles 19 and 37.

[47]According to the findings of the Court, a certain Mr B had forced the applicant, Miss Y, a mentally handicapped young woman who had just turned sixteen, to follow him to his room, to undress and to have sexual intercourse with him (ECtHR, *X and Y v. the Netherlands*, no. 8978/80, judgment of 26 March 1985, Series A no. 91, §§ 7, 8). According to the Government of the Netherlands, under Dutch civil law at the relevant time, it would have been possible to bring before or file with the Netherlands courts, on behalf of Miss Y: an action for damages against Mr B, for pecuniary or non-pecuniary damage; an application for an injunction against Mr B, to prevent repetition of the offence; a similar action or application against the directress of the children's home (ECtHR, ibid., § 25).

[48]ECtHR, *X and Y v. the Netherlands* (n. 47), § 27.

[49]Cf. ECtHR, *X and Y v. the Netherlands* (n. 47), § 24: 'Recourse to the criminal law is not necessarily the only answer.'

[50]ECtHR, *Stubbings and Others v. the United Kingdom*, nos. 22083/93, 22095/93, judgment of 22 October 1996, § 64, RJD 1996–IV, 1488.

[51]ECtHR, *Stubbings* (n. 50), § 65.

statutory time-limit.'⁵² When acknowledging that there is an obligation for the States Parties to deter private individuals from assaulting and offending others effectively by criminal law and criminal prosecution, the judgments consistently emphasise the severity of the wrongdoing.⁵³ This implies that the States' reaction to lesser violations may require no more than providing the victim with civil-law remedies granting redress or compensation; in other cases it will be administrative action which is required, such as police protection – the effectiveness of which was contested by the applicants in the *Osman* case.⁵⁴ Such a conclusion not only finds reinforcement in rulings on the Contracting States' (explicit)⁵⁵ duty to protect the right to life under Article 2,⁵⁶ but also becomes more valid in light of the judgment in the leading case of *X and Y v. the Netherlands*. There the Court observed 'that the choice of the means calculated to secure compliance with Article 8 in the sphere of the relations of individuals between themselves is in principle a matter that falls within the Contracting States' margin of appreciation. In this connection, there are different ways of ensuring 'respect for private life', and the nature of

---

⁵²ECtHR, *Stubbings* (n. 50), § 66. One major cause of complaint had been the scheme of limitations on civil remedies.
⁵³See ECtHR, *A. v. the United Kingdom*, no. 25599/94, judgment of 23 September 1998, § 22, *Reports* 1998–VI, p. 2699, where the heavy beating of a nine-year old with a garden cane was considered to be a case falling under Article 3 ECHR: 'The Court considers that the obligation on the High Contracting Parties under Article 1 of the Convention to secure to everyone within their jurisdiction the rights and freedoms defined in the Convention, taken together with Article 3, requires States to take measures designed to ensure that individuals within their jurisdiction are not subjected to torture or inhuman or degrading treatment or punishment, including such ill-treatment administered by private individuals (see, *mutatis mutandis*, the *H.L.R. v. France,* no. 24573/94, judgment of 29 April 1997, § 40, *Reports* 1997–III, p. 758). Children and other vulnerable individuals, in particular, are entitled to State protection, in the form of effective deterrence, against such serious breaches of personal integrity (see, *mutatis mutandis*, the X and Y v. the Netherlands (n. 47), §§ 21 – 27, pp. 11 – 13; *Stubbings* (n. 50), §§ 62 – 64; and also the United Nations Convention on the Rights of the Child, Articles 19 and 37).'
⁵⁴See above at n. 29. See also ECtHR, *López Ostra v. Spain*, no. 16798/90, judgment of 9 December 1994, §§ 51–58, A 303-C, (failure to protect neighbouring residents against emissions from a waste-treatment plant in Lorca); *Öneryıldız* (GC) (n. 31), §§ 89–90, 97–110 (lack of precautions against illegal building of houses in the slum quarter of Kazım Karabekir in Ümraniye, a district of Istanbul, adjacent to a municipal rubbish tip, in consequence of which a methane explosion on the site led to a land-slide destroying houses and killing thirty-nine people); *Budayeva* (n. 31), §§ 128–137, 147–160 (insufficient measures taken by authorities against mud-slides in the town of Tyrnauz).
⁵⁵See above at n. 29.
⁵⁶See, for example, ECtHR, *Calvelli and Ciglio* (n. 29), § 51: '[...], if the infringement of the right to life or to personal integrity is not caused intentionally, the positive obligation imposed by Article 2 to set up an effective judicial system does not necessarily require the provision of a criminal-law remedy in every case. In the specific sphere of medical negligence the obligation may for instance also be satisfied if the legal system affords victims a remedy in the civil courts, either alone or in conjunction with a remedy in the criminal courts, enabling any liability of the doctors concerned to be established and any appropriate civil redress, such as an order for damages and for the publication of the decision, to be obtained. Disciplinary measures may also be envisaged.'

the State's obligation will depend on the particular aspect of private life that is at issue. Recourse to the criminal law is not necessarily the only answer.'[57]

3.3.1 The base-line argument for the Contracting States' positive obligations to secure the Convention's fundamental rights and freedoms in relations between private individuals

This observation, in the case *X and Y v. the Netherlands*, is an important starting point in the Court's line of argument, showing that criminal-law solutions are not always necessary. It is connected to what might be called the base-line of argument which the Strasbourg Judges, albeit in the context of different rights and freedoms, do not tire of expressing and which in the judgment in the case of *X and Y v. the Netherlands* for Article 8 reads: 'The Court recalls that although the object of Article 8 is essentially that of protecting the individual against arbitrary interference by the public authorities, it does not merely compel the State to abstain from such interference: in addition to this primarily negative undertaking, there may be positive obligations inherent in an effective respect for private or family life (see the Airey judgment of 9 October 1979, Series A no. 32, p. 17, para. 32). These obligations may involve the adoption of measures designed to secure respect for private life even in the sphere of the relations of individuals between themselves.'[58]

Thus, the base-line actually is a triple line:

First, the existence of negative obligations under the Convention is clear and cannot be the object of doubt. The Convention lays down such duties of non-interference on the public authorities, and not on private persons, whose behaviour, in general,[59] is not attributable to the States Parties.[60] In other

---

[57]ECtHR, *X and Y v. the Netherlands* (n. 47), § 27. See also ECtHR, *Verliere v. Switzerland*, no. 41953/98, decision of 28 June 2001, ECHR 2001–VII, where the Court found that effective protection was afforded by the Swiss legislature insofar as '[b]oth civil and criminal remedies – supported by penalties for breach – were available to anyone who considered that their personality rights had been infringed.'

[58]ECtHR, *X and Y v. the Netherlands* (n. 47), § 23.

[59]I.e. absent special reasons for attributing it to public authorities. See as a judgment which is interpreted as containing an exception from the rule that private acts do not fall directly into the sphere of a Contracting State's responsibility: ECtHR, *Costello-Roberts* (n. 2), §§ 27–28, where the Court found that in the particular case of corporal punishment of a seven-year old pupil, 'which relates to the particular domain of school discipline, the treatment complained of although it was the act of a headmaster of an independent school, is none the less such as may engage the responsibility of the United Kingdom under the Convention if it proves to be incompatible with Article 3 or Article 8 or both' (at § 28). But cf. ECtHR, *Storck* (n. 3), § 103, where the *Costello-Roberts* judgment is referred to as a case in which the respondent State's responsibility was based on 'its obligation to secure to pupils their rights guaranteed by Articles 3 and 8 of the Convention' and where, in the context of §§ 100–108 of the *Storck* judgment, this obligation is apparently considered as a 'positive obligation'.

[60]See, as a recent example concerning Article 1 of Protocol No. 1 to the Convention: ECtHR, *Bennich-Zalewski v. Poland*, no. 59857/00, judgment of 22 April 2008, § 94, where the Court

words, there is no *unmittelbare Drittwirkung* of Conventions rights,[61] no 'immediate third-party effect', or more precisely, no direct binding effect on private persons: Private persons are privileged, not burdened, by the Convention's guarantee of rights and freedoms.

Second, positive obligations are conceivable as flowing from the States' duty to respect private life, an example of which is given in the *X and Y v. the Netherlands* judgment. Article 8 with its demand for 'respect' offers a textual link to which positive obligations can be attached easily, albeit not so clearly as in the explicit cases of Articles 2 and 4.[62] But Article 8 was only the first in a row of rights and freedoms which the ECtHR has interpreted as a source of positive obligations, and which include Article 3 (prohibition of torture and inhuman or degrading treatment)[63], Article 5 (right to liberty and security),[64] Article 9 (freedom of thought, conscience and religion),[65] Article 10 (freedom of expression),[66] Article 11 (freedom of assembly and association),[67] Article 1

---

came to the conclusion that '..., having regard to the *institutional and operational independence* of the Izolacja company *from the State*, the latter must be taken to be *absolved from responsibility under the Convention for that company's acts and omissions*' (emphasis added by the author).

[61] *Grabenwarter* (2009), § 19, para. 14 (see also § 17, paras. 6–10); *Ehlers*, (2009), § 2, para. 48; *Harris/O'Boyle/Warbrick* (2009), 20. *Contra*: *Clapham* (1993a), 167 et seq.; *Clapham* (1993b). See also: *Alkema* (1988); *Drzemczewski* (1979).

[62] Above at n. 28 et seq. as to Article 2(1), first sentence (protection of life); at n. 35 et seq. as to Article 4 (prohibition of slavery and forced labour).

[63] Where positive obligations were seen to be attached to Article 3, the Court drew on Article 1, according to which the High Contracting Parties *shall secure* to everyone within their jurisdiction the rights and freedoms defined in Section I of the Convention. As to Article 3 see, for example: ECtHR, *A. v. the United Kingdom* (n. 53), § 22; *Z and Others v. the United Kingdom*, no. 29392/95, judgment of 10 May 2001, § 73, RJD 2001–V, 1, ('The obligation on High Contracting Parties under Article 1 of the Convention to secure to everyone within their jurisdiction the rights and freedoms defined in the Convention, taken in conjunction with Article 3, requires States to take measures designed to ensure that individuals within their jurisdiction are not subjected to torture or inhuman or degrading treatment, including such ill-treatment administered by private individuals […]'; the case concerned children being neglected and abused by their parents). See also ECtHR, *Costello-Roberts* (n. 2), § 26, but see also *supra*, n. 59, as to the interpretation of the *Costello-Roberts* judgment as an instance of attributing private acts to the State.

[64] ECtHR, *Storck* (n. 3), §§ 89, 100–108 (also see § 92); *Ilaşcu and Others v. Moldova and Russia* [GC], no. 48787/99, judgment of 8 July 2004, §§ 332–352 and 464, RJD 2004–VII. Cf. ECtHR, *Nielsen v. Denmark*, no. 10929/84, judgment of 18 November 1988, §§ 63, 72–73, Series A 144 (and the dissenting opinion of Judge Carillo Salcedo).

[65] *Otto-Preminger-Institut v. Austria*, no. 13470/87, judgment of 20 September 1994, § 47, Series A 295-A; EcomHR, *X v. the United Kingdom*, no. 8160/78, decision of 12 March 1981, DR 22, 27 (36–37); *Konttinen v. Finland*, no. 24949/94, decision of 3 December 1996, DR 87, 68 (75)

[66] ECtHR, *Özgür Gündem v. Turkey*, no. 23144/93, judgment of 16 March 2000, § 43, RJD 2000–III; *VGT Verein gegen Tierfabriken v. Switzerland*, no. 24699/94, judgment of 28 June 2001, §§ 44–47, RJD 2001-VI, 243; EComHR, *Rommelfanger v. the Federal Republic of Germany*, no. 12242/86, decision of 6 September 1989, DR 62, 151 (160); *De Geillustreerde Pers N.V. v. the Netherlands*, no. 5178/71, decision of 12 October 1973, § 88, DR 8, 5 (14).

[67] ECtHR, *Plattform 'Ärzte für das Leben' v. Austria*, no. 10126/82, judgment of 21 June 1988, § 32, Series A 139; *Wilson & the National Union of Journalists and Others v. the United*

of Protocol 1 to the ECHR (protection of property).[68] However, again and again judgments will point out that the border between negative and positive obligations cannot be drawn precisely.[69] Furthermore, in fulfilling positive obligations under the Convention, the Contracting States enjoy a certain margin of appreciation.[70]

Kingdom, no. 30668/96, 30671/96 and 30678/96, judgment of 2 July 2002, § 41, ECHR 2002–V; Ouranio Toxo v. Greece, no. 74989/01, judgment of 20 October 2005, § 37; Bączkowski and Others v. Poland, no. 1543/06, judgment of 3 May 2007, § 64 (obiter); Balçık and Others v. Turkey, no. 25/02, judgment of 29 November 2007, §§ 47–48 (obiter).

[68]ECHR Öneryildiz v. Turkey, no. 48939/99, judgment of 18 June 2002, § 135; GC ('In the present case there is no doubt that the causal link established between the gross negligence attributable to the State and the loss of human lives also applies to the engulfment of the applicant's house. In the Court's view, the resulting infringement amounts not to "interference" but to the breach of a positive obligation, since the State officials and authorities did not do everything within their power to protect the applicant's proprietary interests'); Sovtransavto Holding v Ukraine., no. 48553/99, judgment of 25 July 2002, §§ 96 ff., ECHR 2002–VII; cf. also ECtHR, Raimondo v. Italy, no. 12954/87, judgment of 22 February 1994, §§ 31–33, Series A 281–A; Broniowski v. Poland, no. 31443/96, judgment of 2004, §§ 143, ECHR 2004–V; Rosenzweig and Bonded Warehouses LTD. v. Poland, no. 51728/99, judgment of 28 July 2005, §§ 48ff. As to Article 6(2): EComHR, X v. Germany, no. 2413/65, decision of 16 December 1966; Ensslin, Baader and Raspe v. Germany, no. 7572/76, decision of 8 July 1978, DR 14, 64 (112–113); Guy Jespers v. Belgium, no. 8403/78, decision of 29 September 1982, DR 22, 100 (126–127).

[69]See ECtHR, Maurice v. France, no. 11810/03, judgment of 6 October 2005, § 114: 'While the essential object of Article 8 is to protect the individual against arbitrary interference by the public authorities, it does not merely require the State to abstain from such interference: there may in addition be positive obligations inherent in effective "respect" for family life. The boundaries between the State's positive and negative obligations under this provision do not always lend themselves to precise definition; nonetheless, the applicable principles are similar. In both contexts regard must be had to the fair balance that has to be struck between the competing interests of the individual and the community as a whole, and in both contexts the State is recognised as enjoying a certain margin of appreciation (see, for example, Nuutinen v. Finland, no. 32842/96, judgment of 27 June 2000, § 127, ECHR 2000–VIII, and Kutzner v. Germany, no. 46544/99, judgment of 26 February 2002, §§ 61 and 62, ECHR 2002–I). Furthermore, even in relation to the positive obligations flowing from the first paragraph, "in striking [the required] balance the aims mentioned in the second paragraph ... may be of a certain relevance" (see Powell and Rayner v. the United Kingdom, no. 9310/81, judgment of 21 February 1990, § 41, Series A no. 172, p. 18).' Identical wording in: ECtHR, Draon v. France, no. 1513/03, judgment of 6 October 2005, § 105. See also, e.g.; ECtHR, Mikulić v. Croatia, no. 53176/99, judgment of 7 February 2002, § 58, RJD 2002–I; Cf. recently. ECtHR, Emonet and Others v. Switzerland, no. 39051/03, judgment of 13 December 2007, § 67, see also § 63.

[70]See as further and recent reference: ECtHR (GC), Odièvre v. France, no. 42326/98, judgment of 13 February 2003, § 46, ECHR 2003–III: 'The Court reiterates that the choice of the means calculated to secure compliance with Article 8 in the sphere of the relations of individuals between themselves is in principle a matter that falls within the Contracting States' margin of appreciation. In this connection, there are different ways of ensuring 'respect for private life', and the nature of the State's obligation will depend on the particular aspect of private life that is at issue' (quoting ECtHR, X and Y v. the Netherlands [n. 47], § 24). See also the Odièvre judgment at § 49: '...The French legislation thus seeks to strike a balance and to ensure sufficient proportion between the competing interests. The Court observes in that connection that the States must be allowed to determine the means which they consider to be best suited to achieve the aim of reconciling those interests. Overall, the

Third, such positive obligations can extend to relations between private individuals *inter se*.

3.2.2 The Velosa Barreto *case: Revealing two dimensions of positive obligations*

The ECtHR has been reluctant to explore the Convention's influence on private legal relations in the abstract. Instead, it has proceeded case by case, describing it as 'not [...] desirable, let alone necessary, to elaborate a general theory concerning the extent to which the Convention guarantees should be extended to relations between private individuals *inter se*.'[71] Nevertheless, analysis of the Court's case-law reveals a certain 'scheme' for dealing with positive obligations in the sphere of interpersonal relations. The judgment in the case of *Velosa Barreto v. Portugal* is considered to be paradigmatic:[72] The applicant, Mr *Velosa Barreto*, alleged that the Portuguese courts, by not allowing him to terminate the lease on the house he owned, had infringed his right to respect for his private and family life guaranteed under Article 8 ECHR.

In its approach to the *Velosa Barreto* case the Court acknowledges that Article 8 may give rise to positive obligations, 'particularly the obligation to ensure respect for private and family life even in the sphere of interpersonal relations.'[73] This proves that it firmly stands on the triple base-line just described above. However, it adds an important qualification: 'In this matter as in others a fair balance must be struck between the general interest and the interests of the people concerned (...)'.[74] Thus, there are limits to positive obligations resulting from the necessity of balancing interests.

The judgment then shows a *two-step test* when investigating whether barring the applicant from terminating the lease actually amounted to a breach of positive obligations under Article 8 ECHR.[75]

The Court first evaluates the *abstract legal situation* in Portugal, finding that the legislation applied in the case pursued a legitimate aim, namely the social protection of tenants, and that it intended to promote the economic

---

Court considers that France has not overstepped the margin of appreciation which it must be afforded in view of the complex and sensitive nature of the issue of access to information about one's origins, an issue that concerns the right to know one's personal history, the choices of the natural parents, the existing family ties and the adoptive parents.'

[71] ECtHR, *VGT Verein gegen Tierfabriken* (n. 66), § 46.

[72] *Krieger* (n. 45) para. 78.

[73] ECtHR, *Velosa Barreto v. Portugal*, no. 18072/91, judgment of 21 November 1995, § 23, Series A 334, with reference to ECtHR, *Airey v. Ireland*, no. 6289/73, judgment of 9 October 1979, § 32, Series A 32, p. 17; *X and Y v. the Netherlands* (n. 47), § 23.

[74] ECtHR, *Velosa Barreto* (n. 73), § 23 referring to ECtHR, *B. v. France*, no. 13343/87, judgment of 25 March 1992, § 44, Series A 232–C, p. 47; *Keegan v. Ireland*, no. 16969/90, judgment of 26 May 1994, § 49, Series A 290, p. 19. See also, e.g.: ECtHR, *Mikulić* (n. 69), § 58; *Odièvre v. France* (n. 70), §§ 40–49.

[75] *Krieger* (n. 45), para. 78.

well-being of the country and the protection of the rights of others.[76] In pursuit of these aims, the Portuguese legislature was, in the eyes of the Court, entitled to make the termination of a lease subject to the condition that the landlord 'needs the property in order to live there.'[77] This was not in dispute before the Court.[78] So far the legal situation is compatible with Article 8, even if its consequences are that the owner of a home, which he has rented to a third party, is not free to retrieve his property at will. The Court is of the opinion that effective protection for respect for private and family life cannot require the existence in national law of legal protection enabling each family to have a home for themselves alone, and especially, that Article 8 does not go so far as to place the State under an obligation to give a landlord the right to recover possession of a rented house on request and in any circumstances.[79]

This result of an analysis of the abstract legal situation, however, does not paint the full picture. In order to complete it, one needs to know how the abstract rule of Portuguese law *actually is applied*. We need to know what the Portuguese courts require of a landlord when the law subjects the termination of a lease to the condition that he show that he needs the property in order to live there. Only then can we fully understand the abstract rule as a rule 'in operation'. Only then can we furthermore judge whether *in the specific case* the Portuguese court interpreted the requirement so restrictively that it amounted to a lack of respect for the applicant's family life – in other words: a breach of positive obligations under Article 8. Therefore, it is consistent for the ECtHR, after finding the abstract rule of Portuguese law to be in conformity with the Convention standards, to ask whether, in applying this rule restricting the termination of leases, the Portuguese courts infringed the applicant's right to respect for his private and family life.[80] In this regard, the Court found that by denying the applicant a right to terminate the lease, the Portuguese courts acted neither arbitrarily nor unreasonably, and did not fail to discharge their obligation to strike a fair balance between the parties' respective interests.[81] Rather, the Portuguese courts reached their conclusion after duly considering the various questions of fact and of law submitted to them and after conducting a careful analysis of the arguments put forward by the applicant. The courts then set out at length, and in detail, the reasons for their decision.[82]

---

[76]ECtHR, *Velosa Barreto* (n. 73), § 25.
[77]Article 1096(1), lit. A of the Portuguese Civil Code as quoted by the ECtHR, *Velosa Barreto* (n. 73), § 16.
[78]ECtHR, *Velosa Barreto* (n. 73), § 26.
[79]ECtHR, *Velosa Barreto* (n. 73), § 24.
[80]ECtHR, *Velosa Barreto* (n. 73), § 26.
[81]ECtHR, *Velosa Barreto* (n. 73), § 30.
[82]ECtHR, *Velosa Barreto* (n. 73), § 29, in particular pointing out that both courts took account of the fact that Mr Velosa Barreto's situation had improved during the proceedings, since two of his wife's aunts and her brother had in the meantime left the house he was living in, leaving more room for his own household.

Having retraced the Court's line of argument in the *Velosa Barreto* case, one might wonder if it truly involves a case of positive obligations. Is not the essential question whether the *freedom* of the house owner to terminate a lease is allowed *to be restricted* through a State's civil legislation? Is this not a clear case of the State's *interference* with a freedom rather than a problem of positive obligations? The ECtHR, by its very approach to the case,[83] obviously does not think so. On closer inspection this proves to be correct. One must take heed not to narrow down the perspective to Article 8 ECHR but to include all the relevant rights and freedoms at stake. Then it can easily be conceded that a law forbidding the owner of a house to terminate a lease in certain cases does interfere with the landlord's freedom. However, the freedom thus concerned is, as the *Velosa Barreto* judgment itself shows,[84] the right to the peaceful enjoyment of possessions guaranteed by Article 1(1) of Protocol 1 to the ECHR. It is not, at least not specifically, the right to respect for family life guaranteed by Article 8. Instead, this right, in a conflict between landlord and tenant over the termination of their contract, might serve as a *justification* for alleviating or even lifting restrictions on the property of the landlord who wishes to use it as a home for his family. Article 8 might demand, as the Court puts it, 'legal protection enabling [*sic!*] each family to have a home for themselves alone.'[85] This indeed is a *positive effect*, which would *privilege* the applicant (the landlord!), albeit by pushing back limitations – but not limitations on the right to respect for family life, but limitations on the use of property. While this proves the questions raised by the case under Article 8 ECHR and Article 1 of Protocol 1 to the ECHR to be interwoven, it appears convincing to consider the problem under Article 8 to be one of 'enabling' or 'promoting' family life, and thus to concern *positive obligations*.

The Court's two-step test mirrors *two dimensions of positive obligations* under the Convention which extend to private interpersonal relationships: The Contracting States can be required to act positively in furtherance of Convention rights and freedoms, first, through their legislatures enacting laws and, second, through their administrative and, especially, through their judicial institutions applying these laws – or other laws which can be understood to intend the protection of ECHR guarantees. Or put in the negative: The Contracting States can violate their positive obligations either when their law-making institutions altogether fail to bring their domestic laws in accordance with the 'positive' requirements immanent in the Convention's rights and freedoms, or when public authorities, in applying the law, do not meet the standards set by the Convention. The failure in both cases can take the form of not providing *due protection* against non-state actors (or other

---

[83]See above at n. 73.
[84]ECtHR, *Velosa Barreto* (n. 73), §§ 35–38, where the Court speaks of a 'restriction' and an 'interference'.
[85]ECtHR, *Velosa Barreto* (n. 73), § 24.

non-state sources[86]) who threaten the rights and freedoms, or the form of not sufficiently *promoting the realisation* of these guarantees.

3.4 Positive obligations and legislation

This distinction between insufficient protection against non-state actors and the failure to enact enabling or enhancing legislation is of importance. In the past, at least, there seems to be a different handling of positive obligations in two groups of cases. In one of these, the compatibility with domestic legislation is challenged on the grounds of *shortcomings in promoting the realisation* of Convention guarantees (hereinafter also referred to as: 'Group I'). In the other, domestic laws are alleged *to provide insufficient protection* of rights and freedoms *against private interference* (hereinafter also referred to as: 'Group II').

3.4.1 Group I: Shortcomings in promoting the realisation of Convention guarantees by legislation

The very first case in which positive obligations were acknowledged to be immanent in Article 8 ECHR was the case of *Marckx v. Belgium*.[87] The applicants, an unmarried woman and her daughter, complained of provisions in the Belgian Civil Code which stated that no legal bond between an unmarried mother and her child resulted from the mere fact of birth. Maternal affiliation of an 'illegitimate' child, the Code provisions stated, could only be established by means either of a voluntary recognition by the mother or of legal proceedings taken for the purpose.[88] Furthermore, the establishment of the maternal affiliation of an 'illegitimate' child had limited effects with regards to both the extent of his family relationships and to the rights of the child and his mother in the matter of inheritance on intestacy and voluntary dispositions. In the context of the maternal affiliation of an 'illegitimate' child, Belgian legislation did not employ the concepts of 'family' and 'relative'. Even once such affiliation had been established, it in principle created a legal bond with the mother alone. The child did not become a member of the mother's family. The law, inter alia, excluded him from that family regarding inheritance rights on intestacy, restricted his ability to inherit from his parents on intestacy, and limited a parent's voluntary dispositions *inter vivos* in favour of an 'illegitimate' child to no more than the child's entitlement in cases of inheritance on intestacy.[89]

[86]Cf. ECtHR, *Budayeva* (n. 31), §§ 128–137, 147–160, and *supra*, n. 54.
[87]ECtHR, *Marckx v. Belgium*, no. 6833/74, judgment of 13 June 1979, Series A 31, see especially § 31.
[88]ECtHR, *Marckx*, (n. 88), § 14.
[89]ECtHR, *Marckx*, (n. 88), §§ 15–18.

The ECtHR found there to be violations of Article 8 of the ECtHR in the Belgian Civil Code's scheme of legal relations between parents and 'illegitimate' children[90] on the basis of quite an ambitious understanding of the contents of 'positive obligations inherent in an effective "respect" for family life'. 'This means,' the Court says, 'amongst other things, that when the State determines in its domestic legal system the regime applicable to certain family ties such as those between an unmarried mother and her child, it must act in a manner calculated to allow those concerned to lead a normal family life. As envisaged by Article 8, respect for family life implies in particular, in the Court's view, the existence in domestic law of legal safeguards that render possible as from the moment of birth the child's integration in his family. In this connection, the State has a choice of various means, but a law that fails to satisfy this requirement violates paragraph 1 of Article 8 without there being any call to examine it under paragraph 2.'[91] Belgian family law was insufficient in *furthering* the 'illegitimate' child's integration.

Since this judgment of 1979 the Court has, *mutatis mutandis*, relied on the principle worded in this paragraph in various other cases.

Only a few months later, in the case of *Airey v. Ireland*, the Court held that the applicant, who had been trying to obtain a decree of judicial separation from her husband (also known as a divorce *a mensa et thoro*) on the grounds of his alleged physical and mental cruelty to her and their children, had been the victim of a violation of Article 8. The Court took account of the legal situation in Ireland according to which, as regards marriage, husband and wife were in principle under a duty to cohabit but were entitled, in certain cases, to petition for a decree of judicial separation. In the eyes of the Court, this amounted to recognition of the fact that the protection of their private or family life would sometimes necessitate their being relieved from the duty to live together. Effective respect for private or family life, as the judgment must be understood, *positively* obliged Ireland to make this means of protection effectively accessible, when appropriate, to anyone who might wish to have recourse thereto. As it was not effectively accessible to the applicant, she was unable to seek recognition in law of her *de facto* separation from her husband and had therefore been the victim of a violation of Article 8.[92] Irish law, it can be said, failed to install an effective legal 'safety valve' for marital relations, one which would have released the couple from the duty to cohabit, and which would have resolved an otherwise unsolvable personal conflict.

---

[90]For details see ECtHR, *Marckx* (n. 88), §§35–37, 44–47, where the Court deals with questions of a violation of Article 8 taken alone; cf. also §§ 50–53, 61 as to there being no violation of Article 8 taken alone in the case of restricted patrimonial rights (however, there was found to be a violation of Article 14 in conjunction with Article 8, see §§ 54–59, 62).
[91]ECtHR, *Marckx* (n. 88), § 31. Cf. also the dissenting opinion of Judge Sir Gerald Fitzmaurice, *ibid.*, §§ 6, 7 (footnote 5).
[92]ECtHR, *Airey v. Ireland*, no. 6289/73, judgment of 9 October 1979, § 33, Series A 32, recalling the *Marckx* judgment at § 31.

In 1997, almost two decades later,[93] the principle worded in the *Marckx* judgment[94] was essential in determining the standard to be applied in the case of *X, Y and Z v. the United Kingdom*,[95] where the applicants' complaint was that domestic law did not enable X, a female-to-male transsexual who had undergone gender reassignment surgery in the Contracting State and who lived there as part of a family relationship (namely, with Y and her child Z), to be registered as the father of a child. In contrast to the European Commission of Human Rights,[96] the Court denied that there was an obligation under Article 8 to grant parental rights to transsexuals. The Court also did not see a common European standard with regard to the granting of parental rights to transsexuals. Nor did it recognise a generally shared approach amongst the High Contracting Parties with regard to the manner in which the law should reflect the social relationship between a child, conceived after the mother's impregnation with sperm from an anonymous donor, and the person who performs the role of father. Therefore, the Court found the law to be in a transitional stage and concluded that the respondent State had to be afforded a wide margin of appreciation.[97] This, however, did not absolve the respondent State from having to strike a fair balance between the competing interests of the individual and of the community as a whole.[98] At stake were a general interest in maintaining a coherent system of family law which places the best interests of the child at the forefront, on the one hand, and the disadvantages suffered by the applicants as a result of the refusal to recognise X in law as Z's 'father'.[99] Scrutiny of this balancing brought the Court to the final conclusion 'that Article 8 cannot, in this context, be taken to imply an obligation for the respondent State formally to recognise as the father of a child a person who is not the biological father.' Thus, the fact that the law of the United Kingdom did not allow special legal recognition of the relationship between X and Z did not amount to a failure to respect family life within the meaning of Article 8.[100]

It is essential to note that the balancing of interests is part of the investigation into whether or not positive obligations exist. Where the balancing of

---

[93]See also: ECtHR, *Kroon and Others v. the Netherlands*, no. 18535/91, judgment of 27 October 1994, §§ 28–40 (esp. § 32), Series A 297-C, (the case concerned the problem that Dutch law did not allow a mother to have entered in the register of births any statement that her husband at the time of her child's birth was not this child's father, this legal situation making it impossible for the biological father to recognise the child). The *Kroon* judgment, at § 32, expressly relies only on ECtHR, *Keegan* (n. 74), § 50, which itself, however, refers to ECtHR, *Marckx* (n. 88), § 31.
[94]*Supra* at n. 92.
[95]ECtHR, *X, Y and Z v. the United Kingdom*, no. 21830/93, judgment of 22 April 1997, §§ 41–44, RJD 1997–II.
[96]ECtHR, *X, Y and Z* (n. 95), § 30.
[97]ECtHR, *X, Y and Z* (n. 95), § 44.
[98]ECtHR, *X, Y and Z* (n. 95), § 41; see also the discussion of the interests ibid., at §§ 45–52.
[99]ECtHR, *X, Y and Z* (n. 95), §§ 46–47.
[100]ECtHR, *X, Y and Z* (n. 95), § 52.

interests is discussed, the judgment does not refer to Article 8(2) and thus cannot be understood as exploring a justification for an assumed interference with Article 8. This is spelled out more clearly in the Court's judgment in the case of *Rees v. the United Kingdom*, where it says: '*In determining whether or not a positive obligation exists*, regard must be had to the fair balance that has to be struck between the general interest of the community and the interests of the individual, the search for which balance is inherent in the whole of the Convention (…).'[101] The *Rees* judgment goes on to point out that '[i]n striking this balance the aims mentioned in the second paragraph of Article 8 may [*sic!*] be of a certain relevance, although this provision refers in terms only to "interferences" with the right protected by the first paragraph – in other words is concerned with the negative obligations flowing therefrom (…).'[102]

The Court's scheme for the evaluation of cases of allegedly insufficient promotion of Convention rights, as described here, can also be seen in more recent cases.

In *Odièvre v. France*, for example, the applicant complained of, under French law, being unable to obtain identifying information about her natural family and having thereby been prevented from finding out her personal history.[103] This complaint was examined under Article 8 ECHR as to its compatibility with the right to respect for private life.[104] The Court pointed to its established case-law 'that although the object of Article 8 ECHR is essentially that of protecting the individual against arbitrary interference by the public authorities, it does not merely compel the State to abstain from such interference: in addition to this primarily negative undertaking, there may be positive obligations inherent in an effective respect for private life. These obligations may involve the adoption of measures designed to secure respect for private life even in the sphere of the relations of individuals between themselves

---

[101]ECtHR, *Rees v. the United Kingdom*, no. 9532/81, judgment of 17 October 1986, § 37, Series A 106 (emphasis added) with reference to the *James and Others v. the United Kingdom*, no. 8793/79, judgment of 21 February 1986, Series A no. 98, p. 34, para. 50, and the *Sporrong and Lönnroth v. Sweden*, no. 7151/75 and 7152/75, judgment of 23 September 1982, Series A no. 52, p. 26, para. 69. See also ECtHR, *Cossey v. the United Kingdom*, no. 10843/84, judgment of 27 September 1990, § 37.

[102]ECtHR, *Rees* (n. 102), § 37 with reference to ECtHR, *Marckx* (n. 88), § 31

[103]ECtHR (GC), *Odièvre* (n. 70), §§ 13–14, 24.

[104]ECtHR (GC), *Odièvre* (n. 70), §§ 28 f. The perspective of family life does not apply according to the judgment, since the applicant's claim to be entitled, in the name of biological truth, to know her personal history was based on her inability to gain access to information about her origins and related identifying data: Article 8 protects a right to identity and personal development, and the right to establish and develop relationships with other human beings and the outside world. Matters of relevance to personal development include details of a person's identity as a human being and the vital interest protected by the Convention in obtaining information necessary to discover the truth concerning important aspects of one's personal identity, such as the identity of one's parents – and, as the judgment points out, also birth, and in particular the circumstances in which a child is born (the applicant had been denied information as to whether three sons had been born to her biological parents).

(...)'.[105] It then emphasises the impossibility of precisely defining the boundaries between the State's positive and negative obligations under Article 8. From here it points to the essential guideline for the evaluation of the case: Whether looking at the positive or the negative obligations, 'regard must be had to the fair balance which has to be struck between the competing interests; and in both contexts the State enjoys a certain margin of appreciation.' The Court then goes on to weigh the interests involved in cases in which a mother has given birth anonymously and the child, as an adult, seeks to trace its origins and find out about its biological family.[106] The core question was: Does the anonymously born child's 'right to know imply an obligation to divulge' on the side of the biological mother – and indirectly also on the side of the family.[107] The Court shows the answer to involve the interests not only of the child seeking the information but also of the biological mother as the respondent to the claim for information, and of third parties. Non-consensual disclosure could entail substantial risks, not only for the mother herself, but also for the adoptive family who brought up the applicant, and her natural father and siblings, each of whom also has a right to respect for his or her private and family life.[108] But things become even more complex when the general interest at stake is taken into account: The French legislature, the Court points out, has consistently sought to protect the mother's and child's health during pregnancy and birth and to avoid abortions, in particular illegal abortions, and children being abandoned other than under the proper procedure. The right to respect for life is thus one of the aims pursued by the French system. Consequently, 'a higher-ranking value guaranteed by the Convention' comes into play.[109] The ECtHR emphasises the single State's margin of appreciation as well as the complex and sensitive nature of the issue of access to information about one's origins. The judges find a diversity of practice among the legal systems and traditions of the Contracting States. They report that new French legislation will facilitate searches for information about a person's biological origins, possibly enabling the applicant to obtain the information she was seeking.[110] Before this background it is hardly surprising that the Court finds there to have been no violation of Article 8 of the Convention.[111, 112]

---

[105]ECtHR (GC), *Odièvre* (n. 70), § 40.

[106]ECtHR (GC), *Odièvre* (n. 70), §§ 41 et seq.

[107]ECtHR (GC), *Odièvre* (n. 70), § 45.

[108]ECtHR (GC), *Odièvre* (n. 70), § 44.

[109]ECtHR (GC), *Odièvre* (n. 70), § 45.

[110]ECtHR (GC), *Odièvre* (n. 70), §§ 46–49.

[111]ECtHR (GC), *Odièvre* (n. 70), § 49. Cf. also ECtHR, *Mikulić* (n. 69), §§ 56–66, where the Court investigated whether Croatia had violated its *positive obligations* under Article 8 ECHR (ibid., § 59). The applicant was trying to prove that the man whose daughter she alleged to be actually was her biological father. But Croatian law provided her with no other way of establishing this than judicial proceedings before a civil court, which lacked any means of compelling the alleged father to comply with a court order for DNA tests to be carried out. This, in the opinion of

What is troubling in the *Odièvre* case is the complexity of interests. The judgment obviously reacts by acknowledging a margin of appreciation open to the respondent State when dealing with the problem of access to information about one's biological family. But it is not only this. The difficulty in finding a solution is captured in the Court's question: '[D]oes the right to know imply an obligation to divulge?'[113] There is a conflict between the applicant's wish to find out about her family and the possible preference of the members of her biological family to remain anonymous. Fulfilling the one wish necessarily, as far as this goes, encroaches upon the other. Disturbingly, both interests fall within the scope of Article 8 ECHR, which, in principle, requires the State to respect them both. This seems to mean squaring the circle: The State must not pry into the confidential private sphere of the family members, and at the same, time it must enable the applicant to know about her roots. Whichever way the State goes, it either negatively interferes with the family members' sphere of confidentiality, or it denies the applicant 'the right to know', thus failing positively to promote the realisation of a Convention guarantee in her favour. The key to a solution, of course, is that both of the conflicting rights involved are subject to limitation according to Article 8(2) ECHR, which opens a way to 'balancing' the positions. Quite probably, it is exactly this 'blurredness' of the legal situation, in which the State is put by Article 8 ECHR, which makes the Court at the outset state that '[t]he boundaries between the State's positive and negative obligations under Article 8 do not lend themselves to precise definition.'[114]

Before turning to cases in which domestic legislation allegedly failed to provide protection *against interference* with Convention rights and freedoms from non-state sources (Group II, see below), it appears advisable to take a look at a case in a grey zone. In *Keegan v. Ireland*[115] the applicant had

---

the Court, was only in conformity with the principle of proportionality if it provided alternative means enabling an independent authority to determine the paternity claim speedily. As no such procedure was available to the applicant, domestic law did not strike a fair balance between the right of the applicant to have her uncertainty as to her personal identity eliminated without unnecessary delay and that of her supposed father not to undergo DNA tests. Consequently, the Court considered that the protection of the interests involved was not proportionate and found the Croatian authorities, having failed to secure to the applicant the 'respect' for the applicant's private life to which she was entitled under the Convention, to have violated Article 8 of the Convention.

[112]See also ECtHR, *Tysiąc v. Poland*, no. 5410/03, judgment of 20 March 2007, especially §§ 103–130, where the Court – having assessed the case (especially) against the positive obligations of the State to secure the physical integrity of mothers-to-be (ibid., § 107) – found that it had not been demonstrated that Polish law contained any effective mechanisms capable of determining whether the conditions for obtaining a lawful abortion had been met in the applicant's case (ibid., § 124). It created for the applicant a situation of prolonged uncertainty. The authorities were held to have failed to comply with their positive obligations to secure to the applicant the effective respect for her private life (ibid., § 129).

[113]ECtHR (GC), *Odièvre* (n. 70), § 45.

[114]ECtHR (GC), *Odièvre* (n. 70), § 40.

[115]ECtHR, *Keegan* (n. 74).

instituted proceedings before the Irish courts to be appointed guardian of his biological daughter, to whom his former fiancée had given birth after the relationship had broken down. Only as guardian would the applicant under Irish law have been able to challenge the adoption of his child, for which the mother had made arrangements. The applicant, *inter alia*, maintained that the State failed to respect his family life by facilitating the secret placement of his daughter for adoption without his knowledge or consent and by failing to create a legal nexus between himself and his daughter from the moment of birth.[116] It is hardly surprising that in this case the Court found the obligations inherent in Article 8 to be 'closely intertwined'.[117] The State was actively involved in the adoption process; thus, there was more than just a deficiency in the way that the biological father was permitted to participate in the adoption proceedings or in the way that he could establish a permanent relationship with his daughter. In the Court's eyes, '[t]he fact that Irish law permitted the secret placement of the child for adoption without the applicant's knowledge or consent, leading to the bonding of the child with the proposed adopters and to the subsequent making of an adoption order, amounted to an interference with his right to respect for family life.'[118] Although one might discern positive obligations involved in this setting, the Court obviously regards these as overridden by the State's (active!) interference. 'Such interference is permissible only if the conditions set out in paragraph 2 of Article 8 are satisfied.'[119] It considered it as 'not necessary to examine whether Article 8 imposed a positive obligation on Ireland to confer an automatic but defeasible right to guardianship on natural fathers such as the applicant.'[120]

The Keegan case is mentioned here to show how well justified it is when the Court time and again repeats its insight[121] that the boundaries between the State's positive and negative obligations under this provision do not lend themselves to precise definition.[122] This is so even in cases in which the applicant alleges the respondent State not to have fulfilled its positive obligation to promote the realisation of a Convention guarantee.[123]

---

[116]ECtHR, *Keegan* (n. 74), § 46.
[117]ECtHR, *Keegan* (n. 74), § 51.
[118]ECtHR, *Keegan* (n. 74), § 51.
[119]ECtHR, *Keegan* (n. 74), § 51.
[120]ECtHR, *Keegan* (n. 74), § 52. The court (ibid., §§ 53–55) found the State not to have met the requirements of Article 8(2) ECHR.
[121]Already mentioned *supra* at n. 69.
[122]As expressly pointed out by ECtHR, *Keegan* (n. 74), § 49.
[123]As an example of how difficult it is to distinguish negative from positive obligations cf. also ECtHR, *Uçar v. Turkey*, no. 52392/9, judgment of 11 April 2006, § 137–141: In the absence of a legislative framework providing concrete and effective protection against a violation of Article 8 ECHR, the Court held that, in the circumstances of the case, the detention of Cemal Uçar in police custody for nine days without contact with his family constituted a violation of Article 8 (ibid., § 141). What is interesting, the State is not regarded to have prevented Cemal Uçar and the applicant, his father, from communicating, although Cemal Uçar had been detained by the police. This quite probably rests on the Court's observation that there was nothing in the case file

3.4.2 Group II: Insufficient protection provided by legislation against private interferences

The second group of cases involving positive obligations starts with the case of *Young, James and Webster v. The United Kingdom*. It was decided on 13 August 1981,[124] somewhat more than two years after *Marckx v. Belgium*. Mr Young, Mr James and Mr Webster were former employees of the British Railways Board ('British Rail'). In 1975, a 'closed shop' agreement was concluded between British Rail and three trade unions, providing that thenceforth membership of one of those unions was a condition of employment. The applicants failed to satisfy this condition and were dismissed in 1976.[125] The Court summarises a 'closed shop' as being 'an undertaking or workplace in which, as a result of an agreement or arrangement between one or more trade unions and one or more employers or employers' associations, employees of a certain class are in practice required to be or become members of a specified union. The employer is not under any legal obligation to consult or obtain the consent of individual employees directly before such an agreement or arrangement is put into effect. Closed shop agreements and arrangements vary considerably in both their form and their content; one distinction that is often drawn is that between the "pre-entry" shop (the employee must join the union before engaged) and the "post-entry" shop (he must join within a reasonable time after being engaged), the latter being more common.'[126] At the time of the decision, the institution of the closed shop had been of long standing in the United Kingdom. In the years before, closed shop arrangements had become more formalised and the number of employees covered thereby had increased (3.75 million in the 1960s and 5 million in 1980, approximately).[127]

Since the 1920s the British courts had recognised the legitimacy of the trade union object of advancing the union's interests even to the point of enforcing the dismissal, or a ban on the hiring, of non-union employees. However, it was an unlawful conspiracy at common law to pursue a closed shop against individuals beyond the point which the courts regarded as the defence of genuine trade union interests.[128] The Industrial Relations Act 1971 had then

---

which would prove that the applicant and his son had requested to be authorised to contact each other and that their requests had been dismissed (*ibid.*, § 140). The judgment points to the absence of pertinent regulations and finds the Government not to have specified the means at Cemal Uçar's disposal which would have *enabled* him to communicate rapidly with his family following his detention in police custody. It is furthermore obviously regarded as part of the State's *inaction* that after the disappearance of his son the applicant had received no reply to his numerous petitions as to his son's whereabouts for more than one month did not amount to an interference with the applicant's right under Article 8 (*ibid.*, § 138).
[124]ECtHR, *Young, James and Webster v. The United Kingdom*, nos. 7601/76, 7806/77, judgment of 13 August 1981, Series A 44.
[125]ECtHR, *Young, James and Webster* (n. 125), § 12 (see also §§ 29–31).
[126]ECtHR, *Young, James and Webster* (n. 125), § 13.
[127]ECtHR, *Young, James and Webster* (n. 125), § 13.
[128]ECtHR, *Young, James and Webster* (n. 125), § 14 with reference to *Huntley v. Thornton* [1957] 1 All England Law Reports 234; *Morgan v. Fry* [1967] 2 All England Law Reports 386.

made the operation of the majority of closed shops unlawful,[129] but it was repealed by the Trade Union and Labour Relations Act 1974 ('TULRA'), which however did not fully restore the pre-1971 conditions as it maintained the protection against unfair dismissal.[130] Subsequent modifications of the law led to the legal situation at the time of the case that the dismissal of an employee for refusal to join a specified union in a closed shop situation was to be regarded as fair for the purposes of the law on unfair dismissal. However, effective 15 August 1980, this rule became subject to three exceptions whereby such dismissals were regarded as unfair under certain conditions.[131]

All three applicants had been dismissed by British Rail after they had declared that they were not willing to join one of the trade unions with which British Rail had concluded a closed shop agreement.[132] The applicants alleged that the treatment to which they had been subjected gave rise, *inter alia*, to violations of Article 11 of the Convention. It is this provision on which the ECtHR's judgment concentrates when trying the merits of the case.[133] Before, however, it deals with the problem of whether responsibility could be attributed to the respondent State, the United Kingdom.[134] This was not at all clear since it had not been an (immediate) interference by the State which had caused the applicants' dismissals. Rather, it was the British Railway Board ('British Rail') which had given the applicants notice of their dismissal. The Court does not embark on an investigation of whether these dismissals might be attributable to the United Kingdom herself. There did seem to be cause for answering this question as the applicants had argued that the State might be

---

[129] ECtHR, *Young, James and Webster* (n. 125), §§ 16–18.

[130] ECtHR, *Young, James and Webster* (n. 125), §§ 20–22.

[131] These conditions being: (a) the employee objects on grounds of conscience or other deeply-held personal conviction to being a member of any or a particular union; or (b) the employee belonged, before the closed shop agreement or arrangement came into effect, to the class of employees covered thereby and has not been a member of a union in accordance therewith; or (c) in the case of a closed shop agreement or arrangement taking effect after 15 August 1980, either it has not been approved by the vote in a ballot of not less than 80 per cent of the employees affected or, although it is so approved, the employee has not since the balloting been a member of a union in accordance therewith. See ECtHR, *Young, James and Webster* (n. 125), § 24 (see also § 23).

[132] ECtHR, *Young, James and Webster* (n. 125), §§ 33–35; 36–39; 40–44. The ECtHR distinguishes facts of the later case of *Sibson v. the United Kingdom* from the *Young, James and Webster* case, coming to the conclusion that Mr Sibson was not subjected to a form of treatment striking at the very substance of the freedom of association guaranteed by Article 11 ECHR (ECtHR, *Sibson v. the United Kingdom*, no. 14327/88, judgment of 20 April 1993, § 29).

[133] One of the focal questions was whether Article 11 ECHR guarantees not only freedom of association, including the right to form and to join trade unions, in the positive sense, but also, by implication, a 'negative right' not to be compelled to join an association. See ECtHR, *Young, James and Webster* (n. 125), §§ 51–55, see also the concurring opinion of Judges *Ganshof an der Meersch, Bindschedler-Robert, Liesch, Gölcüklü, Matscher, Pinheiro, Farinha* and *Pettiti* and the dissenting opinion of Judge *Sørensen*, joined by Judges *Thòr Vilhjàlmsson* and *Lagergren*.

[134] ECtHR, *Young, James and Webster* (n. 125), § 48.

responsible on the ground that it should be regarded as employer or that British Rail was under its control.[135] But the Court sees no call for such an examination as it regards the State's responsibility clearly to be established on a different basis:

> Under Article 1 (art. 1) of the Convention, each Contracting State 'shall secure to everyone within [its] jurisdiction the rights and freedoms defined in ... [the] Convention'; hence, if a violation of one of those rights and freedoms is the result of non-observance of that obligation in the enactment of domestic legislation, the responsibility of the State for that violation is engaged. Although the proximate cause of the events giving rise to this case was the 1975 agreement between British Rail and the railway unions, it was the domestic law in force at the relevant time that made lawful the treatment of which the applicants complained. The responsibility of the respondent State for any resultant breach of the Convention is thus engaged on this basis. ...[136]

As such, the Court considers the State's responsibility for the 'treatment of the applicants' to result from the legal framework it had set up for closed shop agreements to operate. It is irrelevant whether British Rail might possibly be regarded as part of the State. The closed shop agreement could just as well have been concluded between a private employer and a trade union. For the three applicants it amounted to a threat of dismissal involving loss of livelihood simply because they were not willing to join one of the trade unions involved in the 'closed shop'; this was especially oppressive since the applicants had been engaged by British Rail before any obligation to join a particular trade union had been introduced.[137] When the Court finds there to have been an interference with Article 11 ECHR,[138] it does not in any way qualify the closed shop agreement or the resultant dismissals as immediate acts of the State. Nonetheless it considers the State as responsible. Obviously, in the Court's eyes, this responsibility was established by a lack of protective provisions in the State's legal order, a lack of legal safeguards against employees being compelled to join trade unions against their will. The basis of such responsibility – if it is independent of any immediate involvement of the State in bringing about the specific situation of compulsion – can only be *positive obligations* binding the State.

Positive obligations resulting from the Convention were also involved in a line of cases beginning with the *Marckx* case, as seen above (Group I). But there is a decisive difference in the way in which the Court deals with these obligations in the *Young, James and Webster* case. Here, the respondent

---

[135]ECtHR, *Young, James and Webster* (n. 125), § 49.
[136]ECtHR, *Young, James and Webster* (n. 125), § 49.
[137]ECtHR, *Young, James and Webster* (n. 125), § 55.
[138]ECtHR, *Young, James and Webster* (n. 125), § 55.

State's responsibility is acknowledged for the reason of having given non-State actors leeway to behave in a way which *de facto* infringes a right guaranteed by the Convention. Yet in *Young, James and Webster* these two elements, the State's responsibility and the infringement by a private legal subject, do not automatically add up to a violation of the Convention right. Rather, the Court merely concludes that there has been an 'interference',[139] nothing more, and then goes on to investigate the possibility of a *justification* under Article 11(2) ECHR.[140] The *Young, James and Webster* judgment concentrates on whether the interference was 'necessary in a democratic society',[141] eventually finding that the detriment suffered by the three applicants 'went further than was required to achieve a proper balance between the conflicting interests of those involved and cannot be regarded as proportionate to the aims being pursued'.[142]

As shown above, in the *Marckx* line of cases (Group I), the balancing of interests is part of the investigation into whether or not positive obligations exist.[143] It is *not* a matter of justifying an interference *after* such an interference has been clearly established – and thus not an instance of applying Article 8(2) ECHR. The concept of 'interference' as such is strictly linked to the negative obligations flowing from a Convention right. Clauses in the Convention's provisions allowing the Contracting States to restrict rights and freedoms are therefore not considered to apply to positive obligations.[144]

In contrast, the *Young, James and Webster* judgment, after finding there to have been an interference (on the basis of positive obligations), applies paragraph 2 of Article 11, which defines the scope of restrictions on the freedom of association. Thus, positive obligations here serve the sole purpose of establishing responsibility for a *prima facie* violation of a Convention right, which is only the first step in the two-step test of asking 1) whether there has been an interference, and 2) whether this is justified. This test defines the traditional judicial technique employed by the Court in the case of *negative* Convention obligations.

The constructive idea behind the *Young, James and Webster* judgment might be brought to the surface more clearly by looking at a fairly recent judgment expressly relying on this case. In *VgT Verein gegen Tierfabriken v. Switzerland* the applicant association wished to have a television commercial broadcast by the Swiss Radio and Television Company (*Schweizerische Radio- und Fernsehgesellschaft – 'SRF'*). The intention of the television spot was to induce consumers to eat less meat for the sake of protecting animals. Therefore, the applicant association sent a videocassette to the Commercial

---

[139]ECtHR, *Young, James and Webster* (n. 125), §§ 55, 57.
[140]ECtHR, *Young, James and Webster* (n. 125), §§ 58–65.
[141]ECtHR, *Young, James and Webster* (n. 125), §§ 62–65.
[142]ECtHR, *Young, James and Webster* (n. 125), § 65.
[143]*Supra*, at n. 102.
[144]*Supra*, at n. 103.

Television Company (*AG für das Werbefernsehen* – '*AGW*') responsible for television advertising. AGW, however, declined to broadcast the commercial in light of its 'clear political character'.[145]

In its judgment, the ECtHR observes that AGW is a company established under Swiss private law. Under Article 1 ECHR, therefore, the issue arose whether the company's refusal to accept the commercial fell within the respondent State's jurisdiction. The Swiss Government had pointed out that AGW, when deciding whether or not to acquire advertising, was acting as a private party enjoying contractual freedom.[146] The Court, relying on its *Marckx* judgment,[147] starts out by saying that 'in addition to the primarily negative undertaking of a State to abstain from interference in Convention guarantees, 'there may be positive obligations inherent' in such guarantees. The responsibility of a State may then be engaged as a result of not observing its obligation to enact domestic legislation.'[148] However, as already mentioned,[149] it refuses to theorise on the extent to which the Convention guarantees should be extended to relations between private individuals *inter se*.[150] Then it focuses on sec. 18 of the Swiss Federal Radio and Television Act, which prohibits 'political advertising'. Both AGW and the Swiss Federal Court had relied on this provision. The ECtHR concludes:

> Domestic law, as interpreted in the last resort by the Federal Court, therefore made lawful the treatment of which the applicant association complained (see *Marckx* and *Young, James and Webster*, cited above). In effect, political speech by the applicant association *was prohibited*. In the circumstances of the case, the Court finds that the responsibility of the respondent State within the meaning of Article 1 of the Convention for any resultant breach of Article 10 may be engaged on this basis.[151]

Consequently, the Court considered the refusal to broadcast the applicant association's commercial – although it was the act of a private entity – to amount 'to an 'interference by public authority' in the exercise of the rights guaranteed by Article 10.'[152] From here the Court went on to investigate whether the interference was justified under Article 10(2) ECHR, thus applying the qualifying clause. Therefore, it applied a test which would normally be used to evaluate whether a State Party had failed to fulfil its negative obligations, i.e. the duty to respect a Convention guarantee.

---

[145] *VGT Verein gegen Tierfabriken* (n. 66), §§ 8 et seq.
[146] *VGT Verein gegen Tierfabriken* (n. 66), § 44.
[147] ECtHR, *Marckx* (n. 88), § 49.
[148] *VGT Verein gegen Tierfabriken* (n. 66), § 45.
[149] *Supra*, at n. 71.
[150] *VGT Verein gegen Tierfabriken* (n. 66), § 46.
[151] *VGT Verein gegen Tierfabriken* (n. 66), § 47 (emphasis added).
[152] *VGT Verein gegen Tierfabriken* (n. 66), § 48.

If we reconsider the situation within Switzerland, this can be reconstructed quite consistently. Swiss law contained a provision prohibiting 'political advertising' on television. Such a provision qualifies the rights under Article 10 ECHR. It restricts the SRF in what they are allowed to broadcast. It also bars AGW, as the company specially incorporated under private law in order to deal with all aspects of the acquisition and organisation of television advertising for SRF, from performing, perhaps even from concluding, a contract on the broadcasting of a political commercial. As such, one could say that it was sec. 18 of the Swiss Federal Radio and Television Act which closed this 'channel' of broadcasting, and AGW was only complying with this provision. In other words, Swiss law strictly predetermined AGW's reaction to the applicant company's request to have its commercial broadcast. They had no choice but to decline. Consequently, it is convincing to retrace this behaviour to the enactment of the provision, and to hold the Swiss State responsible for the refusal to broadcast the spot.

This is exactly where the case differs from that of *Young, James and Webster*. There British law merely *did not forbid* closed-shop agreements. It 'allowed' them, but it did not prescribe them. Unions and employers had the *option* of concluding such an agreement. In other words, the law gave them freedom, to decide for themselves how to design a collective agreement. This, however, actually amounts to the law's respecting the *liberty* of unions and employers, and it is therefore quite difficult to attribute their choice of a closed-shop agreement to the State and consider it in any way to be an interference by public authority. Rather, this is the typical constellation in which a case under the Convention can arise only insofar as positive obligations are concerned – in the specific case: positive obligations to protect workers unwilling to join a union against *de facto* being forced into membership.

The factual constellation of *Young, James and Webster* is more similar to the kind found in *X and Y v. the Netherlands*,[153] where Dutch criminal law was considered to be insufficient in its protection against rape. There the Netherlands were found to have failed to fulfil their positive obligations under Article 8 ECHR because the Dutch Criminal Code contained no specific provision determining it to be an offence to make sexual advances to the mentally handicapped.[154] An *interference* by a public authority is not established. Different from *VgT Verein gegen Tierfabriken*, the act of a private person is not attributed to the respondent state. In *X and Y v. the Netherlands*, the Court rather finds there to exist a gap in Dutch criminal law. The Netherlands *failed to provide* an effective deterrence against rape and thus sufficient practical protection of the applicant Y's private life. As a

---

[153]*Supra*, at n. 47 et seq.
[154]ECtHR, *X and Y v. the Netherlands* (n. 47), § 28.

consequence, the Court found Y to have been the victim of a violation of Article 8 ECHR.[155]

In this context the Convention is read as leaving it up to the Contracting States to choose 'the means calculated to secure compliance with Article 8 in the sphere of the relations of individuals between themselves', this being 'in principle a matter that falls within the Contracting States' margin of appreciation.'[156] The Court underlines that 'there are different ways of ensuring 'respect for private life', and the nature of the State's obligation will depend on the particular aspect of private life that is at issue.' Recourse to criminal law 'is not necessarily the only answer.'[157] The State is obliged to act as the protector of potential rape victims, standing on their side. As the defender of Article 8 ECHR, it has different means in its hands. From these it must choose one or several. In some cases the State may, to a certain degree, even leave it up to private individuals to protect themselves against interference by other private parties. Thus it has discretion – albeit only insofar as practical and effective protection is achieved. In *X and Y v. the Netherlands*, the Court is only able to establish a violation because it judges effective deterrence against rape to be 'indispensable', thus leaving the protector no option of inaction. Furthermore, in the Court's eyes such deterrence 'can be achieved only by criminal-law provisions; indeed, it is by such provisions that the matter is normally regulated.'[158] The State's discretion thus is narrowed down. It needs to resort to criminal law.[159] It has not done so. Therefore, it has violated a positive obligation under Article 8 ECHR.

The question of justification under Article 8(2) does not arise. Instead, the issue of what a State is able to do is part of the investigation into its arsenal of protective means. A violation of positive obligations under the Convention can only be established where a balancing of the interests involved (which needs to take the aspects mentioned in qualification clauses such as Article 8(2) ECHR into account)[160] proves that the State clearly failed to perform its role as the defender of Convention guarantees against infringements by

---

[155]ECtHR, *X and Y v. the Netherlands* (n. 47), § 30. Cf. also ECtHR, *Schüssel v. Austria*, no. 42409/98, decision of 21 February 2002: 'The Court recalls that Article 8 taken in conjunction with the obligation to secure the effective exercise of Convention rights imposed by Article 1 of the Convention, may involve a positive obligation on the State to provide a measure of protection for an individual's private life in relation to the exercise by third parties of the right to freedom of expression bearing in mind the duties and responsibilities referred to in Article 10. The absence of a remedy in relation to the publication of information relating to private affairs may constitute a lack of respect for private life (…).'

[156]ECtHR, *X and Y v. the Netherlands* (n. 47), § 24.

[157]ECtHR, *X and Y v. the Netherlands* (n. 47), § 24.

[158]Cf. ECtHR, *X and Y v. the Netherlands* (n. 47), § 27.

[159]ECtHR, *X and Y v. the Netherlands* (n. 47), § 27, implies that consistency might also be required: 'Moreover, …, this is in fact an area in which the Netherlands has generally opted for a system of protection based on the criminal law.'

[160]See *supra*, at n. 102.

private individuals, by either being completely idle although action is called for, or having chosen from its options one which is definitely ineffective or impractical.

3.5 Failure of state authorities other than the legislature to fulfil positive obligations

Breaches of positive obligations are not limited to a State's failure to enact legislative provisions effecting protection of rights guaranteed under the Convention. Administrative agencies and the courts can fall short as well when they apply existing law.

3.5.1 Failure of administrative authorities to comply with positive obligations

Positive obligations may require administrative authorities to respond to an individual's request or obvious need for protection against the activity of other individuals or other private entities. The *Osman* case[161] examined above is one example. There are others: In *López Ostra v. Spain* [162] the ECtHR found that a Spanish municipality had failed to protect neighbouring residents against emissions from a waste-treatment plant. In the case of *Öneryıldız v. Turkey*[163] a methane explosion on the site of a municipal rubbish tip led to a land-slide destroying houses and killing thirty-nine people. The deaths and destruction were attributed to a lack of precautions against the illegal building of houses in the slum quarter of Kazım Karabekir in Ümraniye, a district of Istanbul adjacent to the rubbish tip. The Court found the circumstances of the case to 'give rise to a violation of Article 2 of the Convention in its substantive aspect.'[164] Similarly, in *Budayeva and Others v. Russia*, the authorities were considered to have 'failed to discharge the positive obligation to establish a legislative *and administrative* framework designed to provide effective deterrence against threats to the right to life as required by Article 2 of the Convention' because the measures taken by authorities against mud-slides in the town of Tyrnauz, in the Elbrus District of the Republic of Kabardino-Balkariya, Russia, were regarded as insufficient.[165] In *Guerra and Others v. Italy*[166] a factory had been producing fertilisers and caprolactam releasing large quantities of inflammable gas and

---

[161]*Supra*, at n. 29 et seq.
[162]ECtHR, *López Ostra* (n. 54), §§ 51–58.
[163]ECtHR (GC), *Öneryıldız* (n. 31), §§ 89–90, 97–110.
[164]ECtHR (GC), *Öneryıldız* (n. 31), § 110.
[165]ECtHR, *Budayeva* (n. 31), §§ 128–137, 147–160 (quotation taken from § 159, emphasis added).
[166]ECtHR, *Guerra and Others v. Italy*, no. 14967/89, judgment of 19 February 1988, ECHR.

other toxic substances, including arsenic trioxide. At one time in the past, following the explosion of the scrubbing tower for the ammonia synthesis gases, several tonnes of potassium carbonate and bicarbonate solution, containing arsenic trioxide, had escaped and 150 people had to be hospitalised on account of acute arsenic poisoning. The ECtHR held that the direct effect of the toxic emissions on the applicants' right to respect for their private and family life meant that Article 8 ECHR was applicable.[167] The rights guaranteed, however, were not interfered with by public authorities. The respondent state was held to have breached Article 8 ECHR by not communicating to the applicants essential information which would have enabled them to assess the risks they and their families might run if they continued to live in Manfredonia, a town particularly exposed to danger in the event of an accident within the confines of the factory.[168]

Of a different nature is the case of *I v. Finland*.[169] The applicant, who worked in the same (public) hospital where she was treated, complained that the district health authority had failed in its duties to establish a register from which her confidential patient information could not be disclosed.[170] The Court considered that the general provisions in Finnish legislation aimed at protecting sensitive personal data, had they been applied strictly, 'would have constituted a substantial safeguard for the applicant's right secured by Article 8 of the Convention, making it possible, in particular, to police strictly access to any disclosure of health records.'[171] The hospital's health record, however, was insufficient. It was not possible to retroactively clarify the use of patient records. Furthermore, the prevailing regime in the hospital allowed for the records to be read also by staff not directly involved in the applicant's treatment.[172] Consequently, the Court found that the State failed in its positive obligation under Article 8(1) ECHR to ensure respect for the applicant's private life.[173]

In the case *Botta v. Italy* the ECtHR shows that the Court tries to keep the scope of positive obligations within limits. Relying on Article 8 ECHR, Mr Botta asserted his right to gain access to the beach and the sea at a place distant from his normal place of residence during his holidays. The Court considered this allegation to concern 'interpersonal relations of such broad and indeterminate scope that there can be no conceivable direct link between the measures the State was urged to take in order to make good the omissions of

---

[167]ECtHR, *Guerra and Others* (n. 167), § 57.
[168]ECtHR, *Guerra and Others* (n. 167), § 60. Interesting is the test the Court applies: It considered it necessary only to ascertain whether the national authorities took the necessary steps to ensure effective protection of the applicants' right to respect for their private and family life as guaranteed by Article 8 (ibid., § 58, with reference to ECtHR, *López Ostra* (n. 54), § 55).
[169]ECtHR, *I v. Finland*, no. 20511/03, judgment of 17 July 2008,
[170]ECtHR, *I v. Finland* (n. 170), § 26.
[171]ECtHR, *I v. Finland* (n. 170), § 40 (as to the special sensitivity of medical data, see § 38).
[172]ECtHR, *I v. Finland* (n. 170), § 41.
[173]ECtHR, *I v. Finland* (n. 170), § 48.

the private bathing establishments and the applicant's private life.' Article 8 ECHR was, therefore, considered inapplicable.[174]

3.5.2 Failure of courts of justice to comply with positive obligations

The discussion of the ECtHR's *Von Hannover* judgment in Chapter 2 has already shown positive obligations under the Convention to reach down to the Contracting State's courts of justice.

3.5.2.1 Cases outside the field of tort law

While the *Von Hannover* judgment dealt with (tort) law protection of the right to autonomy as to one's image, the Convention has been seen to affect the way domestic courts deal with contractual relations between private parties. In *van Kück v. Germany*,[175] the applicant brought civil proceedings against her private health insurance company. She claimed reimbursement of medical expenses accrued for gender reassignment measures, namely hormone treatment and gender reassignment surgery.[176] Before the ECtHR she alleged that, in the context of the dispute with the insurance company, the German courts had failed to give appropriate consideration to her transsexuality.[177] Although a violation of the right to a fair hearing under Article 6(1) ECHR had already been established,[178] the Court examined whether or not the German courts had failed to discharge the State's *positive obligations* under Article 8 when assessing whether the medical expenses, the reimbursement of which the applicant was claiming, had been necessary.[179] It found that no fair balance had been struck between the interests of the private health insurance company, on the one side, and the interests of the individual, on the other,[180] because the courts had placed the burden on the applicant to prove the medical necessity of her hormone treatment and gender reassignment surgery. As one of the most intimate areas of private life was concerned, this appeared to be disproportionate.[181] Consequently, Article 8 ECHR had been violated.[182] It is remarkable that positive obligations under Article 8 are regarded to influence the burden-of-proof rules in contract law. These rules,

---

[174]ECtHR, *Botta v. Italy*, no. 21439/93, judgment of 24 February 1998, § 35, ECHR 1998–I.
[175]ECtHR, *van Kück v. Germany*, no. 35968/97, judgment of 12 June 2003, ECHR 2003–VII.
[176]ECtHR, *van Kück* (n. 176), § 53.
[177]ECtHR, *van Kück* (n. 176), § 73.
[178]ECtHR, *van Kück* (n. 176), §§ 46–65.
[179]ECtHR, *van Kück* (n. 176), § 75. It is unclear why the Court in the end concludes that the German authorities overstepped the margin of appreciation afforded to them 'under paragraph 2 of Article 8', as this paragraph would not be directly applicable in the context of positive obligations.
[180]ECtHR, *van Kück* (n. 176), §§ 79–85.
[181]ECtHR, *van Kück* (n. 176), § 82.
[182]ECtHR, *van Kück* (n. 176), § 86.

while affecting court proceedings, are understood to be part of substantive law. Convention law, then, quite excitingly trickles down into the contractual relations of private parties.

Even more amazing is the case of *Pla and Puncernau v. Andorra*.[183] It concerned the Andorran courts' interpretation of a testamentary disposition drafted in 1939 and executed in 1995. The Andorran High Court of Justice had inferred a negative intention on the part of the testatrix and concluded that since she did not expressly state that she was not excluding adopted sons this meant that she did intend to exclude them. The ECtHR found that this interpretation of the testamentary disposition appeared over contrived and contrary to the general legal principle that where a statement is unambiguous there is no need to examine the intention of the person who made it.[184] The Court is aware that it is not dealing with the compatibility of Andorran statutory provisions with the Convention, but essentially with the act of a private person.[185] This is probably what induces it to point to the Contracting States' positive obligations under the Convention.[186] It almost seems as though the Court saw itself under the obligation to step in and protect the heirs and the testatrix's last will:

> Admittedly, the Court is not in theory required to settle disputes of a purely private nature. That being said, in exercising the European supervision incumbent on it, it cannot remain passive where a national court's interpretation of a legal act, be it a testamentary disposition, a private contract, a public document, a statutory provision or an administrative practice appears unreasonable, arbitrary or, as in the present case, blatantly inconsistent with the prohibition of discrimination established by Article 14 and more broadly with the principles underlying the Convention (…).[187]

In this context the Court analyses the Andorran High Court of Justice's interpretation of the testamentary disposition in question to have had 'the effect of depriving the first applicant of his right to inherit under his grandmother's estate and benefiting his cousin's daughters in this regard.'[188] Since the testamentary disposition, as worded by the testatrix, made no distinction between biological and adopted children the ECtHR saw no necessity to

---

[183]ECtHR, *Pla and Puncernau v. Andorra*, no. 69498/01, judgment of 13 July 2004, ECHR 2004–VIII. For a thorough critical analysis of the the judgment see *Kay* (2005).

[184]ECtHR, *Pla and Puncernau* (n. 184), § 58.

[185]ECtHR, *Pla and Puncernau* (n. 184), §§ 43–44.

[186]ECtHR, *Pla and Puncernau* (n. 184), § 43 (concerning Article 8), § 62 (unclear as to which right is referred to).

[187]ECtHR, *Pla and Puncernau* (n. 184), § 58.

[188]ECtHR, *Pla and Puncernau* (n. 184), § 60 (where the effects for the second applicant are also shown).

interpret it as excluding adopted sons, and continues: 'Such an interpretation therefore amounts to the judicial deprivation of an adopted child's inheritance rights.'[189] This sentence seems to qualify the Andorran High Court of Justice's failure as an interference – at least with Article 14 in conjunction with Article 8 ECHR. Then again, the Court points to the States' positive obligations and, with a view to wills, says:

> [A]ny interpretation, if interpretation there must be, should endeavour to ascertain the testator's intention and render the will effective, while bearing in mind that 'the testator cannot be presumed to have meant what he did not say' and without overlooking the importance of interpreting the testamentary disposition in the manner that most closely corresponds to domestic law and to the Convention as interpreted in the Court's case-law.[190]

This need not be explored any further as it is the influence of the Convention on tort law which is the concern.

3.5.2.2 Cases within the field of tort law

Let us now turn to the *Von Hannover* judgment once again. In the Court's opinion, sec. 23(1) KUG had 'to be interpreted narrowly to ensure that the State complies with its positive obligation under the Convention to protect

---

[189]ECtHR, *Pla and Puncernau* (n. 184), § 60.

[190]§ 62. See also the dissenting opinion Judge *Garlicki*, ibid., according to whom the authors of the Convention did not intend this instrument to possess a 'third-party effect' (he refers to see *Drzemczewski* (1979), p. 168). He concedes that according to the ECtHR's case-law there nevertheless 'may be certain positive obligations of the State to adopt measures designed to secure respect for Convention rights, even in the sphere of the relations of individuals between themselves' (quoting ECtHR, *X and Y v. the Netherlands* (n. 47), § 23); this he addresses as an 'indirect third-party effect'. His conclusion that the testatrix's will ought to have been respected (which he obviously understands as excluding adopted sons from becoming heirs) rests on his position that 'it seems equally obvious that the level of protection against a private action cannot be the same as the level of protection against State action. The very fact that, under the Convention, the State may be prohibited from taking certain action (such as introducing inheritance distinctions between children – see *Marckx v. Belgium*, no. 6833/74, judgment of 13 June 1979, Series A no. 31; *Vermeire v. Belgium*, no. 12849/87, judgment of 29 November 1991, Series A no. 214-C; and *Mazurek v. France*, no. 34406/97, judgment of 01 February 2000, ECHR 2000–II) does not mean that private persons are similarly precluded from taking such action. In other words, what is prohibited for the State need not necessarily also be prohibited for individuals. This is particularly visible in regard to 'purely' private-law relations, such as inheritance. The whole idea of a will is to depart from the general system of inheritance, that is, to discriminate between potential heirs. But at the same time, the testator must retain a degree of freedom to dispose of his/her property and this freedom is protected by both Article 8 of the Convention and Article 1 of Protocol No. 1. Thus, in my opinion, the rule should be that the State must give effect to private testamentary dispositions, save in exceptional circumstances where the disposition may be said to be repugnant to the fundamental ideals of the Convention or to aim at the destruction of the rights and freedoms set forth therein. As in respect of all exceptional circumstances, however, their presence must be clearly demonstrated and cannot be assumed.'

private life and the right to control the use of one's image.'[191] Secs. 22, 23 KUG protect the individual's right to his or her image and restrict the possibility of other private parties publicly to present and disseminate a person's images; thus they form part of non-contractual private-law relations and stand as part of German *Deliktsrecht*, tort law.

The criteria on which the German courts based their decisions, i.e. the requirements they had set up for the protection against a person's image publicly being shown or disseminated, were not regarded as sufficient to protect the applicant's private life effectively. Recall that the German courts held that the applicant, as an 'absolute' figure of contemporary society could – in the name of freedom of the press and the public interest – not rely on the protection of her private life unless she was in a secluded place out of the public eye and, moreover, succeeded in proving it. Where that was not the case, she had to accept being photographed at almost any time, systematically, and that the photos could then be very widely disseminated even if the photos and accompanying articles related exclusively to details of her private life.[192]

Considering that the decisive factor in balancing the protection of private life against freedom of expression should lie in the contribution that the published photos and articles make to a debate of general interest,[193] the Court observed that the photographs concerned made no such contribution since the applicant exercised no official function and the photos and articles related exclusively to details of her private life. The public did not have a legitimate interest in knowing where the applicant was and how she behaved generally in her private life even if she appeared in places that could not always be described as secluded and despite the fact that she was well known to the public. Even if such a public interest existed, those interests had to yield to the applicant's right to the effective protection of her private life.[194]

Thus, it was *the interpretation and application of a provision of private law* by the German courts which failed to fulfil positive obligations arising under Article 8 ECHR and which amounted to a violation of the Convention by the Federal Republic of Germany. The domestic courts are state authorities whose behaviour is attributed to the Contracting States. It is not only their (active) interference with a right guaranteed by the ECHR that can establish the responsibility of the State, but also the courts' failure to protect these rights effectively can also mean that a State violates the Convention insofar as a positive obligation to provide such protection exists.

The case of *Storck v. Germany*[195] shows[196] that the ECtHR is willing to dig deeply into the details of domestic law when assessing whether the domestic

---

[191]ECtHR, *Von Hannover v. Germany*, no. 59320/00, judgment of 24 June 2004, § 72 (see also § 78), ECHR 2004–VI.
[192]ECtHR, *Von Hannover* (n. 192), § 74.
[193]ECtHR, *Von Hannover* (n. 192), §§ 60, 63–64, 76.
[194]ECtHR, *Von Hannover* (n. 192), §§ 76–77.
[195]ECtHR, *Storck* (n. 3).
[196]See Chapter 1, at n. 45 et seq.

courts have complied with positive obligations. In Chapter 1 we saw that the Court found the Bremen Court of Appeal to have 'failed to interpret the provisions of civil law relating to the applicant's compensation claims in contract and tort in the spirit of Article 5.'[197] It was the then applicable limitation clause of the BGB which was found to have been too narrowly construed.[198]

The ECtHR reiterates that 'it is not its function to deal with errors of fact or law allegedly committed by the national courts and that it is in the first place for the national authorities, notably the courts, to interpret national law.'[199] Yet it considers itself as competent 'to examine whether the effects of such an interpretation are compatible with the Convention.'[200] Under this heading, it seems quite problematic that the Court essentially requires the German civil courts to interpret the BGB's limitation clause for tort claims parallel to its own interpretation of the six-month time-limit under Article 35(1) ECHR.[201] This potentially amounts to a *detailed prescription of how to construe provisions of domestic law*. It is therefore hardly consistent with the limitation of its power of review which the Court had just confirmed two paragraphs before.[202]

Nevertheless, if the courts belong to the 'public authorities', and thus to a Contracting State's 'public agents', it is quite clear that positive obligations can 'come down' on the courts if and insofar as the State has decided to place the courts in a position enabling them to fulfil these obligations. Therefore, the ECtHR is, in principle, right when it says:

> In securing the rights protected by the Convention, the Contracting States, notably their courts, are obliged to apply the provisions of national law in the spirit of those rights. Failure to do so can amount to a violation imputable to the State of the Convention Article in question. In this connection, the Court reiterates that the Convention is intended to guarantee not rights that are theoretical or illusory but rights that are practical and effective (see, mutatis mutandis, Artico v. Italy, judgment of 13 May 1980, Series A no. 37, pp. 15–16, § 33, and Von Hannover v. Germany, no. 59320/00, § 71, ECHR 2004–VI).[203]

The applicant's complaint that the Bremen Court of Appeal failed to interpret the provisions of civil law relating to her claim in the spirit of Article 5(1) ECHR is then described as 'closely linked' not only to the question of whether the applicant had a fair trial within the meaning of Article 6(1) ECHR, but

---

[197]ECtHR, *Storck* (n. 3), § 99.
[198]See *supra*, Chapter 1, at n. 58 et seq.
[199]ECtHR, *Storck* (n. 3), § 93.
[200]ECtHR, *Storck* (n. 3), § 93 with reference to ECtHR, *Platakou v. Greece*, no. 38460/97, judgment of 11 January 2001, § 37, ECHR 2001–I.
[201]ECtHR, *Storck* (n. 3), §§ 95–96. See *Cremer* (2008) 562 (577–579).
[202]See *supra*, at n. 200.
[203]ECtHR, *Storck* (n. 3), § 93.

also 'to the question whether the State complied with its possible positive obligations' under Article 5(1) ECHR.[204] The judgment as such, however, is not all too clear in the way it deals with positive and negative obligations under the Convention. Although it finds that the Bremen Court of Appeal failed to interpret the provisions of civil law relating to the applicant's compensation claims in contract[205] and in tort in the spirit of Article 5 ECHR, it quite amazingly concludes that there 'has therefore been an interference imputable to the respondent State with the applicant's right to liberty as guaranteed by Article 5(1) of the Convention.'[206] This sounds as though the rejection of the applicant's compensation claims had the (potential) of breaching a negative obligation and of (actively) violating the duty *to respect* the applicant's right to liberty. Yet, nowhere does the judgment then deal with the question of whether the German Appellate Court's failure to interpret and apply domestic law in conformity with the Convention could be justified.[207] This seems to imply that, in truth, the duty to construe domestic law in the light of the ECHR flows from the positive obligations under the Convention. If we keep in mind that the *Storck* case deals with a tort claim, aimed at compensation for damages, this is remarkable because it means that this provision, dealing with tortious conduct *post delictum*, falls within the scope of positive obligations *to protect* Convention rights. This seems plausible insofar as provisions allowing claims for damages have the potential of deterring the behaviour to which such a claim is a reaction. Among others, the case of *I v. Finland*, discussed above, hints that the ECtHR might possibly allow a State not to foresee *preventive* action against a private person's conduct which invades the rights of others if it provides effective repressive sanctions, for instance, in the form of compensation for damages. But this is an *a contrario* argument as the Court notes that the mere fact that the domestic legislation provided the applicant with an opportunity to claim compensation for damages caused by an alleged unlawful disclosure of personal data *was not sufficient* to protect her private life.[208]

---

[204]ECtHR, *Storck* (n. 3), § 92.

[205]Insofar ECtHR, *Storck* (n. 3), §§ 97–98, comes to the conclusion that the Court of Appeal's finding that there was a contractual relationship by which the applicant had consented to her stay and treatment at the clinic must be considered arbitrary. This part of the judgment is not convincing, as the Bremen Court of Appeal was investigating the applicant's claim on the hypothetical assumption that a contract had been concluded in order to examine whether the applicant might have a right to compensation under contract law; the hypothesis as such was not arbitrary, but *lege artis*, and even potentially beneficial to the applicant as contractual claims were then not yet time-barred; see *Cremer* (n. 202), 579.

[206]ECtHR, *Storck* (n. 3), § 99.

[207]As far as questions of justification of an interference with the applicant's rights are discussed, this pertains exclusively to her detention and treatment as such, not to the domestic courts' decisions on her *compensation claims*; ECtHR, *Storck* (n. 3), §§ 109–113, 151–153. See *Cremer* (n. 202), 580.

[208]ECtHR, *I v. Finland* (n. 170), § 47. Doubts whether tort law can of itself suffice are, however, justified with a view to ECtHR, *Tysiąc* (n. 113), § 125. There the Court found that the provisions

3.6 The remaining uncertainty as to the relation of positive and negative obligations under the Convention in cases of controversies between private parties

Despite the ECtHR's impressive jurisprudence in the field of cases arising over controversies between private individuals, the Court again and again repeats that the boundaries between the State's positive and negative obligations under the Convention do not lend themselves to precise definition.[209] This is hardly surprising as we can discern constellations of private controversies where *each* of the parties can – at least in relation to the State – rely on a right under the Convention.[210] We need only to consider the *Von Hannover* case with Princess Caroline's right to respect for her private life under Article 8 conflicting with the press's freedom of expression under Article 10. A solution of the conflict can well require restrictions of one or the other, or both of the competing rights – as the House of Lords judgment on *Campbell v. MGN Ltd.* shows. In this English case we saw that the Members of the House used the principle of proportionality in different ways when they undertook to balance the rights involved. The ECtHR's case-law in contrast does not, in a sufficiently clear and reconstructable way, connect the balancing test and proportionality. With all caution as to the difficulty of keeping track of the Court's case-law, one might say that the closest it has yet come to

---

of the civil law on tort as applied by the Polish courts did not afford the applicant, who had unsuccessfully sought to have therapeutical abortion, a procedural instrument by which she could have vindicated her right to respect for her private life. The civil law remedy was, the Court stated, solely of a retroactive and compensatory character, and could only, and if the applicant had been successful, have resulted in the courts granting damages to cover the irreparable damage to her health which had come to light after the delivery.

[209] ECtHR, *X, Y and Z v. the United Kingdom* (n. 96), § 41; *Keegan* (n. 74), § 49; *Von Hannover* (n. 192), § 57; *Mikulić* (n. 69), § 58; *van Kück* (n. 176), § 71; *Karhuvaara und Iltalehti v. Finland*, no. 53678/00, judgment of 16 November 2004, § 42, ECHR 2004–X; *White v. Sweden*, no. 42435/02, judgment of 19 September 2006, § 20; *Gurgenidze v. Georgia*, no. 71678/01, judgment of 17 October 2006, § 38; *Pfeifer v. Austria*, no. 12556/03, judgment of 15 November 2007, § 37. Interestingly, ECtHR, *A v. Norway*, no. 28070/06, judgment of 9 April 2009, does not contain this reservation as to the impossibility of precisely defining the boundaries between negative and positive obligations; rather the court only investigates whether the unfavourable outcome of defamation proceedings against a man on whom the paper had focused its reporting of a murder which he had not committed was a violation of positive obligations under Article 8 ECHR (*ibid.*, § 67). It is noteworthy that the presumption of innocence under Article 6(2) ECHR is considered not to be directly applicable, but is taken into account in the balancing of the rights under Articles 8 and 10 ECHR (ECtHR, *White v. Sweden, ibid.*, § 21; *A v. Norway, ibid.*, §§ 46–47).

[210] Some scholars tend to regard all problems of *mittelbare Drittwirkung* of Convention rights to be solvable under the heading of positive obligations. See, for example: *Grabenwarter* (2009), § 19, para. 14–15; *Holoubek* (1997), 251 ff.; *Szczekalla* (2002), 900 et seq. See also van Dijk / van Hoof/ van Rijn/ Zwaak (2006), 28–32 (who rightly point out that the Contracting States are free to acknowledge Drittwirkung within their national legal systems).

structuring its balancing test by applying the principle of proportionality is in its judgment in the case of *Karhuvaara und Iltalehti v. Finland*.²¹¹ The case primarily concerned criminal convictions of the editor-in-chief of a newspaper – and thus clear instances of interference by public authorities with rights under Article 10 ECHR. But it went beyond this insofar as the domestic courts ordered the editor and the publishing company to pay damages to a politician because they had reported on the criminal trial of her husband. In laying down the general principles of law to be applied in the case, the Court mentions that it must determine whether an interference with the right to freedom of expression was 'proportionate to the legitimate aims pursued' and whether the reasons adduced by the national authorities to justify it were 'relevant and sufficient'.²¹² As such, it expressly addresses the aspect of proportionality. However, the need to balance the *protection* of private life – which the reader will easily classify as an aspect of positive obligations – against the freedom of expression is only mentioned three paragraphs later.²¹³ The Court²¹⁴ points to the difficulties of distinguishing positive and negative obligations under the Convention, but then examines the specific case under the heading of Article 10(2) ECHR, i.e. the clause qualifying the freedom of expression. This is very likely the reason why the ensuing evaluation can be read as putting the principle of proportionality to work – with the conclusion reading:

> The Court considers that such severe penalties, viewed against the background of a limited interference with the private life of Mrs A. (...), disclose a striking disproportion between the competing interests of protection of private life and freedom of expression.²¹⁵

The investigation does not shed much light on Article 8 ECHR. The application of the general principles does not mention positive obligations to protect the right to respect for private life at all. The Court is content with stating that the interference with the right to freedom of expression 'pursued a legitimate aim, namely the protection of the reputation and rights of others, within the meaning of Article 10(2) of the Convention.'²¹⁶ Moreover, it speaks of the news reports as an 'interference' with the politician's private life, a term usually used for acts of public authorities, and even seems to doubt whether or not there actually was such an 'interference.'²¹⁷ Although we can detect the

---

²¹¹ECtHR, *Karhuvaara und Iltalehti* (n. 210), §§ 37–55.
²¹²ECtHR, *Karhuvaara und Iltalehti* (n. 210), §§ 39.
²¹³ECtHR, *Karhuvaara und Iltalehti* (n. 210), §§ 42.
²¹⁴As already indicated at and in n. 210.
²¹⁵ECtHR, *Karhuvaara und Iltalehti* (n. 210), §§ 53.
²¹⁶ECtHR, *Karhuvaara und Iltalehti* (n. 210), §§ 43.
²¹⁷ECtHR, *Karhuvaara und Iltalehti* (n. 210), §§ 44: 'In these circumstances, especially as Mrs A. as a politician had to tolerate more from the press than 'the average citizen' (...), the interference

court's awareness that freedom of expression is restricted for privacy protection, there is no clarification of how exactly this restriction of a Convention right relates to positive obligations existing in relation to another, competing, Convention right. Nevertheless, we should keep the structure of the *Karhuvaara und Iltalehti* judgment in mind.

From the constellations of a conflict of rights guaranteed under the Convention, which we have just discussed, we can distinguish cases in which only one of the private parties can point to Convention rights. One example is the *Storck* case, where the applicant alleged her detention and medical treatment to have violated her rights under Articles 5(1) and 8(1) ECHR, but the private clinic's position showed no connection to a Convention right.[218]

However, if the boundaries of positive and negative obligations cannot be clearly distinguished, how do these obviously different categories of obligations relate? This is a question which might be answered with the help of structures we can hope to find in the case-law of the German Federal Constitutional Court. The Karlsruhe Court has dealt with cases of *mittelbare Drittwirkung* of basic rights for more than half a century. An investigation into its jurisprudence promises insights into the mechanisms which we might recognise also to exist at the ECHR level.

---

with her private life, assuming there was an interference within the meaning of Article 8, must in any event be regarded as limited.' See also *ibid.*, § 47, where the Court accepts the domestic courts' finding that the nationwide publication in the Iltalehti newspaper 'was capable of infringing Mrs A.'s privacy to a greater degree than the previous publication of the same facts in a local newspaper with a more limited circulation.' But it goes on to find: 'While this interpretation appears to be in line with the domestic case-law (see paragraphs 26–28 above) and cannot therefore be regarded as arbitrary, it is likewise not sufficient to justify the applicants' conviction.'

[218]Interestingly, in cases concerning restrictions on the freedom of expression by court decisions for the purpose of protecting another person's reputation or aspects of his right to privacy, the ECtHR seems only to rely on Article 10(2) ECHR without mentioning Article 8 ECHR. See, e.g., ECtHR, *Prager and Oberschlick v. Austria*, no. 15974/90, judgment of 26 April 1995, Series A no. 313; *Bladet Tromsø and Stensaas v. Norway* [GC], no. 21980/93, judgment of 20 May 1999, § 59, §§ 49–73, ECHR 1999–III; ECtHR, *News Verlags GmbH & CoKG v. Austria*, no. 31457/96, judgment of 11 January 2000, ECHR 2000–I; *Krone Verlag GmbH & Co. KG v. Austria*, no. 34315/96, judgment of 26 February 2002; *Krone Verlag GmbH & Co. KG v. Austria (no. 2)*, no. 40284/98, judgment of 6 November 2003; *Independent News and Media and Independent Newspapers Ireland Limited v. Ireland*, no. 55120/00, judgment of 16 June 2005, §§ 109–132. An exception is ECtHR, *Karhuvaara und Iltalehti* (n. 210), §§ 44 (cf. also the quote in n. 217). In contrast, where a person allegedly negatively affected in aspects of privacy or defamed by media publications was unsuccessful with judicial remedies, the ECtHR necessarily examines whether Article 8 ECHR (especially a positive obligation under this article) was violated balancing this right with the right under Article 10 ECHR; see, e.g., ECtHR, *Von Hannover* (n. 192); *Pfeifer* (n. 210), no. 12556/03, judgment of 15 November 2007.

Chapter 4:
Drittwirkung of constitutionally guaranteed basic rights in the German legal order

4.1 Starting out with hypotheses

The preceding chapter has shown that, while the impact of the rights guaranteed under the Convention on legal relations of private persons *inter se* is accepted at both the European level and within the domestic legal orders of the Contracting States, as exemplified by Germany and the United Kingdom, the structure of this impact is anything but clear. As the German courts have had more than half a century of experience with *mittelbare Drittwirkung der Grundrechte*, third-party effects of basic rights under the *Grundgesetz*, looking into their rich case-law promises insights into the details of how such effects come about.[1] These insights might prove transferable to the understanding of the Convention rights. In other words, and more precisely, by an analysis of German constitutional law we might see structures of the effects of rights and freedoms which we can *redetect* at the European level. In this comparative approach one must, of course, always be aware that our aim cannot, and must not, be a *transfer of structures* from the constitutional sphere to that of the ECHR. This would *force* something upon the Convention law. A single Contracting State's legal order must not have such an effect on a human rights treaty, the validity of which rests on the consent of all of the States Parties. Therefore, our aim must rather be to *recognise* structures. 'Recognising', as part of 'understanding', has a subjective touch,

---

[1]See, as to the scholarly debate on Drittwirkung, especially: *Adomeit, Klaus/Spinti, Henning (1987)*, p. 873, 876; *Bölke (2005)*, p. 67–86; *Calliess (2006)*, p. 321–330; *Canaris (1989)*, p. 161–172; *Canaris (1999)*, p. 1–98; *Canaris (1984)*, p. 201–246; *Diederichsen (1998)*, p. 71–260; *Dolderer (2000)*; *Dreier (1994)*, p. 505–513; *Erichsen (1996)*, p. 527–533; *Eschenbach /Niebaum (1994)*, p. 1079–1082; *(Di) Fabio (2005)*, p. 87–119; *Hager (1994)*, p. 373–383; *Hermes, Georg (1990)*, p. 1764–1768; *Hillgruber (1991)*, p. 69–86; *Klein (1989)*, p. 1633–1640; *Kleine-Cosack, (2005)*, p. 51–66; *Looschelders/Roth (1995)*, p. 1034–1046; *Lücke, (1999)*, p. 377–384; *Neuner (2007)*, p. 159–176; *Oeter (1994)*, p. 529–563; *Pfeifer (2005)*, p. 5–21; *Roth (1996)*, p. 544–577; *Roth (1998)*, p. 563–567; *Ruffert (2001)*; *Ruffert (2009)*, p. 389–398; *Sachs (2006)*, p. 385–401; *Schnapp (2000)*, p. 937–943; *Spielmann (2004)*, p. 371–375; *Starck (2005)*, p. 23–50; *Schwabe (1971)*; *Schwabe (1975)*, p. 442–470; *Schulze-Fielitz (2008)*, p. 52–57; *Wiedemann, (1990)*, p. 691–695.

as does any analysis of case-law aiming at finding common structures in various judgments delivered during a time span of more than fifty years, as hermeneutics teaches us.[2] This is true even within one and the same legal system. Therefore I have decided to present my understanding of *mittelbare Drittwirkung der Grundrechte* under the German *Grundgesetz* in the form of working hypotheses, which, after their exposition in detail in the course of the following chapter, will hopefully appear convincing to the reader. These working hypotheses are the following:

1) My aim is to demonstrate that the *Bundesverfassungsgericht's Lüth* judgment can be interpreted as showing that civil court judgments in private-law cases are acts by an institution exercising *public power*, which, when they decide a controversy using a provision of private law limiting private autonomy, *interfere* with the exercise of basic rights guaranteed by the constitution;

2) From this starting point, which I believe could have been reached by reading the *Lüth* judgment on the day it was handed down, the full relevance of *mittelbare Drittwirkung* of basic rights becomes visible through a *re-constructive reading*, as I would like to call it. By this, I mean an interpretative approach to understanding the judgment from a *present-day point of view*, informed of the development of constitutional interpretation by the *Bundesverfassungsgericht*. Such a re-constructive reading can make clear that

   a) making decisions in private-law controversies requires state (civil) courts to balance the constitutional rights of the private parties involved if, and insofar as, both parties are bearers of constitutional rights;
   b) what is required in such cases is a 'balancing' of conflicting constitutional rights, meaning that the freedoms of one of the parties is restricted in order to protect the other party's freedom;
   c) through the protection afforded to one party by restricting the other party's freedom, positive obligations under the constitution in the form of duties to protect ('*Schutzpflichten*') are fulfilled, which stem from constitutionally guaranteed basic rights;
   d) the restriction of the other party's freedom simultaneously involved needs to comply with the requirements of proportionality;
   e) the civil court's position being that of an umpire of the private-law controversy puts it into a special position as it is called upon to decide the case according to private law but, at the same time, it is required to interpret private law provisions limiting private autonomy;
   f) this 'umpire role' is characterised by the following traits:

[2]Cf. *Hans-Georg Gadamer* (1993), 57 et seq.; *Gadamer, Hans-Georg* (1990), 270 et seq. (see also as to the relevance of the application of a text in which the reader is interest, *ibid.*, 312 et seq., 330 et seq.).

i) the provisions limiting private autonomy are in need of interpretation involving judicial creativity, albeit within the limits of legal methodology;

ii) under the German *Grundgesetz* it is the civil courts' task to interpret the limiting provisions 'in the light of the constitution', which means they must strike the necessary balance between the discernible constitutional right *restricted* by the limiting provision, on the one hand, and the discernible constitutional right *protected* by the limiting provision, on the other;

iii) in striking this balance, the competent civil court itself is authorised by the legal order to decide what 'dose' of protection is necessary in any given case;

iv) the 'dose' of protection for one right being *pre-determinative* of the intensity of the necessity of restricting the other right under the rules composing the principle of proportionality.

3) In sum, the re-constructive reading of the *Lüth* judgment grants the civil courts a special function in the protection of constitutional rights in the context of private law. The constitutional requirement of respecting the value system defined by constitutionally guaranteed basic rights puts them in the position of defining the required dose of protection *as the judicial institutions for solving private-law conflicts and controversies.* This 'umpire role' for private litigation is their prime function. Constitutional law does not intend to alienate civil judges from this task, which includes preserving the consistency of the private-law order (*Privatrechtsordnung*). It only demands the courts to keep the private-law order and the outcomes of single dispute-resolving decisions consistent with constitutional requirements.

4.2 The German *Bundesverfassungsgericht's Lüth* Case

Fifty-two years ago the German *Bundesverfassungsgericht* delivered its judgment in the Lüth case.[3] This judgment deals with a problem that was highly controversial then and has remained so ever since: Do constitutionally guaranteed fundamental (or basic) rights (*Grundrechte*) have an impact on, and if so, how do they influence, private law?

In nuce, the Court gives a summary of the literary discussion of this problem as it had developed up until the judgment, showing two extreme views: Some scholars put forward the thesis that constitutional rights were directed exclusively against the state while others argued that constitutional rights, or at least some, and the most important, of them, applied to private law relationships between every one (*jedermann*), i.e. even between private individuals.

---

[3]*Bundesverfassungsgericht*, judgment of 15 January 1958 –1 BvR 400/51–, BVerfGE 7, 198–230 – *Lüth*.

4.2.1 The objective value system of constitutional rights as the reason for their radiating effect

The *Lüth* judgment was to become, and has remained, the leading case in the solution of this controversy. Nevertheless, the Court saw no reason to discuss the question of *Drittwirkung*, third-party effects of constitutional rights, comprehensively. It did, however, give a fundamental answer: The *Grundgesetz* (*Grundgesetz*) has established an *objective value order* by guaranteeing basic rights, thus principally strengthening and reaffirming the binding force of these rights. This *value system*, which is centred on individuals freely developing their personalities and on their dignity, rests on a fundamental decision made by the constitution and must therefore be valid for all branches of law, sending its guiding impulses to the legislature, the administrative agencies and the judiciary. In the eyes of the Court the natural consequence ('*selbstverständlich*') is that this value system also influences private law: No provision of codified private law can be in contradiction to this value system; every single norm must be interpreted in its spirit. The normative content of basic rights as objective norms 'unfolds within private law', as the Court says, 'through the medium of the provisions which directly govern this field of law.'[4]

Clearly the *Bundesverfassungsgericht* defined the relationship between private law and constitutional rights with special regard to the *Bürgerliches Gesetzbuch (BGB)*. The Hamburg Regional Court's (*Landgericht*) judgment challenged by Mr *Lüth*'s constitutional complaint had relied on sec. 826 BGB.[5] As the first comprehensive codification of a universal private law for Germany,[6] the *Bürgerliches Gesetzbuch* entered into force in 1900, under the Constitution of the German Empire of 1871. The BGB had, notwithstanding amendments made in the course of time, continued to be valid during the Weimar period with its (democratic and republican) Constitution of 1919[7] and the Nazi regime during the years between 1933 and 1945, and has remained in force under the *Grundgesetz* of 1949.[8] From a historical perspective, keeping in mind perversions of law during the Nazi period,[9] one can

---

[4] *Bundesverfassungsgericht* (n. 3), 205 – *Lüth*.
[5] *Bundesverfassungsgericht* (n. 3), 201–202 – *Lüth*.
[6] For a brief overview see *Heinrichs* (2010), *Einleitung*, §§ 4–5 (cf. §§ 9–16 as to renovations to the BGB).
[7] *Verfassung des Deutschen Reichs* of 11 August 1919 (*Reichsgesetzblatt* p. 1383). According to its Article 178 statutes (*Gesetze*) and statutory instruments (*Verordnungen*) remained in force insofar as they were not incompatible with the Constitution.
[8] According to Article 123 of the *Grundgesetz* law in force before the *Bundestag* (Federal Parliament) first convenes shall remain in force insofar as it does not conflict with the *Grundgesetz*.
[9] Cf. as to whether there was 'law' in the Third Reich: *Dworkin* (1986), 101–108; see also *Hart* (1994), 200, 208–212, 303–304. Hart addresses the problem of post-war German courts dealing with cases from 1933 through 1945. In this context, it is interesting to see the German legal

say that the *Bürgerliches Gesetzbuch* in essence 'survived' in different legal contexts, and especially, in different *constitutional* contexts. Ever since 1949 the *Bürgerliches Gesetzbuch*, ranking as a Federal statute[10] within the hierarchy of norms in the Federal Republic of Germany, has been subordinate to the *Grundgesetz* – this *'Grundgesetz'* being the constitution of a democratic state, which was founded on respect for human dignity and basic rights and was meant to contrast sharply with the injustice and arbitrariness of the Nazi regime.

Against this background the *Bundesverfassungsgericht*'s intention in 1958 becomes clear when it addresses 'old law' and 'new law' saying: 'Just as new legal rules must be in harmony with the value system of the constitutional rights, the contents of existing older legal rules are made to align with this value system; from which it receives a specific constitutional-law content, which, from then on, determines its interpretation.'[11]

---

philosopher Gustav Radbruch move from a quite strictly positivist concept of law to a concept more open to natural law ideas. See *Radbruch* (1999), 82 [81]: '*Vermag niemand festzustellen, was gerecht ist, so muß jemand festsetzen, was rechtens sein soll, und soll das gesetzte Recht der Aufgabe genügen, den Widerstreit entgegengesetzteer Rechtsanschauungen durch einen autoritativen Machtspruch zu beenden, so muß die Setzung des Rechts einem Willen zustehen, dem auch eine Durchsetzung gegenüber jeder widerstrebenden Rechtsanschauung möglich ist. Wer Recht durchzusetzen vermag, beweist damit, daß er Recht zu setzen berufen ist. ...*' See also ibid., 83 [82]: '*Das Recht gilt nicht, weil es sich wirksam durchzusetzen vermag, sondern es gilt, wenn es sich wirksam durchzusetzen vermag, weil es nur dann Rechtssicherheit zu gewähren vermag. Die Geltung des positiven Rechts wird also gegründet auf die Sicherheit, die ihm allein zukommt, ...*' (italics in original). *Radbruch* considers the three sides of the idea of law ('die drei Seiten der Rechtsidee'), which are legal certainty, justice and expediency (*Rechtssicherheit, Gerechtigkeit* and *Zweckmäßigkeit*), to be equivalent (*ibid.*, 84 [83]). However the judge's professional duty (*Berufspflicht*) is '*den Geltungswillen des Gesetzes zur Geltung zu bringen, das eigene Rechtsgefühl dem autoritativen Rechtsbefehl zu opfern, nur zu fragen, was Rechtens ist, und niemals, ob es auch gerecht sei. ... wie ungerecht immer das Recht seinem Inhalt nach sich gestalten möge – es hat sich gezeigt, daß es einen Zweck stets, schon durch sein Dasein erfüllt, den der Rechtssicherheit. ... Auch wenn [der Richter], weil das Gesetz es so will, aufhört, Diener der Gerechtigkeit zu sein, bleibt er noch immer diener der Rechtssicherheit. ..., das Gesetz [hat] aber nicht nur als Niederschalg der Gerechtigkeit seinen Wert, sondern auch als Bürgschaft der Rechtssicherheit, ...*' (ebd., 84 f. [83 f.]). After World War II *Radbruch* backed off from the rigidity of this view with his famous 'formula' (*Radbruchsche Formel*): '*Der Konflikt zwischen der Gerechtigkeit und der Rechtssicherheit dürfte dahin zu lösen sein, daß das positive, durch Satzung und Macht gesicherte Recht auch dann den Voprrang hat, wenn es inhaltlich ungerecht und unzweckmäßig ist, es sei denn, daß der Widerspruch des positiven Gesetzes zur Gerechtigkeit ein so unerträgliches Maß erreicht, daß das Gesetz als "unrichtiges Recht" der Gerechtigkeit zu weichen hat*' (Radbruch (1946), 105 [107]; a similar statement is to be found in the article '*Fünf Minuten Rechtsphilosophie*', published in the *Rhein-Neckar-Zeitung* on 12 Sep. 1945, p. 3: '*...; es kann Gesetze mit einem solchen Maß von Ungerechtigkeit und Gemeinschädlichkeit geben, daß ihnen die Geltung, ja der Rechtscharakter abgesprochen werden muß*').

[10]See Article 125 of the *Grundgesetz*.
[11]*Bundesverfassungsgericht* (n. 3), 205 – *Lüth*.
[12]*Bundesverfassungsgericht* (n. 3), 205–206 – *Lüth*.

According to the Court, disputes over such rules, i.e. rules of private law, nevertheless do not lose their private-law nature. The object of interpretation and application still is private law, even though its interpretation must remain consistent with the constiution, i.e. public law.[12]

4.2.2 The Bundesverfassungsgericht's solution: 'the balancing of legal values'

What does it mean in practice for every single norm to be interpreted in the spirit of the constitutional value system?

At first sight, it seems clear that the influence of constitutional rights will be stronger when a written provision of private law is open to interpretation. Depending on the wording of a norm, the interpretative margin varies. Especially in the case of '*Generalklauseln*,' the margin can be wide. An example of such a blanket norm is sec. 138(1) of the *Bürgerliches Gesetzbuch*, according to which any legal transaction is void which is contrary to '*die guten Sitten*' (*contra bonos mores*; contrary to public morals).[13] The *Bundesverfassungsgericht* confirms that the *Generalklauseln* are the inroads ('*Einbruchstellen*'[14]) of constitutional rights into private law.[15] Although the radiating effect ('*Ausstrahlungswirkung*'[16]) of constitutional rights does not exclusively 'flow through' these norms,[17] the focus does lie on the *Generalklauseln*, as they quite often refer to normative standards outside private law, even outside the law as such:[18] The '*gute Sitten*' (public morals; *bona fides*) are perhaps the most obvious example. In the *Lüth* case the Hamburg Regional Court had, as mentioned above, applied sec. 826 BGB, which under the heading '*Vorsätzliche sittenwidrige Schädigung*' ('Intentional damage contrary to public morals') sets up the rule that a person who, in a manner contrary to public morals, intentionally inflicts damage on another person is liable for compensation to the other person ('*Wer in einer gegen die guten Sitten verstoßenden Weise einem anderen vorsätzlich Schaden zufügt, ist dem anderen zum Ersatz des Schadens verpflichtet*').

---

[13]As to the interpretation of this provision of the BGB being influenced by constitutional rights see: *Bundesverfassungsgericht*, decision of 19 October 1993 –1 BvR 567, 1044/89–, BVerfGE 89, 214 (229–234); cf. also *Schwabe* (1975), 449; *Schulze-Fielitz* (2008), 54.

[14]A term of *Günter Dürig's* (see *Dürig* (1954), 525).

[15]*Bundesverfassungsgericht* (n. 3), 206 – *Lüth*; cf. also: *Hager* (1994), 376.

[16]*Bundesverfassungsgericht* (n. 3), 207 – *Lüth*.

[17]*Bundesverfassungsgericht* (n. 3), 206 – *Lüth*: '*Der Rechtsprechung bieten sich zur Realisierung dieses Einflusses vor allem die, "Generalklauseln", …*' (Translation: 'It is the blanket norms which *more than other norms* offer the judiciary the possiblity of realising this influence [sc. of constitutional rights on private law], …' – emphasis added).

[18]*Bundesverfassungsgericht* (n. 3), 206 – *Lüth* ('*… "Generalklauseln", die, …, zur Beurteilung menschlichen Verhaltens auf außer-zivilrechtliche, ja zunächst überhaupt außerrechtliche Maßstäbe, wie die, "guten Sitten", verweisen*').

A judge called on to apply sec. 826 BGB must, according to the *Bundesverfassungsgericht*, see that this norm of private law is influenced by constitutional rights. The 'valve' opening its interpretation for this radiating effect is the phrase '*die guten Sitten*'. The judge must observe and respect the resultant 'modification of private law'.[19] This, in the eyes of the Justices of the Court,[20] is the immediately binding effect of constitutional rights on the civil courts brought about by Article 1(3) of the *Grundgesetz*.[21] This binding effect creates the need for a 'balancing of legal values' ('*Güterabwägung*'), as the *Lüth* judgment shows:

4.2.3 The 'balancing of legal values' in the Lüth case

Mr *Erich Lüth*, acting as the president of the Hamburg Press Club in 1950, publicly called for a boycott on the film '*Unsterbliche Geliebte*' because it was written and directed by Mr *Veit Harlan*, the man who in 1940 had directed the anti-Semitic Nazi propaganda film 'Jud Süß'. Mr *Lüth* pointed to a criminal judgment by the Hamburg Criminal Chamber of the Regional Court (*Schwurgericht*) ruling on charges of a crime against humanity against Mr *Harlan*, saying, *inter alia*, Mr *Harlan* had been only formally acquitted by this judgment. Two companies, one of which had produced the film '*Unsterbliche Geliebte*', the other of which was distributing it, successfully brought action against Mr *Lüth* before the Hamburg Regional Court (*Landgericht*). This civil court issued an injunction against Mr *Lüth*, and ordered him to refrain both from calling on cinema owners and film distributors not to include Mr *Harlan*'s film '*Unsterbliche Geliebte*' in their programmes and from appealing to the German public not to see the film.[22]

The *Bundesverfassungsgericht* found this judgment to violate Mr *Lüth's*[23] freedom of speech as guaranteed by Article 5(1), first sentence, of the *Grundgesetz*.[24] The civil judges did not recognise the special importance

---

[19]*Bundesverfassungsgericht* (n. 3), 206 – *Lüth*: '*Der Richter hat kraft Verfassungsgebots zu prüfen, ob die von ihm anzuwendenden materiellen zivilrechtlichen Vorschriften in der beschriebenen Weise grundrechtlich beeinflußt sind; trifft das zu, dann hat er bei Auslegung und Anwendung dieser Vorschriften die sich hieraus ergebende Modifikation des Privatrechts zu beachten.*'

[20]*Bundesverfassungsgericht* (n. 3), 206, cf. 215 – *Lüth*.

[21]'*Die nachfolgenden Grundrechte binden Gesetzgebung, vollziehende Gewalt und Rechtsprechung als unmittelbar geltendes Recht.*' (Official translation 1994: 'The following basic rights shall bind the legislature, the executive and the judiciary as directly enforceable law.'). Critical of Güterabwägung is *Diederichsen* (1998), 238.

[22]See the facts as established by *Bundesverfassungsgericht* (n. 3), 199–201, 222–223 – *Lüth*.

[23]*Bundesverfassungsgericht* (n. 3), 213 – *Lüth*, states that it was undisputed that Mr *Lüth* acted as a private individual and not as a representative of the Hamburg State (at the time of the call for the film boycott Mr *Lüth* had been Director of the Senate of the *Freie und Hansestadt Hamburg* and head of the city state's press office; see ibid., 199).

[24]*Bundesverfassungsgericht* (n. 3), 199, 230 – *Lüth*.

which the constitutional right to freedom of speech has even in cases where it conflicts with private interests.[25] They thus failed to strike the right balance. If we look at the *Bundesverfassungsgericht*'s '*Güterabwägung*', we can see that the Justices collected a substantial number of arguments in Mr *Lüth*'s 'pan' of the 'judicial scales': He had no immoral motives. There were no economic interests on his side: Mr *Lüth* was not one of Mr *Harlan*'s competitors;[26] rather, he wanted to prevent him from being celebrated as a representative of contemporary German film makers. Mr *Lüth* was worried that the public abroad might gain the (false) impression that German cultural life had not changed since Nazi times and that the German people did not sincerely condemn the cruel persecution of Jews.[27] He was fighting Mr *Harlan* as an exponent of a cultural development which he rejected, intending to avert the danger of Nazi influence on German film from the start. *Speaking* against Mr *Harlan*'s re-entering the public stage could not convincingly be separated from *calling on the public* to prevent Mr *Harlan*'s reappearance; the Regional Court's attempt to do so was wrong.[28] In so doing, Mr *Lüth* was acting in a way consistent with his previous efforts for German–Jewish reconciliation.[29]

All this was not outweighed by the arguments on behalf of the two companies and Mr *Harlan*:[30] Rejecting their economic and professional interests, the *Bundesverfassungsgericht* saw no justification for demanding that Mr *Lüth* refrain from expressing his opinion that Mr *Harlan* ought to be excluded from contributing to 'representative' German film making. The value of freedom of speech for a liberal democracy was considered to be higher. Only public debate could produce a public opinion, enabling individuals to form their single views. Additionally, anyone attacked by an opinion publicly expressed had the right to fight back with the same means, i.e. the means in intellectual debates.[31] The *Bundesverfassungsgericht* is not convinced by the Regional Court's argument that Mr *Harlan* could rely on Article 2 of the *Grundgesetz*[32] and that this constitutional right protected him

---

[25] *Bundesverfassungsgericht* (n. 3), 230 – *Lüth*.
[26] *Bundesverfassungsgericht* (n. 3), 215 – *Lüth*.
[27] *Bundesverfassungsgericht* (n. 3), 216 – *Lüth*.
[28] *Bundesverfassungsgericht* (n. 3), 217 – *Lüth*.
[29] *Bundesverfassungsgericht* (n. 3), 218 – *Lüth*.
[30] It should not be overlooked that, as to rights and interests competing with Mr *Lüth*'s freedom of expression, the *Bundesverfassungsgericht* is mostly concerned with the position of Mr *Harlan*, and only briefly mentions the two companies. This is amazing since it had been the two companies who had brought the case in the civil courts and who thus had been the plaintiffs in the civil proceedings.
[31] *Bundesverfassungsgericht* (n. 3), 218–219 – *Lüth*.
[32] Of Article 2 of the *Grundgesetz* only § 1 can be relevant here, which reads: '*Jeder hat das Recht auf die freie Entfaltung seiner Persönlichkeit, soweit er nicht die Rechte anderer verletzt und nicht gegen die verfassungsmäßige ordnung oder das Sittengesetz verstößt.*' (Official translation 1994: 'Everybody has the right to self-fulfilment in so far as they do not violate the rights of others or offend against the constitutional order or morality.').

both against public institutions and against private individuals who might seek to prevent him from resuming his profession. Article 2 of the *Grundgesetz* affords no such absolute protection, as the Constitutional Justices point out.[33]

That the state, public authority, was and is allowed to act against Mr *Harlan* only within the bounds of the law, is indisputable. But from this nothing can be derived as to what individual citizens have a right to do or say vis-à-vis Mr *Harlan*.[34]

The *Bundesverfassungsgericht* then considers whether the Regional Court's judgment might be understood to establish that Mr *Lüth* had infringed the essence (*'Kern'*) of Mr *Harlan's* personality as an artist (*'künstlerische Persönlichkeit'*), which for reasons of violating human dignity necessarily was contrary to public morals: If the Regional Court could truly be thus interpreted, the Constitutional Justices say, then its judgment would not rest on a sufficient factual basis.[35] Mr *Harlan's* possibilities for performing his art and for developing as a human being were far from completely being destroyed by Mr *Lüth's* opinions, and expressions thereof. Mr *Lüth* possessed no means of coercion. All he could do was appeal to his audience's sense of responsibility and morals. Furthermore, the *Bundesverfassungsgericht* dismisses the allegation that Mr *Lüth* had made an objectively untrue statement by saying that the Hamburg Criminal Chamber of the Regional Court (*Schwurgericht*) had acquitted Mr *Harlan* of charges of a crime against humanity only formally.[36] The Criminal Chamber found that the film '*Jud Süß*' had indeed amounted to a tendentious influence on public opinion in an anti-Semitic way, qualifying it as an act of 'aggression'.[37] As such, it found Mr *Harlan's* participation in the making of the film to show the objective and subjective elements of a crime against humanity; however, as Mr *Harlan* would have risked life and limb had he refused to co-operate with the Nazis, especially '*Reichspropagandaminister*' Goebbels,[38] the Chamber held him to be excused (*entschuldigt*) – though *not* justified (!) – by necessity (*entschuldigender Notstand*) and acquitted him on these grounds.[39] When

---

[33]*Bundesverfassungsgericht* (n. 3), 219–220 – *Lüth*.
[34]*Bundesverfassungsgericht* (n. 3), 220 – *Lüth*: '*Daß der Staat, die öffentliche Gewalt, nur in den Schranken der Gesetze gegen Harlan vorgehen durfte und darf, ist selbstverständlich. Daraus folgt aber nichts dafür, was der einzelne Bürger gegenüber Harlan unternehmen und äußern darf.*'
[35]*Bundesverfassungsgericht* (n. 3), 220–221 – *Lüth*.
[36]*Bundesverfassungsgericht* (n. 3), 221–228 – *Lüth*.
[37]*Bundesverfassungsgericht* (n. 3), 222 – *Lüth*.
[38]See the quotations from the judgment of the Criminal Chamber in *Bundesverfassungsgericht* (n. 3), 223–225 – *Lüth*.
[39]*Bundesverfassungsgericht* (n. 3), 226 – *Lüth*.

Mr *Lüth* spoke of a 'formal acquittal' and 'moral condemnation', this was not a statement of fact ('formal acquittal' especially as such being no legal term). Instead, it was an admissible summarising, valuing characterisation of the Criminal Chamber's judgment.[40]

Finally, the *Bundesverfassungsgericht* regarded the form and manner in which Mr *Lüth* publicly put forward his opinion to be allowed. One of the essential arguments which the Court relied on was that films were a mass medium and that whoever, like the producer and distributor of a film, stepped onto the public stage and appealed to the public using the name of a well-known artist, such as Mr *Harlan*, had to tolerate being criticised in public.[41]

4.3 Analysis and critique of the *Bundesverfassungsgericht*'s thesis that basic rights radiate into private law as objective norms

4.3.1 Judgments by civil courts as interventions into basic rights of parties

It has already been said above that the *Bundesverfassungsgericht* found the Hamburg Regional Court's judgment to violate Mr *Lüth's* freedom of speech as guaranteed by Article 5(1), first sentence, of the *Grundgesetz*.[42] In the tenor of their judgment the Constitutional Justices not only[43] expressly stated this violation, but also quashed the judgment and referred the case back to the Regional Court for retrial.[44] This makes it obvious that the *Bundesverfassungsgericht* qualified the Regional Court's judgment as incompatible not merely with the '*objective* value system' established by the guarantee of constitutional rights but also with *individual* constitutional rights, '*subjective*' basic rights as German lawyers would say.

The *Bundesverfassungsgericht* points out that there is a link between the 'subjective' and the 'objective' dimensions of constitutional rights: If a judge does not observe the 'modifications of private law'[45] and if his judgment in a civil case 'is based on the neglect of the constitution's influence on private law

---

[40]*Bundesverfassungsgericht* (n. 3), 227 – *Lüth*.

[41]*Bundesverfassungsgericht* (n. 3), 228–229. – *Lüth* At the end of its judgment (ibid., 229–3230), the Court points out that others, including 48 university professors from Göttingen, the Swiss newspaper, Neue Zürcher Zeitung, and Members of the German Federal Parliament, the *Deutscher Bundestag*, had also protested against Mr *Harlan's* comeback.

[42]See *supra* note 24.

[43]As required by sec. 95(1), first sentence, of the *Gesetz über das Bundesverfassungsgericht (Bundesverfassungsgerichtsgesetz–BVerfGG)*.

[44]*Bundesverfassungsgericht* (n. 3), 199 – *Lüth*. Such a decision is made under sec. 95(2) *BVerfGG*.

[45]See in main text at note 19 above.

norms, he not only violates objective constitutional law by misconstruing the contents of a norm guaranteeing a basic right (as an objective norm); rather, through his judgment he also, as a bearer of public authority, violates a basic right the compliance with which each citizen can, as of constitutional law, demand of the judiciary power.'[46]

This means that, in such a constellation, the judgment in a civil case is an unjustified *interference* with a constitutionally guaranteed basic right. Why would this appear to be plausible?

At first glance, there can be 'technical' reasons: A judge called upon to adjudicate over a claim can grant the claim to the plaintiff, for instance, award payments for the compensation of damages or, as in the *Lüth* case, prohibit the defendant from performing certain actions. The judgment, in the case of *res judicata*, becomes enforceable. Thus the plaintiff can avail himself or herself of public authority in order to realise vis-à-vis the defendant what according to private law is his or her right. The private right seems to be 'backed up' by public authority. 'Technically', it is even the judgment, and not the private right as such, which is enforceable. In the light of Article 1(3) of the *Grundgesetz*[47] the civil court's judgment is an act of the judiciary which is *bound* by the basic rights guaranteed by the constitution. Therefore, it appears logical that the judgment can *violate* basic rights by disobeying their binding effect.

It is exactly this which the *Bundesverfassungsgericht* expresses at the outset of its discussion of the merits of the *Lüth* case:

> The [sc. Regional Court's] judgment forbids the complainant to make utterances through which he might influence others in such a way that they take over his opinion as to the reappearance of [Mr] Harlan and accordingly adapt their behaviour with respect to the films created by him. Objectively this means restricting the complainant in the free expression of his opinion. For this pronouncement the Regional Court gives the reason that it regards the complainant's utterances as a tortious act within the meaning of sec. 826 BGB vis-à-vis the plaintiffs, and that it consequently, on the grounds of the provisions of private law [*bürgerliches Recht*], acknowledges these [sc. the plaintiffs] to have a right to require [the complainant] to refrain from the utterances. Thus the private law right which the Regional Court assumes to exist leads, by force of the

---

[46]*Bundesverfassungsgericht* (n. 3), 206–207 – *Lüth*: '*Verfehlt er [sc. der Richter] diese Maßstäbe [sc. der durch die grundrechtliche Beeinflussung bewirkten Modifikation des Privatrechts] und beruht sein Urteil auf der Außerachtlassung dieses verfassungsrechtlichen Einflusses auf die zivilrechtlichen Normen, so verstößt er nicht nur gegen objektives Verfassungsrecht, indem er den Gehalt der Grundrechtsnorm (als objektiver Norm) verkennt, er verletzt vielmehr als Träger öffentlicher Gewalt durch sein Urteil das Grundrecht, auf dessen Beachtung auch durch die rechtsprechende Gewalt der Bürger einen verfassungsrechtlichen Anspruch hat.*'
[47]See note 21 above.

court judgement, to *a pronouncement of public power restricting the complainant's freedom to express his opinion.*[48]

Yet it is not sufficient to point to the mere 'formality' or 'technicality' that a claim, based on a private law right, is awarded by a judgment delivered by a state court. Even though under Article 1(3) of the *Grundgesetz* there can be no doubt that the state court is bound by the basic rights which are guaranteed in the constitution, the substance and extent of this binding effect is dependent upon the *contents* of the basic right (or basic rights) in question. As the *Lüth* judgment puts it, the 'pronouncement of public power' in the form of a court judgment 'can only violate the complainant's basic right under Article 5(1), first sentence, of the *Grundgesetz* if the private law provisions applied are, as to their contents, influenced by the *Grundgesetz* norm in such a way that they no longer support the judgment.'[49] In other words: From a purely technical perspective we cannot explain what a basic right substantively demands of a civil judge. Rather, we must – just as the Federal Constitutional Justices in the *Lüth* judgment did[50] – move on to a substantial investigation of the influence of basic rights on private law provisions.

The *Bundesverfassungsgericht's* understanding of what the immediately binding effect of constitutional rights (Article 1(3) of the *Grundgesetz*) means with regard to the civil courts has already been shown:[51] It is the civil judge's duty to observe and respect the 'modification of private law' resulting from the influence of constitutional law on private law, or, more precisely, from the radiating effect of the objective value system emanating from the constitution's guarantee of basic rights.[52] But how is this to be conceived? How precisely does constitutional law attach to private law? This is not at all made clear by the *Lüth* judgment.

The main problem – then and now – is how constitutionally guaranteed basic rights binding all branches of government, '*öffentliche Gewalt*' (public power, see Article 93(1) no. 4a in combination with Article 1(3) of the *Grundgesetz*), can influence legal relationships between private individuals. The *Bundesverfassungsgericht* does give a clue to its solution: Although it emphasises that private law does not change its nature when it is influenced by constitutional law as part of public law,[53] it highlights the *Generalklauseln* (blanket norms), as seen above.[54] But the *Lüth* judgment does not address them immediately. In its search for private law norms especially ('*vor allem*') susceptible to constitutional law influence, it rather first draws larger circles

---

[48]*Bundesverfassungsgericht* (n. 3), 203–204 – *Lüth* (emphasis added by the author).
[49]*Bundesverfassungsgericht* (n. 3), 204 – *Lüth*.
[50]*Bundesverfassungsgericht* (n. 3), 204 et seq. – *Lüth*.
[51]See notes 19 et seq.
[52]*Bundesverfassungsgericht* (n. 3), 204–207 – *Lüth*. See *supra* at notes 4 et seq.
[53]*Bundesverfassungsgericht* (n. 3), 205–206 – *Lüth*. See *supra* at note 12.
[54]See *supra* at notes 13 et seq; cf. also *Dreier* (1994), 510; *Dolderer* (2000), 205 f.

expressly including those provisions of private law 'which contain peremptory norms and thus constitute part of the *ordre public* – in a broad sense – i.e. the principles which, for reasons of the common good, are to be compulsory for the arrangement of legal relationships between individuals and are therefore placed outside the reach of private parties' voluntary disposition'.[55] The Court considers such provisions – among which it obviously counts the *Generalklauseln* of the BGB – to be closely related to public law: They *supplement* public law;[56] and this, the Constitutional Justices say, of necessity exposes them with special intensity to the influence of constitutional law.[57]

This appears to be quite plausible: Private law according to common understanding rests on *Privatautonomie*, i.e. on the principle that private individuals are free to deal with their own affairs, to interact with others, and especially to conclude contracts with others. They are free to make up their own rules as long as those who are to be bound agree.[58]

Peremptory norms, whether of a public or of a private law nature, set limits on private individuals' freedom – theoretically, so that the free development of each individual is compatible with everyone else's liberty.[59] If we leave aside customary law,[60] such norms are enacted by the legislature. It is hardly by pure chance that the *Bundesverfassungsgericht* speaks of '*Vorschriften*', literally translated: 'prescriptions'. Quite apparently the Constitutional Justices were considering *codified* private law norms. The legislature is, according to Article 1(3) of the *Grundgesetz*, bound by constitutionally guaranteed basic rights. Legislation on private law relationships is seldom self-executing. It needs to be applied by the civil courts when they decide disputes arising from private law. Judicial decisions are authoritative. They rely on public authority which the civil judge derives, formally, not only from being appointed by the state but also from holding a position which defines him as the 'umpire' of disputes between private individuals. No less importantly, the judge in deciding such controversies draws substantive authority from being exclusively guided and bound by the law, i.e. legal rules guaranteed (and mostly enacted) by the state.[61] In administering justice the judge brings the law's contents to bear on private individuals. If its contents

---

[55]*Bundesverfassungsgericht* (n. 3), 206 – *Lüth*.

[56]*Bundesverfassungsgericht* (n. 3), 206 – *Lüth*: '*Diese Bestimmungen haben nach ihrem Zweck eine nahe Verwandtschaft mit dem öffentlichen Recht, dem sie sich ergänzend anfügen.*'

[57]*Bundesverfassungsgericht* (n. 3), 206 – *Lüth*: '*Das muß sie in besonderem Maße dem Einfluß des Verfassungsrechts aussetzen.*'

[58]Cf. Also *Classen* (1998), 69 et seq. (pointing out that private parties act under private law, as specified by the courts, private parties not being immediately bound by the *Grundgesetz*).

[59]See *Kant*, (1797/98), § B *Was ist Recht*, 336–337, esp. 337: '*Das Recht ist also der Inbegriff der Bedingungen, unter denen die Willkür des einen mit der Willkür des anderen nach einem allgemeinen Gesetze der Freiheit zusammen vereinigt werden kann.*'

[60]Which however must, whether by the legislature or by the courts of justice, somehow be endorsed by the legal system and thus receive some form of governmental support.

[61]See Articles 20(3) and 97 of the *Grundgesetz*.

(as in tort law) is to make one person liable to another or to give one person the right to demand that another refrain from committing a certain act, then not only that legal provision itself can be seen as restricting the liberty of one individual on behalf of the other; but also *the civil court* applying the norm *is* – even if we abstract from the powers and authority of a judgment in a technical sense[62] – *also actively involved* in this (normative) restriction of liberty. This involvement is quite essential. As the *Bundesverfassungsgericht* once put it: Throughout Europe, judges have never merely been '*la bouche qui prononce les paroles de la loi*'.[63] The judges are not reduced to just reading what the law says from the books. Their judgment must tell the parties in a controversy what the law says *in their specific, single case*. The abstract rules written down, for instance, in the *Bürgerliches Gesetzbuch*, are in need of being interpreted in order to 'connect' to the particular facts of the case. They need to be 'brought to life' for the parties by the civil judge.

Some of these provisions can be understood to do no more than ascertain and reinforce the obligations voluntarily entered into by private individuals – thus form *enabling* conditions and the necessary prerequisites of *Privatautonomie*.

Others, especially peremptory norms, define the bounds within which private individuals can move and decide freely, or can interact with others. A written norm, just like every text, gives the interpreter a margin of interpretation, which appears especially wide in the case of written *Generalklauseln* (blanket norms). *Ex officio* the interpreter of written peremptory norms of private law – such as sec. 138(1) or sec. 836 BGB with their vague references to '*die guten Sitten*' – is the civil judge when called upon to decide a case. It is therefore the civil judge's task to narrow down the margin of interpretation left by such norms and to determine the limits of *Privatautonomie*; there is quite some power in the judge's hand to draw these limits tight or to leave them lax. This by itself shows that the legislator and the judge work together to limit the *Privatautonomie* of private individuals. There is even a further element in this 'co-operation': Remembering what was said above, we see that judicial decisions seldom are solely declaratory acts. Instead the judge most frequently delivers an *enforceable* judgment mobilising public authority on behalf and at the request of the successful party. The judgment need not remain a theoretical analysis of what the law says in the specific case; enforcement ensures compliance with the private law provisions in practice. All in all, there is a kind of division of labour between the maker of peremptory

---

[62]See *supra* after n. 46.

[63]*Bundesverfassungsgericht*, decision of 8 April 1987 –2 BvR 687/85–, BVerfGE 75, 223 (243–244). The literal quotation is from *Montesquieu*, De L'Esprit des Lois, II.2, Œuvres complètes, préface de George Vedel, présentation et notes de Daniel Oster, Paris 1964, 528 [589]; the complete sentence reads: '*Mais les juges de la nation ne sont, comme nous avons dit, que la bouche qui prononce les paroles de la loi; des êtres inanimés qui n'en peuvent modérer ni la force ni la rigueur.*'

private law norms and the civil courts. From this point of view it should be no surprise that a civil court's judgment ordering, on the grounds of peremptory private law norms, the defendant to refrain from certain behaviour can interfere with constitutionally guaranteed basic rights. In the *Lüth* case there ought not to have been any doubt that the injunction against expressing an opinion and propagating a boycott against a film, was an interference with the defendant's freedom of speech.

The *Bundesverfassungsgericht*'s reasons seem consistent with this view. They are quite in line with the – by now – classical test applied to cases of an alleged violation of a basic right when they proceed from (1) acknowledging the *possibility* of a civil court's violation of a constitutional right by not (sufficiently) observing the right's impact on the interpretation of a private law norm, to (2) analysing the *limits* which the constitution imposes on the freedom of speech guaranteed under Article 5(1) of the *Grundgesetz*. The Court looks at Article 5(2), according to which the rights laid down in Article 5(1) are subject, *inter alia*, to the limitations embodied in the provisions of acts of general legislation (*'finden ihre Grenzen in den Vorschriften der allgemeinen Gesetze'*). It then sets a milestone in the development of the constitutional principle of proportionality as a 'restriction on the possibility to restrict' basic rights (*Schranken-Schranke*):[64] The Court goes to great lengths to prove any *prima facie* conclusion that Article 5(2) limits the freedom of speech to what 'general legislation' (*'allgemeine Gesetze'*) happens to concede as the scope of this liberty as a fallacy.[65] In the Constitutional Justices' eyes the constitution would not be interpreted correctly if freedom of speech were construed to be dependent on what laws enacted under the constitution explicitly allowed or did not forbid. Once again, they underline the essential importance of the freedom to express one's opinion not only for self-fulfilment but also for a democratic state. It is in this light that the restrictive effects of *allgemeine Gesetze* must be seen. So great a value is accorded to freedom of speech that there is a presumption in its favour (*'eine Vermutung für die Freiheit der Rede'*) in all spheres, especially in public life.[66] Under the *Grundgesetz*, laws cannot restrict freedom of speech in a one-sided, unbalanced way (*'einseitig'*). Instead, there is a *'Wechselwirkung'*, an 'interactive' relationship, between 'acts of general legislation' and the basic right:[67] *Allgemeine Gesetze* cannot,

---

[64]The *Lüth* judgment can be seen as the starting point from which the *Bundesverfassungsgericht* continually and with more and more precision developed its understanding of '*Verhältnismäßigkeit*', proportionality, as the principle restricting limitations of constitutional rights by acts of public authority. The next important step was the famous '*Apotheken-Urteil*', judgment of 11 June 1958 –1 BvR 596/56–, BVerfGE 7, 377 [403–413, esp. 405), as to restrictions on the establishment of pharmacies.
[65]*Bundesverfassungsgericht* (n. 3), 207–209 – *Lüth*.
[66]*Bundesverfassungsgericht* (n. 3), 208 – *Lüth*.
[67]See also *Bundesverfassungsgericht* (n. 3), 212 – *Lüth*, where '*das Verhältnis von Zweck und Mittel*' [the relation of object and means] is mentioned. The principle of proportionality is

and must not, simply intrude upon the right to freedom of speech. On the contrary, the force with which they 'push back' this liberty encounters an opposing force which is 'fed' by the 'energy' it receives from the constitutional protection of the basic right. As the *Bundesverfassungsgericht* puts it: 'The relationship between the basic right [sc. guaranteed under Article 5(1) of the *Grundgesetz*] therefore is not to be construed as a one-sided restriction of the basic right's scope through "acts of general legislation" [*"allgemeine Gesetze"*]; there rather is an interaction [*Wechselwirkung*] in the sense that the "acts of general legislation", although the text [sc. of Article 5(2) of the *Grundgesetz*] says that they limit the basic right, must themselves be interpreted with respect to the insight into the basic right's value-defining dimension, and that their effect of restricting the basic right again must be limited.'[68] As such, there are limits to limiting[69] freedom of speech through acts of general legislation – which must be observed by the judiciary.

Especially important, the *Bundesverfassungsgericht* treats private law norms, as far as they have a restricting effect on freedom of speech, as '*allgemeine Gesetze*' within the scope of Article 5(2) of the *Grundgesetz*:[70] 'It would not be conceivable why provisions of private law protecting honour or other essential values [*Güter*] of the human personality should not suffice to set limits [*Schranken zu setzen*] on the freedom to express one's opinion even when criminal norms to the same effect are not enacted.'[71] The Court's final interpretative conclusion reads: 'Even judgments by a civil judge which in applying "acts of general legislation" [*"allgemeine Gesetze"*] of a private law character result in limiting freedom of speech [*einer Beschränkung der Meinungsfreiheit*] can violate the basic right guaranteed under Article 5(1), first sentence, of the *Grundgesetz*.'[72]

---

understood to be a balancing of an interference of a constitutional freedom and an aim, or object, in the public interest, the interference being a means for realising the aim.

[68] *Bundesverfassungsgericht* (n. 3), 208–209 – *Lüth*: '*Die gegenseitige Beziehung zwischen Grundrecht und "allgemeinem Gesetz" ist also nicht als einseitige Beschränkung der Geltungskraft des Grundrechts durch die "allgemeinen Gesetze" aufzufassen; es findet vielmehr eine Wechselwirkung in dem Sinne statt, daß die "allgemeinen Gesetze" zwar dem Wortlaut nach dem Grundrecht Schranken setzen, ihrerseits aber aus der Erkenntnis der wertsetzenden Bedeutung dieses Grundrechts im freiheitlichen demokratischen Staat ausgelegt und so in ihrer das Grundrecht begrenzenden Wirkung selbst wieder eingeschränkt werden müssen.*'

[69] German constitutional lawyers tend to speak of '*Schranken-Schranken*'.

[70] *Bundesverfassungsgericht* (n. 3), 211–212 – *Lüth*.

[71] *Bundesverfassungsgericht* (n. 3), 211 – *Lüth*: '*Es wäre nicht einzusehen, warum zivilrechtliche Vorschriften, die die Ehre oder andere wesentliche Güter der menschlichen Persönlichkeit schützen, nicht ausreichen sollten, um der Ausübung des Grundrechts der freien Meinungsäußerung Schranken zu setzen, auch ohne daß zu dem gleichen Zweck Strafvorschriften erlassen werden.*'

[72] *Bundesverfassungsgericht* (n. 3), 212 – *Lüth*. '*Auch Urteile des Zivilrichters, die auf Grund "allgemeiner Gesetze" bürgerlich-rechtlicher Art im Ergebnis zu einer Beschränkung der Meinungsfreiheit gelangen, können das Grundrecht aus Art. 5 Abs. 1 Satz 1 GG verletzen.*'

The *Bundesverfassungsgericht*'s *Lüth* judgment can therefore be read as supportive of the thesis that:

(1) judgments of civil courts deciding controversies between private individuals can indeed amount to an *intervention* within the protective sphere of a basic right when a provision of private law is applied which restricts a basic right of one of the parties and that
(2) in such a case, there is a *violation* of the relevant basic right by the civil court's judgment when the result the court reaches in interpreting the private law amounts to a restriction of the basic right which is *excessive* – i.e. unbalanced, in modern German legal terminology, '*unverhältnismäßig*', meaning no longer proportionate.

Now, by speaking of proportionality, we are going beyond an interpretation which would have been possible on the day on which the *Lüth* judgment was pronounced. Rather, we are employing 'dogmatic' tools which only fully developed during the years to follow. When we proceed from here to taking a closer look at the balancing of 'positions' in the *Lüth* case, we will apply these modern-day tools and, as a result, clearly turn to the re-constructive reading of the judgment announced at the beginning of this chapter. The re-constructive approach will be most clearly visible when we examine the *Bundesverfassungsgericht*s analysis of Mr *Harlan*'s rights and interests.

4.3.2 The need for balancing

Above it was highlighted that the *Bundesverfassungsgericht* resorted to Article 5(2) of the *Grundgesetz*, which allows limitations on the freedom of speech. This was done in order to show that it is possible and plausible to interpret the *Lüth* judgment as regarding civil court judgments based on restrictive (peremptory) norms of private law as potential interferences with basic rights. Any such interference is in need of constitutional justification. In this context we encountered the thesis that the 'acts of general legislation' ('*allgemeine Gesetze*') within the scope of Article 5(2) of the *Grundgesetz* interact with the guarantee of freedom of speech so that, for reasons of proportionality, their impetus for limiting this liberty is weakened and softened. This theory of '*Wechselwirkung*' between the guarantee of a basic right and its limitations demands anyone applying an 'act of general legislation' to a case, to strike a balance.[73]

---

[73]*Bundesverfassungsgericht* (n. 3), 209 – *Lüth*, where the *Bundesverfassungsgericht* asserts constitutional control over the civil courts and defines the constitutionally required task of balancing the competing tendencies of the basic right and the 'acts of general legislation' as falling within its own range of competence: '*Es muß zu seiner [sc. des Bundesverfassungsgerichts] Kompetenz gehören, den spezifischen Wert, der sich in diesem Grundrecht für die freiheitliche*

The *Bundesverfassungsgericht* defines the concept of 'acts of general legislation' (*'allgemeine Gesetze'*) by eclectically blending different approaches developed for the same term as it was used in Article 118 of the Weimar Constitution of 1919: *'Allgemeine Gesetze'* are those 'which "do not forbid an opinion as such, are not directed against the expression of the opinion as such", rather "serve to protect a legal value deserving protection absolutely, irrespective of any specific opinion," to protect a common value which has priority over freedom of speech activity (...).'[74] Thus, 'acts of general legislation' solve conflicts between free speech and other legal values. The Bundesverfassungsgericht specifies:

> The right freely to express one's opinion must stand back when interests of another person deserving protection and ranking higher are infringed by free speech activity. Whether such overriding interests of others exist must be established on the basis of all the circumstances of the case.[75]

This necessitates a *'Güterabwägung'* in each case, i.e. a balancing of legal values. The balancing exercise is something which Article 5(2) of the *Grundgesetz* demands by defining the limits to freedom of expression as 'acts of general legislation' and which, consequently, is not as such a specific feature of constitutional review of civil court judgments! This is important to see before we take a closer look at the interests weighed against Mr *Lüth's* freedom of speech in the *Bundesverfassungsgericht's* judgment of 1958.

4.3.3 The interests and values in the other side of the judicial scales

As shown above, the *Lüth* judgment attaches great weight to freedom of speech especially in public debates.[76] Here, as the judgment seems to imply, it is extraordinarily difficult for private law norms to set limits to the free expression of opinions. Provisions of private law can count among 'acts of general legislation' (*'allgemeine Gesetze'*).[77] However, the Court addresses the function of a private law norm as *'Schutz des privaten Rechtsguts'*,[78] i.e.

Demokratie verkörpert, allen Organen der Öffentlichen Gewalt, also auch den Zivilgerichten, gegenüber zur Geltung zu bringen und den verfassungsrechtlich gewollten Ausgleich zwischen den sich gegenseitig widerstreitenden, hemmenden und beschränkenden Tendenzen des Grundrechts und der "allgemeinen Gesetze" herzustellen.' See also ibid., 207, as to the limits of constitutional jurisdiction, the *Bundesverfassungsgericht* says it is not the ultimate court of review in civil proceedings (no *'Superrevisionsinstanz'*); rather it is restricted to putting civil court judgments to a constitutional test. Cf. Canaris (1999), 27 et seq. (who favours a strict separation *'Ausstrahlungswirkung'* and *'Superrevisionsproblematik'*).
[74] *Bundesverfassungsgericht* (n. 3), 209–210 – *Lüth.*
[75] *Bundesverfassungsgericht* (n. 3), 210–211 – *Lüth.*
[76] See *supra* after n. 26 and after n. 29.
[77] See *supra* at n. 70 et seq.
[78] *Bundesverfassungsgericht* (n. 3), 212 – *Lüth.*

as the protection of the *private* legal value concerned. When *'allgemeine Gesetze'* are private law norms, the values they refer to seem to be of a *private* nature. As such, in cases like the controversy between Mr *Lüth* and Mr *Harlan*, one party's (constitutionally guaranteed) right to freedom of speech appears to be in need of being balanced against the *private* legal value which the applicable private *'allgemeines Gesetz'* protects.

At this point it might be of some help to see that German legal terminology[79] quite often refers to *'Rechtsgüter'*, legal values. Often legal texts read as if their authors were speaking of something material. There is some temptation in the German language to do so as the word *'Gut'* (pl. *'Güter'*), which here is mostly translated as 'value', also means 'commodity'; one especially common meaning of *'Güter'* is 'goods'. *'Rechtsgut'*, however, is best understood to mean the 'object' of a legal norm in an *immaterial* sense; more precisely it derives from the norm's positive[80] 'objective': What is to be *protected* by the norm? The answer to this question reveals the *'Rechtsgut'*.

If we read the *Lüth* judgment, which are the *'Rechtsgüter'* the *Bundesverfassungsgericht* discusses under the blanket norm of sec. 826 BGB? If the materialistic metaphor is allowed, which *'Rechtsgüter'* might be placed in Mr *Harlan's* 'pan' of the 'judicial scales' when striking a balance with Mr *Lüth's* freedom of speech?

Sec. 826 BGB taken by itself seems to point to a field of non-legal values, as defined by good morals. As we saw above, however,[81] the *Bundesverfassungsgericht* understands *'gute Sitten'* to be one of the 'valves' through which constitutional law 'flows into' private law. The *Grundgesetz*, as the constitution, has the power to influence the meaning and contents of 'good morals'. The *Bundesverfassungsgericht* regards the judge, through Article 1(3) of the *Grundgesetz*, to be bound to respect the fundamental value decisions and the principles of the social order (*'grundsätzliche Wertentscheidungen und soziale Ordnungsprinzipien'*) when determining what is socially required or prohibited in a single case. 'It is within this order of values, which simultaneously is a *hierarchy* of values, that the required balancing of the basic right guaranteed by Article 5(1), first sentence, of the *Grundgesetz* and the rights and legal values restricting its exercise has to be performed.'[82]

Let us turn to the legal values in the 'pan' of the 'judicial scales' used in the *Lüth* judgment's balancing. In order to find them, we must first set aside the other 'pan', so to say, the *Bundesverfassungsgericht's* quite lengthy exploration of Mr *Lüth's* motives for publicly calling for a boycott of Mr *Harlan's*

---

[79]'Legal terminology' here is intended to mean the terminology used in reasons of judicial or administrative decisions and in scholarly comments, not the terminology used in statutes or other acts.

[80]It is not the negative objective of preventing some behaviour which defines the *'Rechtsgut'*.

[81]*Supra* at n. 19.

[82]*Bundesverfassungsgericht* (n. 3), 215 – *Lüth*.

films.[83] The Court discusses these in order to demonstrate the 'weight' of Mr *Lüth*'s right freely to express his opinion under Article 5(1), first sentence, of the *Grundgesetz*. This weight is considered to be the larger, the more speech is used not within a private controversy but in an attempt to influence public opinion. This is thought to be especially so when reverberations on the legal spheres of other private persons are indirect and non-intentional. Special importance is attributed to whether the expression of an opinion aims at contributing to an intellectual struggle in the public forum without pursuing egotistic, especially economic, aims. Such a participation in public debate, so the Court says, is privileged by a presumption in favour of free speech.[84]

It is in the midst of the discussion of Mr *Lüth*'s motives for his public statements (which are understood to be of a purely a moral nature) that Mr *Harlan*'s professional interests ('*die beruflichen Interessen Harlans*') and the economic interests of the film companies employing him ('*die wirtschaftlichen Interessen der ihn beschäftigenden Filmgesellschaftern*') are mentioned.[85] But these interests, which obviously are of a private nature, are not expounded upon here.

It is two pages later[86] that the judgment begins seriously to examine which rights and '*Rechtsgüter*' restrict the basic right guaranteed by Article 5(1), first sentence, of the *Grundgesetz*. Here, the *Bundesverfassungsgericht*, as shown above,[87] considers the Regional Court's argument that Mr *Harlan* could rely on Article 2 of the *Grundgesetz* and that this constitutional right protected him both from public institutions and from private individuals who might seek to prevent him from resuming his profession.

Although the Constitutional Court rejects the Regional Court's evaluation, it does acknowledge that Article 2 of the *Grundgesetz* also belongs to the value system of constitutional rights and essentially influences the conception of what contravenes good morals (within the scope of sec. 826 BGB). However, it points out the difference between an interference with this right by public authorities on the one hand and by private individuals on the other: It is, the Court says, natural ('*selbstverständlich*') that the state, the public power, was permitted to take steps against Mr *Harlan* only within the limits of the laws. But from this no conclusion can be drawn as to what the individual citizen is allowed to do or say in relation to Mr *Harlan*, since every individual is the bearer of the same fundamental rights:[88] In a large community there will unavoidably always be conflicts of interests and rights between individuals. Therefore conflicting rights will constantly have to be balanced

---

[83]See *Bundesverfassungsgericht* (n. 3), 214–219 – *Lüth*.
[84]*Bundesverfassungsgericht* (n. 3), 212 – *Lüth*.
[85]*Bundesverfassungsgericht* (n. 3), 218 – *Lüth*.
[86]*Bundesverfassungsgericht* (n. 3), 219 et seq. – *Lüth*.
[87]See *supra* at n. 32 et seq.
[88]*Bundesverfassungsgericht* (n. 3), 220 – *Lüth*.

and weighed against each other in accordance with the intensity of protection they deserve. The restrictions on the possibilities to free development which result from such balancing must be suffered by the individual. No one can retreat to an allegedly absolute position provided by Article 2 of the *Grundgesetz* in order to fend off any intrusion whatsoever (by other private individuals) as a violation of good morals.[89] The Constitutional Court furthermore rejects the *argumentum a maiore ad minus* used by the *Oberlandesgericht Hamburg* that *a fortiori* an individual citizen was prevented from doing something not even the state had no right to do.[90]

It is obvious that what the *Bundesverfassungsgericht* is saying here does not amount to banning the idea that Article 2 of the *Grundgesetz* is relevant to determining the outcome of a private law dispute. Instead, it is pointing out that the constitutional right does *not directly* apply to the legal relationship between private parties. The *Bundesverfassungsgericht* can be understood as saying that Article 2 of the *Grundgesetz*, though not directly applicable, is nevertheless relevant. It is part of the constitutional value system. Article 2 does not apply to conflicts between individuals in the same manner, and especially not in the same strictness, in which it applies to conflicts between the state and an individual.[91]

This becomes clear when the *Bundesverfassungsgericht* hypothetically considers whether or not the Regional Court's argument (sc. as to Article 2 of the *Grundgesetz*) might be understood to establish that Mr *Lüth* had infringed the essence ('*Kern*') of Mr *Harlan's* personality as an artist ('*künstlerische Persönlichkeit*'), which for reasons of violating human dignity, was contrary to public morals.[92] By denying that there was a sufficient factual basis for such an evaluation of the case,[93] the Federal Constitutional Justices are, at least implicitly, accepting the idea that the need for *protecting* one individual's personality (Article 2(1) of the *Grundgesetz*) and human dignity (Article 1(1) of the *Grundgesetz*) may well *justify* a civil court *in judging* another individual's speech act as a violation of good morals and thus *in restricting the latter individual's freedom of speech* by applying sec. 826 BGB in its judgment. It is the special *need for the protection of a basic right* which – in the light of the constitution's value system – may call for 'activating' sec. 826 BGB as an 'act of of general legislation' within the meaning of Article 5(2)

---

[89]*Bundesverfassungsgericht* (n. 3), 220 – *Lüth*.
[90]*Bundesverfassungsgericht* (n. 3), 220 – *Lüth*.
[91]The *Bundesverfassungsgericht* refrains from positively defining the way in which Article 2(1) of the *Grundgesetz* does influence the answer whether one person has, within the meaning of sec. 826 BGB, inflicted damages on another in contradiction with good morals.
[92]It may well be that the *Bundesverfassungsgericht* was inspired by the way the *Landgericht* had treated Article 2 of the *Grundgesetz* as an absolute protection against any 'high-handed restriction' of this basic right of whatever source it might be (cf. *Bundesverfassungsgericht* (n. 3), 219–220 – *Lüth*). Only human dignity is, according to Article 1(1), first sentence, of the *Grundgesetz*, '*unantastbar*' (inviolable).
[93]*Bundesverfassungsgericht* (n. 3), 220–221 – *Lüth*.

of the *Grundgesetz* – the clause *restricting, inter alia,* the freedom of expression guaranteed by Article 5(1), first sentence, of the *Grundgesetz*.

In the context of Article 2 of the *Grundgesetz,* the Court addressed the collision of interests and rights in social interactions and said that the individual had to suffer the resultant restrictions.[94] The discussion of an interference with Mr *Harlan*'s personality right and dignity by Mr *Lüth*'s call for a boycott reveals that this balancing is, or at least can be, entrusted to the civil courts. This balancing requires the courts to come up with equitable solutions to conflicts between individuals, vested equally with basic rights, so that each of their rights can 'co-exist' and so that the exercise of one of the individual's rights is compatible with the exercise of the other.

This is underlined by the way in which the *Bundesverfassungsgericht* treats the final (legal) value in Mr *Harlan's* 'pan of the scales'. It discusses whether Mr *Lüth* had made an objectively untrue statement by saying that the Hamburg Criminal Chamber of the Regional Court (*Schwurgericht*) had only formally acquitted Mr *Harlan* of charges of a crime against humanity.[95] From today's point of view, it is quite surprising to find that the Court does not connect Mr *Harlan*'s interest in not having to tolerate false statements publicly being made about him with a constitutional right. For, in the meantime, the Court has acknowledged Article 2(1) in combination with Article 1(1) of the *Grundgesetz* to guarantee the *'allgemeines Persönlichkeitsrecht'*.[96] This right, *inter alia,* protects a person against a distorted and untrue image of their person being publicly conveyed insofar as this is of some significance for the development of their personality.[97] At the time of the *Lüth* judgment, however, the Court's case-law had not yet evolved so far. Nevertheless, the *Lüth* judgment discusses the problem of false allegations, and it points out that when Mr *Lüth* spoke of a 'formal acquittal' and 'moral condemnation', this was not a statement of fact, but rather an admissible summarising, valuing characterisation of the criminal judgment.[98] The *Bundesverfassungsgericht* criticises the Hamburg Regional Court's decision for defining too strict a diligence standard for Mr *Lüth*'s speech by requiring of him, even though he was not a lawyer, to be as scrupulous as a 'reader educated in criminal law' (*'strafrechtlich geschulter Leser'*) when commenting on the criminal judgment against Mr *Harlan.* This, according to the Federal Constitutional Justices, amounts to an unacceptable restriction on the right to freedom of speech in a liberal democracy (*'eine unannehmbare Einengung der Redefreiheit in einer freiheitlichen Demokratie'*).[99]

---

[94]See *supra* before n. 92.
[95]*Bundesverfassungsgericht* (n. 3), 221–228 – *Lüth.*
[96]The first case in which the Court spoke of the *'allgemeines Persönlichkeitsrecht'* as a constitutionally guaranteed right was BVerfGE 54, 148 (153).
[97]BVerfGE 99, 185 (194) with reference to BVerfGE 97, 125 (148 f.); 97, 391 (403).
[98]*Bundesverfassungsgericht* (n. 3), 227 – *Lüth.*
[99]*Bundesverfassungsgericht* (n. 3), 227 – *Lüth.*

4.3.4 Proportionality

The balancing of the conflicting interests and rights by the Regional Court's judgment, i.e. by the act of a state judicial institution, was thus overly restrictive on one party's right to freedom of expression. The reason for this was that the other party's 'interest' in preventing false statements from being forwarded to the public *did not require* such restrictions on free speech. Again, from today's constitutional perspective, this interest is an aspect of the '*allgemeines Persönlichkeitsrecht*' as guaranteed by Articles 2(1) and 1(1) of the *Grundgesetz*. The characterisation by Mr *Lüth* of the criminal court's acquittal of Mr *Harlan*, clearly conceivable as being a value judgment and not an assertion of fact, was incapable of creating an untrue or distorted depiction of Mr *Harlan*. Rather, it was a contribution of his opinion to a public debate, the correct response to which would have been putting forward a value argument in Mr *Harlan*'s favour in the same forum.[100] In present-day terminology, the Regional Court's judgment was not a proportionate ('*verhältnismäßig*') limitation ('*Einschränkung*') of Mr *Lüth*'s right under Article 5(1), first sentence, of the *Grundgesetz*. According to the interpretation of constitutional law in the *Lüth* judgment, Mr *Harlan* ought to have defended himself against Mr *Lüth*'s criticism in the public forum, not in the courts, as the *protection* of Article 2(1) and 1(1) of the *Grundgesetz*, through what we today call the '*allgemeines Persönlichkeitsrecht*', did not justify a restriction on Mr *Lüth*'s freedom of speech. The *Grundgesetz* thus gives someone who is publicly criticised by another person a means of protection, even though it is basically not a judicial remedy. The constitution expects criticism to be countered by free speech first.

4.3.5 Balancing defined as an act of deciding how far to restrict one party's constitutionally guaranteed freedom for the sake of protecting the other party's constitutionally guaranteed freedom

Looking back, one cannot help but be surprised: The *Bundesverfassungsgericht* started out by saying that 'acts of general legislation' within the meaning of Article 5(2) of the *Grundgesetz* could restrict freedom of expression in order to protect *private* legal values. But what the Court looks into are essentially – and permitting a modern-day understanding of the interest in not having to tolerate false statements – other constitutionally guaranteed basic rights. The *Lüth* judgment thus gives the impression that the civil judges in deciding a controversy of *private* law (under sec. 826 BGB) are required to discuss the impact of their decisions on the *constitutional* rights of *both* parties. What is decided in terms of private law is, viewed from the perspective of the constitutional value system, of relevance for:

---

[100]*Bundesverfassungsgericht* (n. 3), 219 – *Lüth*.

(1) how far the constitutionally guaranteed freedom of one of the parties is *restricted*, and, as this is done with a view to the other party's benefit;
(2) how far the other party's constitutionally guaranteed freedom is *protected* exactly by acknowledging the private law obligation, or denying the private right, which the other party is alleging, and through the judgment's binding force and enforceability.

Restriction and protection go hand in hand. In controversies between private parties, constitutionally guaranteed basic rights can be discovered on the side of both parties. If the use which one party is making of a basic right excessively burdens the other party's basic rights position, any protection of this burdened party's basic right necessarily requires restricting the first party's basic right. Under the German constitution this is the general situation in private law controversies insofar as the parties are truly private law subjects (and it is not a state or governmental entity acting under private law or from behind a private-law corporate veil), the only exception being that under Article 19(3) of the *Grundgesetz* it is only domestic legal persons which enjoy basic rights protection, foreign corporations are excluded.

It appears quite natural that restricting one party's right for the sake of the protection of another party's right requires balancing. The *Lüth* judgment gives an example of such balancing to the effect that the conflicting (constitutional) rights are restricted no further than is necessary in a democratic society[101]. This seems clearly to point to the relevance of the principle of proportionality in deciding private law disputes in light of constitutional law, but the *Lüth* judgment is silent on this. Therefore, we will have to look at later decisions by the *Bundesverfassungsgericht*.

4.4 The *Bundesverfassungsgericht*'s Commercial Agent Decision

4.4.1 The facts of the case

In 1990 the *Bundesverfassungsgericht* delivered a decision, which can be regarded as confirming the interpretation of *mittelbare Drittwirkung* according to the *Lüth* judgment.[102]

This so-called *Commercial Agent* case (*Handelsvertreter-Fall*) concerned the termination of a contractual relationship between a company producing

---

[101]Cf. *Canaris* (1989), p. 161 (167) ('besondere Form der Verhältnismäßigkeitsprüfung'); in contrast *Diederichsen* (1998), 253 et seq. is sceptical of the usefulness of the principle of proportionality.

[102]*Bundesverfassungsgericht* judgment of 7 Feb. 1990 –1 BvR 26/841–, BVerfGE 81, 242 – *commercial agent*.

and selling wine and champagne, and a commercial agent employed by the company. The contract foresaw that, if it was terminated for any reason caused by the fault of the commercial agent, he would be obliged to refrain from activity for any competitor, of whatever kind, for the duration of two years. In such a case he would receive no compensation of any kind from the company. After the agent in this case concluded a contract with a competitor, he decided to quit his old job and gave the (old) company notice of the termination of his contract. Having been persuaded to continue working for the (old) company, he withdrew this notice. Nevertheless, he started working for the competitor without terminating his contract with the (old) company, which thereupon dismissed the agent instantly.[103]

This former company then brought a prohibitory action against the commercial agent, seeking a court order forbidding him to work in the field of wine sales for two years since the date of his dismissal. This claim, though denied by the court of first instance, was granted by the court of appeals, and then the *Bundesgerichtshof* (the German Federal Court of Justice) confirming this judgment upon review.[104] Against the decisions by the civil courts the commercial agent lodged a constitutional complaint. The civil courts had, he argued, wrongly considered him to be an independent businessman, who had been able to negotiate the terms of his contract freely. In truth, however, up to the time of the conclusion of the contract, he had been an employee. The company had offered him a contract in printed form, which had allowed him no possibility of negotiation. He had not been able to foresee the effect of the restraint-of-competition clause contained therein, which essentially meant the destruction of his livelihood. The sanction (of not being allowed to work in his profession for two years without receiving compensation) applied to him where he only wanted to use his (constitutionally guaranteed) occupational liberty. This was against good morals within the meaning of sec. 138 BGB (which declares legal transactions in violation of good morals to be invalid).[105]

4.4.2 Confirmation and further explication of the re-constructive reading of the Lüth judgment

4.4.2.1 Civil court judgments as interferences with basic rights

The *Bundesverfassungsgericht* regarded the constitutional complaint as wellfounded. The civil court decisions violated Article 12(1) of the *Grundgesetz*, which guarantees occupational liberty. The first aspect confirming the reconstructive interpretation of the *Lüth* judgment can be found at the

---

[103]*Bundesverfassungsgericht* (n. 102), 245–246 – *commercial agent.*
[104]*Bundesverfassungsgericht* (n. 102), 246–248 – *commercial agent.*
[105]*Bundesverfassungsgericht* (n. 102), 248 – *commercial agent.*

beginning of the merits when the Court states that the civil court judgments 'restrict [*beschränken*] the complainant in his occupational liberty (Article 12(1) of the *Grundgesetz*). They are subject to constitutional review [*verfassungsgerichtlicher Kontrolle*] since the judiciary, as all public power, is bound by the basic rights (Article 1(3) of the *Grundgesetz*).'[106] The civil court judgments, though aimed at solving a controversy between private parties and only pronouncing a prohibition of commercial activity which the parties had contractually agreed to, are accorded the effect of restricting the complainant's basic right under Article 12 of the *Grundgesetz*. That the civil courts merely restated the company's private right to demand its former agent to refrain from competition for two years does not matter. Through the civil judgments, *public power* is exercised to the effect of *reinforcing* the private right. Thus, basic rights as guaranteed by the *Grundgesetz* apply.

4.4.2.2 Restrictive constitutional review of decisions by regular courts

As seen above, in the *Lüth* judgment, the *Bundesverfassungsgericht* was very much aware that disputes over restrictive statutory rules of private law do not lose their private-law nature, even though the interpretation of private law is required to comply with the constitution, and thus with public law: The object of interpretation and application still essentially are the private-law provisions as such.[107] This awareness can equally be detected in the *Commercial Agent* decision: The *Bundesverfassungsgericht* points out that its review of decisions by the regular courts is restricted to examining whether constitutional law has been violated. This rule had (and has) been developed and upheld in a number of *Bundesverfassungsgericht* decisions ever since the *Lüth* judgment.[108] In the *Commercial Agent* case, the Court refers to the consistent case-law according to which there is a violation of constitutional law (which the *Bundesverfassungsgericht* must correct) if decisions by the civil courts show failures of interpretation which are based on a fundamentally wrong conception of the meaning of a basic right, especially of the extent of its protective sphere, and which in their substantive meaning are of some gravity in the case which is to be decided.[109]

---

[106] *Bundesverfassungsgericht* (n. 102), 253 – *commercial agent*.
[107] See *supra* at n. 12.
[108] See esp. *Bundesverfassungsgericht*, BVerfGE 18, 85 (92 f.). The restriction of constitutional review to the control of violations of the constitution is extended to all decisions by regular courts; it is not reserved for civil court decisions.
[109] *Bundesverfassungsgericht* (n. 102), 253 – *commercial agent*.

4.4.2.3 The especially severe interference in the case of a prohibition of working in one's trade leads to stricter scrutiny

Then the *Bundesverfassungsgericht* emphasises that the civil court decisions restrict the complainant's occupational liberty in a way which comes close to an interference with the choice of a profession[110] – which, under Article 12(1) of the *Grundgesetz*, is considered to be typically more severe than a mere regulation of the exercise of a profession.[111] The complainant was professionally specialised in the wine trade. By enjoining the complainant from any commercial activity in the field of wine sales the courts therefore barred him from exercising his profession so broadly and to such an extent as to endanger his livelihood, because the complainant was not likely to find equivalent employment in another field. That he would be forced to give up his profession was not improbable; and yet, compensation by his former employer was excluded.[112]

The significance of this paragraph can only be fully realised if one takes into account that the *Bundesverfassungsgericht* had, in the time between *Lüth* and the *Commercial Agent* case, not only underlined that it could review the decisions by regular courts only according to the standards of constitutional norms, but had also made the Court's powers to intervene (*'Eingriffsmöglichkeiten des Bundesverfassungsgerichts'*) dependent upon the *intensity* of infringements of basic rights: The more intensively a civil court judgment, through its outcome, affects the basic rights sphere of the unsuccessful party to the proceedings, the stricter the requirements for justifying (*'Begründung'*) this interference (*'Eingriff'*) will be, and the further the examination by the *Bundesverfassungsgericht* will be allowed to go; in cases of the highest intensity of an interference, the Court even considers itself to be competent to replace the civil court's assessment of how its judgment affects constitutional rights by its own evaluation.[113]

In the *Commercial Agent* case the Court, however, does not draw immediate conclusions from the intensity of the restrictions on the complainant's occupational liberty.

---

[110]*Bundesverfassungsgericht* (n. 102), 253 – *commercial agent*.

[111]See the *Bundesverfassungsgericht*'s '*Apotheken-Urteil*', *supra*, n. 64.

[112]*Bundesverfassungsgericht* (n. 102), 253 – *commercial agent*.

[113]*Bundesverfassungsgericht*, decision of 11 May 1976 –1 BvR 671/70–, BVerfGE 42, pp. 143 et seq. (pp. 148–149), pointing to its judgment of 5 June 1973 – 1 BvR 536/72–, BVerfGE 35, 202 – *Lebach* – obviously as an example of such strict scrutiny. However, the *Lebach* judgment only rather tentatively intensified the abstract standard of constitutional review by saying that a regular court's decision could be 'censured' if the court could not have reached the decision it did find if it had applied the typical criteria for the evaluation of a case like the one before it which resulted from the radiation of the basic rights ('*Ausstrahlung der Grundrechte*'). In essence, the *Lebach* judgment detailedly balances the right to protection of one's personality (Article 2(1) in combination with Article 1(1) of the *Grundgesetz*) with the freedom of broadcasting (Article 5(1), second sentence, of the *Grundgesetz*) for cases in which a television station wants to report on a crime committed and to include personal information on the offender.

4.4.2.4 The Janus-headed nature of civil court judgments: Burdening one party for the sake of protecting the other

The *Bundesverfassungsgericht* rather expressly turns to the private-law nature of the controversy at the heart of the case decided by the civil courts: 'The legal basis for this extensive restriction on the complainant's professional activity is not primarily to be found in acts of the state. Rather, the complainant himself contractually agreed to a corresponding obligation. Such a self-commitment by a private legal act leads to a restriction of professional mobility, but at the same time is done in exercise of individual liberty.'[114] The Court goes on to show that individuals who make use of their occupational liberty as guaranteed by Article 12(1) of the *Grundgesetz* regularly need to enter into temporary or long-term legal relations. In the context of private law, this is done by concluding contracts, in which both parties reciprocally limit their freedom for their mutual benefit: 'On the foundation of private autonomy, which is a structural element of a liberal order of society, the parties to a contract define their legal relations autonomously. It is they who decide how their controversial interests are to be reconciled appropriately, and who thereby simultaneously, without coercion by the state, make dispositions of positions guaranteed to them by basic rights. The state must basically respect the regulations made within the framework of private autonomy.'[115]

In the next argumentative step it takes, the Court expressly refers to the *Lüth* judgment, which had, as shown above, dealt with civil court decisions in a tort case. The *Commercial Agent* case in contrast concerns contract law. Therefore, and consistently, the *Bundesverfassungsgericht* addresses the limits of private contracting:

> Private autonomy exists only within the framework of the laws valid and applicable, and these are themselves limited by basic rights. The *Grundgesetz* does not want to be a value-neutral order; rather it has made objective fundamental decisions in first chapter on basic rights, which are valid for all sectors of law, including private law. No provision of the civil code must stand in contradiction to the principles expressed in the basic rights. This especially holds true for those provisions of private law which contain peremptory norms and thereby set limits for private autonomy (cf. BVerfGE 7, 198 [205 et seq.; consistent holding]).

In using the *Lüth* judgment (BVerfGE 7, 198), the Court puts private contracting into the context of the legal order: Freedom to design the contents of contracts exists only within the limits of what state-made private-law norms

---

[114] *Bundesverfassungsgericht* (n. 102), 253–254 – *commercial agent.*
[115] *Bundesverfassungsgericht* (n. 102), 254 – *commercial agent.*

say. These must be in conformity with the *Grundgesetz* as the constitution, especially with the basic rights guarantees. The requirement of conformity with the constitution, however, does not merely restrict the legislator from enacting statutes which excessively encroach upon private autonomy. Rather, the basic rights of the *Grundgesetz* may well call for the fixing of strict rules in order to protect private autonomy. The resulting limits on what private parties can do can be essential, the Court says, because it is a prerequisite of private autonomy that the conditions for autonomy (*'Selbstbestimmung'*) exist truly and in fact. Where one of the parties is so much stronger than the other as to be, *de facto*, able to define the contents of a contract unilaterally, there is the complete opposite of autonomy: i.e. *Fremdbestimmung*, one party being controlled by the other. Where there is not even an approximate balance of strength and powers (*'Kräftegleichgewicht'*) between the parties, state rules must intervene in order to secure the protection of basic rights.[116] The Bundesverfassungsgericht sees objective constitutional principles involved here:

> Legal provisions protecting against social and economic imbalances here lead to the realisation of the objective fundamental value decisions of the [sc. *Grundgesetz*'s] basic rights chapter and simultaneously the *Grundgesetz*'s principle of the social state (Article 20(1), Article 28(1) of the *Grundgesetz*).[117]

Later on the *Commercial Agent* decision underlines that '[l]egal restrictions of private autonomy are necessary for the protection and balancing of basic rights positions even when contractual parity is essentially disturbed otherwise' than by the fact that employees are (typically) in a situation of social dependency.[118]

The *Bundesverfassungsgericht* considers it impossible to derive immediately from the constitution a precise answer to the question when an imbalance calls for protective legislation. Factual constellations can be manifold. The Court concedes a wide margin of appreciation to the legislator, who, on the other hand, must remain passive when obstacles obviously prevent private parties from a truly autonomous, i.e. reciprical, settlement of their affairs. It then points out something which up to then and ever since has not been said with such clarity:

> Then, however, [sc. the legislator] must beware that any limitation of contractual freedom for the protection of one party simultaneously interferes with the other party's freedom.[119]

---

[116]*Bundesverfassungsgericht* (n. 102), 255 – *commercial agent*.

[117]*Bundesverfassungsgericht* (n. 102), 255 – *commercial agent*.

[118]*Bundesverfassungsgericht* (n. 102), 260 – *commercial agent*.

[119]*Bundesverfassungsgericht* (n. 102), 255 – *commercial agent*. Cf. for the situation under the ECHR: *Fenwick/Phillipson* (2006), 661, 676.

This is exactly what had been the focal point of the re-constructive reading of the *Lüth* judgment. Private law is not just the sum of norms which private legal subjects set up by agreement or by custom. Private autonomy is essential, but state-made private-law norms set to autonomous regulation limits and, as they limit liberty, *interfere with basic rights*. The *Commercial Agent* judgment is precise in this:

> If the validity of a contract clause is restricted for the sake of the occupational freedom of a party working for an entrepreneur, this effects an interference ['*Eingriff*'] with the occupational freedom of the entrepreneur.[120]

The legal provision making such a restriction thus is Janus-headed, a stern face looking at the entrepreneur whose constitutionally protected occupational liberty suffers a limitation – a smiling face looking at the commercial agent whose autonomy in occupational matters is preserved. Article 12(1) of the *Grundgesetz*, which guarantees occupational liberty, applies to both the entrepreneur and the commercial agent, but the entrepreneur's liberty is curbed while the commercial agent's liberty is protected. In designing the legal restriction on contracting the legislator must pay due respect to the competing basic rights positions involved and find a balance between them, the scope of legislative discretion being wide.[121]

4.4.2.5 The law can assign the task of balancing basic rights to the civil court judges

Even if the legislator abstains from enacting peremptory norms of contract law for special spheres of life or for special forms of contracts, the *Bundesverfassungsgericht* does not regard the practice of contracting as being the object of a limitless free play of forces. It points to the *Lüth* judgment and to those 'general clauses' of private law which guard against excess burdening, such as sec. 138 BGB, which declares legal transactions which contravene good morals as void, or sec. 242 BGB, which requires the performance of obligations according to what good faith requires in the light of common usage. As shown above,[122] the *Lüth* judgment underlined that basic rights were to be respected in interpreting and applying such general clauses. In the *Commercial Agent* case the *Bundesverfassungsgericht* adds: 'The corresponding constitutional task of granting protection ("*Schutzauftrag der Verfassung*") here is assigned to the judge who is to give effect to the objective

---

[120]*Bundesverfassungsgericht* (n. 102), 255 – *commercial agent*.
[121]*Bundesverfassungsgericht* (n. 102), 255 – *commercial agent*: 'Der Gesetzgeber muss diesen konkurrierenden Grundrechtspositionen ausgewogen Rechnung tragen. Insoweit besitzt er eine weite Gestaltungsfreiheit.'
[122]*Supra* at n. 14.

fundamental value decisions of the basic rights in cases of disturbed contractual parity ("*Vertragsparität*") by using the means of private law and who fulfils this task in manifold ways (…).'[123]

It is essential to note that the *Bundesverfassungsgericht* considers the legislator to be competent to hand down the task of granting the protection required by basic rights such as Article 12(1) of the *Grundgesetz* to the civil judges by enacting 'general clauses', which restrict the free play of private autonomy and which in 1958 the *Lüth* judgment characterised as being close to public law norms.[124] In the Constitutional Justices' eyes, obviously neither basic rights nor the principle of democracy require parliamentary statutes as such to anticipate what kind of conflicts might arise between private legal subjects and to spell out specific solutions well-balanced to the competing basic rights – even though this is the Court's principled point of view in cases involving public power interferences with basic rights.[125] It is true, when the Court addresses the rules of the HGB governing the legal relation between an entrepreneur and a commercial agent after the termination of their contract, it criticises the provisions of the HGB precisely for their inflexibility and one-sidedness in indiscriminately burdening the commercial agent by strictly ruling out any right of his to compensation during a two-year period of non-competition following a termination of contract for reasons caused by his fault.[126] The Court also mentions the possibility of changing the Commercial Code to include a set of differentiating answers to the question of whether, and if so, how much compensation a commercial agent ought to be accorded.[127] Establishing a '*Generalklausel*', a blanket norm, however, is evidently regarded as an equally valid legislative option. By this, the *Commercial Agent* decision implies that passing the '*Schutzauftrag*' on to the civil judges does not substantially change the task of solving the conflict between the colliding basic rights positions of private parties. Rather, using the general clause, the judges will regularly be in an even better position to find an equitable solution on a case-by-case basis. In the course of proceedings a single case will unfold before their eyes, and this will allow them delicately to balance the basic rights involved and, when judging whose right is to prevail, to

[123]*Bundesverfassungsgericht* (n. 102), 256 – *commercial agent* (see also *ibid.*, 262, where the Court acknowledges it to be constitutional to create a *Generalklausel* for the solution of problems of compensation payments during a non-competititon period, thus allowing for differential solutions – which, one must add, it would be for the civil courts to design).
[124]*Supra* at no. 55 to n. 57.
[125]For a more detailed discussion of this problem, see infra, at n. 274.
[126]*Bundesverfassungsgericht* (n. 102), 262–263 – *commercial agent*.
[127]*Bundesverfassungsgericht* (n. 102), 262–263 – *commercial agent*. The Court takes into account to what extent the commercial agent might be obliged to compensate the entrepreneur for damages resulting from the fault of his which has led to the termination of the contract. It also raises the question how to avoid creating incentives for the entrepreneur to provoke a situation in which the instant termination of the contract would be allowed.

tailor their decision to the details of the conflict. Deciding whose basic right is to take priority is exactly what the '*Schutzauftrag der Verfassung*' requires.

4.4.2.6 The civil courts are bound by duties to protect basic rights (grundrechtliche Schutzpflichten)

We should stop for a moment to reflect on the phrase '*Schutzauftrag der Verfassung*'. If we translate it as the 'constitutional task of granting protection', it shows that, where the legislator does not enact special rules, it is the judge to whom the constitution places the duty of ensuring that basic rights are protected in the realm of private law. '*Auftrag*', however, means more than just a task; it designates a *mission*, a mission to protect basic rights in controversies between private legal subjects. If the *Bundesverfassungsgericht* speaks of such a '*Schutzauftrag*' in the year 1990, it must be doing so in awareness of the development of its case-law as to '*grundrechtliche Schutzpflichten*', duties to protect deriving from constitutionally guaranteed basic rights.[128] While the *Lüth* judgment could not foresee this development, it did by itself come quite close to considering duties to protect when it looked at Mr *Harlan's* side of the case and asked which of his positions might have outweighed Mr *Lüth's* freedom of speech.[129]

The *Bundesverfassungsgericht* first came to acknowledge the existence of constitutional duties to protect when deciding on the constitutionality of a statute reforming the criminal rules on abortion.[130] Interestingly enough, in this context, the Court was able to leave undecided whether the unborn child was the bearer of a right to life (and thus a right to be protected against an abortion) or whether the unborn child merely benefited from the objective norms of the constitution as it could point, *inter alia*, to the *Lüth* judgment in which, as shown above, the constitutionally guaranteed basic rights had been acknowledged to form an objective value system ('*objektive Wertordnung*').[131] For the purposes of abstract norm control (Article 93(1), no. 2, of the *Grundgesetz*), it could content itself with investigating whether, and to what extent, the basic rights norms in their objective substance required the state to

---

[128] The *Grundgesetz* expressly defines certain protective duties in Article 1(1), 2nd sentence, (human dignity); Article 6(1) (marriage and family); Article 6(4) (mothers). The *Bundesverfassungsgericht* has addressed the right to establish private schools as a *Schutzpflicht* (see judgment of 8 April 1987 –1 BvL 8, 16/84–, BVerfGE 75, 64 [67 et seq.]). Cf. *Ruffert* (2001), § 7 IX 1. 252, who rightly stresses the essential importance of the '*Schutzpflichtendogmatik*'.

[129] See *supra* at n. 76 et seq., and after n. 99.

[130] *Bundesverfassungsgericht*, judgment of 25 February 1975 –1 BvF 1, 2, 3, 4, 5, 6/74–, BVerfGE 39, 1, at 41 et seq. – *abortion I*. The Court relied on Article 2(2), first sentence, of the *Grundgesetz* both by itself and in combination with Article 1(1), 2nd sentence, of the *Grundgesetz*. Article 1(1), 2nd sentence, puts all governmental power under the obligation to respect and to *protect* human dignity. By saying that human life, where it exists, must be accorded human dignity, the Court brings the right to life in contact with the obligation to protect human dignity in Article 1(1), 2nd sentence, and concludes that there is a duty to protect life.

[131] *Bundesverfassungsgericht* (n. 130), 41.

protect unborn life.[132] Subsequent decisions recognised duties to protect constitutional rights other than the right to life.[133] However, for quite some time the argument remained rooted in the objective value system of the constitution.[134] Only eventually did the Court also acknowledge protective duties to correspond with an individual *right* to protection.[135] However, the content of such a right to protection in most cases appears almost non-justiciable due to its vagueness – as it is regularly a matter for the legislator to decide[136] how much protection ought to be provided.[137]

All of this points towards the '*Schutzauftrag der Verfassung*' being immediately linked to '*grundrechtliche Schutzpflichten*'. Both the mission of protecting basic rights and protective duties seem quite clearly to originate in the basic rights of the *Grundgesetz*. This becomes clearer when we take a closer look at the legislation in the field of relations between private parties (we will need to return to the judges and their role shortly).

---

[132]*Bundesverfassungsgericht* (n. 130), 41–42.

[133]It is interesting to note that not only liberties guaranteed by the *Grundgesetz* in the form of basic rights can generate duties to protect. *Bundesverfassungsgericht*, decision of 4 December 1993 –1 BvR 258/86–, BVerfGE 89, 276, interprets Article 3(2), first sentence, of the *Grundgesetz* ('Men and women shall have equal rights.') as containing a duty to protect (see *ibid.*, at 285–286). Interestingly, only after the decision was the *Grundgesetz* changed by adding a second sentence to Article 3(2): '*Der Staat fördert die tatsächliche Durchsetzung der Gleichberechtigung von Frauen und Männern und wirkt auf die Beseitigung bestehender Nachteile hin.*' ('The state shall promote the effective realisation of equal rights for women and men and take steps to eliminate existing disadvantages.').

[134]*Bundesverfassungsgericht*, decision of 8 August 1978 –2 BvL 8/77–, BVerfGE 49, 89 (140, 141–142) – *Kalkar I*; BVerfGE 53, 30 (57) – *Mülheim-Kärlich*; decision of 14 January 1981–1 BvR 612/72–, BVerfGE 56, 54 (71, 80–82) – *Fluglärm* (air-traffic noise); 16 December 1983 –2 BvR 1160, 1565, 1714/83–, BVerfGE 66, 39 (61) – *Nachrüstung* (new arms deployment).

[135]It did so when regarding a constitutional complaint alleging a violation of protective duties to be admissible: After pointing out that the right to life is not only a negatory right, but also contains an objective value judgment and creates duties to protect, *Bundesverfassungsgericht*, decision of 29 October 1987 –2 BvR 624, 1080, 2029/83–, BVerfGE 77, 170 (214–215) – *chemical weapons depots*, continues: 'If these protective duties are violated, this simultaneously is a violation of the basic right under Article 2(2), first sentence, of the *Grundgesetz*, in defence against which the person concerned can raise a constitutional complaint.' A few lines below this quotation, the Court speaks of the '*mit einer solchen Schutzpflicht verbundene grundrechtliche Anspruch*', the basic rights claim connected with such a protective duty.

[136]But cf. *Bundesverfassungsgericht*, judgment of 16 October 1977 –1 BvQ 5/77–, BVerfGE 46, 160 (164–165) – *Schleyer*, where the Court concedes, as it seems, to all state authorities a wide scope of discretion as to how to fulfil their obligation to protect life (ibid., 164; in the case, *Hanns Martin Schleyer* had been kidnapped by terrorists, who threatened to 'execute' their victim if, among other things, ten terrorists detained in German prisons were not released). However, it continues that the choice of means might possibly narrow down to one specific means 'if an effective protection of life cannot be achieved otherwise' (ibid., 164–165). In the specific case, such a situation was denied to exist. Especially in administrative law, most likely in police law, cases the discretion of administrative authorities can be reduced to zero ('*Ermessensreduktion auf Null*').

[137]*Bundesverfassungsgericht* (n. 130), 44; decision of 14 January 1981–1 BvR 612/72–, BVerfGE 56, 54 (71) – *Fluglärm* (air-traffic noise); n. 135, BVerfGE 77, 170 (214–215) – *chemical weapons depots*. See also *infra*, n. 274.

4.4.2.7 Distinguishing the duty to protect and the duty to respect occupational liberty (Article 12(1) of the Grundgesetz) in the Commercial Agent case

The *Commercial Agent* case itself is special in that the civil court judgments upholding the contract clause forbidding the commercial agent any competitive activity without a right to compensation rested on an explicit provision of statutory law, Sec. 90a of the Code of Trade (*Handelsgesetzbuch*; HGB); the *Bundesverfassungsgericht* concluded that the judgments violated the complainant's rights under Article 12(1) of the *Grundgesetz* if sec. 90a HGB, more specifically: the second sentence of its second paragraph, was unconstitutional.[138]

Sec. 90a(1) HGB expressly allowed contracts between commercial agents and employers to place restrictions on the commercial agent in the case of a contract terrmination, albeit, for no longer than two years and, under the condition that the employer compensate the agent with an appropriate amount of money. Any derogation from these limitations to the disadvantage of the commercial agent was explicitly ruled out (sec. 90a(4) HGB). However, according to sec. 90a(2), second sentence, HGB the agent had no right to compensation if the employer terminated the contract for an important reason caused by the agent's fault. The civil courts had simply applied these provisions to the complainant's case, brushing aside his argument that sec. 90a(2), second sentence, HGB was unconstitutional, and pointing to the contractual agreement as emanating from private autonomy.[139] The civil courts, in the eyes of the *Bundesverfassungsgericht*, had not sufficiently taken into account that the legislator intended sec. 90a HBG to ameliorate the situation of commercial agents who were economically dependent and typically lacked the bargaining power they would need in order to be able to negotiate the terms of their contracts with businesses freely.[140]

The *Bundesverfassungsgericht* draws on this protective intention, but finds sec. 90a HGB, as already hinted at above,[141] to be unconstitutional insofar as the second sentence of its second paragraph strictly rules out *any* right to compensation during the two-year period of non-competition when the termination of the contract is caused by a fault of the commercial agent. The rigidity of this exclusion is unjustifiable in the eyes of the Constitutional Justices: 'Such a sanction is not necessary to encounter the competitive disadvantages of the entrepreneur terminating the contract; for the commercial agent it is, in many cases, intolerable because of its drastic consequences; in its generality it thus has a disproportionate effect.'[142]

This sounds as though the Court considered sec. 90a(2), second sentence, HGB to be a disproportionate *restriction* on the commercial agent's

[138] See *Bundesverfassungsgericht* (n. 102), 263, see also 259–260 – *commercial agent*.
[139] *Bundesverfassungsgericht* (n. 102), 259–260 – *commercial agent*.
[140] *Bundesverfassungsgericht* (n. 102), 260–261, see also 256–259 – *commercial agent*.
[141] *Supra*, at n. 126.
[142] *Bundesverfassungsgericht* (n. 102), 263 – *commercial agent*.

occupational liberty under Article 12(1) of the *Grundgesetz*. However, it is not perfectly clear whether the provision can be regarded as an interference with Article 12(1) in the strict sense. It does not apply automatically, but only in cases in which the commercial agent has agreed to a non-competition period following the termination of his contract with the entrepreneur. Nevertheless, in such cases it is a strict rule. But it must be seen in the context of the whole scheme sec. 90a HGB designs: A non-competition period can be foreseen in a contract, but for no longer than two years and with the condition that the commercial agent is to be compensated for having to refrain from business in his former field of activity. These limits on contractually established non-competition periods confine the entrepreneur in the pursuit of his interests[143] and thus restrict his occupational liberty while at the same time saving the commercial agent from having to concede more, i.e. from accepting a longer non-competition period and less than appropriate, or even no, compensation. The *Commercial Agent* decision can be understood to regard some kind of protection for commercial agents as a consitutional requirement in order to fulfil the duty to protect, as laid out in Article 12(1) of the *Grundgesetz*.[144] Such protection, however, necessitates a restriction of the entrepreneur's occupational freedom and autonomy.[145] The balance of the protective scheme which the legislator has chosen is disrupted by sec. 90a(2), second sentence, HGB, which rules out compensation where a fault on the side of the commercial agent leads to the termination of the contract. As such, this provision thwarts the law's initial intention to protect commercial agents and even adds a burden to their professional freedom.

4.5 Tracing duties to protect and duties to respect basic rights in cases concerning statutory norms regulating private-law relations

4.5.1 Statutory protection against unfair dismissals: The Kleinbetriebsklausel I case and the exceptionally sole relevance of protective duties (Schutzpflichten)

While the *Commercial Agent* decision speaks of the '[l]egal restrictions of private autonomy ... necessary for the protection and balancing of basic rights positions'[146] without mentioning the term '*Schutzpflicht*', other decisions by the *Bundesverfassungsgericht* do use the concept. A prominent example is a

---

[143]The entrepreneur must want the commercial agent to refrain from competitive activity after the termination of the contract or else the non-competition clause would not be included in the contract.

[144]See *Bundesverfassungsgericht* (n. 102), 256–258 – *commercial agent*. Cf. also *Hillgruber* (1991), 75f.

[145]See *supra* at n. 119.

[146]*Bundesverfassungsgericht* (n. 102), 260 – *commercial agent*. Full quote *supra* at n. 118.

decision of 1998,[147] in which the Court was called upon to decide on the constitutionality of the German *Kündigungsschutzgesetz* (Act Against Unfair Dismissals), which was amended to exempt operational units of businesses and administrations with five or less employees from the restrictions on dismissals defined in the *Kündigungsschutzgesetz*. It is apparent that the Act Against Unfair Dismissals is a state-made law regulating the autonomy of private legal subjects in the sphere of labour law, a sector of private law. The law's basic intention is to protect employees against being fired arbitrarily or discriminatorily, at the will of their employers.[148] In an analysis of the constitutional setting for such legislation we would, after reading the *Commercial Agent* decision, expect a balancing of each side's basic rights positions to be called for: A statute limiting an employer's possibilities to dismiss an employee interferes with the employer's occupational liberty under Article 12(1) of the *Grundgesetz*.[149] This interference can, however, be justified. On the one hand, justification can be founded on the demands of the principle of the social state (Article 20(1) and Article 28(1), first sentence, of the *Grundgesetz*). More importantly in our context, a reason justifying the burdening of employers can be the need to protect the employees' occupational freedom under Article 12(1) of the *Grundgesetz*, who are considered to be the structurally weaker group. It is clear that protecting the basic rights positions of the employees can only be achieved by restricting the basic rights positions of employers. The Court leaves no room for doubts:

> Private-law regulations limiting contractual freedom concern the balancing of conflicting interests, which are regularly tied to basic rights. This also is the case here. The employee's interest in preserving his workplace, protected by Article 12(1) of the *Grundgesetz*, is confronted with the employer's interest to give work only to employees who meet his requirements, and to limit their number to what he defines. He thereby regularly makes use of his occupational freedom within the meaning of Article 12(1) of the *Grundgesetz*, at least however of his freedom of economic activity, which is protected by Article 2(1) of the *Grundgesetz*. The legislator is thus confronted with the problem of practical concord [*praktische Konkordanz*]. The conflicting basic rights positions need to be conceived of in their inter-relatedness [*Wechselwirkung*] and to be

---

[147] *Bundesverfassungsgericht*, decision of 27 January 1998 –1 BvL 15/87–, BVerfGE 97, 169 – *Kleinbetriebsklausel I*.

[148] See *Bundesverfassungsgericht* (n. 147), 179, see also 177.

[149] *Bundesverfassungsgericht* (n. 147), 175, emphasises that Article 12(1) of the *Grundgesetz* is directed against the state, and that it neither conveys a right to be provided with a job of one's choice nor provides a guarantee for the existence of an employment one has chosen; finally, Article 12(1) does not give immediate protection against losing one's job in consequence of private dispositions.

limited in such a way as to be effective for all those concerned to the greatest extent possible [...].¹⁵⁰

In light of this exposition of the basic rights conflict, it might be surprising to read in the *Kleinbetriebsklausel I* decision that the amendment of the *Kündigungsschutzgesetz* could violate Article 12(1) of the *Grundgesetz only* if the legislature had not sufficiently fulfilled their *duty to protect* employees against being dismissed by their employers.¹⁵¹ On second thought it is obvious why only positive obligations under Article 12(1) of the *Grundgesetz*, in the form of a duty to protect, come into play: The *Bundesverfassungsgericht* was examining the question whether the *lifting* of restrictions on dismissals was constitutional. For the employers, freedom was gained. For the employees, there was no limitation of their liberty, existing employment relations were not automatically affected by the new statute;¹⁵² only the protection which peremptory state-made norms provided against dismissal by employers was reduced. But the main point is that the statute was evidently examined as to whether it might violate *Schutzpflichten*.

4.5.2 The legal father's right to know the paternity of his child: Restricting the child's informational autonomy for the protection of the father's personality right and the relevance of the principle of proportionality (Verhältnismäßigkeit, Übermaßverbot)

Another case also demonstrates how the legislative solution of conflicts between private persons involves both the fulfilment of duties to protect the basic rights of one group and restrictions on the basic rights of others. This constitutional complaint case, decided in 2007,¹⁵³ concerns the right of a man to find out whether a child, whose father he is legally considered to be, is biologically descended from him. The complainant had acknowledged the paternity of a child with whose mother he had had sexual intercourse during the period of conception defined by law. For three years after the child's birth he cohabited with the mother, who was the child's sole guardian. Four years after their separation he started a first, although unsuccessful, attempt to contest paternity of the child. One year later he had his saliva and chewing gum allegedly used by the child genetically examined. The laboratory found that the possibility that the two persons whose material had been examined were father and child could be excluded by 100 percent. With the result of this DNA diagnosis, the complainant again brought proceedings to contest paternity. The results of the examination, however, were not admitted as proof nor

---

¹⁵⁰*Bundesverfassungsgericht* (n. 147), 176 – *Kleinbetriebsklausel I.*
¹⁵¹*Bundesverfassungsgericht* (n. 147), 176 – *Kleinbetriebsklausel I.*
¹⁵²*Bundesverfassungsgericht* (n. 147), 175–176 – *Kleinbetriebsklausel I.*
¹⁵³*Bundesverfassungsgericht*, judgment of 13 February 2007 –1 BvR 421/05–, BVerfGE 117, 202 – *paternity.*

as part of the complainant's allegations (*Parteivortrag*) since the genetic analysis had been conducted secretly and in violation of the child's right to informational autonomy protected by Article 2(1) in combination with Article 1(1) of the *Grundgesetz* (*Recht auf informationelle Selbstbestimmung*).[154] In its decision on the subsequent constitutional complaint, the *Bundesverfassungsgericht* found that the family courts had not violated the complainant's basic rights. However, the Court did hold that the legislator violated Article 2(1) in combination with Article 1(1) of the *Grundgesetz* by failing to provide a formal procedure which would enable a legal father to clarify the paternity of his, legally considered, child and to have the child's descent from the legal father established, whether positively or negatively, without any consequences for the child's legal status being attached to such establishment.

Considering the situation of a child's legal father with doubts as to whether he was the biological parent, the *Bundesverfassungsgericht* recognised the man's right to know whether or not a child is descended from him as an aspect of his personality right under Article 2(1) in combination with Article 1(1) of the *Grundgesetz*.[155] Such a right includes the possibility of clarifying and establishing the child's descent in a formal procedure. This procedural component is qualified as an aspect of a protective duty (*Schutzpflicht*) anchored in Article 2(1) in combination with Article 1(1) of the *Grundgesetz*.[156]

Yet, the constellation of interests in such cases is complex and multi-faceted. Interests not only of the father and the child, but also of the mother are at stake. One quintessential aspect of the *Bundesverfassungsgericht*'s judgment is that the legislator must not leave the settlement of interests to the free play of forces: The father must not resort to some kind of self-help to find out about the child's genetic connection to him if the mother, as the sole guardian, does not consent. If the man asks a laboratory to make a genetic analysis of the DNA of the child, of whom he is not the guardian, and does so secretly, without the guardian's consent, this, the *Bundesverfassungsgericht* makes clear, constitutes a violation both of the child's personality right under Article 2(1) in combination with Article 1(1) of the *Grundgesetz* and of the mother's parental care and custody right protected under Article 6(2) of the *Grundgesetz*.[157] Nevertheless, the state is under an obligation, arising under Articles 2(1) and 1(1) of the *Grundgesetz* as a protective duty (*Schutzpflicht*), to allow the father to know, for certain, the paternity of the child. As only the

---

[154] *Bundesverfassungsgericht* (n. 153), 207–211 – *paternity*.
[155] *Bundesverfassungsgericht* (n. 153), 226 – *paternity*.
[156] *Bundesverfassungsgericht* (n. 153), 227, 242 (see also 232, 237) – *paternity*.
[157] *Bundesverfassungsgericht* (n. 153), 227–229 – *paternity*. Article 6(2) of the *Grundgesetz* declares the care and upbringing of children to be the natural right of parents and a duty primarily incumbent upon them and calls upon the state shall to watch over them in the performance of this duty. The Court underlines that the child has to be protected against any attempt of the father's to have its DNA tested secretly (ibid., 229).

data collected by DNA testing will allow secure knowledge, the child's right to informational autonomy, protected as an aspect of the child's personality right under Articles 2(1) and 1(1) of the *Grundgesetz*, must suffer an *interference*.[158] The right to informational autonomy is not absolute. Article 2(1) of the *Grundgesetz* expressly guarantees the free development of one's personality only insofar as one does not violate the rights of others and does not contravene the constitutional order or the laws of morals (*das Sittengesetz*). The *Bundesverfassungsgericht* gives the man's right to know his child's descent priority over the child's right to withhold such information: 'Since data are concerned which can stand in relation to data of the man who is the child's legal father, the child's right not to disclose these data is less worthy of protection in relation to him. In this constellation of basic rights, the legal father's right to know the child's paternity needs to be accorded greater weight than the child's right to informational autonomy, especially since the legislator can only fulfil and honour its obligation under Article 2(1) in combination with Article 1(1) of the *Grundgesetz* if it provides a procedure in which, with the aid of the child's genetic data in comparison with the legal father's data, it can be clarified whether the child is really descended from him.'[159]

If we put together what the *Bundesverfassungsgericht* tells us about the basic rights conflict in the factual constellation of the case, it becomes evident that the procedure the Court considers to be required by constitutional law will help the man to realise his personality right by learning whether or not the child is descended from him. The procedure, obviously conceived of as some kind of proceedings before state courts, will, however, at the same time demand the child to tolerate having a DNA analysis made. This means that the child will be *compelled* to submit genetic material as samples for genetic testing – allowing for the collection of very sensitive data. The exposure of such data in the procedure envisaged is clearly addressed in the *Bundesverfassungsgericht*'s judgment as '*Einschränkungen*' and

---

[158]*Bundesverfassungsgericht* (n. 153), 230–231, 232 – *paternity*. *Ibid.*, 230–231, the judgment reads: 'Neither can the child's right to informational autonomy justify continuously withholding from its legal father the knowledge of the paternity of the child. The right to informational autonomy protects the right autonomously to pass on and use personal data. In cases where paternity is in doubt, however, it is only these data which can, through comparison with the genetic data of the father, give information on the child's descent. Unrestricted protection of the child's genetic data against being brought to the father's knowledge would therefore mean for him the withholding of the knowledge of his own data as well as, in many cases, simultaneously the impossibility of gaining access to information on the paternity of the child, since he is not necessarily able to know whether the mother of the child had sexual intercourse with other men during the time of conception. The father's legitimate interest in knowing the true paternity of the child is reinforced by the existence of obligations resting on him as the legal father. In case the mother has the sole right of custody for the child, she can furthermore by exercising the child's right to informational autonomy prevent the man from learning of the paternity of the child as long as he lacks a procedure to clarify the [child's] descent.'
[159]*Bundesverfassungsgericht* (n. 153), 232 – *paternity*.

'*Beschränkungen*', i.e. restrictions, of the right to informational autonomy as guaranteed under Articles 2(1) and 1(1) of the *Grundgesetz*.[160] Such restrictions, the Court says, can be required by procedural law,[161] 'if, taking into account the basic rights of others, such as here the father's basic right to know the paternity, this is justified and proportionate [*gerechtfertigt und verhältnismäßig*]'.[162]

Emphasis must be placed here on the fact that the Court expressly addresses the question of *proportionality*.[163] The child can be compelled to disclose data, which is an interference with his right under Article 2(1) and 1(1) of the *Grundgesetz*. This compulsion, however, must prove proportionate. The *Bundesverfassungsgericht* connects the principle of proportionality to the principle of the *Rechtsstaat*.[164] To answer the question of whether or not an interference with a basic right, which guarantees a liberty, is proportionate a four-part test has evolved.

(1) The interference needs to serve a public interest purpose.

(2) The interfering measure of governmental power must promote this interest; it must be an apt ('*geeignet*') means.

(3) The public interest goal must, furthermore, not be achievable by a means less intrusive on the basic right: Among several equally effective means, the one with the least degree of interference must be chosen. This is what the requirement means that the interference needs to be 'necessary' ('*erforderlich*').

(4) Finally, the interference must be appropriate ('*angemessen*'); the restriction on the basic right must not be grossly disproportionate in comparison to the measure's positive effect; it must be a tolerable burden for the rights bearer; and, moreover, the burden must be in a balance with what is gained by burdening.[165]

If we apply the four-part test to the paternity case, we can see: (1) The public interest is that of protecting and promoting the legal father's right to know

---

[160]*Bundesverfassungsgericht* (n. 153), 228–229 – *paternity*.

[161]The Court points to sec. 372a of the German Code of Civil Procedure (*Zivilprozessordnung*), which concerns examinations for the purpose of establishing paternity.

[162]*Bundesverfassungsgericht* (n. 153), 228–229 – *paternity*.

[163]See, i.a.: *Lerche* (1961); *Grabitz* (1973), 568; *Dechsling* (1989); *Lücke* (1974), 769; *Wend* (1979), 414 ff. Cf. also *Wittig* (1968), 817 (819 et seq.) (as to the derivation of the principle of proportionality from the prohibition of arbitrariness).

[164]*Bundesverfassungsgericht*, decision of 7 April 1964 –1 BvL 12/63–, BVerfGE 17, 306 (313) – *lift-arranging agency*; decision of 15 December 1965 –1 BvR 513/65–, BVerfGE 19, 342 (348–349) – *Wencker* (the principle of proportionality derives from 'the *Rechtsstaatsprinzip*, essentially even from the very nature of the basic rights, which, as expressions of the citizen's general right to freedom in relation to the state, are allowed to be restricted by public power no further than is imperative for the protection of public interests'); decision of 7 April 1964 –1 BvL 12/63–, BVerfGE 55, 159 (165) – *falconer licence*; judgment of 24 April 1985 –2 BvF 2, 3, 4/83 und 2/84–, BVerfGE 69, 1 (35) – *conscientious objectors against military service*.

[165]See *von Münch (2000)*, para. 55.

his child's descent, i.e. the fulfilment of a protective duty, or positive obligation, under Articles 2(1) and 1(1) of the *Grundgesetz*. (2) The means of providing a (court) procedure, in which the child can be compelled to submit to DNA testing, is evidently able to achieve this aim; the corresponding restrictions on the child's right to informational autonomy under Articles 2(1) and 1(1) of the *Grundgesetz* therefore suit the purpose. (3) It appears to be without an alternative and thus necessary; however, one ought to conceive of the possibility that such a genetic examination and analysis might unavoidably produce results which go beyond the mere clarification of paternity; if, for instance, the test had the potential of disclosing genetic defects and such information were not needed for the purpose of establishing paternity, the collection of such excessive data would appear excessive and thus 'not necessary'; these data would have to be withheld from the father. (4) On these conditions, the burden on the child appears tolerable since the man is the *legal* father and there consequently are legal ties between the two; the legal father especially has obligations, one of the relevant ones being to provide or contribute to the child's maintenance.[166]

Thus, the case of the legal father's seeking certainty as to the paternity of a child shows that:

(1) in controversies between private parties whose basic rights stand in conflict, the positive constitutional obligations in the form of duties *to protect* one of the parties' basic rights may call for a solution in the form of *restricting* the other party's basic right and that
(2) this restriction, if brought about by a legislative act, must comply with the requirements of proportionality.

4.6 Proportionality and practical concord in judicial case-by-case decisions on conflicting basic rights of private parties

4.6.1 The prima facie *relevance of proportionality when the courts are called upon to solve a basic rights conflict*

Let us return to the *Commercial Agent* decision. There the *Bundesverfassungsgericht* taught us that the conflict between basic rights positions in private-law relations need not be solved immediately by the legislature.[167] Legislation, instead, can restrict itself to enacting blanket norms, thereby passing the '*Schutzauftrag*' on to the civil judges.[168] This, of course, does not change the nature of the conflict between private parties' basic rights

---

[166]Cf. *Bundesverfassungsgericht* (n. 153), 232 – *paternity*.
[167]*Supra*, at n. 122 to n. 127. Cf. also *Hermes* (1990), 1767.
[168]Cf. *Oeter* (1994), 535 f.; Cf. *Hillgruber* (1991), 84 Cf. Contra: *Dolderer* (2000), § 5 B II 3. p. 216.

positions.[169] Therefore, the task of solving this conflict does not change substantially. Although the Court does not expound on this question in the *Commercial Agent* case, the structural equivalence of the basic rights problem to be solved also points towards the relevance of the principle of proportionality, independent of whether or not the legislature or the courts are competent. The *Bundesverfassungsgericht* does touch upon this aspect, albeit only briefly and only with regard to the legislature, when it describes legislative discretion for the regulation of non-competition clauses to be limited in two directions because basic rights positions are concerned both on the entrepreneur's side and on the commercial agent's side: 'In such a situation of inter-relatedness [*Wechselbeziehung*], neither the restriction of freedom nor the protection of freedom must be disproportionate [*unverhältnismäßig*].'[170]

Here the *Commercial Agent* case connects to the case of the legal father's right to know the paternity of his legally considered child, which has also shown us that the *legislative* protection of one party's basic right[171] through restrictions on the other party's basic right[172] must respect the principle of proportionality: The public purpose pursued is to fulfil the positive constitutional obligation to protect the first party's basic right; the means used to achieve this purpose must not be excessive.[173] If this is so, and if the nature of the basic rights conflict does not change when the legislator entrusts it to the civil courts, it is quite astonishing to find that the principle of proportionality is hardly mentioned in the *Bundesverfassungsgericht*'s review of civil-court cases.[174]

Naturally, there can be cases, similar to the *Kleinbetriebsklausel I* case, in which the essential question is simply that of 'under-protectiveness'. Such an omission of protection can occur when the civil courts *refuse* to restrict one party for the sake of protecting the other. In such cases there seems, at least *prima facie*, to be no need for applying the principle of proportionality as there has not been a restriction on any of the party's rights.

4.6.2 The exclusion of the principle of proportionality as a standard for the constitutional review of civil-court judgments in the Bundesverfassungsgericht's Mephisto case

However, there are cases, like the *Lüth* judgment, in which the civil courts, for the sake of protecting one of the parties in a controversy, apply a provision

---

[169]Cf. *Dolderer* (2000), § 5 B I, p. 206; cf. *Schwabe* (1971), 69 ('vertraglich bedingte Gesetzesbefehle').

[170]*Bundesverfassungsgericht* (n. 102), 261 – *commercial agent*.

[171]I.e. the father's personality right.

[172]I.e. the child's right to informational autonomy. Additionally, the mother's right of parental care and custody was affected.

[173]*Supra*, at n. 166.

[174]Disregarding the danger of being repetitive, one must underline that the *Commercial Agent* decision addresses aspects of proportionality only when dealing with the *legislative* solution of the conflict; see *Bundesverfassungsgericht* (n. 102), 261, 263 – *commercial agent*.

of private law which restricts the other party's basic right position, but there is no application of the principle of proportionality. A prominent example of this is the *Bundesverfassungsgericht*'s *Mephisto* decision of 1971.[175] The case concerned a constitutional complaint against civil court judgments which enjoined a publishing company from publishing the book '*Mephisto* Roman einer Karriere' ('*Mephisto* Novel of a Career') by Klaus Mann. The case was brought before the civil courts by the adopted son and sole heir of the actor and director *Gustaf Gründgens*. The novel tells the story of *Hendrik Höfgen*, who denies his political conviction and sheds all human and ethical bonds in order to make a career as an artist in a pact with the rulers of national-socialist Germany.[176] *Klaus Mann* used *Gustaf Gründgen* to model his character *Hendrik Höfgen*. While the district court rejected the claim against the publisher, the court of appeals and the *Bundesgerichtshof* granted the injunction. In their eyes, the novel violated *Gustaf Gründgens'* honour, his reputation, his social esteem and denigrated his memory. Even though the novel was not intended as a biography nor as a historical study of the world of German theatre in the 1920s and 1930s, the description of the appearance and life of *Gustaf Gründgens* in the person of *Hendrik Höfgen* would lead the public to believe that *Hendrik Höfgen's* personal experiences, actions and motives were true for the real person *Gustaf Gründgens*. The courts assumed that readers would be unable to distinguish between fiction and fact, especially as what had been added to the picture of *Gustaf Gründgen's* life was not only possible, but well believable.[177]

In line with the *Lüth* judgment, the *Bundesverfassungsgericht* regards the interpretation and application of private law as a matter entrusted to the civil courts, which cannot be reviewed as arbitrariness (and thus a violation of Article 3(1) of the *Grundgesetz* guaranteeing equal protection before the law). Then the Court expressly refers, *inter alia*, to the standards developed in the *Lüth* judgment, and asks whether the civil court decisions are founded on a fundamentally wrong conception of the relevance of basic rights or whether the result of the interpretation of private law violates basic rights.[178]

The *Mephisto* judgment sets a milestone for the constitutional protection of the freedom of art by extending the personal scope of this basic right to a work of art's sphere of impact ('*Wirkbereich*'). Looking back to the time of the national-socialist rule in Germany, the Court points out that the personal freedom of the artist is not sufficient to secure the freedom of art; without the protection of the presentation, publication and distribution of a work of art

---

[175]*Bundesverfassungsgericht*, decision of 24 February 1971 –1 BvR 435/68–, BVerfGE 30, 173 – *Mephisto*.
[176]See the summary in *Bundesverfassungsgericht* (n. 175), 174 – *Mephisto*.
[177]See the summary of the court of appeal's account of facts by *Bundesverfassungsgericht* (n. 175), 178.
[178]*Bundesverfassungsgericht* (n. 175), 188 – *Mephisto*.

the guarantee would remain theoretical.[179] Article 5(3) of the *Grundgesetz* permits the artist, without interference by public power, to choose his subject-matter for a work of art, including topics of present-day relevance, and freely to make creative decisions according to the internal rules of art.[180] The basic right not only protects the artist, but also protects the people who serve as intermediaries between the artist and public. For example, in the case of a book, the intermediary whose right is protected would be the publisher.[181]

Although the *Grundgesetz* does not attach a limitation clause to the freedom of art, the *Bundesverfassungsgericht* does not understand the basic right to be without limits. From the *Grundgesetz*'s conception of the human being (*Menschenbild*) as an autonomous personality developing within the social community, it concludes that there are restrictions. As Article 5(3) of the *Grundgesetz*, however, does not expressly reserve to the legislator the power to limit the freedom of art, such restrictions can only result from the constitution itself, and need to be found by interpretation. Although the *Bundesverfassungsgericht* discerns a direct link between the freedom of art and the guarantee of the inviolability of human dignity, as the highest value within the system of basic rights, it regards conflicts between Article 5(3) of the *Grundgesetz* and the personality right protected by the constitution as possible.[182] As *Gustaf Gründgens*, alleged to have been defamed by *Klaus Mann's* novel, was already deceased, the Court accords protection only on the grounds of Article 1(1) of the *Grundgesetz*, reserving Article 2(1) for the living.[183]

Thus, in the *Mephisto* case there is a conflict between the publisher's freedom of art and the deceased *Gustaf Gründgens's* human dignity. Again resorting to the *Grundgesetz*'s conception of the human being, the Court sees an inter-relatedness between Articles 5(3) and 1(1) of the *Grundgesetz*, neither of the basic rights being superior *ab initio*.[184] Nevertheless, the conflict needs to be resolved.

> The resolution of the tension between the protection of the personality and the right of freedom of art therefore cannot be based solely on the effects which a work of art has, beyond the artistic sphere, in the social sphere; rather it must take into account art-specific aspects as well. The conception of the human being [*Menschenbild*] forming the basis of Article 1(1) of the *Grundgesetz* is equally co-defined by the guarantee of

---

[179]*Bundesverfassungsgericht* (n. 175), 188–189 – *Mephisto*.

[180]*Bundesverfassungsgericht* (n. 175), 190 – *Mephisto*.

[181]*Bundesverfassungsgericht* (n. 175), 191 – *Mephisto*.

[182]*Bundesverfassungsgericht* (n. 175), 193 – *Mephisto*.

[183]*Bundesverfassungsgericht* (n. 175), 194 – *Mephisto* ('The basic right guaranteed by Article 2(1) of the *Grundgesetz* indispensably requires the existence of a person who is able to act, be it potentially or in future.').

[184]*Bundesverfassungsgericht* (n. 175), 195 – *Mephisto*.

liberty in Article 5(3), first sentence, of the *Grundgesetz* as it is, in reverse, influenced by the value judgment of Article 1(1) of the *Grundgesetz*. The individual's claim to social esteem and respect does not rank superior to the freedom of art, just as art must not indifferently disregard the human being's general claim to being respected.

The decision whether shaping an artistic image according to real-life personal data raises the danger of a severe intrusion into the personality sphere of the person depicted, and thus forms an obstacle to publishing the work of art, can only be taken by balancing all the circumstances of the individual case. In so doing, attention must be paid to how far the 'image', in comparison with the 'original', appears to have become so independent, by the artistic shaping of the subject-matter and its insertion into the overall organism of the work of art, that what is individual, personally intimate, has been objectified for the benefit of the general, symbolic dimension of the 'character'. If, however, such an evaluation, which takes into consideration what is art-specific, shows the artist to have drawn, or even to have intended to draw, a 'portrait' of the 'original', it will depend on the extent of artistic alienation or the degree and intensity of 'distortion' for the reputation, or for the memory, of the person concerned.[185]

The *Bundesverfassungsgericht* thus calls for a balancing of the conflicting basic rights, but it does not mention the principle of proportionality. The Court continues by pointing to its restricted power to review civil court decisions. This balancing, as the two paragraphs quoted above show,[186] is required by constitutional law, and is entrusted to the civil courts:

---

[185]*Bundesverfassungsgericht* (n. 175), 195 – *Mephisto*: '*Die Lösung der Spannungslage zwischen Persönlichkeitsschutz und dem Recht auf Kunstfreiheit kann deshalb nicht allein auf die Wirkungen eines Kunstwerks im außerkünstlerischen Sozialbereich abheben, sondern muß auch kunstspezifischen Gesichtspunkten Rechnung tragen. Das Menschenbild, das Art. 1 Abs. 1 GG zugrunde liegt, wird durch die Freiheitsgarantie in Art. 5 Abs. 3 Satz 1 GG ebenso mitgeprägt wie diese umgekehrt von der Wertvorstellung des Art. 1 Abs. 1 GG beeinflußt ist. Der soziale Wert- und Achtungsanspruch des Einzelnen ist ebensowenig der Kunstfreiheit übergeordnet wie sich die Kunst ohne weiteres über den allgemeinen Achtungsanspruch des Menschen hinwegsetzen darf. Die Entscheidung darüber, ob durch die Anlehnung der künstlerischen Darstellung an Persönlichkeitsdaten der realen Wirklichkeit ein der Veröffentlichung des Kunstwerks entgegenstehender schwerer Eingriff in den schutzwürdigen Persönlichkeitsbereich des Dargestellten zu befürchten ist, kann nur unter Abwägung aller Umstände des Einzelfalles getroffen werden. Dabei ist zu beachten, ob und inwieweit das "Abbild" gegenüber dem "Urbild" durch die künstlerische Gestaltung des Stoffs und seine Ein- und Unterordnung in den Gesamtorganismus des Kunstwerks so verselbständigt erscheint, daß das Individuelle, Persönlich-Intime zugunsten des Allgemeinen, Zeichenhaften der "Figur" objektiviert ist. Wenn eine solche, das Kunstspezifische berücksichtigende Betrachtung jedoch ergibt, daß der Künstler ein "Porträt" des "Urbildes" gezeichnet hat oder gar zeichnen wollte, kommt es auf das Ausmaß der künstlerischen Verfremdung oder den Umfang und die Bedeutung der "Verfälschung" für den Ruf des Betroffenen oder für sein Andenken an.*'
[186]*Supra*, at n. 185.

This balancing is in the first place assigned to the competent courts in the context of applying and interpreting private-law provisions. The civil judge's task in such cases consists in specifying the limits of one party's basic rights sphere in relation to that of the other party – respecting the general prohibition of arbitrariness (Article 3(1) of the *Grundgesetz*).[187]

The *Mephisto* decision does not bind the civil court decisions to the principle of proportionality. Instead, the *Bundesverfassungsgericht*, pointing to its restricted powers of control, is only willing to apply Article 3(1) of the *Grundgesetz*. Consequently, the standard for reviewing civil court decisions which balance conflicting basic rights is the constitutional prohibition of arbitrary decisions. We have come across the *Bundesverfassungsgerichts's* self-restraint several times before. The Mephisto decision reiterates:

The *Bundesverfassungsgericht* has no power, in the manner of an appellate court [*nach Art eines Rechtsmittelgerichts*], to put its own evaluation of an individual case in the place of that of the competent judge. Rather, in such cases, it can establish a violation of the basic right only if the competent judge either did not realise that the case involves the balancing of competing basic rights spheres, or if his decision is founded on a fundamentally wrong conception of the meaning of the one or of the other of the basic rights, especially of their scopes of protection.[188]

The *Bundesverfassungsgericht* even goes one step further. First it shows that the judgments by the court of appeals and the *Bundesgerichtshof* in the *Mephisto* case abided by the applicable constitutional standards. The civil courts had rightly rejected the complaint that the publisher's right under Article 5(3) of the *Grundgesetz* stood against enjoining it from publishing *Klaus Mann's* novel.[189] Then the Court raises the question whether the injunction might be *out of proportion* [*außer Verhältnis*] to the foreseeable interference with the deceased *Gustaf Gründgens's* claim to respect. And it expressly denies the applicability of the principle of proportionality in cases of conflicting private persons' basic rights:

It is true that the *Bundesverfassungsgericht* has repeatedly emphasised that the principle of proportionality has the rank of constitutional law (...) and must therefore be respected whenever the public power interferes with the citizen's sphere of liberty. However, the present case does

---

[187]*Bundesverfassungsgericht* (n. 175), 197 – *Mephisto*.
[188]*Bundesverfassungsgericht* (n. 175), 197 – *Mephisto*.
[189]*Bundesverfassungsgericht* (n. 175), 197–199 – *Mephisto*. The votes of the Constitutional Justices however were tied so that a violation of the constitution could not be established, *ibid.*, 196; see sec. 15(4), 3rd sentence, BVerfGG.

not concern such an interference. The [sc. civil] courts merely had to adjudicate upon a private-law claim raised by one citizen against the other, i.e., to specify a private-law relationship in an individual case. Nor can those requirements which the constitution demands to be respected in the citizen's relation to the state in cases of interferences with the individual's sphere of liberty be applied analogously in the adjudication on the foundation and extent of a private-law claim. It is the primary object of private law adequately to solve conflicts of interest between legal subjects who legally stand on an equal footing. Accordingly, the *Bundesverfassungsgericht* can review the injunction against the publication [of the novel] only as to whether Article 3(1) of the *Grundgesetz* has been respected.[190]

In the face of the *Mephisto* decision, the re-constructive reading of the *Lüth* judgment thus suffers a severe set-back as it had understood the *Lüth* judgment to address an aspect of proportionality when acknowledging a *Wechselwirkung*, an inter-relatedness, between conflicting private parties' basic rights positions. The *Mephisto* decision strictly denies the applicability of the principle of proportionality, obviously attempting not to intrude too far into the realm of the regular courts.

However, the exclusion of proportionality must seem inconsistent when we look back. With ease, the *Bundesverfassungsgericht* resorted to the principle of proportionality when it examined legislative solutions to basic-rights related conflicts between private parties, as in the case of the legal father's right to know the paternity of the child.

4.6.3 Practical concord – praktische Konkordanz

Before we show that the *Bundesverfassungsgericht* lately might have changed its attitude toward the relevance of proportionality in civil court decisions on controversies between private parties, another conception which has become important in the *Bundesverfassungsgericht*'s relevant case-law needs to be mentioned. It is the principle of *praktische Konkordanz*, practical concord, which also is linked to the principle of proportionality.

The *Bundesverfassungsgericht* used this principle in one of its most far-reaching decisions, which concerned the influence of constitutional rights on private-law relations, in the so-called *Bank Guarantee* cases.[191] The decision concerned two constitutional complaints, the first of which was raised by a young woman who had concluded a guarantee contract with a bank for the payment of her father's debts to the bank. The bank insisted on the guarantee

---

[190]*Bundesverfassungsgericht* (n. 175), 199 – *Mephisto*.
[191]*Bundesverfassungsgericht*, decision of 19 October 1993 –1 BvR 567, 1044/89–, BVerfGE 89, 214 – *bank guarantee*.

contract; otherwise it would not have been prepared to extend the loans to the father, which he needed to run his business. The contract derogated almost all safeguards for the guarantor which the BGB foresees as far as the law declared them dispensable. Thus, the parties had excluded the application of almost all non-peremptory statutory provisions designed to protect the guarantor. The guarantee was limited to 100.000 Deutsche Mark but extended to all pecuniary obligations the father had, or would have in the future, in relation to the bank. The daughter had no occupational training, was unemployed for long periods of time, and was, at the time when the guarantee contract was concluded, earning a monthly salary of 1150 Deutsche Mark from her job at a fish factory.[192] The daughter brought proceedings before the district court (*Landgericht*) with the aim of establishing that the guarantee contract was null and void. The bank raised a counter-claim, in reaction to which the daughter withdrew her claim. The district court granted the counter-claim and ordered the daughter to pay 100.000 Deutsche Mark plus interest to the bank. The court of appeals reversed the judgment and rejected the counter-claim, arguing that the bank had failed to inform the daughter, who was completely inexperienced in banking affairs, of the nature and the extent of the guarantee contract, especially of the risk involved; the representative of the bank had even seriously played down the gravity of the commitment and the risk. The *Bundesgerichtshof* reversed the court of appeals' judgment and, by rejecting the daughter's appeal, restored the district court's judgment. The *Bundesgerichtshof* held that the bank, as the father's creditor, neither had any obligation to inform the daughter as the guarantor, nor was it obliged to make any inquiry into whether the guarantor was well-informed. A person of more than 18 years of age was an adult according to the law and in general should know that concluding a guarantee contract involved a risk of having to pay the debts of the person for whom the guarantee was given. Any expectation on the guarantor's side that she would not have to perform was irrelevant; such an expectation especially could not be construed to be the foundation of the guarantee contract. At the time of the conclusion of the guarantee contract the father was credit-worthy, and the bank representative's assessment had been correct. It would have been for the daughter to observe the ensuing development of her father's business success and to calculate her risk of having to pay the guarantee sum. The possibility of terminating the contract had been brought to her knowledge.[193]

In the second case decided in the *Bank Guarantee* decision, a woman had guaranteed to a bank the repayment of a loan which the bank had granted her husband. The woman herself was without income and assets. She was a housewife taking care of her and her husband's children, who at the time of the guarantee contract were minors. When her husband became unable to pay

---

[192]*Bundesverfassungsgericht* (n. 191), 218–219 – *bank guarantee*.
[193]*Bundesverfassungsgericht* (n. 191), 219 – *bank guarantee*.

the interest rates for the loan, the contract was terminated by the bank, which used a life-insurance contract the husband had given as security to recover part of the loan and demanded the woman to pay the sum not covered by the insurance. The district court granted the bank's claim seeing no reason to consider the guarantee contract void. The woman's appeal was rejected by the court of appeals as was her constitutional complaint by the *Bundesverfassungsgericht*.

Knowing the *Commercial Agent* decision[194] one can hardly be surprised to see that the *Bundesverfassungsgericht* found the *Bundesgerichtshof*, in the first of the two cases, in contrast to have violated the daughter's basic right under Article 2(1) of the *Grundgesetz*. The financial risk, especially the lack of any limit to the debts secured by the guarantee, and the details of her obligations under the contract could hardly have been fully understood even by experienced business people; to the 21-year-old young woman, who was completely inexperienced in business affairs, they were practically unintelligible. In cases of such distinct and clear *inferiority* of one of the parties, the manner in which a contract had been concluded became determinative. Because the *Bundesgerichtshof* denied there to be any obligation on the side of the bank to inform and to explain the risks associated with a guarantee loan, and because the *Bundesgerichtshof* did not consider the insistence and pertinacity of the bank's representative to be relevant, its decision was found to have failed so drastically in securing the basic right of private autonomy that the judgment was quashed.[195]

The *Bundesverfassungsgericht* considers private autonomy to be protected by Article 2(1) of the *Grundgesetz*. But private autonomy, of necessity, is both limited and in need of being structured by legislation. However, the legislator is not completely free to regulate private autonomy, but bound by the objective provisions of basic rights. The legislator 'must open to the individual's autonomy [*Selbstbestimmung*] an appropriate space for being exercised in legal life [*Rechtsleben*]. According to its object of regulation, private autonomy is necessarily dependent on being implemented and enforced by the state. The task of securing it is *quasi* aware of judicial realisation and therefore establishes the legislator's duty to provide means of [individually] designing legal transactions, which are to be treated as legally binding and establish legal positions enforceable even in case of controversy.'[196]

Here, the *Bundesverfassungsgericht* focuses on legislative power: 'By the duty to structure the private legal order [*Ausgestaltung der Privatrechtsordnung*] the legislator is confronted with a problem of practical concord [*praktische Konkordanz*]. Those who are involved in private-law interactions are bearers of basic rights who rank equally and who pursue

---

[194]See *supra*, at n. 102 et seq. *Bundesverfassungsgericht* (n. 191), 232, expressly refers to the Commercial Agent decision, BVerfGE 81, 242 (255).
[195]*Bundesverfassungsgericht* (n. 191), 234–235 – *bank guarantee*.
[196]*Bundesverfassungsgericht* (n. 191), 231–232 – *bank guarantee*.

different interests and manifold contradictory aims. As all those who are involved in private legal interactions enjoy protection under Article 2(1) of the *Grundgesetz* and can equally claim the basic right guarantee of private autonomy, it must not only be the right of the strongest [*Recht des Stärkeren*[197]] that prevails. The conflicting basic rights positions are to be seen in their inter-relatedness [*Wechselwirkung*] and to be limited in such a way as to become effective for all persons involved to the greatest possible extent.'[198]

The reference made to '*Wechselwirkung*', i.e. to the inter-relatedness of basic rights positions, clearly points back to the *Lüth* judgment.[199] There, however, it was used to explain why acts of general legislation within the meaning of Article 5(2) of the *Grundgesetz* could not be used unilaterally and unrestrainedly to deprive the basic right of freedom of expression of its protective force for reasons of public interest. Further analysis of the *Lüth* judgment demonstrated that the public interests involved in the case, in their essence, were constitutionally protected basic rights positions.[200] *Wechselwirkung*, even in the *Lüth* case, actually existed between competing basic rights positions.

By invoking the principle of '*praktische Konkordanz*' (practical concord) in the *Bank Guarantee* cases, the *Bundesverfassungsgericht* is using a term invented by *Konrad Hesse*, a prominent scholar of constitutional law and a former Constitutional Justice. During *Konrad Hesse*'s term as Constitutional Justice, which lasted until 16 July 1987, the Court used the idea of '*Konkordanz*' in some of its cases, indicating that conflicts between different legal values protected equally by the constitution needed to be solved by the balancing and the relative positioning ('*Zuordnung*') of the values concerned, as there was no *ab initio* priority of the one value over the other.[201] The Court

---

[197]Also meaning 'law of the jungle'.

[198]*Bundesverfassungsgericht* (n. 191), 232 – *bank guarantee*.

[199]See *supra*, at n. 67.

[200]See *supra*, at n. 86 et seq.

[201]See *Bundesverfassungsgericht*, decision of 17 December 1975 –1 BvR 63/68–, BVerfGE 41, 29 (51) (concerning the conflict between the right of a *Land* to define the forms of public schools and the constitutionally guaranteed religious freedom of the children, Article 4 of the *Grundgesetz*, and the parents' right to decide questions of their children's religious education; this decision is referred to by *Bundesverfassungsgericht*, decision of 17 December 1975 –1 BvR 428/69?, BVerfGE 41, 65 (78); and decision of 17 December 1975 –1 BvR 548/68–, BVerfGE 41, 88 (106–108) (pointing to differences in the parents' convictions and their choices as to the religious education of their children). See also *Bundesverfassungsgericht*, judgment of 9 February 1982 –1 BvR 845/79–, BVerfGE 59, 360 (381). Furthermore, *Bundesverfassungsgericht*, decision of 16 October 1979 – 1 BvR 647/70 und 7/74–, BVerfGE 52, 223 (240, 242) – *school prayer*, which was taken without *Konrad Hesse* participating. Cf. *Bundesverfassungsgericht*, decision of 13 January 1982 – 1 BvR 848, 1047/77, 916, 1307/78, 350/79 und 475, 902, 965, 1177, 1238, 1461/80 –, BVerfGE 59, 231 (262–263) (where a collision of constitutional values requiring the achievement of 'practical concord' is denied to exist in the relation between the freedom of broadcasting and the principle of the social state).

has since, not infrequently, resorted to the principle of practical concord,[202] once concisely rephrasing it as:

This principle demands to refrain from privileging, and maximizing the realization of, one of the competing legal positions; instead it requires to bring all into a balance (...).[203]

Konrad Hesse describes '*praktische Konkordanz*' as a specific form of problem-solving: Constitutionally protected legal values need to be positioned in relation to one another ('*einander zugeordnet werden*') in such a way as to allow each of them to be realised, or to use a more colourful metaphor, to allow each of them to flourish. Collisions of legal values must not be hastily solved by a mere balancing which would lead to the realisation of only one of the values at the expense of the other. Rather, the principle of 'the unity of the constitution' calls for an *optimisation*: Both legal values need to be limited so that both can gain optimal effectiveness. The delimitations must be proportionate ('*verhältnismäßig*') in every single case, and not go beyond what is required for both legal values to exist in concord.[204] It needs to be underlined that practical concord includes the idea of 'proportionality' ('*Verhältnismäßigkeit*'). However, 'proportionality' in this context means something special. In 'simple' cases the principle of proportionality, which is

---

[202]See, e.g.: *Bundesverfassungsgericht*, decision of 27 November 1990 –1 BvR 402/87–, BVerfGE 83, 130 (143) – *Mutzenbacher*; (n. 147), BVerfGE 97, 169 (176) – *Kleinbetriebsklausel I* ('The conflicting basic rights positions need to be comprehended in their inter-relatedness [*Wechselwirkung*] and to be limited in such a way that for all those involved they become effective to the farthest extent possible'). Cf. also *Bundesverfassungsgericht*, decision of 7 March 1993 –1 BvR 1215/87–, BVerfGE 81, 298 (308) – *national anthem*. From the *Bundesverfassungsgericht*'s more recent case-law there need to be mentioned: *Bundesverfassungsgericht*, decision of 14 March 2006 –1 BvR 2087, 2111/03–, BVerfGE 115, 205 (233–235) – *business and trade secrets*; decision of 23 May 2006 –1 BvR 2530/04–, BVerfGE 116, 1 (21) – *insolvency administrator*. – It might be interesting to know that in the case concerning the legal father's right to have the child's paternity established, the complainant and the Ministry of Justice of the Land of Baden-Württemberg, which intervened on the complainant's behalf, had argued that the courts had not complied with the requirements of bringing competing basic rights positions into a relation of practical concord; see *Bundesverfassungsgericht* (n. 153), 211, 215 – *paternity*.
[203]*Bundesverfassungsgericht*, decision of 16 May 1995 –1 BvR 1087/91–, BVerfGE 93, 1 (21): The *Bundesverfassungsgericht* points out that under Article 7(1) of the *Grundgesetz* it is not only the state's duty to organise a public school system and to create state schools, but the state also has the authority to define educational goals and paths of education. In this the state is independent of the parents. Thus, there can not only be conflicts between school education and parental education; it is unavoidable that within the school there is an especially intensive confrontation of the different religious and philosophical beliefs of the students and the parents. This conflict between different bearers of the right to religious freedom, guaranteed without express limitations, as well as between religious freedom and other constitutionally protected values needs to be solved according to the principle of practical concord.
[204]*Hesse (1993)*, p. 27, para. 72.

essentially concerned with disciplining public power where it is allowed to interfere with basic rights, starts from a *fixed* 'object', 'purpose' or 'goal' to be achieved (e.g. arresting a criminal suspect fleeing from the police). From this starting point, it requires the public authorities to choose among variable means (e.g. running after and holding on to him, tackling him, or shooting him in the leg). Only those means will be proportionate which not only serve the object, purpose or goal, but which, at the same time, are the least invasive on the basic rights concerned (e.g. right to life and physical integrity, Article 2(2), first sentence, of the *Grundgesetz*) and, additionally, are appropriate in the sense of neither being grossly disproportionate nor intolerable (risking the death of someone suspected of having stolen an apple).[205] With great emphasis, *Hesse* points out that 'proportionality' has a different meaning in the context of achieving practical concord between constitutional values: Here 'proportionality' describes the relation between *two (!)* variables. These variables can best be understood to be the *degrees* to which, positively speaking, the conflicting constitutional values can be realised, or to which, negatively speaking, the values need to suffer limitation.[206] Although *Hesse* does not consider the term '*Wechselwirkung*' to be very enlightening, he does admit that it is used by the *Lüth* judgment to show the need for the *relative positioning*, in the case of Article 5(1), first sentence, of the *Grundgesetz*, of the *freedom of expression*, on the one hand, and the *legal values protected by general legislation* within the meaning of Article 5(2) of the *Grundgesetz*, on the other hand. Moreover, practical concord draws the consequence of specific values being *guaranteed by the constitution*[207] by calling for an *optimisation* of *all* conflicting values. Thereby, it points to the solution of the conflict, gives the judges' deliberation a direction (albeit without fixing the solution). By determining *this direction*, '*praktische Konkordanz*', means more than simply 'balancing' values. In *Hesse's* eyes, 'balancing', as a concept, is too vague and indefinite as to prescribe even the tendency of the solution; thus, it does no more than to rephrase the problem.[208]

Above, we saw that in private-law controversies the basic rights positions of private parties can clash and therefore are in need of 'balancing'. Instead of 'balancing' it now appears preferable to apply *Hesse's* concept of '*praktische Konkordanz*'. This especially appears so when we remember that, according to our analysis, the conflict between private parties' basic rights raises the question of how far party A may, in making use of a basic right, intrude on party B's basic right position. From the point of view of public authorities, i.e. the legislature and the courts, this question needs to be restated: Does the state have a *duty to protect* B's basic right by *restricting* A's basic right, and if

---

[205]As to the normal meaning see *supra*, at n. 163 et seq. Cf. also *Hesse* (n. 204), p. 134, para. 318.

[206]*Hesse* (n. 204).

[207]Or, in the case of Article 5(2) of the *Grundgesetz*, of values of a certain quality, i.e. meeting the requirements of general legislation, being declared relevant by the constitution.

[208]*Hesse* (n. 204), p. 27, para. 72; see also *ibid.*, p. 134, para. 319.

so, how far is this restriction required, and allowed, to go?[209] Also shown above was that duties to protect basic rights have been acknowledged by the *Bundesverfassungsgericht*, but they are essentially in need of specification – the German word for such specification being '*Konkretisierung*'.[210] It cannot be strictly derived from the constitution how far the duty to protect party B's basic right reaches. Now, if this is so, we have a *variable* position: Different degrees of protection are conceivable. Simultaneously, it is exactly this (variable) degree of protection which is *decisive* for *whether*, and *how far*, party A's basic right (in use of which A is intruding on party B) can be restricted. In its dependence on the (variable) extent of protection required for party B's right, the restrictability of party A's right is *also a variable*. At the same time, there is no *ab initio* priority of either of the conflicting basic rights. Rather, both equally require the state's attention and respect. This shows that *Hesse's* description of the constellations for the application of the principle of practical concord captures the typical *Drittwirkung* situation with considerable precision: Two variables are in need of 'optimisation'. The goal to be achieved is reminiscent of the Kantian idea of the compatibility of each individual's liberty with every other individual's liberty.[211]

When *Hesse* himself speaks of this optimisation as a *proportionate* relative positioning of the conflicting legal values, the optimising *mechanism* appears to be the principle of proportionality. However, *Hesse* does not say much more other than that a solution has to be sought which allows both legal values to be realised as much as possible. I believe that the idea of proportionality can be taken a step further. When the 'simple' cases of proportionality were described above, the 'simplicity' lay in the object, purpose or goal pursued by state authorities when interfering with a basic right being *fixed*, being a *given datum*; thus there was only *one* variable: the intensity of the basic rights interference. Although the principle of practical concord is considered to promote the solution of cases with *two* variables and therefore requires a *special kind* of 'proportionality', there still is a connection to the 'simple' principle of proportionality. In the *Commercial Agent* case the *Bundesverfassungsgericht* clearly demonstrated that limiting contractual freedom in order to protect one of two parties simultaneously interferes with the other party's freedom.[212] If the constitution requires the state to protect private party B's basic right and the state has discretion, or a margin of appreciation, as to the degree of protection to be afforded, its agents (especially the courts) nevertheless at some point must *determine* how much protection is necessary – at least as a first, preliminary step. If protection against the basic right being interfered with by private party A is what is required, then an affirmative decision that B's protection is called for will, of necessity, mean that

---

[209]Insofar, especially see *supra*, at n. 119.
[210]See *supra*, at n. 128 et seq., and at n. 138 et seq.
[211]See *supra*, at n. 59.
[212]*Bundesverfassungsgericht* (n. 102), 255 – *commercial agent*; see *supra*, at n. 119.

A's basic right must suffer a restriction. According to general principles of the constitution, the extent to which A's liberty is allowed to be restricted depends upon the principle of proportionality. Given a prior (first, preliminary and thus hypothetical) determination of the *degree of protection* required for B, the answer to this question seems to be given by the 'simple' operation of the principle of proportionality, which we have already encountered,[213] and has a considerable range. One component rule is that the constitution allows only the *least restrictive* interference with A's right through which the required degree of protection for B's right can be achieved effectively; different *modes* of limiting A's liberty would have to be tested as to their intensity. It might even be that the principle of proportionality will altogether forbid restricting A's right to the degree necessary to provide the protection *prima facie* presumed to be necessary for the protection of B's right. This can, according to another component rule of the principle of proportionality, especially be so if A would suffer an intolerable loss of liberty, the inviolability of human dignity being an especially important indicator for such intolerability. In cases like these, restricting A's right would go too far. Consequently, the (hypothetical) degree of protection for B's basic right has to be reduced, since this 'dose' of protection defines the 'pressure' on A's basic right. Requiring less protection for B's right, however, will normally be possible because the degree of protection is considered to be variable (although insufficient protection, 'under-protectiveness', might also violate B's basic right; but this is only a minimum standard). The right 'dose' of protection therefore can only be found by a kind of trial-and-error procedure in the application of the principle of proportionality.

When the *Bundesverfassungsgericht* adopts the principle of '*praktische Konkordanz*' for the radiation of basic rights into private-law relations, i.e. for the *Drittwirkung* of constitutionally guaranteed basic rights, and confirms this in the *Guarantee Contract* cases, it can well be understood as the acknowledgement of what *Konrad Hesse* points out: the necessity of *proportionate relative positioning* of basic rights in controversies between private parties who in the context of their controversy can both rely on basic rights positions. The Court can even be shown to have been aware of the element of proportionality contained in the principle of practical concord.[214] Thus proportionality already plays a role in what is often addressed as the blurry idea of a 'balancing' of basic rights.

---

[213]*Supra*, at n. 166.

[214]As far as can be seen, the most explicit importation of *Konrad Hesse's* approach is to be found in a separate opinion of Justice *Johann Friedrich Henschel* to the decision by the *Bundesverfassungsgericht* of 8 March 1988 –1 BvL 9/85 and 43/86–; BVerfGE 78, 38, 54 (56–57): '[Within the realization of practical concord] aspects of proportionality do play a role, as it demands the proportionate positioning of basic rights and values limiting basic rights (...). Nevertheless, both paths to a solution of conflicts [i.e., proportionality, on the one hand, and practical concord, on the other] have their own scope of application, which is not completely

Let us have a look at only one example. Strictly speaking, however, it is not directly connected to our main theme, the *Drittwirkung* of basic rights. The *Bundesverfassungsgericht*'s decision of 27 November 1990 in the *Mutzenbacher* case[215] concerns the placing of the pornographic novel *Josefine Mutzenbacher* on the list of prohibited books by the *Bundesprüfstelle*, the Federal Control Agency competent under the *Gesetz über die Verbreitung jugendgefährdender Schriften* (GjS – Act on Publications Morally Harmful for Adolescents). The consequence of such a listing is that, essentially, such publications are allowed to be sold to adults exclusively, and offences against these restrictions are punishable under criminal law.[216] Therefore, the object of the constitutional complaint against the decision by the *Bundesprüfstelle* and the administrative court decisions upholding it, on which the Court had to decide, was an interference *by the state*, albeit by an authority with discretion.

The underlying dispute is not of a private-law nature. Nevertheless, the state's prohibition of books or other written publications under the GjS raises questions similar to those with which the civil courts are confronted when the basic rights of private parties clash in a private-law controversy. Placing a novel on the list of prohibited books is an intervention in the right to freedom of the press (Article 5(1), second sentence, of the *Grundgesetz*) and, in the *Mutzenbacher* case even more specifically, in the freedom of art (Article 5(3) of the *Grundgesetz*), which is also intended to protect not only 'objective'

---

identical. The principle of proportionality, deriving from the principle of *Rechtsstaat*, has its settled place in cases of authorities interfering with liberty and property, where individual interests and state interests conflict, that is, interests of the general public are to be attained in relation to the individual. In contrast, the achievement of practical concord also pertains to the cases of a controversy between two basic rights limiting each other. Even if this case also concerns the proportionate positioning of basic rights and values limiting basic rights, the special feature is that the value limiting the basic right is, itself, a basic right, thus the interest of one individual stands against the interest of another individual. In this situation both basic rights positions need to be brought to an optimal balance. Prominent is not the interference in the sphere of a basic right but the realisation of both basic rights which are concerned and conflict.' – See also: *Bundesverfassungsgericht* (n. 202), BVerfGE 115, 205 (233–235) – *business and trade secrets* (the case concerned controversies over remuneration payments for access of competitors to a market-dominating telecommunications company's telecommunications network; the *Bundesverfassungsgericht* modifies the standards of proportionality to be applied by the legislator for such a 'multi-polar' legal constellation; interestingly, the Court also addresses the case that the legislator should decide to assign the task of solving the controversy to public authorities; in this respect it describes the situation as especially requiring the bringing about of a practical concord of the competing interests and constitutionally protected rights); *Bundesverfassungsgericht* (n. 202), BVerfGE 116, 1 (21) – *insolvency administrator* (the case concerned restrictions on judicial remedies available to applicants for the post of an administrator in the procedure of corporate insolvency; interestingly, the *Bundesverfassungsgericht* obviously connects the principle of proportionality with the principle of practical concord in cases of 'multi-polar legal relationships').

[215]*Bundesverfassungsgericht*, decision of 27 November 1990 –1 BvR 402/87–, BVerfGE 83, 130 (143) – *Mutzenbacher*.

[216]For more details, see *Bundesverfassungsgericht* (n. 215), 131–132 – *Mutzenbacher*

constitutional values, but also certain other *basic rights*.[217] The *Bundesverfassungsgericht* distinguishes several constitutional values competing with the freedom of art in the case of morally harmful publications:[218] Protecting children and adolescents against moral harm is a constitutional value in itself, incidentally recognised by Article 5(2) of the *Grundgesetz*.[219] Furthermore, the GjS is seen to protect the parents' right to educate their children, which comprises the right to decide what their children shall be allowed to read.[220] Finally, the statute pursues the protection of children's and adolescents' personality right, protected under 'Article 1(1) in combination with Article 2(1) of the *Grundgesetz*'.[221] Their personal development requires protection against sexual dangers and respectfulness in sex education.[222]

The *Mutzenbacher* decision uses the principle of practical concord and underlines its connection with the principle of proportionality in the following words:

> The legislature may, in a situation in which scientific opinions are controversial, adopt the view that publications within the meaning of sec. 1, second sentence, GjS basically have the potential of exerting harmful moral effects on children and adolescents. Taking into consideration the freedom of art it [sc. the legislature] must not, however, determine that in cases of a certain kind of especially harmful publications the protection of juveniles shall always, and without exception, prevail. Rather, if there is a conflict between the freedom of art and another right of constitutional rank, both must, with the aim of optimisation, be brought to an appropriate balance. In this context, *the principle of proportionality is of special importance*[223] (BVerfGE 30, 173 [199][224]). Furthermore, it must be kept in mind that the freedom of art is co-constitutive of the *Grundgesetz*'s conception of the human being. (cf. BVerfGE 30, 177 [193 and 195][225]). In achieving the required concord [*Konkordanz*][226]

---

[217]A further reason for the relevance of *praktische Konkordanz* in the specific case, which however is everything other than atypical, is that the listing of the book interferes with Article 5(3) of the *Grundgesetz*, to which the wording of the constitution attaches no limitation clause. See *supra*, after n. 181.

[218]*Bundesverfassungsgericht* (n. 215), 139–140 – *Mutzenbacher*

[219]Which, however, is a limitation clause applicable only to the rights guaranteed in Article 5(1) of the *Grundgesetz*, and thus not to Article 5(3) of the *Grundgesetz*.

[220]This right not negatively affected by the GjS as *Bundesverfassungsgericht* (n. 215), 139–140 – *Mutzenbacher*, points out.

[221]It is noteworthy that *Bundesverfassungsgericht* (n. 215), 140 – *Mutzenbacher*, refers first to human dignity protected under Article 1 (1) of the *Grundgesetz* and only then to the free development of one's personality protected under Article 2(1), whereas it usually starts with Article 2(1).

[222]*Bundesverfassungsgericht* (n. 215), 140 – *Mutzenbacher*.

[223]Emphasis added by the author.

[224]*Bundesverfassungsgericht* (n. 175) – *Mephisto*.

[225]*Bundesverfassungsgericht*, decision of 3 November 1987 –1 BvR 1257/84, 861/85–, BVerfGE 77, 240 – *Herrnburger Report*.

[226] The Court does not use the term '*praktische*' *Konkordanz*, but obviously means it.

heed must be taken that the freedom of art itself sets limits to the competing constitutional value (cf. BVerfGE 77, 240 [253]). All this requires a balancing of the conflicting interests and forbids assigning to one of them, even if only for a certain kind of publication, a general priority.²²⁷

The Court is silent on abstract component rules constituting the principle of proportionality. When reviewing the application of the *Konkordanz* requirements by the *Bundesprüfstelle* and the administrative courts, the Court expounds on aspects of 'balancing' basic rights specific to conflicts involving the freedom of art. Examples of aspects are, for example, the relevance of interpreting a work of art in an appropriate, art-specific, way (*'werkgerechte Interpretation'*); the actual effects of erotic literature in a society with a tendency to more permissiveness; the importance of evaluating how far morally harmful contents are part of an artistic concept; and finally the reputation a work of art has gained in the eyes of the public.²²⁸

Having sieved through the *Bundesverfassungsgericht*'s case-law, one cannot see that the Constitutional Justices have tried to define an abstract test of proportionality to be applied under the principle of practical concord – at least not any further than by developing specific guidelines for 'optimisation' as in the *Mutzenbacher* case.

I have tried to demonstrate that the proportionality principle can be applied to the solution of conflicts between basic rights positions. This application is special because it involves a dynamic assessment process, as the *Bundesverfassungsgericht*'s interpretation of the constitution implies: Solving a conflict between basic rights by achieving practical concord requires *a trial-and-error procedure* of evaluation, in which the hypothetical and provisional fixing of a level, degree, or 'dose', of protection is the starting point – in the sense of an object pursued when restricting the competing right.

---

²²⁷*Bundesverfassungsgericht* (n. 215), 143 – *Mutzenbacher*: *'Der Gesetzgeber darf sich zwar im Widerstreit der wissenschaftlichen Meinungen für die Auffassung entscheiden, daß Schriften im Sinne des § 1 Abs. 1 Satz 2 GjS grundsätzlich geeignet sind, Kinder und Jugendliche sittlich zu gefährden. Er darf mit Rücksicht auf die Kunstfreiheit jedoch nicht anordnen, bei einer bestimmten Art besonders gefährdender Schriften genieße der Jugendschutz stets und ausnahmslos Vorrang. Gerät die Kunstfreiheit mit einem anderen Recht von Verfassungsrang in Widerstreit, müssen vielmehr beide mit dem Ziel der Optimierung zu einem angemessenen Ausgleich gebracht werden. Dabei kommt dem Grundsatz der Verhältnismäßigkeit besondere Bedeutung zu (BVerfGE 30, 173 [199]). Außerdem ist zu beachten, daß die Kunstfreiheit das Menschenbild des Grundgesetzes ebenso mitprägt, wie sie selbst von den Wertvorstellungen des Art. 1 Abs. 1 GG beeinflußt wird (vgl. BVerfGE 30, 177 [193 und 195]). Bei Herstellung der geforderten Konkordanz ist daher zu beachten, daß die Kunstfreiheit Ausübung und Geltungsbereich des konkurrierenden Verfassungsrechtsgutes ihrerseits Schranken zieht (vgl. BVerfGE 77, 240 [253]). All dies erfordert eine Abwägung der widerstreitenden Belange und verbietet es, einem davon generell – und sei es auch nur für eine bestimmte Art von Schriften – Vorrang einzuräumen.'*
²²⁸*Bundesverfassungsgericht* (n. 215), 146–148 – *Mutzenbacher*.

After the level of protection has been defined, the 'simple' rules of proportionality (aptness of the interference with the competing basic right as a means of realising the object; prohibition of excessive intervention; and appropriateness) are put to work.[229] In a conflict between A and B, the 'dose' of protection of B's basic right is in need of adjustment since there can be two kinds of failure: The *first* is that protection can be insufficient if B suffers serious disadvantages (which fall within the protective sphere, the *Schutzbereich*, of his right) when A exercises his right. In such a case of 'under-protectiveness', more protection is needed. This can only be achieved by limiting A's right more strictly. The consequence, however, can be the *second* kind of failure: Restricting A's competing basic right in order to protect B can be excessive. If, given a specific degree of B's protection, the principle of proportionality proves the restriction on A's right, which is needed to protect B, to be 'over-intrusive', the level of protection has to be reduced. This takes 'pressure' from A's right. If protection is not denied altogether, A's right still needs to be restricted, though less intensively. In order to find out if the restriction on A's right, which achieves this level of B's protection, is constitutional, the proportionality test needs to be applied again. And so forth.

Characterising this evaluation as a trial-and-error procedure is an attempt to clarify and specify the – otherwise blurry – 'balancing' nature of achieving practical concord. It is this which essentially, although only implicitly, is addressed both by *Konrad Hesse* and the *Bundesverfassungsgericht* by the concept of 'optimisation'.

4.6.4 A tendency towards further relevance of proportionality in the context of Drittwirkung

As briefly mentioned above, a fairly recent decision seems to indicate that the *Bundesverfassungsgericht* is moving toward acknowledging that the component rules constitutive of the principle of proportionality operate in the process of achieving the practical concord of basic rights positions which conflict in a private-law controversy.

4.6.4.1 The Caroline von Monaco I case

The decision delivered by the *Bundesverfassungsgericht* in 1998 on the *Caroline von Monaco I* case can be seen as a stepping stone toward this more recent decision. The *Caroline von Monaco I* case was already mentioned in Chapter 2 as proof of the *Bundesverfassungsgericht*'s strict distinction between the '*zivilrechtliches allgemeines Persönlichkeitsrecht*' and the '*verfassungsrechtliches Persönlichkeitsrecht*'.

---

[229]See *supra*, after n. 211. As to the 'simple' principle of proportionality, see *supra*, at n. 166.

We remember that the Court was called upon to decide constitutional complaints raised by a publishing company against civil court judgments ordering it to print counter-statements and a rectification in two of its magazines because of the title pages and cover stories of two of their editions.[230] One of the magazines had reported that Princess Caroline of Monaco was planning to wed again; the other had announced the famous German swimmer Franziska van Almsick was intending to marry. The civil courts had – in procedures of interim judicial relief – applied sec. 11 of the Hamburg Press Act and had ordered a counter-statement by Princess Caroline in the first case, and by Ms van Almsick in the second case, to be placed on the front page of the respective magazines. Ms van Almsick and the man said to be her boyfriend and wedding candidate additionally were successful with their claims and the publishing company had to print a rectification saying that they had no intention to marry.[231] These claims were based on secs. 823 and 1004 BGB and the allegations that the personality rights of the two plaintiffs had been infringed.

In its general considerations, the *Bundesverfassungsgericht* comments on the constitutionality of sec. 11 of the Hamburg Press Act separately from that of secs. 823 and 1004 BGB and their application.

Sec. 11 of the Hamburg Press Act obliges the publisher and the responsible editor of a periodical to print a counter-statement of the person concerned in reaction to a statement of fact which was printed in the periodical. If the amount of text of the counter-statement is inappropriate, there is no such obligation. If, however, its size is equal to that of the original article, it is presumed to be appropriate. The counter-statement must restrict itself to statements of fact, and its content must not violate criminal law. When the editors receive a counter-statement, they must print it in the very next edition of the periodical, placing it in the same part and in exactly the same typescript as the original article; they must not make any insertions and are prohibited from abridging the statement.[232]

In its evaluation the *Bundesverfassungsgericht* starts out by qualifying sec. 11 of the Hamburg Press Act as an act of general legislation, which according to Article 5(2) of the *Grundgesetz* limits the freedom of the press. Then it expressly goes on to discuss the *proportionality* of the provision. In doing so, the Court clearly acknowledges the object of sec. 11 to be the fulfilment of the state's *duty to protect* the general personality right against the impacts of the media on a person's private sphere.[233] Verbatim it speaks of '*eine aus dem allgemeinen Persönlichkeitsrecht folgende Schutzpflicht*'.[234] The right to have a

---

[230]*Bundesverfassungsgericht*, decision of 14 January 1998 –1 BvR 1861/93, 1864/96, 2073/97–, BVerfGE 97, 125 – *Caroline von Monaco I*.

[231]*Bundesverfassungsgericht* (n. 230), 126–130, 130–133, 133–137 – *Caroline von Monaco I*.

[232]*Bundesverfassungsgericht* (n. 230), 145–146 – *Caroline von Monaco I*.

[233]*Bundesverfassungsgericht* (n. 230), 146 – *Caroline von Monaco I*.

[234]*Bundesverfassungsgericht* (n. 230), 146 – *Caroline von Monaco I*.

counter-statement printed is considered as a necessary and appropriate limitation on the freedom of the press (Article 5(1), second sentence, of the *Grundgesetz*) even if it does not require the falsity of the relevant article to have been proven beforehand. It allows the person concerned to have a speedy reaction to an article, restricted to a statement of fact,[235] in the same public forum into which this person has been drawn by the publication of the periodical.[236]

The decision then turns to secs. 823 and 1004 BGB, denying that there are any doubts as to the constitutionality of these provisions.[237] The civil courts had interpreted them as giving a person about whom false statements had been disseminated a right to demand rectification. The *Bundesverfassungsgericht* sees no reason to reprimand this *Rechtsfortbildung*, especially as the right – in parallel to the right to have a counter-statement printed – finds a foundation in the constitutionally guaranteed personality right.[238] As a point of orientation for specifying the right to a rectification, the civil courts had chosen the principle of equality of the publicity effects. Quite remarkably, the Court emphasises that this choice is compatible with the *duty to protect* the basic right (*grundrechtliche Schutzpflicht*).[239] As such, it expressly brings the operation of the general tort clause into a context with positive obligations under the constitution.

The decision shows the Court's awareness that the right to rectification burdens freedom of the press. This is a clear indication that the structure of this right is very similar to the right to have a counter-statement printed. In both cases the person affected by an article in a periodical can demand the editor to include a certain content in one of the next editions for the sake of personality right protection. Nevertheless, the decision does not directly address the principle of proportionality in the context of secs. 823 and 1004 BGB. It only finds that the personality protection under these provisions is not accorded an inappropriately large weight in relation to the freedom of the press.[240] When the Court uses the word 'inappropriate' ('*unangemessen*') it faintly reminds us of the principle of proportionality. However, the appropriateness of an interference with a right is only the last of the four steps of the test.[241] Thus the *Bundesverfassungsgericht* does not seem willing to bring the full force of the principle to bear on the case.

---

[235]However, only insofar as the facts are of some significance for the image of this person's personality; see *Bundesverfassungsgericht* (n. 230), 148 – *Caroline von Monaco I*.

[236]*Bundesverfassungsgericht* (n. 230), 146–148 – *Caroline von Monaco I*.

[237]*Bundesverfassungsgericht* (n. 230), 148 – *Caroline von Monaco I*.

[238]*Bundesverfassungsgericht* (n. 230), 148–149 – *Caroline von Monaco I*.

[239]*Bundesverfassungsgericht* (n. 230), 149 – *Caroline von Monaco I*.

[240]*Bundesverfassungsgericht* (n. 230), 149 – *Caroline von Monaco I*: 'Der Persönlichkeitsschutz überwiegt bei Anwendbarkeit dieses Anspruchs auf Presseveröffentlichungen auch nicht unangemessen zu Lasten der Pressefreiheit.'

[241]See *supra*, at n. 163.

This can also be seen in the specific evaluation of the cases. As far as sec. 11 of the Hamburg Press Act is concerned the Court finds that the civil courts' order to print the counter-statement did not amount to a disproportionate interference with the publisher's freedom of the press.[242] In contrast, the constitutional review of the application of secs. 823 and 1004 BGB does not mention proportionality at all. The closest the decision comes to this principle is when it mentions that the publisher maintained that the rectification must not exceed what is necessary (*'erforderlich'*) in order to redress the interference.[243]

It is surprising to see the Court treat proportionality like a hot potato when reviewing court decisions granting a right to have a rectification of an article printed in a periodical. Yet, at the same time it applies the principle of proportionality with ease where a specific statutory provision of press law, a segment of private law, foresees a right to demand a periodical to print a counter-statement. This might be a reverberation of the *Mephisto* judgment,[244] but it is not all too convincing.

4.6.4.2 The Esra case: recognition of proportionality as an element in balancing competing rights

Let us now turn to the case that might be understood to adopt proportionality as a requirement for balancing competing basic rights more clearly than before.

The facts of this case[245] somewhat resemble those of the *Mephisto* decision. *Maxim Biller* had written the novel *Esra*, telling the love story of Adam and Esra, whose relationship is difficult because of complications from Esra's family, especially her mother and Esra's daughter born during her first, then divorced, marriage.[246] A claim against the publication of the novel was brought by a woman, the first claimant, who had had an intimate relationship with *Maxim Biller* and who had a daughter from her first marriage, and by the first claimant's mother, the second claimant. The civil courts enjoined the publishing company from publishing the book. They found that the claimants' general personality right had been violated and, consequently, could derive a right to demand the publishing company not to publish the novel under secs. 1004 and 823(1) BGB in combination with Article 2(1) of

---

[242]*Bundesverfassungsgericht* (n. 230), 153 – *Caroline von Monaco I*: 'Die in den angegriffenen Entscheidungen getroffenen Anordnungen zu Schriftart und Schriftgröße der Gegendarstellung lassen keine unverhältnismäßige Beeinträchtigung der Pressefreiheit der Beschwerdeführerin erkennen.'
[243]*Bundesverfassungsgericht* (n. 230), 155 – *Caroline von Monaco I*.
[244]See *supra*, at n. 163.
[245]*Bundesverfassungsgericht*, decision of 13 June 2007 –1 BvR 1783/05–, BVerfGE 119, 1 – *Esra*.
[246]*Bundesverfassungsgericht* (n. 245), 2 – *Esra*.

the *Grundgesetz*. Despite a disclaimer in the epilogue of the printed version of the book saying that all figures were invented, similarities with living or deceased persons therefore being accidental and unintended,[247] the civil courts were of the opinion that both claimants could – though only within a circle of acquaintances[248] – individually be identified as two of the main characters of the novel. One prominent reason for possible identification was that the first claimant had, just as the novel's main character, Esra, had, received the *Bundesfilmpreis*, the Federal Film Award, in 1989, and that her mother, just like Esra's mother in the book, had been awarded the Alternative Nobel Prize in the year 2000. The civil courts remained convinced of the relevance of these facts even after *Maxim Biller* had changed the names of the awards into '*Fritz-Lang-Preis*' and '*Karl-Gustav-Preis*' in a second version of the novel. Since intimate details of their lives, and in the case of the first claimant, also of her sexual life, were spelled out in the novel and indistinguishably mixed with fiction, the first claimant's sphere of intimacy (an especially protected aspect of her personality right) and the second claimant's personality right were violated.The publishing company raised a constitutional complaint against the civil courts' judgments.[249]

The *Bundesverfassungsgericht* found the complaint to be only partially well-founded. The civil courts had not infringed the publishing company's rights insofar as they had awarded the first claimant a right to demand the company not publish the novel. They went too far, however, by deciding equivalently in the second claimant's case.

In its decision, the Court, staying consistent with its case-law, regards the novel as a work of art protected under Article 5(3), first sentence, of the *Grundgesetz* and confirms the *Mephisto* judgment's inclusion[250] of the '*Wirkbereich*' of a work of art in the sphere of protection of the freedom of art. Consequently, the publishing company could rely on Article 5(3), first sentence, of the *Grundgesetz*.[251]

Very much in line with its consistent ruling, the Court acknowledges the private-law nature of the controversy underlying the constitutional complaint, the matter therefore basically being for the civil courts to decide. With a view to the applicability of the principle of proportionality, however, it is exciting to read that the court considers the prohibition of the novel to be 'an especially severe interference with the freedom of art'.[252] From the intensity of

---

[247]*Bundesverfassungsgericht* (n. 245), 3 – *Esra*.
[248]*Bundesverfassungsgericht* (n. 245), 25 – *Esra*, found no mistake in the civil courts evaluation that such a person's being identifiable within a limited circle can suffice to activate the personality right, although it emphasises that identifiability of a person as the model for a character in a novel in itself does not constitute a violation of the personality right; additional factors are needed (*ibid.*, 25–26).
[249]*Bundesverfassungsgericht* (n. 245), 4–12 (see also 26) – *Esra*.
[250]See *supra*, at n. 179.
[251]*Bundesverfassungsgericht* (n. 245), 20–22 – *Esra*.
[252]*Bundesverfassungsgericht* (n. 245), 22 – *Esra*.

this '*Eingriff*', the Court derives that it must not restrict itself to investigating whether the civil court judgments are based on a fundamentally false conception of the meaning of Article 5(3), first sentence, of the *Grundgesetz*. Rather, it considers itself bound to examine the compatibility of the judgments with the constitutional guarantee of freedom of art 'on the basis of the specific circumstances of the present case'.[253] This means that it is prepared to review the civil court judgments in detail. However, the Court does point out that, where private claims are brought in the courts, interferences with the freedom of art are not acts of *the state censuring* art,[254] which, it might be added for clarification, would call for a test involving the 'simple' principle of proportionality. Such interferences (by civil court decisions) are to be examined as to 'whether they equally do justice both to the basic rights of artists and the basic rights of those affected by the work of art'.[255] This can be seen as an allusion to the necessity of achieving 'practical concord' of conflicting rights in such controversies between private parties.

We have learned that the constitution in its wording does not show that the freedom of art can be restricted, but that it nevertheless suffers limitation from other provisions of the constitution protecting essential values. This is expressly confirmed in the *Esra* decision,[256] which goes on to show that the personality right protected under Article 2(1) in combination with Article 1(1) of the *Grundgesetz* can run into conflict with the freedom of art.[257] The Court regards the relations between parents and children, especially insofar as they are relevant for the development of the children's personalities, to fall within the scope of this right.[258] Unsurprisingly, the Court finds the two claimants in the civil proceedings respectively to be affected in their personality right.[259] It goes on to explain that it is not only the personality right which can limit the freedom of art, but that also, vice-versa, the freedom of art has the potential to limit the personality right.[260] Here we encounter a variant of what the *Lüth* judgment called '*Wechselwirkung*',[261] which, according to what we have seen above,[262] can be explained with the principle of 'practical concord' and its call for optimising basic rights which collide. The Court, however, only speaks of 'balancing'.[263]

---

[253]*Bundesverfassungsgericht* (n. 245), 22 – *Esra*, interestingly pointing to the separate opinion of Constitutional Justice *Erwin Stein* in the *Mephisto* judgment (n. 175), 173 (201–202).

[254]*Bundesverfassungsgericht* (n. 245), 23 – *Esra*.

[255]*Bundesverfassungsgericht* (n. 245), 23 – *Esra*.

[256]*Bundesverfassungsgericht* (n. 245), 23 – *Esra*.

[257]*Bundesverfassungsgericht* (n. 245), 23–24 – *Esra*.

[258]*Bundesverfassungsgericht* (n. 245), 24 – *Esra*.

[259]*Bundesverfassungsgericht* (n. 245), 24–26 – *Esra*.

[260]*Bundesverfassungsgericht* (n. 245), 26–27 – *Esra*.

[261]See *supra*, at n. 199–200.

[262]*Supra*, after n. 203.

[263]*Bundesverfassungsgericht* (n. 245), 29–30 – *Esra*.

In the eyes of the Constitutional Justices, it is characteristic of novels, in some way or another, to draw on reality. Therefore, a constitutional judgment in cases of conflicts between the freedom of art, used in writing a novel, and the personality rights of real-life persons, to whom the novel is connected, calls for an 'art-specific' evaluation:[264] 'The extent to which the author creates an aesthetic reality separated from real life and the intensity of the violation of the personality right are inter-connected. The stronger the image and the original resemble one another, the more severe is the interference with the personality right. The more the artistic depiction touches those dimensions of the personality right which enjoy specific protection, the stronger the fictionalisation must be in order to exclude a violation of the personality right.'[265]

Using this sliding standard, the Court finds the *Esra* novel not to have interfered with the second claimant's (the first claimant's mother's) personality right in such a way as to justify an injunction against the publishing company on her behalf.[266] In light of the constitutional guarantee of freedom of art, the civil courts needed to establish more than that the second claimant was identifiable as one of the figures and that this figure bore negative character traits. They would have had to prove that the author was inducing the reader to accept parts of the story actually to have happened, and that it was these parts which constituted a violation of the personality right, either because they made defaming, false statements of fact, or because they touched the core of the personality as such and therefore did not belong in the public sphere. In the eyes of the *Bundesverfassungsgericht*, the judgment did not provide any such proof and failed to see that the freedom of art required the legal evaluation to start from the point that the text was fictional.[267]

With regard to the first claimant, the Court, in contrast, found that the novel violated her personality right partly because it infringed her sphere of intimacy and thus a sphere of her personality right belonging to the 'human dignity core' ('*Menschenwürdekern*') of this right, especially by presenting details of her sexual life, and partly because the novel told of the life-threatening illness from which the first claimant's daughter, who herself was identifiable by the details given in the story, was actually suffering.[268] This led the *Bundesverfassungsgericht* to the conclusion that the outcome of the 'balancing' of the competing basic rights must be in favour of the first claimant's personality right, the freedom of art having to stand back.[269]

In this context the *Bundesverfassungsgericht* – and interestingly, only after finding that the first claimant's personality right prevails – touches on the

---

[264] *Bundesverfassungsgericht* (n. 245), 27 – Esra.
[265] *Bundesverfassungsgericht* (n. 245), 30 – Esra.
[266] *Bundesverfassungsgericht* (n. 245), 30–33 – Esra.
[267] *Bundesverfassungsgericht* (n. 245), 33 – Esra.
[268] *Bundesverfassungsgericht* (n. 245), 33–35 – Esra.
[269] *Bundesverfassungsgericht* (n. 245), 34–35 – Esra.

principle of proportionality. The *Bundesgerichtshof*[270] had granted the injunction against the publication of the novel as such (in favour of both claimants, which the *Bundesverfassungsgericht*, as we have seen, considers to go too far). Such a pronouncement required that the parts of the text found to violate the personality right were essential either for the overall composition of the book or for understanding its intention. The court of appeals had already considered the alternative possibility of ordering the publishing company merely to delete those parts of the text which infringed the claimants' personality right before publication; but it had rejected this option. The *Bundesgerichtshof* agrees that it is *not disproportionate* to enjoin the company from publishing the novel altogether. It endorses the court of appeals' view that, if the courts attempted to define those parts which needed to be deleted in order to protect the claimants' personality right, this would interfere with the structure of the novel as it was filled with allusions to, and descriptions of, the claimants, and several variants of such textual changes were conceivable.

The *Bundesverfassungsgericht* agrees with the *Bundesgerichtshof* (as mentioned before, it does not, however, regard the second claimant's personality right to call for a restriction of the publishing company's freedom of art): 'It is not for the courts to make deletions or changes in order to exclude the violation of the personality right as a number of possible variants exist how to make these changes, and the character of the novel would suffer considerable alteration through such interferences. However, the freedom of art requires that violations of the personality right be specified so clearly as to enable the author and the publisher to conclude how they can eliminate the defect.'[271]

It is quite remarkable to see the *Bundesverfassungsgericht* adopt the *Bundesgerichtshof*'s position. Within the context of its own decision the *Bundesverfassungsgericht* is addressing a problem of proportionality after it has established that, in the case, the first claimant's personality right, deriving from Articles 2(1) and 1(1) of the *Grundgesetz*, prevails over the freedom of art, upon which the publisher can rely under Article 5(3) of the *Grundgesetz*. We have seen that this prevalence of the personality right can mean that the personality right *requires protection* against interferences – in the *Esra* case: interference by the publication of the novel. The *Bundesverfassungsgericht*'s 'balancing' thus reveals that there is a *duty to protect* the claimant's personality right. In discussing how the conflicting guarantee of freedom of art must be restricted in order to fulfil this duty, the civil courts used the terminology of the principle of proportionality. The *Bundesverfassungsgericht* adopts this discussion, at least indirectly acknowledging that proportionality must be respected. In the context of its case-law, this is amazing insofar as we saw the Constitutional Justices, in

---

[270]*Bundesgerichtshof*, judgment of 21 June 2005 – VI ZR 122/04–, Neue Juristische Wochenzeitschrift 2005, 2844 – 2848.

[271]*Bundesverfassungsgericht* (n. 245), 35 – *Esra*.

the parallel case of *Klaus Mann's* novel *Mephisto*, strictly and unconditionally refuse to apply the principle of proportionality to the review of civil court decisions in private-law controversies.[272] This position seems to be abandoned in the *Esra* decision; its foundations having been gradually eroded through decisions acknowledging the principle of practical concord.[273] In the *Esra* case, the civil courts as well as the *Bundesverfassungsgericht* are essentially discussing whether the prohibition of publishing the novel places an *excessive* burden on the publisher. This is an element of the 'simple' principle of proportionality, which demands asking the question: Which is the least invasive measure the courts have at their avail in order to provide sufficient protection to one private party's basic right intruded upon by another private party exercising a constitutionally guaranteed liberty?

In the *Esra* case, the substantive problem is how to compare the impact of the alternative measures on the freedom of art: Is a prohibition of the novel a more severe intervention than the deletion of parts of the text? Both the civil courts and the *Bundesverfassungsgericht* do not accept what is superficially obvious. Rather, they take into account that striking out parts of the text means meddling with the author's work of art. In light of the guarantee of the freedom of art they essentially opine that it is not for the courts, even if only by deletions, to rewrite a novel and thus usurp the role of the author. On second thoughts and in awareness of the requirements of the principle of proportionality, it is not surprising to find an injunction against the publication of a novel as such to be less invasive than altering its text – especially as the author retains the right to make changes eliminating the personality right violations, thereby clearing the way for publication.

In sum, the *Esra* decision can be seen as an indication that the *Bundesverfassungsgericht* acknowledges the principle of proportionality to apply when civil courts have to solve a conflict between private parties' competing basic rights.

4.7 Empowering the judges to decide on basic rights conflicts within private-law controversies

In the previous discussion of the relevance of proportionality for the solution of conflicts between private parties' basic rights, we only shortly touched upon the institutional side of the question. We said that the right 'dose' of protection was something which could not be derived from the constitution in the abstract,[274] but was rather in need of being constitutively defined by the legislature or the

---

[272] See *supra*, at n. 190.

[273] See *supra*, at n. 191 et seq.

[274] The reason for this is that a *duty to protect* will point into a certain direction, or might even point to a certain goal in the form of a degree of protection, but as a *positive obligation* it may well be fulfilled in various ways (see especially *Bundesverfassungsgericht* (n. 130), 44 – *abortion I*; n. 136, 164–165 – *Schleyer*. In contrast, a negative obligation, such as the duty to respect a

courts. Before[275] we had seen that the *Bundesverfassungsgericht* judged it to be constitutional for the legislator to pass on the task of protecting basic rights in private controversies to the regular courts. Now this might appear as surprising in light of what is often referred to as the '*Wesentlichkeitslehre*'.[276] The essence of this 'theory' adopted and consistently upheld by the *Bundesverfassungsgericht* is confirmed in a recent decision concerning the question of whether a woman applying for a post as a teacher at a state school could be denied the job because she had declared that she would, for religious reasons, wear a headscarf in class:[277]

> The necessity, as of constitutional law, of a statutory provision follows from the principle of *Parlamentsvorbehalt* [the constitutional require-ment of a matter to be decided by parliament]. The principle of *Rechtsstaat* [rule of law] and the constitutional requirement of demo-cratic rule [*Demokratiegebot*] obligate the legislature itself to determine the rules essential for the realisation of basic rights (...).To which extent the legislature must itself define the guidelines necessary in the rel-evant sphere of life depends on its connection with basic rights [*Grundrechtsbezug*]. Such a duty [sc. to legislate] exists when there is a confrontation of competing liberties [sc. constitutionally] protected as basic rights, and their limits are fluid and difficult to discern.[278]

The Court then addresses a problem raised by the special basic rights con-stellation in the case. As the *Mephisto* and the *Esra* cases show, quite a num-ber of basic rights lack special limitation clauses so that the constellation is not uncommon:

---

constitutionally guaranteed liberty, is clear-cut and definitive, as it requires from the public pow-ers (see Article 1(3) of the *Grundgesetz*) to *refrain* from interference, i.e. not to act, not to initi-ate a causal chain at the end of which the bearer of a basic right would be hindered in exercising the freedom guaranteed.

[275]See *supra* at n. 124.

[276]Essential for its adoption by the *Bundesverfassungsgericht* were controversies over questions of state education. See *Bundesverfassungsgericht*, judgment of 6 December 1972 –1 BvR 230/70 and 95/71–, BVerfGE 34, 165 (192–193) – *Förderstufe*; decision of 27 January 1976 –1 BvR 2325/73–, BVerfGE 41, 251 (259–260); decision of 22 June 1977 –1 BvR 799/76–, BVerfGE 45, 400 (417–418) – *Oberstufenreform*; decision of 21 December 1977 –1 BvL 1/75, 1 BvR 147/75–, BVerfGE 47, 46 (78–79) – *sex education*. See also Bundesverfassungsgericht (n. 134), BVerfGE 49, 89 (127) – *Kalkar I* (concerning the peaceful use of atomic energy); n. 135, BVerfGE 77, 170 (230–231) –*chemical weapons depots*; (n. 215), BVerfGE 83, 130 (142) – *Mutzenbacher*; deci-sion of 25 March 1992 –1 BvR 1430/88–, BVerfGE 85, 386 (403–404) – *telephone trap*; judg-ment of 14 July 1988 –1 BvR 1640/97–; BVerfGE 98, 218 (252) – *spelling reform*; judgment of 6 July 1999 –2 BvF 3/90–, BVerfGE 101, 1 (34) – *regulation on chicken keeping*.

[277]*Bundesverfassungsgericht*, judgment of 24 September 2003 –2 BvR 1436/02–, BVerfGE 108, 282 – *headscarf*.

[278]*Bundesverfassungsgericht* (n. 277), 311 – *headscarf*.

This especially holds true when the basic rights affected – as in the present case, positive and negative freedom of religion as well as the parents' right to educate their children [*elterliches Erziehungsrecht*] – according to the wording of the constitution are guaranteed without a reservation for limiting legislation [*Gesetzesvorbehalt*] and when consequently any provision which intends to regulate this sphere of life must define and specify the limits immanent in the constitution [*verfassungsimmanente Schranken*]. Here the legislature is under the duty itself to determine the limits of the conflicting basic rights guarantees at least insofar as such a definition is essential for the exercise of these liberties [*für die Ausübung dieser Freiheitsrechte wesentlich ist*] (...).

The question when a legislative regulation by parliament is required, can only be judged with a view to the respective thematic field and the peculiarity of the object of regulation affected. The constitutional criteria for this evaluation are to be extracted from the fundamental principles of the *Grundgesetz*, especially the basic rights guaranteed therein (...). It is true that the fact that a regulation is politically controversial does not lead to its having to be considered as essential (...). According to the constitution the restriction of liberties guaranteed by basic rights are reserved for parliament in order to secure that decisions of such far-reaching consequences result from a procedure which gives the public the opportunity to form and represent their opinions and which induces the representation of the people to clarify in public debate the necessity and extent of interferences with basic rights (...).[279]

In light of the '*Wesentlichkeitslehre*' as spelled out here, it might appear doubtful whether or not the civil courts may be entrusted with the task of finding solutions to basic-rights conflicts between private parties on a case-by-case basis. Is it not for the legislature to decide these conflicts?

In the decision of the *Bank Guarantee* cases the *Bundesverfassungsgericht* relied on '*praktische Konkordanz*' in order to explain how conflicts between competing basic rights of private parties are to be resolved with a view to achieving contractual parity, or, put negatively, to avoiding situations of structural inferiority of one of the parties negotiating and concluding a contract.[280] In this context it looks at the provisions of the German Civil Code, the BGB, demonstrating that it was originally designed according to the model of the participants in legal interactions being *formally* equal, but that over time one of the main objects of private law has come to be the restoration of a balance when contractual parity (*Vertragsparität*) is disturbed.[281]

---

[279]*Bundesverfassungsgericht* (n. 277), 311–312 – *headscarf*. Empty brackets indicate the omission of references.
[280]See *supra*, at n. 191 et seq., especially after n. 196.
[281]*Bundesverfassungsgericht* (n. 191), 232–233 – *bank guarantee*.

The *Bundesverfassungsgericht* regards the BGB to contain sufficient safeguards against a contracting party being disadvantaged by structural inferiority. It especially points to the 'general clauses' of sec. 138(1) and sec. 242 BGB[282] and sums up that the scholars of private law are unanimous in that the principle of good faith serves as an immanent limitation on contractual freedom and formed the foundation of the civil judges' competence to review the contents of contracts.[283] Conceding that the conditions for, and the intensity of, such judicial review was debated, the Court is, in terms of constitutional law, content to find that private law as it stands at least has provided 'instruments' enabling a reaction to structural disturbances of contractual parity.[284] It concludes that it is the duty of the civil courts, in interpreting and applying the general clauses of the BGB, to take heed that contracts are not used by one party to force its will upon the other.[285] They must not confine themselves to saying that what the parties have agreed upon is binding ('*Vertrag ist Vertrag*'). Instead, they must investigate whether or not a contractual provision is the result of unequal bargaining power, and if they so find, must use the general clauses of the BGB to intervene and correct the contract. In the eyes of the *Bundesverfassungsgericht*, it is primarily a matter of statutory law [*einfaches Recht*] to define how the civil courts are to proceed and which results they need to achieve in such cases, the constitution allowing for broad leeway. A violation of private autonomy as guaranteed by basic rights is conceivable if the civil courts either do not see the problem of disturbed contractual parity at all or attempt to solve it by employing ineffective or unsuitable means.[286]

Considering what the *Bundesverfassungsgericht* explicates here, we cannot yet be sure of the reason why the solution to basic rights conflicts between private parties are allowed to be founded on general clauses which the civil courts will have to apply by specifying their content to the peculiarities of the single case they are sitting on. Why is it that the rule of law and the principle of democracy do not call for more detailed legislative provisions as in the case of school teachers wearing religious symbols?

The most plausible reason for this seems to be that contractual relations between private individuals are so manifold and various that the reasons for a disturbance of contractual parity, bargaining power being in a severe structural imbalance, are just as unforeseeable as the nature, constellations and details, of conflicts that can ensue. It is only *Generalklauseln* that have the flexibility of being applicable in any such situation as they define principles,

---

[282]See *supra*, at n. 122.
[283]*Bundesverfassungsgericht* (n. 191), 233 – *bank guarantee*.
[284]*Bundesverfassungsgericht* (n. 191), 233–234 – *bank guarantee*.
[285]*Bundesverfassungsgericht* (n. 191), 234 – *bank guarantee*: 'Für die Zivilgerichte folgt daraus die Pflicht, bei der Auslegung und Anwendung der Generalklauseln darauf zu achten, daß Verträge nicht als Mittel der Fremdbestimmung dienen.'
[286]*Bundesverfassungsgericht* (n. 191), 234 – *bank guarantee*.

principia, in the sense of fundamental rules which give binding guidelines to the solution of cases, but simultaneously are in need of specification.

We have found *Konrad Hesse's* analysis of competing constitutional values to be enlightening. Conflicts between them need to be solved by optimisation, which *Hesse* describes as the relative positioning of two values whose realisation can vary; thus there are two variables in the equation and the constitution can do no more than define the direction in which the solution is to be found.[287]

This is exactly what the general clauses of the BGB can do. In their flexibility these provisions can adapt to what constitutional law requires for the solution of basic rights conflicts between private parties. In its decision on the *Bank Guarantee* cases, the *Bundesverfassungsgericht* describes the interaction of basic rights and sub-constitutional law, especially the *Generalklauseln* of the BGB, in the following words:

> In its chapter on basic rights, the *Grundgesetz* contains fundamental constitutional determinants for all spheres of law. These fundamental determinants take effect through the medium of those provisions which immediately rule the respective sphere of law; and they are especially ['*vor allem*'] important for the interpretation of the general clauses [*Generalklauseln*] of private law (cf. BVerfGE 7, 198 [205–206]; 42, 143 [148]). By referring in a completely general way to good morals [*die guten Sitten*], common usage [*die Verkehrssitte*] and good faith [*Treu und Glauben*], sec. 138 and sec. 242 BGB require of the courts a [normative] specification [sc. of the general clauses] according to the standard of value conceptions which are primarily established by the fundamental determinants of the constitution. Therefore, the civil courts are bound by the constitutional duty to respect the basic rights as 'guidelines' when interpreting and applying the general clauses. If they fail to see this and therefore decide against one of the parties, they violate the basic rights of this party (cf. BVerfGE 7, 198 [206–207; consistent ruling]).[288]

This conception of the influence of basic rights on the interpretation and operation of sub-constitutional law very much matches *Hesse's* description

---

[287]See *supra,* after n. 203.

[288]*Bundesverfassungsgericht* (n. 191), 229–230 – *bank guarantee.* The *Bundesverfassungsgericht* has assigned a far-reaching binding effect to its decisions in cases where it pronounces on what the basic rights require of the regular courts; see *Bundesverfassungsgericht,* decision of 6 December 2005 –1 BvR 1905/02–, BVerfGE 115, 51. This was a follow-up decision to the *Bank Guarantee* decision, in which the *Bundesverfassungsgericht,* applying sec. 79(2), 3rd sentence, BVerfGG (see *supra,* n. 43) by double analogy, held that, where judgments by the regular courts were based on an interpretation and application of indefinite legal concepts (*unbestimmte Gesetzesbegriffe*) which the *Bundesverfassungsgericht* had, after the judgments have become final, declared to be unconstitutional, proceedings before the regular courts could be reopened. For a critique of the *Bundesverfassungsgericht's* decision see *Cremer* (2009), p. 741–777.

of the effects of the principle of practical concord. It becomes especially clear, then, that basic rights do not strictly predetermine the outcome of the civil courts' decisions, but merely define 'guidelines'.

The *Lüth* judgment had already exposed the very aptness of *Generalklauseln* as the inroads of basic rights into private law.[289] Of course, however, adaptation to the peculiarities of a case is nothing that comes about by itself. We need institutions to operate these general clauses and to approach each case individually. There is no institution structurally better suited for this task than the civil courts. In their impartiality and in their strict commitment to deciding cases according to the law,[290] it is the courts that are fit for fine-tuning general clauses in order to optimise the conflicting basic rights between private parties. In saying this, one must be aware that the courts have to fulfil this task in obedience to the law, as Article 20(3) of the *Grundgesetz* binds them to 'law and justice'. Only insofar as the legislature (especially through general clauses) opens the law for solving controversies in application of the principle of practical concord, do the judges generally have the corresponding power.[291] The extent of this 'openness' also depends on the 'legal environment' the case is situated in. It would be doubtful to allow the judges to restructure a field of law contrary to the fundamental decisions made by the legislature. Their decisions, as such, must remain consistent within relevant special segments of law and within the system of private law as such (which neither excludes the possibility of constitutional law 'radiating' into private law nor discredits the superiority of constitutional law, which must be respected both by private-law legislation and by court decisions applying and interpreting the law).

The *Bundesverfassungsgericht*'s decision in the *Bank Guarantee* cases has made us concentrate on the problem of private autonomy as protected under Article 2(1) of the *Grundgesetz*. The general clauses of secs. 138(1) and 242 BGB here operate to the effect of restricting one of the parties' contractual freedom with the intention of protecting the other party who lacks the bargaining power necessary in order to have had their concerns and interests respected. This ought not to distract our attention from tort law, for it is mostly tort law which protects privacy against intrusion.

The *Lüth* judgment dealt with a torts claim based on the general provision of sec. 826 BGB.[292] In the *Esra* case sec. 823(1) BGB was applied by the civil courts in combination with sec. 1004(1) BGB. Secs. 823(1) and 826 BGB are central tort provisions of the German Civil Code. The former provision obligates anyone who willingly or negligently illegally does harm to another person's life, physical integrity, health, liberty, property or any other right

---

[289]See *supra*, at n. 15.
[290]See Article 20(3) of the *Grundgesetz*.
[291]Cf. *Classen* (1997), 86.
[292]See *supra*, after n. 18

intentionally to compensate for the resulting damages. Sec. 826 puts the same obligation on someone who, in a manner contrary to public morals, intentionally inflicts damage on another person. If we merely look at these obligations and the corresponding claims, their existence shows that private persons carry responsibility for their conduct in general: They will have to compensate someone who suffers damages caused by their behaviour. Such an obligation puts a burden on the person who inflicts damages, and limits his freedom – for the sake of protecting, at least of indemnifying, the victim. The provisions of the BGB '*Deliktsrecht*' are an indirect means of regulating the activities of private persons by attaching certain consequences to the result of certain behaviour. They are supplemented by an analogous application of sec. 1004(1) BGB. In tort cases, this provision gives the victim the right to demand the person responsible to stop a continuing tortious act, to abate the continuing disturbance resulting from such an act, or to refrain from repeating it.

All three of the provisions quoted, only being a segment of BGB '*Deliktsrecht*', are of general application, the cases to which they apply not being specified in any detail. The operation of these norms does not require there to exist a contractual or *quasi* contractual relation between the actor and the victim. Thus, they regulate private persons' behaviour in a general way.

Furthermore, we have seen that, when sec. 826 BGB applies where someone has done harm contrary to good morals, it opens wide opportunity for interpretation. Similarly where sec. 823(1) BGB attaches the obligation to compensate for an illegal infringement of 'another right', the civil courts require a detailed investigation into whether or not illegality can be established. In both cases it is the civil courts who are placed in a position to specify what these tort provisions say. Again, the justification for entrusting the courts with this task seems to be that case constellations cannot be foreseen in their details.

Under constitutional law, this impossibility of foreseeing cases – just as the infinity of constellations of cases of disturbed contractual parity above – corresponds with the impossibility of making abstract prescriptions for the outcomes of the process of operating the principle of practical concord. If conflicting basic rights positions of private parties are in need of being 'balanced' in the sense of being 'positioned' in relation to one another so as to be optimised, this task can only be performed case-specifically as the solution must be tailored to the details of a controversy and requires adjustment of two variables, i.e. the extent of two freedoms.

Entrusting the civil courts with constitutively solving controversies which involve private parties' conflicting basic rights positions, at first sight, seems to be incompatible with the '*Wesentlichkeitslehre*', i.e. the basic constitutional requirement that parliament decide on questions essential for the realisation of basic rights. Nevertheless, it is not unconstitutional. As we have seen, the constitution requires *practical concord* to be achieved where a private party exercising a basic right runs into conflict with the basic rights position of another private individual. If the achievement of practical concord is only possible on a case-by-case basis, as this very much appears to be so in the field of private law, then it cannot be done by abstract legislation alone, which must confine itself to defining guidelines. The constitution cannot demand of the legislature something which is impossible. Rather, under the constitution's scheme of separation and balancing of powers it is the courts which are best suited to operate the principle of practical concord. The requirement of achieving practical concord exists as a constitutional principle of equal weight and force as the '*Wesentlichkeitslehre*'. Therefore it has the power to modify the 'Wesentlichkeitslehre' to demand no more than legislative guidelines for the solution of private controversies in the form of *Generalklauseln*.

4.8 Summing up

Looking back at this chapter, I hope that I have both demonstrated the hypotheses, which I set up in the beginning, to at least be plausible and also shown:

- that conflicts can arise between private parties which involve conflicting basic rights positions;
- that according to German constitutional law these conflicts, for structural reasons, regularly must be decided in application of 'general clauses' by the civil courts which find themselves in the role of 'basic rights umpires' having to decide whether or not there is a *duty to protect* the basic right of one of the parties (*grundrechtliche Schutzpflicht*) by interfering with and restricting the exercise of the other party's conflicting basic right;
- that this decision requires finding a solution in which the basic rights are 'optimised' in the sense of having been brought into practical concord ('*praktische Konkordanz*');
- that such a solution by 'optimisation' can only be found by a process of trial and error, starting by hypothetically fixing a degree of protection for the basic right encroached upon by one of the parties and by examining whether the restriction which this party's basic right consequently suffers is justifiable according to the specific rules applying to this basic right (for instance, its lack of express limitability) and the ('simple') principle of proportionality.

Chapter 5:
Conclusions

We have embarked on the investigation of the way basic rights under the German Constitution affect private-law relations of private individuals *inter se* in the hope of finding structures which we might then be able to detect in the law of the ECHR and to use in its application. As we have seen, we can reconstruct *mittelbare Drittwirkung* of basic rights as requiring a judge to perform a balancing of competing rights which involves two variables: the 'dose' of protection for the right of one private person needed, on the one hand, and the intensity of a restriction on the other private person's right, the exercise of which negatively affects the first person's right. Dependent on the urgency and the required degree of protection (or the intensity of the duty to protect, the *Schutzpflicht*) the principle of proportionality will allow the judge, in solving the controversy between the private parties, to apply the law in a way that, to a higher or lesser degree, invades the second person's liberty.

5.1 Applicability of the principle of practical concord to cases under the Convention

5.1.1 The example of Karhuvaara and Iltalehti

Looking into the ECtHR's case-law demonstrated that the judgment in *Karhuvaara and Iltalehti v. Finland*[1] simultaneously addressed the protection of privacy, on the one hand, and the proportionality of restrictions on the freedom of expression for the sake of such protection, on the other. It was clear that the case primarily concerned the criminal conviction of the first applicant, the editor-in-chief of a newspaper, for invasion of privacy because the paper had reported on the criminal trial of the husband of a politician. The judgment, therefore, naturally concentrates on Article 10(2) ECHR, as a conviction in reaction to a publication is clearly an interference with freedom of expression by state authorities. The principle of proportionality thus *prima*

---

[1] ECtHR, *Karhuvaara and Iltalehti v. Finland*, no. 53678/00, judgment of 16 November 2004, ECHR 2004-X.

facie operates in a rather conventional way. An additional content of the Finnish court judgments, however, gives the case a slightly unusual colour: The Finnish courts, applying Finnish tort law, ordered the editor-in-chief and the publishing company to pay damages to the politician. Thus, in addition to pronouncing a criminal conviction, they settled a private-law dispute, the outcome of which was an order to compensate. This order was in itself regarded to be an 'interference'[2] so that Article 10(2) ECHR comes into play. This provision allows subjecting the exercise of freedom of expression to 'such formalities, conditions, restrictions or penalties as are prescribed by law and are necessary in a democratic society, …, for the protection of the reputation or rights of others.' As such, there is an explicit qualifying clause aimed at the protection of positions under the category of which privacy – or to comply with the Convention's legal concepts: the right to respect for private life – can be subsumed. Therefore, it seems all the more natural that the ECtHR in this context also discusses aspects of the protection of privacy.

Nevertheless, the Court, in its general considerations, additionally and outside of any clear context with Article 10(2), also points out that '[t]he protection of private life has to be balanced against the freedom of expression guaranteed by Article 10 of the Convention'.[3] Looking at Article 8 ECHR, the Court then describes the two dimensions of this Article: that 'its object is essentially that of protecting the individual against arbitrary interference by public authorities', but that 'in addition to this primarily negative undertaking, there may be positive obligations inherent in effective respect for private or family life'.[4] Here the Court refers not only to the case of *Stjerna v. Finland*,[5] which concerned the question of whether, under Article 8 ECHR, the applicant had a right to change his surname. It also quotes its *Von Hannover* judgment.[6] Thus the Court obviously draws a connection between the positive obligation arising under Article 8 to protect private life and Article 10(2), which allows restricting freedom of expression for the sake of the protection of the reputation or rights of others. Thus, it clearly recognises that the protection of private life and the restriction of freedom of expression are inter-related.

The discussion in *Karhuvaara and Iltalehti* of whether the interference with the rights under Article 10 ECHR was 'necessary in a democratic society' shows two main themes: first, that there is no substantial *need for protecting* the private life of the politician concerned as it is doubtful whether it is

---

[2] ECtHR, *Karhuvaara and Iltalehti* (n. 1), §§ 43, 53.
[3] ECtHR, *Karhuvaara and Iltalehti* (n. 1), § 42.
[4] ECtHR, *Karhuvaara and Iltalehti* (n. 1), § 42.
[5] ECtHR, *Stjerna v. Finland*, no. 18131/91, judgment of 25 November 1994, § 38, Series A no. 299-B, p. 61.
[6] ECtHR, *Von Hannover v. Germany*, no. 59320/00, judgment of 24 June 2004, § 57, ECHR 2004-VI.

affected, and even whether the politician as a person is affected, at all;[7] second, that the fines imposed, especially when taken together with damage payments, could not be justified by the intention behind the applicable provisions to protect parliamentarians, and thus disclosed 'a striking *disproportionality*'.[8] On Justitia's scales, the 'weight' of the need to protect the right to respect for private life was close to null, while the gravity of the interference with the freedom of expression was considerable. The protective interest on the side of the politician was far from balancing the restriction of the applicants' freedom of the press.

If we imagine shifting the perspective of the evaluation under the Convention from that of the applicants to that of the politician, we will have a constellation similar to that of the *Von Hannover* case. We might even hypothesise that the editor-in-chief was acquitted of the criminal charges and the claims for damages were turned down. If we then thought of the politician as the applicant, the first question would be whether under Article 8 there arose a positive obligation to protect her rights. We would find little ground for this. Yet, even assuming that there is a duty to protect, we should quickly realise that criminal sanctions against the editor would be disproportionate and compensation could be no more than minimal as it would otherwise be an excessive burden on freedom of expression under Article 10. Thus the case also 'works the other way around'. The categories of 'positive obligation to protect', on the one side, and 'proportionality of any interference called for in the course of the fulfilment of such an obligation', on the other, would structure the legal problems, showing whether there were a variety of valid evaluations or only one convincing result. The case *needs to* 'work the other way around' – because otherwise its outcome would depend on which of the parties lodges an application to the ECtHR. There is also a deeper reason: The positive obligations to protect bind the state authorities. If they are to fulfil these obligations in a case where A intrudes on B's freedom and B therefore needs to be protected, they will have to stop A from acting in a way that encroaches upon B's freedom. When both parties enjoy rights guaranteed under the Convention, the duty to protect one party's right will require state authorities to restrict the other party's right. Such a restriction, however, needs to comply with the requirements of qualifying clauses such as Article 10(2) ECHR, one of which is adherence to proportionality. One party cannot expect the duty to provide protection against others to go beyond what the state authorities are allowed to do under the Convention. Not only the fulfilment but the *scope and contents* of positive obligations to protect are limited by the principle of proportionality.

In other words, in the light of the *Karhuvaara and Iltalehti* case, the principle of *practical concord*, as structured by the two-variable test, has the potential of also being applied at the level of the ECtHR.

---

[7] ECtHR, *Karhuvaara and Iltalehti* (n. 1), §§ 44, 47.
[8] ECtHR, *Karhuvaara and Iltalehti* (n. 1), §§ 50–54 (emphasis added).

5.1.2 Operating the principle of practical concord under the Convention using the two-variable test

5.1.2.1 Rationalisation of the balancing test

Perhaps *Karhuvaara and Iltalehti* is just too clear a case. Whether viewed from the press's or from the politicians' side, the imbalance is obvious. Let us therefore return to the *Von Hannover* case and try to assess the two-variable test as an analytical tool.

Expressly determining the intensity of the duty to protect a right guaranteed under the Convention, 'calculating' the 'weight' of the need for protection, and thus of the positive obligation, is a first – however, only a first – step in rationalising the balancing test. If we once again retrace the stages of the *Von Hannover* case, the German *Bundesgerichtshof* had attached little weight to the privacy interests of Princess Caroline; if we use Convention law as the common denominator, we can say that the *Bundesgerichtshof* did not extend the positive obligation to protect the right to respect for private life beyond the walls of the home and places of seclusion. The *Bundesverfassungsgericht* expanded the duty to protect to situations of family life in public contexts. The ECtHR, finally, brushed away any argument against protecting Princess Caroline from being photographed in public, which was based on her publicity as such. It acknowledged this celebrity's need to have paparazzi photographs banned from publication against her will. We can easily compare the three judgments by asking which 'dose' of protection for the right to private life was considered as correct.

The second step in the rationalisation of the balancing is assessing the intensity of the restriction on the conflicting right which is necessary to achieve the level of protection required. Logically, this cannot be the first step because the guarantee of a right *quasi* establishes the presumption of liberty and, on the other side of the coin, the necessity of showing a justification for any restriction. Thus, the law encounters the person who exercises a right and thereby intrudes into the sphere of another person's right, by saying, 'In principle, you are free to do as you choose, *but* here you have overstepped a limit.' The justification for the restriction of the right is that it is necessary in order to protect the other person's right (this is exactly the point where the duty to protect connects with restricting the competing right). We can understand the term 'necessary' as in itself containing the principle of proportionality. If we adopt the understanding developed in German constitutional law,[9] this means that 1) the restriction of the right must be capable of advancing the protection of the other's right, 2) it must not exceed what is unavoidable to afford the degree of protection required, and 3) it must not be intolerable or otherwise inappropriate. In the *Von Hannover* case the principle of proportionality

---

[9] As to the understanding of proportionality under German constitutional law, see Chapter 4, 4.5.2, at n. 159 et seq.

rather simply operated to the effect that with every expansion of the obligation to protect Princess Caroline's private life another 'set of photographs' taken from the Princess's private life was excluded from publication.

In the House of Lords' *Campbell v. MGN Ltd.* Case, the principle of proportionality can be used to examine whether the extent to which the publications on the plaintiff's drug addiction and therapy were judged to be tortious behaviour was compatible with the freedom of expression under Article 10 ECHR (under the assumption that the award of damages depends on this extent). Again, we can observe a correspondence with the duty to *protect* 'confidential' information: If positive obligations exist under Article 8 ECHR to prevent the disclosure of information on the details of Ms Campbell's therapy, but not on her drug career as such, then there is no justification for awarding compensation for the publication of the fact that she was addicted to drugs (and thereby interfering with the press's freedom of expression by negatively sanctioning the publication). Again, under the principle of proportionality, the degree of protection, which a judge assumes to be required, predetermines how far the press must suffer a limitation of freedom. Not only does this make it easier to compare the opinions of the single judges, but it also allows reviewing the consistency of each evaluation of the case. This consistency quite obviously depends on compliance with the principle of proportionality, as can be seen by the following examples: A judge who regarded it as correct to protect against disclosure Ms Campbell's private life insofar as any aspect of her therapy was concerned would have to acknowledge a breach of confidence in both the text articles and the photographs as far as they convey such information; consequently, the judge would have to grant compensation for the whole publication. Any other solution would appear inconsistent. A judge who on the one hand saw no ground for reprimanding the text of the article, but on the other hand considered it necessary to prevent the details of Ms Campbell's attendance of therapy sessions, visible only in the secretly taken photographs, from being revealed, would have to allow the publication of the text and could only grant compensation for the printing of the pictures. The degree of protection conceded to the one party and the degree of restriction suffered by the other correspond. The link is the principle of proportionality.

The two variable test thus structures conflicts of human rights in private-law controversies in a rational way. It can therefore be applied at the European level. But then, in consequence of the Human Rights Act 1998, it is also applicable in the context of English tort law insofar as this is influenced by the Convention.

5.1.2.2 The two-variables test as a dynamic instrument

Splitting up the test into a determination of the need for protection and an ensuing investigation of how intensively the intruder's right needs to be cut back enables different results reached by different judges or courts to be compared rationally and criticised. It also describes part of the dynamic process of finding a solution to a case, as this can be imagined as a sequence of trials of defining the correct intensity of protection required for the one right and asking how far the conflicting other right needs to be restricted. Any such trial is undertaken under the proviso that there are ultimate limits to the restriction of rights. In the *Campbell* case for instance, the parties and the House of Lords obviously agreed that barring the press from any report of Ms Campbell's drug affair would have been excessive and grossly disproportionate with a view to freedom of expression.

5.1.2.3 Practical concord can mean that one right might completely yield to another right in a specific case

Of course, there can be cases in which the press must be completely forbidden to publish information or an image because the demands of privacy protection are overwhelmingly strong. We should not be amazed to find such a result in cases of German constitutional law, for instance in the *Esra* case[10] where the courts enjoined the publisher from any further distribution of the roman à clef. This is so, although we have seen *Konrad Hesse* say that conflicts between private parties' basic rights need to be solved by 'optimising' the basic rights in the sense of bringing them into practical concord (*'praktische Konkordanz'*). More and more, German constitutional lawyers tend to describe the basic rights norms as principles, and not as rules[11] within the meaning introduced by Ronald Dworkin.[12] Principles exist, even if and insofar as they conflict. Yet this ought not to induce us to think that when there is a 'conflict' between basic rights, 'optimisation' means that *in each specific case* there must be something left of each of the right's substance. Rather, one of the rights, understood as principles, can very well prevail in the sense of *completely barring the exercise* of the other, conflicting, right, without questioning the existence of the rights as principles.[13]

5.1.2.4 No more than a restatement of judicial intuition?

A critic might comment that up to this point the reconstruction of *mittelbare Drittwirkung* as requiring a trial-and-error approach using two variables (the intensity of protection required, and the dependent variable of proportionate restriction of the conflicting right), is nothing more than the restatement of what judicial intuition has induced judges to do all along (however, if this

[10]See Chapter 4, 4.6.4.2.

[11]Cf. *Alexy* (1985), 104 et seq., who, however, gives a differentiating description of basic rights norms as differently composed of principles and rules. See especially *Sieckmann* (2009) and the very informative article by *Couzinet* (2009).

[12]*Dworkin* (1977), 22–28.

[13]See *Alexy* (n. 11), 79; *Günther* (1988), 255. *Habermas* (1994), 255.

were so, the test could be applied at the Convention level with all the more ease). To such criticism we can reply that our analysis has made it clear that the decisive point is to establish whether and how far a private party's right is in need of protection since this, insofar as such protection is sought against another party exercising rights, predetermines how severely these conflicting rights need to be restricted – even if the principle of proportionality prevents such restrictions from becoming excessive and intolerable. Admittedly, the required 'dose' of protection is nothing that can be calculated with mathematical precision (but this in itself is an insight we gained by sieving through German constitutional law). As the *Von Hannover* case at the different stages of its development shows, not even the national courts necessarily agree on how intensively a celebrity's private life ought to be secured against intrusions. The ECtHR even evaluates the case differently – although the ECHR standards and those of German sub-constitutional and constitutional law are inter-connected, as we have seen:[14] Not only statutes and norms at the level of the *Länder* (the constituent states) but also basic rights and fundamental principles of the *Grundgesetz* principally need to be interpreted in conformity with the Convention guarantees, as interpreted by the Strasbourg Court. This might cast some doubt on describing the civil courts, when they are called upon to solve private-law controversies involving conflicting basic rights, as 'umpires'. Are they not rather 'arbiters'? Aristotle[15] distinguishes these from courts which are bound to apply the rules of law strictly. Arbiters, in contrast to judges, are called upon to achieve equity. Aristotle describes equity as taking into account (*inter alia*) not only the legislative intention more than the wording of a norm, but also the specific constellation of a case and, foremost, a full picture of the persons involved.[16] But does this role of an arbiter expose the courts' decisions in such cases to the danger of *arbitrariness*? If we again look at the different stages of the *Von Hannover* case, imagining that we were reading each judgment singly, by itself, and for the first time, would we consider any one of them as arbitrary? Of course, the judgments will satisfy different people to a respectively different degree, but none of the judgments seems completely unreasonable or arbitrary. None of the judgments can be proven false.[17] Rather, the *Bundesgerichtshof*'s judgment, and even the civil court judgments before, at the one end of the development, very much favoured the freedom of the press, while, at the other end, the ECtHR saw no reason to give the press leeway to invade Princess Caroline's private life by publishing the photographs showing her in private situations within the social sphere.

---

[14] See Chapter 1, 1.4.
[15] *Aristoteles* (1995), 13th Chapter, 1374a 13, p. 72.
[16] *Aristoteles* (n. 15),
[17] Cf. *Sieckmann* (n. 11), 192–210.

5.1.2.5 The potential for acknowledging a certain degree of autonomy of domestic courts when they decide private controversies with implications for Convention guarantees

This variety of valid solutions to a case once again directs our attention to the important feature that there are no schematic solutions to the *Drittwirkung* cases. In other words, the courts do not apply 'rules' in the sense of conditional programmes that might merely require them to establish whether certain conditions are met,[18] in order to find such a rule to be applicable,[19] and then to read the solution of the case from the statute book – as '*la bouche qui prononce les paroles de la loi; des êtres inanimés qui n'en peuvent modérer ni la force ni la rigueur.*'[20] Rather their task can, as we have seen, be understood as what *Konrad Hesse* and the *Bundesverfassungsgericht* call achieving practical concord (*praktische Konkordanz*) between basic rights. Basic rights norms here indeed appear as rules, not principles.[21] Among German constitutional lawyers there is little doubt that this 'operation' is part of complying with constitutional law: The solution of a private-law conflict under the influence of basic rights concerns both the question of whether and how far *duties* to protect basic rights against private invasion exist in a case, and the connected question of whether and how far it is *constitutional* to restrict the private invader. As we saw in Chapter 4,[22] these might appear to be *grundrechtswesentliche Fragen*, questions essential for basic rights, which, according to the jurisprudence of the *Bundesverfassungsgericht*, as a rule, need to be decided by the Federal or *Länder* parliaments ('*Wesentlichkeitslehre*').[23] Principally, the parliaments must not leave such questions undecided. They are barred from simply referring them to the

---

[18]See *Dworkin* (n. 12), 24.

[19]Cf. *Montesquieu* (1964), De L'Esprit des Lois, VI.3, p. 557 ('*Plus le gouvernement approche de la république, plus la manière de juger devient fixe; ... Dans les États despotiques, il n'y a point de loi: le juge est lui-même sa règle. Dans les États monarchiques, il y a une loi: et là où elle est précise, le juge la suit; là où elle ne l'est pas, il en cherche l'esprit. Dans le gouvernement républicain il est de la nature de la constitution que les juges suivent la lettre de la loi. Il n'y a point de citoyen contre qui on puisse interpréter une loi, quand il s'agit de ses biens, de son honneur, ou de sa vie.*')

[20]*Montesquieu* (n. 19), XI.6, p. 589.

[21]See *supra*, at n. 11 et seq.

[22]Chapter 4, 4.6.1, at n. 166 et seq., and 4.4, at n. 258 et seq.

[23]See, e.g., *Bundesverfassungsgericht*, decision of 8 August 1978–2 BvL 8/77–, BVerfGE 49, 89 (126–127) – *Kalkar I* (pointing to Articles 20(3), 80(1) and 59(2), first sentence, of the *Grundgesetz*); decision of 27 November 1990–1 BvR 402/87–, BVerfGE 83, 130 (142) – *Mutzenbacher*; judgment of 24 September 2003–2 BvR 1436/02–, BVerfGE 108, 282 (302, 311–313) – *headscarf* (ibid., 302 reads: 'It is for the democratic legislature of the *Länder* to solve the inevitable tension between a teacher's positive religious freedom, on the one hand, and the States duty to neutrality in matters of philosophy [*Weltanschauung*] and religion, the right of parents to educate [their children] and the students' negative religious freedom'). See also *Bundesverfassungsgericht, 1st Chamber of the Second Senate*, decision of 30 January 2008 –2 BvR 754/07–, 2008 Neue Zeitschrift für Verwaltungsrecht 547 (549).

administrative authorities or the courts of justice. Rather, it is for the parliaments themselves to sufficiently define precise[24] normative solutions.[25] Nevertheless, the *Bundesverfassungsgericht* considers it to be constitutional for the democratically elected legislature to abstain from immediately solving the conflict between basic rights positions in private-law relations, i.e. by an act of its own, and allows parliaments to pass the fulfilment of the *Schutzauftrag* or *Schutzpflicht* on to the civil judges and thus to restrict itself to the enactment of blanket norms. We have found this softening of the *Vorbehalt des Gesetzes* to be justified by the impossibility of prescribing the outcomes of the process of operating the principle of practical concord in the abstract.[26] Practical concord exists as a constitutional principle equal in weight to that of '*Wesentlichkeitslehre*'. The relative 'positioning' of basic rights can only be performed case-specifically; the solution must be tailored to the details of a controversy and simultaneously must comply with the various constitutional duties to protect and to respect that are involved. This is something abstract legislation is unable to achieve. Consequently, it must, of necessity, confine itself to defining guidelines. The constitution cannot demand of the legislature something impossible. Rather, under the constitution's scheme of separation and balancing of powers it is the courts that are best suited to operate the principle of practical concord.

Recalling that situation under the German *Grundgesetz* is important at this point because leaving it up to the courts to find solutions of practical concord in private controversies necessitates relaxing the requirements of the '*Wesentlichkeitslehre*' and modifying what the principle of democratic rule would normally demand. Consequently, blanket norms suffice to empower the courts to solve private controversies along the lines of the constitution. In all this, the basic principle of democracy is not completely set aside. This is essential, because democratic self-government enables people to decide on the solution of conflicts by themselves. The people can make choices for themselves as a community and will solve problems of their society according to their culture.

Turning to the situation under the ECHR, there are 47 Contracting Parties. The Convention itself respects democracy, as the preamble and the qualifying

---

[24]See *Bundesverfassungsgericht*, decision of 14 January 1998–1 BvR 1861/93, 1864/96, 2073/97–, BVerfGE 97, 125 (149) – *Caroline von Monaco I*.

[25]See once again (cf. Chapter 4, 4.7, at n. 262), *Bundesverfassungsgericht* (n. 23), 142 – *Mutzenbacher*: 'To which extent the legislature must itself define the guidelines necessary in the relevant sphere of life depends on its connection with basic rights [*Grundrechtsbezug*]. Such a duty [sc. to legislate] exists when there is a confrontation of competing liberties [sc. constitutionally] protected as basic rights, and their limits are fluid and difficult to discern.'

[26]Of considerable importance is that, insofar as private law is concerned, its basic principle is *Privatautonomie*, thus the idea that private individuals are equal and free autonomously to define their relations with other private individuals. Consequently, state authorities such as the courts are only exceptionally empowered to intervene in private-law relations. Cf. Chapter 4, 4.3.1.

clauses of Articles 6(1), 8(2), 9(2), 10(2) and 11(2) prove. Thus, it ought to be susceptible to the diversity of solutions for private-law controversies involving Convention rights. When in *Karhuvaara and Iltalehti* the ECtHR says,

> that its task is not to review the relevant law and practice *in abstracto*, but to determine whether the manner in which they were applied to or affected the applicant gave rise to a violation of the Convention (…). In particular, it is not the Court's task to take the place of the domestic courts. It is primarily for the national authorities, notably the courts, to resolve problems of interpretation of domestic legislation (…)[27]

the Court is obviously willing to respect that domestic law is reserved for the Contracting States' courts to interpret. The domestic courts' task itself stands in the context of democratic rule insofar as the judges will bring statutes enacted by parliament (or, perhaps, even laws created through referenda) to bear on single cases.

When the ECtHR in *Karhuvaara and Iltalehti* continues by saying that '[t]he Court's role is confined to ascertaining whether the effects of such an interpretation are compatible with the Convention,'[28] one might assume that the Court will content itself with examining whether or not there is a clear case of a Convention violation by domestic courts. Respect for solutions reached in the context of domestic law appears to be necessary where judicial decisions in controversies between private parties require the 'balancing' of rights guaranteed under the Convention, because this 'balancing' is influenced both by the provisions of domestic law as defined in the process of legislation in a democratic society, *and by the details of the case.* As seen above, its outcome can vary, especially where the spectrum of non-arbitrary judgments by the courts is wide. In the *Pla and Puncernau* judgment (quite astonishingly[29]) the ECtHR seems prepared to be tolerant toward how a Contracting State's courts will construe and apply domestic law. It even gives good reasons for such tolerance:

> [T]he domestic courts are evidently better placed than an international court to evaluate, in the light of local legal traditions, the particular context of the legal dispute submitted to them and the various competing

---

[27]ECtHR, *Karhuvaara and Iltalehti* (n. 1), § 49, referring to ECtHR, *Padovani v. Italy*, no. 13396/87, judgment of 26 February 1993, § 24, Series A no. 257-B, p. 20; and afterwards to ECtHR, *Pérez de Rada Cavanilles v. Spain*, no. 28090/95, judgment of 28 October 1998, § 43, ECHR 1998-VIII, p. 3255. Similar: ECtHR, *Pla and Puncernau v. Andorra*, no. 69498/01, judgment of 13 July 2004, § 46, ECHR 2004-VIII, referring to *Winterwerp v. the Netherlands*, no. 6301/73, judgment of 24 October 1979, § 46, Series A no. 33, p. 20; *Iglesias Gil and A.U.I. v. Spain*, no. 56673/00, judgment of 29 April 2003, § 61, ECHR 2003-V; and *Slivenko v. Latvia* [GC], no. 48321/99, judgment of 9 October 2003, § 105, ECHR 2003-X.

[28]ECtHR, *Karhuvaara and Iltalehti* (n. 1), § 49.

[29]Cf. Chapter 3, 3.5.2.2), at n. 183 et seq.

rights and interests (...). When ruling on disputes of this type, the national authorities and, in particular, the courts of first instance and appeal have a wide margin of appreciation.[30]

This preference for the 'local' decision sounds convincing. Will it not be the trial judge who can look the parties in the eyes and understand the circumstances they live in? Will it not be harder for judges to tailor the solution of a case to the details of the facts, the farther they are away from the 'scene'? If there necessarily is a variety of sound, non-arbitrary solutions of private controversies over conflicting Convention rights and choosing among them *depends on who decides*,[31] why not leave the choice to the court closest to the parties and the setting in which their dispute has arisen? This has the practical advantage of paying attention to detail. Detail matters. The specific constellation of a conflict determines both variables of the test involved in bringing conflicting rights into practical concord: The details will show how *vulnerable* the first party is, whose position is encroached upon by the second party's exercising certain rights. The details will also be decisive for assessing the impact which limiting this second party's rights for the sake of protecting the first party will have. In the context of German constitutional law the *Bundesverfassungsgericht* has been aware of this advantage of the regular courts; simultaneously, its self-restraint shows respect for the system of private law and its specific characteristics: The *Bundesverfassungsgericht* denies to be competent to review civil court decisions as to their consistency with sub-constitutional, especially private, law. Rather the Constitutional Justices restrict their review to whether decisions by the civil courts show failures of interpretation which are based on a fundamentally wrong conception of the meaning of a basic right, especially regarding the extent of its protective sphere, and which in their substantive meaning are of some gravity in the case which is to be decided.[32] At the European level, the ECtHR seems to take a similar position when in *Pla and Puncernau* it says:

> Accordingly, an issue of interference with private and family life could only arise under the Convention if the national courts' assessment of the facts or domestic law were manifestly unreasonable or arbitrary or blatantly inconsistent with the fundamental principles of the Convention.[33]

As the *Storck* case – as well as the *Pla and Puncernau* case itself! – showed,[34] such self-restraint is not always practiced. It would nevertheless be called for

---

[30]ECtHR, *Pla and Puncernau* (n. 27), § 46, referring to ECtHR, *De Diego Nafría v. Spain*, no. 46833/99, judgment of 14 March 2002, § 39.
[31]Cf. again *Sieckmann* (n. 11), 192–210. See also *Lord Browne-Wilkinson* (1998), 22.
[32]See *supra*, 4.4.2.2 at n. 108 et seq., p. 178.
[33]ECtHR, *Pla and Puncernau* (n. 27), § 46.
[34]Chapter 3, 3.5.2.2, at n. 195 et seq.

as one cannot expect the solutions to similar private-law controversies over conflicting Convention rights to coincide throughout the 47 Contracting States of the ECHR, whose historical backgrounds and legal cultures vary considerably. Thus it would be wise for the ECtHR to practise a considerable degree of self-restraint when examining applications arising out of private-law controversies.[35] This is not only a question of wisdom. The insights gained in the course of analysing *Drittwirkung* under German constitutional law have shown us that self-restraint would be the best way that the Court could adapt its examination of applications under the Convention to the structures of human rights. Deference, though not subordination, to the domestic courts' decisions in private-law controversies is something called for by the very nature of the human rights impact on relations of private parties *inter se*.

5.1.3 Have we got it all wrong?

Perhaps even such a self-restrained review of domestic court decisions by the ECtHR could raise doubts. Up to now we have not answered the basic question of whether the Court has been right to acknowledge that human rights influence relations between private persons and can thus be violated when civil courts decide cases under their national private law. Admittedly, in light of the Court's jurisprudence, one can hardly imagine that the Strasbourg judges will stop examining the merits of applications insofar as the application of substantive (private) law by the domestic courts is alleged to have violated rights guaranteed under the Convention. So, the question is highly theoretical. Nevertheless, one might ask whether there could be a fundamental reason to deny the Court's power of review. The *Von Hannover* case might show why. Here the Court found the German courts violated the applicant's right to respect for her private life[36] because they had not handled the provisions of German law in a way 'sufficient to protect the applicant's private life effectively'.[37] The two-variables test for *Drittwirkung* cases helps to see clearly that the 'dosage' of protection said to be required by Article 8 ECHR has necessary implications for the competing right under Article 10. If the Convention demands protecting Princess Caroline more intensively against the publication of her image, it simultaneously *requires* restricting the press's freedom of expression. It is true that the German courts themselves had forbidden the republication of certain photographs and thus had drawn limits to freedom of the press under Article 5 of the *Grundgesetz*, but this

---

[35]Such self-restraint might put those at ease who would be inclined to support their country's withdrawal from the Strasbourg court, as considered by Lord Hoffmann, Human Rights and the House of Lords, 1999 MLR 159–166 (164–166).

[36]ECtHR, *Von Hannover* (n. 6), § 80.

[37]ECtHR, *Von Hannover* (n. 6), § 74.

freedom still expanded quite far, as pictures showing the Princess in private situations in public could be published at liberty. The *Von Hannover* judgment must be understood as saying that, from the Convention's point of view, the German courts had interpreted the freedom of the press too expansively. This might not contradict Article 53 ECHR, which says:

> Nothing in this Convention shall be construed as limiting or derogating from any of the human right and fundamental freedoms which may be ensured under the laws of any High Contracting Party or under any other agreement to which it is a Party.

This provision might in itself show that the framers of the Convention were not aware of the possibility that human rights could be understood to affect the legal relations of private individuals *inter se* – at least when their behaviour, insofar as it relates to a conflict between them, is respectively protected under the Convention.[38] Here, protecting one right necessitates restricting another.

Upon closer examination, however, Article 53 ECHR must not be read as an obstacle to applying the Convention to cases of such private controversies. Even if we shun going deep into philosophy, we can see why with the help of some thoughts of *Immanuel Kant*'s. To him *Recht* (right, law) is the sum of the conditions allowing individuals to co-exist peacefully according to a general law of freedom.[39] Freedom, as independence from any other's coercive will, is the only innate right *Kant* is willing to accept. But this holds true only of freedom insofar as it is compatible with everyone else's freedom according to a general law.[40] Innate freedom thus is conceived of as something limited in itself from the very beginning. Like the pieces of a jigsaw puzzle, every

---

[38]Cf. the dissenting opinion Judge *Garlicki* in ECtHR, *Pla and Puncernau* (n. 27), verbatim quote above in Chapter 3, 3.5.2.1, n. 190. See also van Dijk / van Hoof/ van Rijn/ Zwaak (2006), 31.

[39]*Kant* (1797/98), § B Was ist Recht?, 337: '*Das Recht ist also der Inbegriff der Bedingungen, unter denen die Willkür des einen mit der Willkür des anderen nach einem allgemeinen Gesetze der Freiheit zusammen vereinigt werden kann.*'

[40]*Kant* (1797/98), Einteilung der Rechtslehre, B. Allgemeine Einteilung der Rechte, 345–346: '*Freiheit (Unabhängigkeit von eines anderen nötigender Willkür), sofern sie mit jedes anderen Freiheit nach einem allgemeinen Gesetz zusammen bestehen kann, ist dieses einzige, ursprüngliche, jedem Menschen, kraft seiner Menschheit, zustehende Recht. – Die angeborne Gleichheit, d.i. die Unabhängigkeit, nicht zu mehrerem von anderen verbunden zu werden, als wozu man sie wechselseitig auch verbinden kann; mithin die Qualität des Menschen, sein eigener Herr (sui iuris) zu sein, imgleichen die eines unbescholtenen Menschen (iusti), weil er, vor allem rechtlichen Akt, keinem Unrecht getan hat; endlich auch die Befugnis, das gegen andere zu tun, was an sich ihnen das Ihre nicht schmälert, wenn sie sich dessen nur nicht annehmen wollen; dergleichen ist, ihnen bloß seine Gedanken mitzuteilen, ihnen etwas zu erzählen oder zu versprechen, es sei wahr und aufrichtig, oder unwahr und unaufrichtig (veriloquium aut falsiloquium), weil es bloß auf ihnen beruht, ob sie ihm glauben wollen oder nicht; – alle diese Befugnisse liegen schon im Prinzip der angebornen Freiheit, und sind wirklich von ihr nicht (als Glieder der Einteilung unter einem höheren Rechtsbegriff) unterschieden.*'

individual's freedom needs to fit in with every other individual's freedom. Where someone is pressing too hard, encroaching upon another in a way incompatible with the concord of everyone's freedom, such coercion can principally be warded off by each negatively affected individual, who are even allowed to use force (*Zwang*). The reason for this is that the intruder is stepping in the other's way, preventing him from making use of his freedom. This means the intruder is coercing the other. If this other individual reacts and forces the intruder to step back and retreat from the sphere of freedom he has invaded, such force *neutralises* the intruder's act of coercion. In consequence, the situation in which all individuals can live in freedom is restored.[41] This hypothetical situation is, of course, thought of outside the context of a state, understood as the institutional organisation of a society under rules of public law.[42] *Kant* sees the individuals enter such a state, democratically creating powers of government under whose rule they, from then on, live.[43]

We need not pursue this any further. The philosophical *excursus* shows that individual freedom is always liberty within limits. The Convention itself acknowledges this. We need only point to Articles 8(2) and 10(2), with which we have been dealing with all along. These clauses foresee that the Contracting States' public authorities may restrict the rights guaranteed, *inter*

---

[41]*Kant* (1797/98), § D., 338–339 '*Das Recht ist mit der Befugnis zu zwingen verbunden: Der Widerstand, der dem Hindernisse einer Wirkung entgegengesetzt wird, ist eine Beförderung dieser Wirkung und stimmt mit ihr zusammen. Nun ist alles, was Unrecht ist, ein Hindernis der Freiheit nach allgemeinen Gesetzen; der Zwang aber ist ein Hindernis oder Widerstand, der der Freiheit geschieht. Folglich: wenn ein gewisser Gebrauch der Freiheit selbst ein Hindernis der Freiheit nach allgemeinen Gesetzen (d.i. unrecht) ist, so ist der Zwang, der diesem entgegengesetzt wird, als Verhinderung eines Hindernisses der Freiheit mit der Freiheit nach allgemeinen Gesetzen zusammen stimmend, d.i.recht: mithin ist mit dem Rechte zugleich eine Befugnis, den, der ihm Abbruch tut, zu zwingen, nach dem Satze des Widerspruchs verknüpft.*'

[42]*Kant* (1797/98), § 43, 429: '*Der Inbegriff der Gesetze, die einer allgemeinen Bekanntmachung bedürfen, um einen rechtlichen Zustand hervorzubringen, ist das öffentliche Rechts. – Dieses ist also ein System von Gesetzen für ein Volk d.i. ein Menge von Menschen, oder für eine Menge von Völkern, die im wechselseitigen Einflusse gegen einander stehend, des rechtlichen Zustandes unter einem sie vereinigenden Willen, einer Verfassung (constitutio) bedürfen, um dessen, was Rechtens ist, teilhaftig zu werden. – Dieser Zustand der einzelnen im Volke, in Verhältnis untereinander, heißt der bürgerliche (status civilis) und das Ganze derselben, in Beziehung auf seine eigene Glieder, der Staat (civitas), welcher, seiner Form wegen, als verbunden durch das gemeinsame Interesse aller, im rechtlichen Zustande zu sein, das gemeine Wesen (res publica latius sic dicta) genennt wird, im Verhältnis ber auf andre Völker seine Macht (potentia) schlechthin heißt (daher das Wort Potentaten), was sich auch wegen (anmaßlich) angeerbter Vereinigung ein Stammvolk (gens) nennt, und so, unter dem allgemeinen Begriffe des öffentlichen Rechts, nicht bloß das Staats- sondern auch ein Völkerrecht (ius gentium) zu denken Anlaß gibt: welches dann, weil der Erdboden eine nicht grenzenlose, sondern sich selbst schließende Fläche ist, beides zusammen zu der Idee eines Völkerstaatsrechts (ius gentium) oder des Weltbürgerrechts (ius cosmopoliticum) unumgänglich hinleitet: so., daß, wenn unter diesen drei möglichen äußere Freiheit durch Gesetze einschränken Prinzip fehlt, das Gebäude aller übrigen unvermeidlich untergraben werden, und endlich einstürzen muß.*'

[43]*Kant* (1797/98), 430.

alia, for the purpose of protecting 'the rights and freedoms of others', as Article 8(2) says.[44] It is very likely that the framers of the Convention, when putting down what is now Article 53, had in mind only conflicts arising in relations between bearers of Convention rights, on the one side, and public authorities, on the other. In this 'vertical' dimension, the 'horizontal' relations of the private individuals *inter se* come into view only as justifications for the public authorities' acts setting limits to individual freedom. But the moment positive obligations are acknowledged to exist under the Convention, and quite rightly so as Chapter 3 demonstrates, a balancing becomes necessary as soon as – in the 'horizontal' dimension – the freedoms of individuals conflict.

With the *excursus* on *Kant* in mind, one can understand the balancing itself, insofar as it limits the freedom of the person who intrudes upon another's sphere, to be the restoration of the overall concord of freedom: *praktische Konkordanz*. It is part of the ECHR's vision of reinforcing fundamental freedoms as the 'foundation of justice and peace' in a twofold way: on the one hand, by securing 'a common understanding and observance of human rights' at the international level, especially through the ECtHR, and on the other, by strengthening 'an effective political democracy'.[45] Thus, the intention and scheme of the Convention as such – not only single qualifying clauses such as Article 8(2) and 10(2) – imply that such practical concord of individual freedom is at the heart of it all. But if this is so, and the balancing of competing freedoms lends itself to various outcomes which are nevertheless neither false nor arbitrary, then solutions of controversies involving conflicting Convention rights at the European level may well differ from what the domestic courts have judged to be right. Such differences do not contradict Article 53 ECHR.[46]

5.2 Outlook

Tort law is also concerned with balancing competing freedoms. Therefore, it is not really astonishing that for more than fifty years under the *Grundgesetz* the basic rights have had a considerable impact on the scope and operation of sec. 823(1) BGB and other provisions of *Deliktsrecht*. Similarly, that cases arising out of private controversies and settled by domestic courts in the exercise of their judicial powers can raise questions of human rights must not be a surprise. Both the United Kingdom and Germany have opened their domestic legal orders to the influence of the Convention and require their national provisions of law to be interpreted and applied in conformity with its standards.[47] The consequence is that the guarantee of rights and freedoms under

---

[44]Article 10(2) speaks of 'the reputation or rights of others.'
[45]See the Preamble of the Convention.
[46]See also *Alkema* (1988), 43.
[47]See *supra*, Chapter 1.

the Convention are required to be observed by the domestic courts. Tort law is not excluded from such observation. The German courts may for some time have been somewhat forgetful of the ECHR. They were, it might appear, rather absorbed by what the *Bundesverfassungsgericht* revealed to be demanded by the *Grundgesetz* and its basic rights. But with the recent *Caroline von Monaco III* decision, the Karlsruhe Court has fine-tuned German constitutional and tort law to comply with the developments at the level of European human rights protection. The British courts have, in an impressive way, for many years, even before the Human Rights Act 1998, been attentive to the ECtHR's jurisprudence.[48] However, they have been reluctant to 'invent' any new tort under English common law – such as breach of privacy, or infringement of the personality right.[49] Instead, as documented by the House of Lords' *Campbell* judgment, breach of confidence now also comprises cases of misuse of information, including images. Thereby English law grants considerable protection to important aspects of privacy.

However, in the long run, an expansion of tort-law protection for matters at least partially concerning privacy may be required by the Convention. We need only look into the ECtHR's judgment in the case of *Tysiąc v. Poland*,[50] where the Court reiterates that 'private life' is 'a broad term, encompassing, inter alia, aspects of an individual's physical and social identity including the right to personal autonomy, personal development and to establish and develop relationships with other human beings and the outside world'.[51] The Court points out 'that private life includes a person's physical and psychological integrity and that the State is also under a positive obligation to secure to its citizens their right to effective respect for this integrity'.[52]

---

[48]See Lord Nicholls in: *Campbell v. MGN Ltd* [2004] UKHL 22, § 16; and Chapter 2, 2.6.7. Also cf. *Sir Neill* (1997). Contrast *Wright* (2001), 24–7, 33.

[49]Cf. *Markesinis/ Unberath* (2002), 392–505 (especially 406–412, 472–505); *Markesinis/ Fedtke* (2006), 130–132, who call for adapting English law. See also *Markesinis* (1997), 43–4, 382–437; *Markesinis* (2001), 131–218, 321–8. As to breach of confidence see *Barendt* (2005), 239–46; *Fenwick/Phillipson* (2006), 720–70, 869–70.

[50]ECtHR, *Tysiąc v. Poland*, no. 5410/03, judgment of 20 March 2007, § 107.

[51]ECtHR, *Tysiąc* (n. 49), § 107, referring to ECtHR, *Pretty v. the United Kingdom*, no. 2346/02, judgment of 29 April 2002, § 61, ECHR 2002-III. Mention might be made of ECtHR, *van Kück v. Germany*, no. 35968/97, judgment of 12 June 2003, § 69, Reports 2003-VII, where with a view to Article 8 embracing aspects of an individual's physical and social identity, elements such as, for example, gender identification, name and sexual orientation and sexual life fall are said to fall within the personal sphere protected by Article 8. The Court, *ibid.*, further points out that Article 8 also protects a right to personal development, and the right to establish and develop relationships with other human beings and the outside world. Likewise, although a right to self-determination had not yet been recognised as being contained in Article 8, the notion of personal autonomy was an important principle underlying the interpretation of its guarantees. Moreover, the very essence of the Convention being respect for human dignity and human freedom, protection was given to the right of transsexuals to personal development and to physical and moral security (ibid., with reference to ECtHR, *I. v. the United Kingdom*, no. 25680/94, judgment of 11 July 2002, § 70, and *Christine Goodwin v. the United Kingdom*, no. 28957/95, judgment of 11 July 2002, § 90).

[52]ECtHR, *Tysiąc* (n. 49), § 107, referring to ECtHR, *Glass v. the United Kingdom*, no. 61827/00,

In the specific case, the ECtHR includes State regulations on abortion within the scope of Article 8 ECHR, insofar as they concern a therapeutic abortion, and sees the need to assess these regulations 'against the positive obligations of the State to secure the physical integrity of mothers-to-be'.[53] In the context of this investigation the Strasbourg Judges also look into the provisions of the Polish civil law on tort, finding that these, as applied by the Polish courts, 'did not afford the applicant' – who did not manage to have an abortion and whose eyesight in consequence of giving birth, as foreseen by three ophthalmologists, deteriorated badly[54] – 'a procedural instrument by which she could have vindicated her right to respect for her private life'. The Court found that the civil law remedy being solely of a retroactive and compensatory character allowed her, if successful, only to receive compensation for the irreparable damage to her health which had come to light after delivery.[55]

Although abortions pose special problems under German constitutional law,[56] at least prima facie such a case would quite clearly fall within the scope of BGB tort law. For, as shown above, sec. 823(1) BGB is – in the light of Articles 2(1) and 1(1) of the *Grundgesetz* – interpreted to include the general personality right, which guarantees autonomy in the meaning of self-determination. This flexibility, as we have seen, stems from the words 'infringement of … another right' being open for specification by interpretation, and identifies the provision as the *deliktsrechtliche Generalklausel*, the general clause, or blanket norm, of tort law. Where a woman wished to have a therapeutic abortion and a doctor de facto prevented such an abortion by denying her a certificate that the legal conditions were fulfilled, there thus might be a tort under sec. 823(1) BGB. Whether this is truly so in the specific case, however, would depend on a complicated balancing. The courts would have to consider the woman's personality right (Articles 2(1) and 1(1) of the *Grundgesetz*) and the doctor's right to perform his profession (protected

---

judgment of 9 March 2004, §§ 74–83, ECHR 2004-II; *Sentges v. the Netherlands*, no. 27677/02, decision of 8 July 2003; *Pentiacova and Others v. Moldova*, no. 14462/03, decision of 4 January 2005, ECHR 2005-.I; *Nitecki v. Poland*, no. 65653/01, decision of 21 March 2002; *Odièvre v. France* [GC], no. 42326/98, judgment of 13 February 2003, ECHR 2003-III.
[53] ECtHR, *Tysiąc* (n. 49), § 107.
[54] ECtHR, *Tysiąc* (n. 49), §§ 9, 15–16.
[55] ECtHR, *Tysiąc* (n. 49), § 125.
[56] *Bundesverfassungsgericht*, judgment of 25 February 1975–1 BvF 1, 2, 3, 4, 5, 6/74–, BVerfGE 39, 1 – *abortion I*; judgment of 28 May 1993–2 BvF 2/90 und 4, 5/92–, BVerfGE 88, 203 – *abortion II*. Cf. especially *Bundesverfassungsgericht*, decision of 12 November 1997–1 BvR 479/92 und 307/94–, BVerfGE 96, 375 (393 et seq., 399 et seq.) – *child as damage*, in which problems of awarding compensation to parents in the case of a failed sterilisation and subsequent birth of a child, and in the case of flawed advice on the parents' genetic dispositions before they decided to have a child are discussed. In neither of the cases did Court reprimand the civil courts' damage awards. These questions, however, did appear doubtful in the light of the judgment of 28 May 1993. This contained an *obiter dictum* that a child could not be regarded as 'damage' within the meaning of private-law rules of compensation (BVerfGE 88, 203 [295–296]; see also the dissenting opinion of Constitutional Justices Mahrenholz and Sommer, ibid., 338 [358]).

under Article 12 of the *Grundgesetz*). Perhaps even the doctor's freedom of conscience (Article 4 of the *Grundgesetz*), will play a role. For constitutional reasons, some influence will even have to be accorded to the unborn child's dignity protected under Article 1(1) of the *Grundgesetz*. The balancing will furthermore be influenced by Article 8 ECHR and the ECtHR's *Tysiąc* judgment.

German tort law through the *Generalklausel* is thus able to absorb requirements both of constitutional law and of the Convention. The *Bundesverfassungsgericht* has even judged it to be constitutional for the civil courts to award monetary compensation for '*immaterielle Schäden*', non-physical damages, caused by violations of the personality right.[57] The civil courts had granted such claims although the BGB, in principle, excludes monetary compensation for any non-pecuniary damage. This is different only in cases (expressly) stipulated by law (see sec. 253(1) BGB). The civil courts thus went beyond the limits of what statutory law allowed. The *Bundesverfassungsgericht* interpreted the *Bundesgerichtshof* as merely acknowledging a single additional exception to the rule that monetary compensation is excluded. For this exceptional case the *Bundesgerichtshof* had found there to be a cogent and stringent demand in light of the development of the conditions of society ('Entwicklung der Lebensverhältnisse') and also of a '*jus superveniens*' of higher rank, namely Articles 1 and 2(1) of the *Grundgesetz*.[58]

However, the civil courts have applied this exception clause, created by *Rechtsfortbildung*, sparingly and restrictively, as the table of judgments granting compensation in cases of personality right violations at the end of this book shows. Monetary compensation is awarded only if, and insofar as, other methods of redressing a violation, such as an order of rectification, forbearance or counter-statement, are insufficient.[59] The reason for this is that

---

[57]*Bundesverfassungsgericht*, decision of 14 February 1973 -1 BvR 112/65-, BVerfGE 34, 269 (286–292) – *Soraya*.

[58]*Bundesverfassungsgericht* (n. 56), 292 – *Soraya*. Before (*ibid.*, 273–275), the Court had pointed out that the *Bundesgerichtshof* had originally relied on an analogy to sec. 847 BGB (according to which compensation in the form of damages for pain and suffering were to be paid in cases of tortuous infringements of body, health, or freedom; see *Bundesgerichtshof*, judgment of 14 February 1958 –I ZR 151/56– (*Herrenreiter*), 1958 Neue Juristische Wochenschrift 827 = BGHZ 26, 349). The Bundesgerichtshof had, however, abandoned this analogy. Instead, it argued that under the influence of the value system of the *Grundgesetz* the protection of the personality under private law would be incomplete if a violation would not trigger sanctions adequate to the non-pecuniary infringement; excluding non-pecuniary damages in such cases would amount to denying any sanction; the function of such sanctions was satisfaction more than compensation; therefore a high degree of fault was required (see *Bundesgerichtshof*, judgment of 19 September 1961 – VI ZR 259/60– (*Ginsengwurzel*), 1961 Neue Juristische Wochenschrift 2059 = BGHZ 35, 363). – Today monetary compensation for non-pecuniary damages is regarded as an emanation of the mandate to protect under Articles 2(1) and 1(1) of the *Grundgesetz* (*Bundesgerichtshof*, judgment of 15 November 1994 - VI ZR 56/94–1995 Neue Juristische Wochenschrift 861 = BGHZ 128, 1 [15]).

[59]*Rixecker* (2006), para. 232.

the fundamental general BGB rule governing awards of compensation for damages is that of *Naturalrestitution, restitutio in integrum*, i.e. the person who owes *Schadensersatz* to another is obliged to restore the situation which would exist if the ground for his obligation to compensate had not occurred (sec. 249(1) BGB).

In further developing English law to include more aspects of the general personality right under tort law, whether by the courts, who have up to now withstood any temptation to 'invent' a new tort, or by an act of Parliament, the definition of the legal consequences of such a tort will be essential. Money payments as compensation might come close to permitting people to 'sell' their privacy. Giving them a subsidiary character, as in German law, stresses *restitutio in integrum* as the apt sanction and correction of a violation of the personality right and might well, at least partially, prevent the commercialisation of this right. But these are questions that would need an in-depth analysis requiring a book of its own.

Quite probably, we would again see that the provisions of national law in different states have become interwoven under the ECHR in consequence of the domestic legal orders' receptivity for the requirements of the Convention guarantees.

Hopefully, the present study has shown that there are convincing reasons to compare tort law and explore its human rights dimensions.

Addendum

Total of: 120 cases
Limited to cases where a violation of personal rights can be affirmed in principle.
Sorted according to the different types of violations and according to the amount of damage (ascending).

Covert recordings and observations: 7 cases ➜ 5.83 %

Court of law	Date	Type of violation of personal rights	Extent of damage
AG Aachen	11.11.2003	Video observation	Omission
AG Berlin-Mitte	18.12.2003	Video observation	Omission
AG Berlin-Spandau	06.01.2004	Video observation	Omission
AG Mölln	06.10.1998	Secret AIDS test	None (minimum limit)
AG Sieburg	29.09.2004	Observation by a private investigator	None
KG Berlin	25.04.2003	Unauthorized film recordings of how a prohibited circumcision is volunteered by a physician	None (true testimony; social relevance)
OLG Köln	05.07.2005	Secretly produced film recordings (without consent of the respondent) about the damaging of washing machines	Exclusionary rule

Defamation and slight: 9 cases ➜ 7.5 %

Court	Date	Type of violation of personal rights	Extent of damage
AG Aachen	31.05.2002	Spitting someone into the face	None (minimum limit)
AG Greiz	18.04.2002	Slander	None (minimum limit)
AG Hamburg	27.10.2005	Undesired calls	None (minimum limit)
LG Heidelberg (2 O 173/07)	11.12.2007	Unrequested telephone calls for business purposes	Lawyer's fees
AG Frankfurt	14.12.2004	Stadium bans for hooligan	None
OLG Köln (15 U 64/07)	18.09.2007	Stage play that describes in detail the circumstances of the murder of a 14-year old girl, while deviating from the truth in a distorting and defamatory manner	—

OLG Frankfurt am Main	26.08.1999	Offensive inquiry as to sexual activities and preferences	None
LG Hildesheim	04.06.2004	Slander	285 €
LAG Rheinland-Pfalz	04.10.2005	Severe defamation	Ca. 20,000 €

Transfer of data or knowledge: 2 cases → 1.6%

Court of law	Date	Type of violation of personal rights	Extent of damage
OLG Karlsruhe	25.02.2000	Communication of oral and written knowledge about the claimant to neighbors	—
OLG Jena	18.08.2004	Divulging telephone data and addresses that lead to harassment of the claimant	1,000 €

Violation of due diligence or duty of disclosure: 6 cases → 5 %

Court of law	Date	Type of violation of personal rights	Extent of damage
OLG Koblenz (6U81/08)	24.04.2008	Suggestion that the claimant abused his daughter vis-à-vis a person who is not concerned with this child's best interest	—
OLG München	26.04.2002	Detailed expert opinion on alleged personality disorders which lead to the revocation of the physical custody of her child	—
LG Karlsruhe	13.07.2004	Accommodation of a prisoner together with one other prisoner in a very small cell	650 €
OLG Frankfurt am Main	26.04.2002	Violation of the physician's obligation to inform by not pointing out the possible loss of procreative capacity	15,000 DM (compensation for personal suffering) + 3,000 DM
OLG Frankfurt am Main (4 W 12/07)	21.08.2007	Instigation of a circumcision of a child that is not yet able to give consent without having the right of custody	10,000 €

			150,000.00 €
OLG Frankfurt am Main (19 U 8/07)	2.10.2007	Gross negligence of the appraiser within the scope of generating an anthropological opinion to determine an offender in a legal proceeding on the basis of which the claimant is serving a prison sentence for a felony he did not commit	destruction

Violation of personal rights within the employment: 33 cases → 27.5 %

Court of law	Date	Type of violation of personal rights	Extent of damage
BAG	06.06.1984	Questionnaire with questions that invade the privacy	None (minimum limit)
BAG	18.12.1984	Forwarding the personnel file to third parties	None
BAG	04.04.1990	Access to the personnel file	None
LAG B – W	29.09.2000	Allegation of harassment and mobbing (substantiated assertion of facts is missing)	None
LAG Berlin	07.11.2002	Mobbing (substantiated assertion of facts is missing)	None
LAG Berlin	06.03.2003	Mobbing (but not systemic)	None
LAG Berlin	15.07.2004	Mobbing (substantiated assertion of facts is missing)	Termination agreement
LAG Berlin	26.08.2005	Mobbing	None
LAG Bremen	17.10.2002	Mobbing (substantiated assertion of facts is missing)	None (employer has offered extension)
LAG Düsseldorf	29.06.1992	Employer does not extend contract because of a pregnancy	Recall
LAG Hamm	19.03.1986	The statement is passed on to the supervisor and exposes him	None
LAG Hessen	28.09.1988	Slanderous facts in the personnel file (substantiated assertion of facts is missing)	None
LAG Hessen	24.08.2001	Mobbing (substantiated assertion of facts is missing)	

Court	Date	Subject	Outcome
LAG Köln	07.01.1998	Unauthorized warning letter	Removal from personal file
LAG Köln	19.09.2005	Mobbing (but not systemic)	None
LAG München	28.09.2006	Mobbing (substantiated assertion of facts is missing)	None
LAG Rheinland-Pfalz	28.09.2000	Allocation of work that is damaging to health, even thought the employer knows about the disability	None (the suffering was not important to the employer)
LAG Rheinland-Pfalz	15.12.2003	Mobbing (substantiated assertion of facts is missing)	None
LAG Rheinland-Pfalz	10.03.2004	Mobbing (but not systematically)	None
LAG Rheinland-Pfalz	26.01.2005	Mobbing	None
LAG Rheinland-Pfalz	17.03.2005	Mobbing (but not systematically)	None
LAG Rheinland-Pfalz	03.05.2006	Mobbing (substantiated assertion of facts is missing)	None
LAG Rheinland-Pfalz	02.08.2007	Mobbing	None
LAG Rheinland-Pfalz	30.08.2007	Mobbing (substantiated assertion of facts is missing)	None
LAG Sachsen	17.02.2005	Mobbing (substantiated assertion of facts is missing)	None
LAG Berlin	01.11.2002	Mobbing	8,000 €
LAG B – W (6 Sa 93/06)	28.06.2007	Mobbing	10,000 €
BAG (8 AZR 709/06)	16.05.2007	Mobbing	20,000 €
LAG B – W	12.06.2006	Mobbing and unemployment	Ca. 20,000 €
BAG (8 AZR 593/06)	25.10.2007	Mobbing	Compensation for personal suffering (+) dismissal to the trier of fact
LAG Hamburg	11.02.1987	Discrimination upon employment	Six times the gross salary held out in prospect
ArbG Dresden	07.07.2003	Mobbing	40,000 €
ArbG Ludwigshafen	06.11.2000	Occupation not according to contract	51,900 DM

Violation of the right to personal rights due to unauthorized publications and untrue reporting: 63 cases → 52.5 %

Court of law	Date	Type of violation of personal rights	Extent of damage
KG Berlin	15.05.2007	Deliberate incomplete reporting that generates a wrong impression	—
KG Berlin	15.06.2007	Reporting with untrue facts	—
KG Berlin	18.12.2007	Copy of an image + title: 'the terrorist lives here'	—
LG Berlin (Beschluss, beiderseitige Erledigungserklärung)	12.12.1991	Stating a false telephone number in a red-light ad	None (withdrawn)
LG Berlin	11.11.1999	Publication of photos that may lead to the impression that this would be prostitution	None
LG Berlin	03.07.2001	Reporting with circumstantial evidence	None
LG Berlin	17.02.2005	Inadmissible reporting about a person in a book	None
LG Hamburg	21.01.2005	Transmission of film material without consent	Omission
LG Heilbronn (6 O 55/07 Hg)	05.07.2007	Publication of offensive caricatures and statements	None
OLG Frankfurt am Main	13.08.2001	Publication of a press release about a serious crime that took place 20 years ago by publishing a photo of the offender without giving the name of the offender without current cause	None
OLG Frankfurt (11 U 71/06 und 11 U 72/06)	22.05.2007	Identifying reporting on television about a murder	Omission
OLG Frankfurt am Main (11 U 9/07)	30.10.2007	Identifying reporting for an unlimited period of time about a felon without cause (beyond the current reporting)	Omission
OLG Hamburg (7 U 21/07)	8.4.2008	Suspicion reporting about a former Federal Chancellor	Omission
OLG Hamm	22.03.1999	Unauthorized forwarding of images to an advertising paper	Satisfaction obtained from other forms than compensation for personal suffering

Court	Reference	Date	Description	Outcome
OLG Jena		02.10.2001	Violation of honor and personal identity through allegations in campaign brochures	No compensation for personal suffering because of low circulation
OLG Karlsruhe		17.05.2002	Suspicion reporting in advertising paper (untrue allegation of facts by not mentioning that so far there is only a suspicion)	—
OLG München		10.05.1996	Press cutting 'Sumpf der Korruption' (Swamp of corruption) with subsequent listing of the names of ten liquidators with the largest turnovers	Omission
OLG München		20.08.1999	Report in a newspaper of a lawyer having set up 'contracts like in a brothel'	(has demonstrated by demanding too much money that he was asking for monetary compensation and not compensation for violation of his personal rights)
BGH	(IV ZR 182/58)	18.03.1959	Mentioning of a publically known artist in an advertisement	—
BGH	(I ZR 44/66)	20.03.1968	Publishing of a novel (Mephisto) without corresponding clarifying preface	Omission
BGH	(VI ZR 121/73)	02.07.1974	Unauthorized distribution of nude photos	(conclusive agreement to general publishing)
BGH	(I ZR 73/82)	17.05.1984	Use of the name of a deceased scientist in an advertisement. The advertisement objected to is evaluated by the average reader as a deception (fraud)	Omission
BGH	(VI ZR 226/02)	25.11.2003	Television program about the mismanagement by a hospital director, whose professional competence was questioned and could lead to the suspicion of embezzling public funds (one-sided interpretation)	—
BGH	(VI ZR 265/04)	06.12.2005	Presentation of the corpse of a close relative (mother) in a TV report	—

Court	Date	Description	Amount
AG Berlin-Mitte	22.03.1995	Disclosure of the salary of a celebrity	1500 DM
AG Nürnberg	20.08.1999	Publication of a photo as contact ad	1,700 DM
OLG Frankfurt	12.07.1991	Unauthorized use of a photo on the cover of a book	2,000 DM
BGH (VI ZR 108/78)	26.06.1979	Unauthorized advertisement with the photo of the claimant	Probably 3050 DM (Trier of fact)
BGH (VI ZR 183/64)	18.01.1966	Publication of a false obituary	Probably 5,000 DM (Trier of fact)
OLG München	18.01.2002	Distribution of flyers with untrue allegation of facts in the run-up to parliamentary elections	5.000 DM
OLG München	31.05.1976	Disclosure of name and photo in a press-cut without consent of the concerned party	5,000 DM compensation for personal suffering
OLG Karlsruhe	26.05.2006	Publication of words which should have remained among those participating in the discussion	2,500 € each
OLG Karlsruhe	11.12.2002	Broadcasting of the tape recording of a group therapy session on the radio without consent.	3,000 €
KG Berlin	11.11.2002	Illegal suspicion reporting	3,000 €
LAG Hamm	03.09.1997	Publication of an offensive article	4,000 DM + omission
ArbG Cottbus (1 Ca 1779/06)	05.04.2007	Circulation of a suspicion (pedophilia)	5,000 €
BGH (Ib ZR 44/63)	15.01.1965	Publication of claimant's photos in connection with captions and tickers without consent	10,000 DM
BGH (VI ZR 127/66)	05.01.1968	Press-clip (listing and publication of untrue allegations while violating the duty of journalistic scrutiny	10,000 DM
LG Bonn	04.06.1992	Reporting with a pseudonym that is actually the correct name of another person who will now be associated with the deed	10,000 DM
OLG Koblenz	29.09.1988	Publication of a newspaper ad under a different name, offering prostitution	5,000 € compensation for personal suffering + expenses for a new telephone connection

Court	Date	Subject	Award
BGH (VI ZR 28/83)	22.01.1985	Emission of a nude photo on television without the consent of the person pictured	10,500 DM (Trier of fact)
OLG München	28.06.2002	Report of a previous suspended sentence with untrue allegation of facts	6,200 € compensation for personal suffering + 500 € material damage
LG Hamburg	23.12.1993	Presentation by the press as 'adulterer' damaging the reputation	15,000 DM
OLG München	01.12.2000	Disclosure of details from the intimate and private life in a newspaper without anonymizing the person and without consent of the person concerned	15,000 DM
LAG Hamburg	03.04.1991	Publication of a discriminating advertisement	2 monthly salaries as compensation for personal suffering + 7,000 DM
OLG München	09.08.2002	Publishing of nude photos (prominent)	5,000 € twice (2 press agencies)
LG Bonn	12.06.1995	Reporting about the parents of a 'murderer', even though the case was only in the phase of preliminary investigation	20,000 DM
OLG München	22.10.2003	Publishing of the photo of a custodian of a felon, mixing him up with the offender	10,000 €
BGH (I ZR 49/97)	01.12.1999	Use of the writing, signature and photo of a celebrity for advertising purposes and business correspondence without consent	Licence fee
BGH (I ZR 226/97)	01.12.1999	The photo of the body double who looks deceptively similar to a famous person, lies the image of this person. This was used without consent for advertising purposes	License fee
BGH (VI ZR 332/94)	05.12.1995	Reporting on the title page about a celebrity who allegedly has cancer so that this gave the impression that the person really had cancer	More than 20,000 DM (Trier of fact)
BGH (VI ZR 223/94)	12.12.1995	A repeated and persistent violation of rights of the own image, in order to achieve economic advantages	Probably 20,000 DM (Trier of fact)

Court	Date	Description	Amount
BGH (VI ZR 56/94)	15.11.1994	Untrue allegation of facts on the cover page with the intentional aim of increasing circulation and gains	30,000 DM
LG Trier	26.10.1995	Photo of a catholic priest in connection with the allegation of sexual abuse of minors	30,000 DM
OLG Koblenz	20.12.1996	Unauthorized publication of a photo in a newspaper; mix-up of photos due to gross negligence.	20,000 €
BGH (VI ZR 38/03)	09.12.2003	Publication of untrue allegation of facts which violates the privacy	20,000 €
OLG Frankfurt am Main	04.07.1991	Negative press-clip, listing of untrue allegations of facts and suspicions	Frustrated expenditures of up to 110,000 DM + 10,000 DM
BGH (VI ZR 285/91)	14.04.1992	Publishing of the photo of a famous actor and television moderator for advertising purposes without consent	demanded 120,000 DM (recommitted to the trier of fact)(however as explicit obligation due to enrichment law)
OLG Hamburg (7 UF 23/05)	15.05.2007	Unauthorized commercial use of the name of a celebrity (satiric word game)	61,200 € (especially license fee)
OLG Hamm	04.02.2004	Targeted vilification of a minor in television show to increase viewer quotas	70,000 €
BGH (VI ZR 255/03)	05.10.2004	Repeated publishing of photos of children of celebrities	150,000 DM
LG Hamburg	27.10.2006	Use of images for advertising purposes without consent	203,109,14 € (license fee and lawyer's fee)
BGH (VI ZR 323/95)	26.11.1996	Untrue allegation of facts in a TV report about a gynecologist	Over 50,000 DM (Trier of fact) + 500,000 € material damage (public impact)

Bibliography

Adomeit, Klaus/Spinti, Henning (1987), 'Zur Kontrolle zivilgerichtlicher Urteile durch das BVerfG', *Juristenzeitung*, pp. 873–877.

Adorján, Johanna (2008), 'Das Leben der anderen', *Frankfurter allgemeine Zeitung Sonntagszeitung*, 27 January 2008, p. 23.

Alexy, Robert (1985), *Theorie der Grundrechte*, 1st ed., Suhrkamp-Verlag, Baden-Baden, Frankfurt am Main.

Alkema, Evert Albert (1988), 'Third-Party Applicability or "Drittwirkung"', in: Franz Matscher et al. (eds.), Protecting Human Rights: the European dimension, studies in honour of Gérard J. Wiarda, Heymann, Cologne et al., pp. 33–45.

Aristoteles (1995), *Rhetorik*, in: Sieveke, Franz G.: 'translation, bibliography, explanations and a post-script', Book I, 5th ed., UTB, Munich.

Bleckmann, Albert (1994), 'Verfassungsrang der EMRK?', *Europäische Grundrechte-Zeitschrift*, pp. 149–155.

Bölke, Dorothee (2005), *die Konsequenzen der Entscheidungen des EGMR aus der Sicht der Medien*, in: Stern, Klaus/Prütting, Hans (Editor), 'Das Caroline Urteil des EGMR und die Rechtsprechung des BVerfG. Vertragsveranstaltung des Instituts für Rundfunkrecht an der Universität zu Köln vom 29.04.2005', C.H. Beck-Verlag, Munich, pp. 67–86.

Breuer, Marten (2005), 'Karlsruhe und die Gretchenfrage: Wie hast du's mit Strasbourg', *Neue Zeitschrift für Verwaltungsrecht*, pp. 412–414.

Browne-Wilkinson, The Rt Hon The Lord (1998), The Impact on Judicial Reasoning, in: The Impact of the Human Rights Bill on English Law, The Clifford Chance Lectures Volume III, Clarendon Press, Oxford, pp. 21–23.

Brudermüller, Gerd (2010), § 1357 BGB, in: Palandt, Otto (Begr.), 'Bürgerliches Gesetzbuch', 69th ed., C.H. Beck-Verlag, Munich.

Buschle, Dirk (2005), 'Ein neues »Solange«?', *Verwaltungsblätter für Baden-Württemberg*, pp. 293–297.

Calliess, Christian (2006), 'Die grundrechtliche Schutzpflicht im mehrpoligen Verfassungsrechtsverhältnis', *Juristenzeitung*, pp. 321–330.

Canaris, Claus-Wilhelm (1984), 'Grundrechte und Privatrecht', *Archiv für die civilistische Praxis* 184, pp. 201–246.

Canaris, Claus-Wilhelm (1989), 'Grundrechtswirkungen und Verhältnismäßigkeitsprinzip in der richterlichen Anwendung und Fortbildung', *Juristische Schulung*, pp. 161–172.

Canaris, Claus-Wilhelm (1999), 'Grundrechte und Privatrecht – eine Zwischenbilanz-, *Schriftenreihe der Juristischen Gesellschaft zu Berlin*, Issue 159, pp. 1–98.
Clapham, Andrew (1993a), *Human Rights in the Private Sphere*, 1st ed., Clarendon Press, Oxford.
Clapham, Andrew (1993b), The 'Drittwirkung' of the Convention, in: R. St. J. Macdonald et al. (eds.), The European System for the Protection of Human Rights, 1st ed., Kluwer Law International, The Hague, 163–206.
Coing, Helmut (1947), *Die obersten Grundsätze des Rechts- ein Versuch zur Neugründung des Naturrechts*, Schriften der Süddeutschen Juristen-Zeitung, Schneider- Verlag, Heidelberg.
Coing, Helmut (1954), 'Anmerkung zu BGH, Urteil vom 25.5.1954, I ZR 211/53', *Juristenzeitung*, p. 700.
Couzinet, Daniel (2009), 'Die Prinzipientheorie der Grundrechte', *Juristische Schulung*, pp. 603–608.
Cremer, Hans-Joachim (2004), 'Zur Bindungswirkung von EGMR-Urteilen', *Europäische Grundrechte-Zeitschrift*, pp. 683–700.
Cremer, Hans-Joachim (2008), 'Freiheitsentzug und Zwangsbehandlung in einer Privatklinik, Rechtskraftdurchbrechung und (mittelbare) Drittwirkung der EMRK – Der Fall Waltraud Storck vor dem Europäischen Gerichtshof für Menschenrechte', *Europäische Grundrechte-Zeitschrift*, pp. 562–581.
Cremer, Hans-Joachim (2009), *Rückwirkung der Bürgschaftsentscheidung? – Die doppelt analoge Anwendung von § 79 Abs. 2 Satz 3 BVerfGG durch das Bundesverfassungsgericht und ihre Folgen*, in: Butzer, Hermann/Kaltenborn, Markus/Meyer, Wolfgang (Hrsg.), 'Organisation und Verfahren im sozialen Rechtsstaat, Festschrift für Friedrich E. Schnapp', Duncker & Humblot, Berlin, pp. 741–777.
Cremer, Hans-Joachim (2010), *Chapter 32* in: Grothe, Rainer (ed.), Grote, Rainer/Marauhn, Thilo, 'EMRK/GG Konkordanzkommentar', 2nd ed. (forthcoming), Mohr/Siebeck-Verlag, Tübingen,
Dechsling, Rainer (1989), *Das Verhältnismäßigkeitsgebot*, Vahlen, Munich.
Denecke, Johannes (1953), Vorbemerkung II vor § 1, in: Mitglieder des BGH (Editor), 'Das Bürgerliche Gesetzbuch mit besonderer Berücksichtigung der Rechtsprechung des Reichsgerichts und des Bundesgerichtshofes', 10th ed., de Gruyter, Berlin.
Diederichsen, Uwe (1998), 'Das Bundesverfassungsgericht als oberstes Zivilgericht – ein Lehrstück der juristischen Methodenlehre', *Archiv für die civilistische Praxis*, pp. 71–260.
Dijk, Pieter van/Fried van Hoof/Arjen van Rijn/Leo Zwaak (2006), *Theory and Practice of the European Convention on Human Rights*, Intersentia, Antwerpen and Oxford.
Dolderer, Michael (2000), *Objektive Grundrechtsgehalte*, Duncker & Humblot, Berlin.
Dreier, Horst (1994), 'Subjektiv-rechtliche und objektiv-rechtliche Grundrechtsgehalte', *Juristische Ausbildung*, pp. 505–513.
Drzemczewski, Andrew (1979), 'The European Human Rights Convention and Relations between Private Parties', *Netherlands International Law Review, Issue 2*, pp. 163–181.
Dürig, Günter (1958), *Art. 1 Abs. III, § 127*, in: Günter Dürig/Theodor Maunz, 'Grundgesetz: Kommentar', Beck- Verlag, Munich.
Dürig, Günter (1956), *Grundrechte und Zivilrechtsprechung*, in: Theodor Maunz

(ed.), 'Vom Bonner Grundgesetz zur gesamtdeutschen Verfassung, Festschrift für Nawiasky', Isar-Verlag, Munich, pp. 157–190.

Dürig, Günter (1954), *Freizügigkeit*, in: Neumann, Franz Leopold/Nipperdey, Hans Carl/Scheuner, Ulrich, 'Die Grundrechte', vol. II, Duncker & Humblot, Berlin, pp. 507–534.

Dworkin, Ronald (1977), *Taking Rights Seriously*, Harvard University Press, Cambridge, Massachusetts.

Dworkin, Ronald (1986), *Law's Empire*, Fontana Press, Cambridge, Massachusetts, London.

Dylan, Bob (2004), *Chronicles, Volume One*, Simon & Schuster, New York.

Ehlers, Dirk (2009) in: Ehlers Dirk (Editor), '*Europäische Grundrechte und Grundfreiheiten*', 3rd ed., De Gruyter- Verlag, Berlin.

Enneccerus, Ludwig/Lehmann, Heinrich (1954), *Lehrbuch des bürgerlichen Rechts, Band 2: Recht der Schuldverhältnisse*, fourth ed., Siebeck Mohr Verlag, Tübingen.

Enneccerus, Ludwig/Nipperdey, Hans Carl (1952), *Allgemeiner Teil des Bürgerlichen Rechts*, 14th ed, Siebeck Mohr Verlag, Tübingen.

Erichsen, Hans-Uwe (1996), 'Die Drittwirkung der Grundrechte', *Juristische Ausbildung*, pp. 527–533.

Eschenbach, Jürgen/Niebaum, Frank (1994), 'Von der mittelbaren Drittwirkung unmittelbar zur staatlichen Bevormundung', *Neue Zeitschrift für Verwaltungsrecht*, pp. 1079–1082.

Eser, Albin (1994), '§ 7 StGB', in: Schönke, Adolf/Schröder, Horst, *Strafgesetzbuch*, 24th ed., C. H. Beck-Verlag, Munich.

Esser, Robert (2005), 'Die Umsetzung der Urteile des Europäischen Gerichtshofs für Menschenrechte im nationalen Recht – ein Beispiel für die Dissonanz völkerrechtlicher Verpflichtungen und verfassungsrechtlicher Vorgaben?', *Der Strafverteidiger*, pp. 348–355.

Di Fabio, Udo, *Impulsreferat*, in: Stern, Klaus/Prütting, Hans (Editor), 'Das Caroline-Urteil des EGMR und die Rechtsprechung des BVerfG, Vertragsveranstaltung des Instituts für Rundfunkrecht an der Universität zu Köln vom 29.04.2005.', C.H. Beck-Verlag, Munich, pp. 87–119.

Fenwick, Helen/Phillipson, Gavin (2006), *Media Freedom under the Human Rights Act*, Oxford University Press, Oxford, New York.

Fiedler, Wilfried (2000), *Quantitative und qualitative Aspekte der Einordnung der Bundesrepublik Deutschland in völkerrechtliche Verträge*, in: Rudolf, Geiger (Editor), 'Völkerrechtlicher Vertrag und staatliches Recht vor dem Hintergrund zunehmender Verdichtung der internationalen Beziehungen', Nomos-Verlag, Baden-Baden, pp. 11–21.

Frowein, Jochen Abraham (1986), 'Der europäische Menschenrechtsschutz als Beginn einer europäischen Verfassungsrechtsprechung', *Juristische Schulung* (JuS), pp. 845–851.

Frowein, Jochen Abraham (1987), *Das Bundesverfassungsgericht und die Europäische Menschenrechtskonvention*, in: Fürst, Walther (Editor), 'Festschrift für Wolfgang Zeidler', Band 2, de Gruyter-Verlag, Berlin, pp. 1763–1774.

Frowein, Jochen Abraham (1996) in: Frowein, Jochen Abraham/Peukert, Wolfgang (Editor), *Europäische Menschenrechtskonvention, EMRK-Kommentar*, 2nd ed., Engel-Verlag, Kehl/Strasbourg/Arlington.

Frowein, Jochen Abraham (2005), *Die traurigen Missverständnisse – Bundesverfassungsgericht und Europäischer Gerichtshof für Menschenrechte*, in:

Dicke, Klaus/Hobe, Stefan/Meyn, Karl/Peters, Anne/Tietje, Christian (Editor), 'Weltinnenrecht, Liber amicorum, Festschrift für Jost Delbrück', Duncker & Humblot, Berlin, pp. 279–287.

Frowein, Jochen Abraham (2007), *The Binding Force ECHR Judgments and ist Limits*, in: Breitenmoser, Stefan/Ehrenzeller, Bernhard/Sassòli, Marco/Stoffel, Walter (Hrsg.), 'Human Rights, Democracy and the Rule of Law, Festschrift für Luzius Wildhaber', Nomos-Verlag, Baden-Baden 2007, pp. 261–269.

Frowein, Jochen Abraham (2009) in: Frowein, Jochen Abraham/Peukert, Wolfgang (Editor) *Europäische Menschenrechtskonvention*, 3rd ed., Engel-Verlag, Kehl am Rhein.

Gadamer, Hans-Georg (1990), *Wahrheit und Methode*, Gesammelte Werke Band 1: Hermeneutik, 6th ed., Mohr Siebeck-Verlag, Tübingen.

Gadamer, Hans-Georg (1993), *Vom Zirkel des Verstehens*, in: Gadamer, Hans-Georg, 'Wahrheit und Methode, Ergänzungen und Register', Gesammelte Werke Band 2: Hermeneutik, 2nd ed., Mohr Siebeck-Verlag, Tübingen.

Gamm, Freiherr von, Friedrich Otto (1955), 'Zur praktischen Anwendung des allgemeinen Persönlichkeitsrechts', *Neue Juristische Wochenschrift*, pp. 1826–1827.

Gerste, Ronald D. (2008), 'Ärzte fordern mehr Offenheit von McCain', *Neue Zürcher Zeitung*, 6 October 2008, p. 2.

Götting, Hans-Peter (1995), *Persönlichkeitsrechte als Vermögensrechte*, Mohr Siebeck Verlag, Tübingen.

Grabenwarter, Christoph (2009), '*Europäische Menschenrechtskonvention*', 4th ed., C.H. Beck Verlag, Munich.

Grabitz, Eberhard (1973), 'der Grundsatz der Verhältnismäßigkeit in der Rechtsprechung des Bundesverfassungsgerichts', *Archiv des öffentlichen Recht 98*, pp. 568–616.

Grupp, Klaus / Stelkens, Ulrich (2005), 'Zur Berücksichtigung der Gewährleistungen der Europäischen Menschenrechtskonvention bei der Auslegung deutschen Rechts', *Deutsches Verwaltungsblatt*, pp. 133–143.

Günther, Klaus (1988), *Der Sinn für Angemessenheit*, Suhrkamp-Verlag, Frankfurt am Main.

Habermas, Jürgen (1994), *Faktizität und Geltung*, 4th ed., Suhrkamp, Frankfurt am Main.

Hager, Johannes (1994), 'Grundrechte im Privatrecht', *Juristenzeitung*, pp. 373–383.

Hamann, Andreas,(1956), *Das Grundgesetz für die Bundesrepublik Deutschland vom 23. Mai 1949,* Verlag Luchterhand, Neuwied.

Harpwood, Vivianne (2009), *Modern Tort Law*, 7th ed., Routledge-Cavendish, Abingdon.

Hart, H.L.A. (1994), The Concept of Law, 2nd ed., Oxford University Press, Oxford.

Heimerich, Hermann (1956), 'Der Mißbrauch von Tonbandaufnahmen', *Der Betriebsberater*, pp. 249–252.

Heinrichs, Helmut (2010), Einleitung, §§ 4–5, in: Palandt, Otto (Begr.), 'Bürgerliches Gesetzbuch', 69th ed., C.H. Beck-Verlag, Munich.

Heldrich, Andreas (2006), 'EGBGB Art. 16', in: Palandt, Otto (Begr.) Bürgerliches Gesetzbuch, C.H. Beck Verlag, Munich.

Hermes, Georg (1990), 'Grundrechtsschutz durch Privatrecht auf neuer Grundlage? Das BVerfG zu Schutzpflichten und mittelbarer Drittwirkung der Berufsfreiheit', *Neue Juristische Wochenzeitschrift,* pp. 1764–1768.

Hesse, Konrad (1993), *Grundzüge des Verfassungsrechts der Bundesrepublik Deutschland*, 19th ed., C. F. Müller-Verlag, Heidelberg.

Hillgruber, Christian (1991), 'Grundrechtsschutz im Vertragsrecht – zugleich: Anmerkung zu BVerfG NJW 1990, S. 1469', *Archiv für die civilistische Praxis*, pp. 69–86.

Hoffmeister, Frank (2001), 'Die Europäische Menschenrechtskonvention als Grundrechtsverfassung und ihre Bedeutung in Deutschland', *Der Staat 40* (2001), pp. 349–381.

Hoffmann-Riem, Wolfgang (2009), 'Die Caroline II-Entscheidung des BVerfG – Ein Zwischenschritt bei der Konkretisierung des Kooperationsverhältnisses zwischen den verschiedenen betroffenen Gerichten', *Neue Juristische Wochenschrift*, pp. 22–23.

Holoubek, Michael (1997), *Grundrechtliche Gewährleistungspflichten*, Springer Verlag, Vienna.

Hubmann, Heinrich (1953), *Das Persönlichkeitsrecht*, Verlag Böhlau, Münster.

Imhof, Kurt (2008), 'Als die Privatsphäre verloren ging – Die Gefährdung der Öffentlichkeit durch entbettete Medien', *Neue Zürcher Zeitung*, 3 October 2008, B3.

Jescheck, Hans-Heinrich (1988), 'Lehrbuch des Strafrechts – Allgemeiner Teil', 4th ed., Duncker & Humblot, Berlin.

Kadelbach, Stefan (2005), 'Der Status der Europäischen Menschenrechtskonvention im deutschen Recht', *Juristische Ausbildung*, pp. 480–486.

Kant, Immanuel (1797/98), *Die Metaphysik der Sitten*, in: Weischedel, Wilhelm (Editor), 'Werkausgabe in zwölf Bänden', Band VIII, Suhrkamp, Frankfurt a.M..

Kay, Richard S. (2005), The European Convention on Human Rights and the Control of Private Law, 2005 *European Human Rights Law Review*, 466–79.

Klein, Eckart, (1989), 'Grundrechtliche Schutzpflichten des Staates', *Neue Juristische Wochenzeitschrift*, pp. 1633–1640.

Klein, Eckart (2004), 'Anmerkung zu BverfG, Beschluss v. 14. 10. 2004 – 2 BvR 1481/04', *Juristenzeitung*, pp. 1176–1178.

Kleine-Cosack, Michael (2005), *Die Rechtstellung des Europäischen Gerichtshofs für Menschenrechte aus der Sicht der deutschen Praxis – Fragwürdiger Kompetenzstreit zwischen EGMR und Bundesverfassungsgericht*, in: Stern, Klaus/Prütting, Hans (Editor), 'Das Caroline-Urteil des EGMR und die Rechtsprechung des BVerfG. Vertragsveranstaltung des Instituts für Rundfunkrecht an der Universität zu Köln vom 29.04.2005', C.H. Beck-Verlag, Munich, pp. 51–66.

Krieger, Heike (2006), *Funktionen von Grund- und Menschenrechten*, in: Grote, Rainer/Marauhn, Thilo, 'Konkordanzkommentar zum europäischen und deutschen Grundrechtsschutz', Mohr Siebeck, Tübingen.

Lerche, Peter (1961), *Übermaß und Verfassungsrecht*, Heymann, Cologne, Berlin, Munich, Bonn.

Looschelders, Dirk/Roth, Wolfgang (1995), 'Grundrechte und Vertragsrecht: Die verfassungskonforme Reduktion des § 565 II 2 BGB', *Juristenzeitung*, pp. 1034–1046.

Lucke, Jörg (1974), 'die Grundsätze der Verhältnismäßigkeit und Zumutbarkeit', *Die öffentliche Verwaltung*, pp. 769–771.

Lücke, Jörg (1999), 'Die Drittwirkung der Grundrechte an Hand des Art. 19 III GG', *Juristenzeitung*, pp. 377–384.

Marauhn, Thilo, (2005), *Kommunikationsgrundrechte*, in: Ehlers (ed.), 'Europäische Grundrechte und Grundfreiheiten', 2nd ed., de Gruyter, Berlin.

Markesinis, Sir Basil/Fedtke, Jörg (2006), *Judicial Recourse to Foreign Law*, Routledge Cavendish, New York.

Meyer-Ladewig, Jens/Petzold, Herbert (2005), 'Die Bindung deutscher Gerichte an Urteile des EGMR – Neues aus Straßburg und Karlsruhe', *Neue Juristische Wochenschrift*, p 15–20.

Markesinis, Basil S. (1997), *Foreign Law and Comparative Methodology: A Subject and a Thesis*, Hart Publishing, Oxford.

Markesinis, Basil S. (2001), *Always on the Same Path, Essays on Foreign Law and Comparative Methodology*, Volume II, Hart Publishing, Oxford and Portland, Oregon.

Markesinis, Basil S. (2003), *Comparative Law in the Courtroom and Classroom*, Hart Publishing, Oxford and Portland, Oregon.

Markesinis, Basil S./Jorg Fedtke (2009), *Engaging with Foreign Law*, Hart Publishing, Oxford and Portland, Oregon.

Markesinis, Basil S./Unberath, Hannes (2002), *The German Law of Torts – A Comparative Treatise*, 4th ed, Hart Publishing, Oxford.

Michael, Lothar (2007), Pressefreiheit und Schutz der Privatsphäre im Spiegel nationalen und spezifisch europäischen Verfassungsrechts, Jahrbuch des Öffentlichen Rechts der Gegenwart Neue Folge, Vol. 55, pp. 357–375.

Montesquieu, Charles–Louis de Secondat (1964), *De L'Esprit des Lois*, in: Vedel, Georges/Daniel Oster (Editor): 'Oeuvres complètes de Montesquieu', préface de George Vedel, présentation et notes de Daniel Oster, Editions du Seuil, Paris.

von Münch, Ingo (2000), *Vorbemerkungen zu den Art. 1–19 GG*, in: Ingo von Münch/Philip Kunig, 'Grundgesetz-Kommentar', vol. 1, 3rd ed., C.H. Beck-Verlag, Munich.

Murphy, John (2007), *Street on Torts*, 12th ed., Oxford University Press, Oxford.

Neil, Brian (1999), *Privacy: a challenge for the next century*, in: Markesinis, Basil (Editor), 'Protecting Privacy, the Clifford Chance Lectures', Vol. 4, Oxford University Press, Oxford.

Neil, Brian (1997), *The Influence of the European Convention of Human Rights and the American Constitution on the English Law of Defamation*, in: Basil S. Markesinis, Law Making, Law Finding, And Law Shaping The Divers Influences, The Clifford Chance Lectures Volume II, Oxford University Press, Oxford, pp. 53–67.

Neuner, Jörg (2007), *Die Einwirkung der Grundrechte auf das deutsche Privatrecht*, in: Neuner, Jörg (Editor) 'Grundrechte und Privatrecht aus rechtsvergleichender Sicht', Mohr Siebeck-Verlag, Tübingen, pp. 159–176.

Nipperdey, Hans Carl (1954), *Die Würde des Menschen*, in: Neumann, Franz L./Nipperdey, Hans Carl/Scheuner, Ulrich, 'Die Grundrechte', vol. II, Duncker & Humblot, Berlin, pp. 1–50.

Oeter, Stefan (1994), ' "Drittwirkung" der Grundrechte und die Autonomie des Privatrechts – ein Beitrag zu den funktionell-rechtlichen Dimensionen der Drittwirkungsdebatte', *Archiv des öffentlichen Recht* 119, pp. 529–563.

Peukert, Wolfgang (2009), in: Frowein, Jochen Abraham/Peukert, Wolfgang, 'Europäische Menschenrechtskonvention, EMRK-Kommentar', 3rd ed., Verlag Engel, Kehl am Rhein.

Pfeifer, Karl-Nikolaus (2005), *Das Caroline-Urteil des EGMR und die Rechtsprechung des Bundesverfassungsgerichts – Begrüßung und Einführung*, in: Stern, Klaus/Prütting, Hans (Editor), 'Das Caroline-Urteil des EGMR und die Rechtsprechung des BVerfG. Vertragsveranstaltung des Instituts für

Rundfunkrecht an der Universität zu Köln vom 29.04.2005.', C.H. Beck-Verlag, Munich, pp. 5–21.

Radbruch, Gustav (1945), 'Fünf Minuten Rechtsphilosophie', *Rhein-Neckar-Zeitung,* 12 September 1945, p. 3.

Radbruch, Gustav (1946), 'Gesetzliches Unrecht und übergesetzliches Recht', *Süddeutsche Juristenzeitung,* pp. 105–108.

Radbruch, Gustav (1999), *Rechtsphilosophie (1932), Studienausgabe,* ed. by Dreier, Ralf u. Paulson, Stanley L., 3rd ed., C.F. Müller-Verlag, Heidelberg.

Ress, Georg (1987), *Verfassungsrechtliche Auswirkungen der Fortentwicklung völkerrechtlicher Verträge,* in: Fürst, Walter/Herzog, Roman/Umbach, Dieter C. (Editor), 'Festschrift für Wolfgang Zeidler', Band 2, de Gruyter, Berlin, pp. 1775–1798.

Ress, Georg (1996), 'Wirkung und Beachtung der Urteile und Entscheidungen der Straßburger Konventionsorgane', *Europäische Grundrechte-Zeitschrift,* pp. 350–353.

Rixecker, Roland (2006), *Anhang zu § 12 BGB: das allgemeine Persönlichkeitsrecht,* in: Rebmann, Kurt/Säcker, Franz Jürgen/Rixecker, Roland (Editor), 'Münchener Kommentar zum Bürgerlichen Gesetzbuch', vol. 1, 5th ed., Munich.

Rohleder, Kristin (2009), *Grundrechtsschutz im europäischen Mehrebenensystem,* Nomos-Verlag, Baden-Baden.

Roth, Wolfgang (1996), 'Die Überprüfung fachgerichtlicher Urteile durch das Bundesverfassungsgericht und die Entscheidung über die Annahme einer Verfassungsbeschwerde', *Archiv des öffentlichen Recht* 121, pp. 544–577.

Roth, Wolfgang (1998), 'Die verfassungsgerichtliche Überprüfung verfassungskonformer Auslegung im Wege abstrakter Normenkontrolle', *Neue Zeitschrift für Verwaltungsrecht,* pp. 563–567.

Ruffert, Matthias (2001), *Vorrang der Verfassung und Eigenständigkeit des Privatrechts,* Moor Siebeck-Verlag, Tübingen.

Ruffert, Matthias (2009), 'Die Rechtsprechung des Bundesverfassungsgerichts zum Privatrecht', *Juristenzeitung,* pp. 389–398.

Sacco, Rodolfo (2001), *Einführung in die Rechtsvergleichung,* 1st ed., Nomos-Verlag, Baden-Baden.

Sachs, Michael (2006), *Grundrechtliche Schutzpflichten und wirtschaftliche Beziehungen Privater,* in: Bauer, Hartmut (Editor), 'Festschrift für Reiner Schmidt, Wirtschaft im offenen Verfassungsstaat', C.H. Beck-Verlag, Munich, pp. 385–401.

Schnapp, Friedrich (2000), 'Grundrechtsbindung nichtstaatlicher Institutionen', *Juristische Schulung,* pp. 937–943.

Schulze-Fielitz, Helmuth (2008), 'Das Lüth-Urteil – nach 50 Jahren', *Juristische Ausbildung,* pp. 52–57.

Schwabe, Jürgen (1971), *Die sogenannte Drittwirkung der Grundrechte,* Goldmann Wilhelm GmbH-Verlag, Munich.

Schwabe, Jürgen (1975), 'Bundesverfassungsgericht und "Drittwirkung" der Grundrechte', *Archiv des öffentlichen Recht* 100, pp. 442–470.

Sieckmann, Jan (2009), *Recht als normatives System,* first ed., Nomos-Verlag, Baden-Baden.

Sommermann, Karl-Peter (1989), 'Völkerrechtlich garantierte Menschenrechte als Maßstab der Verfassungskonkretisierung', *Archiv des öffentlichen Rechts* 114, pp. 391–422.

Spielmann, Christoph (2004), 'Die Verstärkungswirkung der Grundrechte', *Juristische Schulung*, pp. 371–375.

Sprau, Hartwig (2010), '§ 823 BGB' in: Palandt, Otto (Begr.), Bürgerliches Gesetzbuch, 69th ed., C.H. Beck-Verlag, Munich.

Stadler, Rainer (2008), 'Im Glashaus der Mediengesellschaft', *Neue Zürcher Zeitung*, 3 October 2008, B1.

Starck, Christian (2005), *Das Caroline-Urteil des EGMR und seine verfassungsrechtlichen Konsequenzen*, in: Stern, Klaus/Prütting, Hans (Editor), 'Das Caroline-Urteil des EGMR und die Rechtsprechung des BVerfG. Vertragsveranstaltung des Instituts für Rundfunkrecht an der Universität zu Köln vom 29.04.2005.', C.H. Beck-Verlag, Munich, pp. 23–50.

Steinberger, Helmut (1992), *Allgemeine Regeln des Völkerrechts*, in: Isensee, Josef/Kirchhof, Paul, 'Handbuch des Staatsrechts', Band. VII, 1st ed., C.F. Müller-Verlag, Heidelberg, § 173, pp. 525–570.

Szczekalla, Peter (2002), Die sogenannten grundrechtlichen Schutzpflichten im deutschen und europäishen Recht, Duncker & Humblot, Berlin.

Tomuschat, Christian (1993), *Freedom of Association*, in: MacDonald, Ronald St. J./Matscher, Franz/Petzold, Herbert (eds.), 'The European System for the Protection of Human Rights', Dordrecht et al., Nijhoff Verlag, pp. 493–513.

Walter, Christian (1999), 'Die Europäische Menschenrechtskonvention als Konstitutionalisierungsprozeß', *Zeitschrift für ausländisches Öffentliches Recht und Völkerrecht 59*, pp. 961–983.

Warren, Samuel D./Brandeis, Louis D. (1890), 'The right to privacy', *4 Harvard Law Review*, pp. 193–220.

Weber, Albrecht (2006), *Grundrechtsschutz in Europa – Kooperation oder Kooperationsverweigerung*, in: Akyürek, Metin/Schäffer, Heinz (ed.), 'Staat und Recht in europäischer Perspektive, Festschrift für Heinz Schäffer', C.H. Beck Verlag, Munich, Vienna, pp. 911–922.

Weller, Marc-Philippe (2009), *Die Vertragstreue*, Mohr-Siebeck, Tübingen.

Wernicke, Kurt Georg (1950), *Article 1 Entstehungsgeschichte*, in: Dolzer, Rudolf/Abraham, Hans-Jürgen, 'Bonner Kommentar zum Grundgesetz', Loseblatt-Ausgabe, Stand: Dezember 2009, C.F. Müller-Verlag, Heidelberg, Hamburg.

Wendt, Rudolf (1979), 'Der Garantiegehalt der Grundrechte und das Übermaßverbot', *Archiv des öffentlichen Rechts 104*, pp. 414–474.

Wiedemann, Herbert (1990), 'Anmerkung zu BVerfG, Beschluss vom 07.02.1990 – 1 BvR 26/84', *Juristenzeitung*, pp. 691–695.

Wittig, Peter (1968), 'Zum Standort des Verhältnismäßigkeitsgrundsatz im System des Grundgesetzes', *Die öffentliche Verwaltung*, pp. 817–825.

Woller, Hans (2010), 'Das Private und das Politische', *Neue Zürcher Zeitung*, 13 January 2010, p. 21.

Wright, Jane (2001), *Tort Law and Human Rights*, Hart Publishing, Oxford and Portland, Oregon.

Zitzmann, Marc (2008a), 'Was ist der Sarkozysmus?', *Neue Zürcher Zeitung*, 16 January 2008, p. 45.

Zitzmann, Marc (2008b), 'Form und Inhalt – Kalkulierte Selbstinszenierung – Frankreichs Präsident, sein Privatleben, seine Politik', *Neue Zürcher Zeitung*, 30 January 2008, p. 43.

Index

human dignity 48; under the ECHR 241; under the *Grundgesetz* 48–55, 156–7; 161, 173–4, 184, 196, 206, 208, 216, 242; human dignity core 216; and human rights 103, 106
Human Rights Act 1998 11–14, 20–3, 30–1, 95, 102–8, 111, 230, 241

image: protection of one's image *see Kunsturhebergesetz*
informational autonomy 189–94
internet 1–3
interrelatedness of conflicting basic rights positions *see Wechselwirkung*

journalistic margin *see* editorial discretion
just satisfaction 82

Kahn, Oliver 4
Kant, Immanuel 165, 205, 238–40
KUG *see Kunsturhebergesetz*
Kunsturhebergesetz 43–7, 50–1, 57, 65, 67–9, 79–80, 83–7, 89, 91, 93, 99, 146–7; *abgestuftes Schutzkonzept* 6; *absolute Person der Zeitgeschichte* (figure of contemporary society *par excellence*) 44–5, 47, 67–8, 79–80, 83–5, 147; and general personality right 45, 67–8; *neues abgestuftes Schutzkonzept* 83–7, 89; public interest 85, 147; *relative Person der Zeitgeschichte* (relative figure of contemporary society, relatively public figures) 67, 80, 83–5, 99

legal values: 169–74, 175, 202, 207–9, 215, 222; and practical concord 202–10; *Rechtsgut (-güter)* 170–2; *see also* balancing; *Grundrechte*; *Wechselwirkung*
libel 94
liberty *see* right to liberty
limitation of basic rights *see* restriction; *see also* balancing
limitation of claims 14–15, 18–19; and ECHR 18–19, 148

malicious falsehood 94
margin of appreciation: under ECHR (especially for fulfilling positive obligations) 73–4, 80, 110, 121, 124, 130, 132–3, 141, 144, 236; for legislature under the Grundgesetz 181–2, 185, 194; *see also* positive obligations under the ECHR
McCain, John 3
medical data 143
medical treatment 56, 61–2, 75, 98, 121; *see also* psychiatric clinic
medication 16–21
mittelbare Drittwirkung see Drittwirkung
Mosley, Max 3

national-socialist regime in Germany 48, 112–13, 156, 195
neues abgestuftes Schutzkonzept see Kunsturhebergesetz
Nipperdey, Hans Carl 61–2, 70

occupazione acquisitiva see accessione invertita
oikos 3
online searches 1

parent(s) 4–5, 25–6, 56–7, 64, 70, 123–5, 128–30, 131, 189–93, 194, 202, 203, 208, 215, 220, 233, 242; *see also* general personality right
personality right *see* general personality right
politicians 6, 45, 62, 66, 75–6, 79, 92, 151, 226–9; *see also* celebrities; public figures
positive obligations under the ECHR: and legislation 128–52; fulfillment by administrative action 121, 142–4; fulfilment (and non-fulfilment) by domestic courts 69, 79–80, 144–50; fulfilment by enacting criminal law 117–22, 140–1; fulfilment by enacting tort law 121, 149; fulfilment by foreseeing civil-law remedies 120–1; interpretation of domestic law in conformity with ECHR 34, 37, 80, 105–6, 148–9, 232, 240; legislative promotion of the realisation of ECHR guarantees 128–34; legislative protection against private interferences 127–8, 135–42; margin of appreciation 73–4, 80, 110, 121, 124, 130, 132–3, 141, 144; protection against non-state actors

UNIVERSITIES AT MEDWAY LIBRARY